Deleuze and Guattari

Also available from Bloomsbury

Who's Afraid of Deleuze and Guattari?, Gregg Lambert
Schizoanalysis and Ecosophy, edited by Constantin V. Boundas
Deleuze and Becoming, Samantha Bankston
Deleuze and Art, Anne Sauvagnargues
Deleuze and Becoming, Samantha Bankston
Ecosophical Aesthetics, edited by Colin Gardner and Patricia MacCormack

Deleuze and Guattari

Selected Writings

Kenneth Surin
Duke University, USA

BLOOMSBURY ACADEMIC
LONDON • NEW YORK • OXFORD • NEW DELHI • SYDNEY

BLOOMSBURY ACADEMIC
Bloomsbury Publishing Plc
50 Bedford Square, London, WC1B 3DP, UK
1385 Broadway, New York, NY 10018, USA
29 Earlsfort Terrace, Dublin 2, Ireland

BLOOMSBURY, BLOOMSBURY ACADEMIC and the Diana logo are
trademarks of Bloomsbury Publishing Plc

First published in Great Britain 2020
This paperback edition published in 2021

Copyright © Kenneth Surin, 2020

Kenneth Surin has asserted his right under the Copyright,
Designs and Patents Act, 1988, to be identified as Author of this work.

For legal purposes the Acknowledgments on p. ix constitute
an extension of this copyright page.

Cover design by Maria Rajka
Cover image © Getty Images

All rights reserved. No part of this publication may be reproduced or
transmitted in any form or by any means, electronic or mechanical, including
photocopying, recording, or any information storage or retrieval system,
without prior permission in writing from the publishers.

Bloomsbury Publishing Plc does not have any control over, or responsibility for,
any third-party websites referred to or in this book. All internet addresses given
in this book were correct at the time of going to press. The author and publisher
regret any inconvenience caused if addresses have changed or sites have ceased
to exist, but can accept no responsibility for any such changes.

A catalogue record for this book is available from the British Library.

A catalog record for this book is available from the Library of Congress.

ISBN: HB: 978-1-3501-0310-8
PB: 978-1-3502-5955-3
ePDF: 978-1-3501-0309-2
eBook: 978-1-3501-0311-5

Typeset by Integra Software Services Pvt. Ltd

To find out more about our authors and books visit www.bloomsbury.com
and sign up for our newsletters.

For Alastair and Rebecca

Contents

Preface		viii
Acknowledgments		ix
Abbreviations		x
1	The "Epochality" of Deleuzean Thought …	1
2	Deleuze's Three Ontologies	15
3	Was Deleuze a Materialist?	23
4	Force as a Deleuzean Concept	31
5	On Producing the Concept of the Image-Concept	41
6	"A Question of an Axiomatic of Desires": The Deleuzean Imagination of Geoliterature	51
7	"Existing Not as a Subject but as a Work of Art"—The Task of Ethics? or Aesthetics?	73
8	The Socius and Life	85
9	"1000 Political Subjects …"	91
10	The Radical Event?	117
11	On Producing (the Concept of) Solidarity	125
12	What Is Becoming-Animal? The Politics of Deleuze and Guattari's "Strange Notion"	139
13	The Society of Control and the Managed Citizen	147
14	The Undecidable and the Fugitive: *Mille Plateaux* and the State-Form	163
15	"Reinventing a Physiology of Collective Liberation": Going "Beyond Marx" in the Marxism(s) of Negri, Guattari, and Deleuze	173
16	Mao's "On Contradiction," Mao-Hegel/Mao-Deleuze	191
Notes		203
Bibliography		238
Index		251

Preface

This collection of sixteen essays (five previously unpublished) contains essays I've written on Gilles Deleuze and Félix Guattari in the last couple of decades. The first essay (Chapter 14) was published in 1991, the most recent in 2018.

Nearly every essay was written in response to invitations to give lectures or conference presentations, as well contributions to journals or essay collections. The task of revising the essays to efface all traces of oral delivery or obvious conformity to the prescribed agenda of a journal issue or book collection would have been impossible. I've limited myself to forms of updating that remain within the realm of plausibility, the addition and removal of paragraphs here and there, and of course correcting typographical errors. Where the same passages are to be found in more than one essay, I've allowed them to stand so as not to compromise the flow or coherence of my argument in that particular essay.

The essays range fairly widely. One (Essay 1), for a commemorative issue of *Theory, Culture and Society* shortly after Deleuze's death, is an attempt, futile of course, to assess his philosophical legacy. Four (Essays 2, 3, 4, 5) deal fairly specifically with Deleuzean themes and concepts—his ontologies (Essay 2), his materialism (Essay 3), his concept of force (Essay 4), and his theory of the image-narrative-concept (Essay 5). A couple deal with his relation to other thinkers (Essays 11 [Raymond Williams] and 15 [Antonio Negri]). One deals with Deleuze and literature (Essay 6), another with Deleuze and ethics/aesthetics (Essay 7). The remaining essays deal with themes in political philosophy, especially Marxism.

I am grateful to Janell Watson for much help given in countless ways while most of these essays were written. My indebtedness to others is expressed in the individual essays.

Acknowledgments

I thank the publishers for permission to reprint material from the following articles and book chapters:

"The Epochality of Deleuzean Thought," *Theory, Culture, and Society* 14 (1997), pp. 9–21.

"Force," in *Gilles Deleuze: Key Concepts*, ed. Charles J. Stivale (Montreal: McGill-Queen's University Press, 2005), pp. 19–30.

"On Producing the Concept of the Concept-Image," in *Releasing the Image: From Literature to New Media*, ed. Robert Mitchell and Jacques Khalip (Palo Alto: Stanford University Press, 2011), pp. 171–80, 266–7.

"'A Question of an Axiomatics of Desires': The Deleuzean Imagination of Geoliterature," in *Deleuze and Literature*, ed. Ian Buchanan and John Marks (Edinburgh: Edinburgh University Press, 2000), pp. 167–93.

"'Existing Not as a Subject but as a Work of Art': The Task of Ethics or Aesthetics?," in *Deleuze and Ethics*, ed. Nathan Jun and Daniel W. Smith (Edinburgh: Edinburgh University Press, 2011), pp. 142–53.

"1000 Political Subjects," in *Deleuze and the Social World*, ed. Adrian Parr and Ian Buchanan (Edinburgh University Press, 2006), pp. 57–78.

"On Producing (the Concept) of Solidarity," *Rethinking Marxism* 23 (2010), pp. 446–57.

"Control Societies and the Managed Citizen," *Junctures* 8 (2007), pp. 11–25.

"The Undecidable and the Fugitive: *Mille Plateaux* and the State-Form," *SubStance*, #66 (1991), pp. 102–13.

"'Reinventing a Physiology of Collective Liberation': Going 'Beyond Marx' in the Marxism(s) of Negri, Guattari, and Deleuze," *Rethinking MARXISM*, 7 (1994), pp. 9–27.

"Mao's "On Contradiction," Mao-Hegel/Mao-Deleuze." *CLCWeb: Comparative Literature and Culture* 20.3 (2018): <https://doi.org/10.7771/1481-4374.3248>

Abbreviations

References to the works below are given in the text using the following abbreviations. The abbreviations are followed by two paginations, the first to the English translation cited in the Bibliography, the second to the French original, also given in the Bibliography. Translations that have been modified on occasion will be acknowledged as such.

AO   Deleuze, Gilles, and Guattari, Félix. (1977) *Anti-Oedipus*, trans. Robert Hurley, Mark Seem, and Helen R. Lane (New York: Viking).

B   Deleuze, Gilles. (1988) *Bergsonism*, trans. Hugh Tomlinson and Barbara Habberjam (New York: Zone Books).

CLU   Guattari, Félix, and Negri, Antonio. (1990) *Communists Like Us: New Spaces of Liberty, New Lines of Alliance*, trans. Michael Ryan (New York: Semiotext(e)).

D   Deleuze, Gilles, and Parnet, Claire. (1987) *Dialogues*, trans. Hugh Tomlinson and Barbara Habberjam (New York: Columbia University Press).

DI   Deleuze, Gilles. (2004) *Desert Islands and Other Texts*, ed. Sylvère Lotringer, trans. Michael Taomina (New York: Semiotext(e)).

DR   Deleuze, Gilles. (1994) *Difference and Repetition*, trans. Paul Patton (New York: Columbia University Press).

ECC   Deleuze, Gilles. (1997) *Essays Critical and Clinical*, trans. Daniel W. Smith and Michael A. Greco (Minneapolis: University of Minnesota Press).

EPS   Deleuze, Gilles. (1990) *Expressionism in Philosophy: Spinoza*, trans. Martin Joughin (New York: Zone Books).

ES   Deleuze, Gilles. (1991) *Empiricism and Subjectivity: An Essay on Hume's Theory of Human Nature*, trans. Constantin V. Boundas (New York: Columbia University Press, 1991).

F   Deleuze, Gilles. (1986) *Foucault*, trans. Seán Hand (Minneapolis: University of Minnesota Press).

FLB   Deleuze, Gilles. (1993) *The Fold: Leibniz and the Baroque*, trans. Tom Conley (Minneapolis: University of Minnesota Press).

KCP	Deleuze, Gilles. (1983) *Kant's Critical Philosophy: The Doctrine of the Faculties*, trans. Hugh Tomlinson and Barbara Habberjam (Minneapolis: University of Minnesota Press).
LS	Deleuze, Gilles. (1990) *The Logic of Sense*, trans. Mark Lester with Charles Stivale, ed. Constantin V. Boundas (New York: Columbia University Press).
M	Deleuze, Gilles. (1989) *Masochism: Coldness and Cruelty*, trans. Jean McNeil and Aude Willm (New York: Zone Books).
MI	Deleuze, Gilles. (1986) *Cinema 1: The Movement-Image*, trans. Hugh Tomlinson and Barbara Habberjam (Minneapolis: University of Minnesota Press, 1986).
N	Deleuze, Gilles. (1995) *Negotiations, 1972–1990*, trans. Martin Joughin (New York: Columbia University Press).
NP	Deleuze, Gilles. (1983) *Nietzsche and Philosophy*, trans. Hugh Tomlinson (New York: Columbia University Press).
PI	Deleuze, Gilles. (2001) *Pure Immanence: Essays on a Life*, trans. Anne Boyman, intro. John Rajchman (New York: Zone Books).
PS	Deleuze, Gilles. (2000) *Proust and Signs: The Complete Text*, trans. Richard Howard (Minneapolis: University of Minnesota Press).
SPP	Deleuze, Gilles. (1988) *Spinoza: Practical Philosophy*, trans. Robert Hurley (San Francisco: City Lights).
TI	Deleuze, Gilles. (1989) *Cinema 2: The Time-Image*, trans. Hugh Tomlinson and Robert Goleta (Minneapolis: University of Minnesota Press).
TRM	Deleuze, Gilles. (2006) *Two Regimes of Madness: Texts and Interviews 1975–1995*, ed. David Lapoujade, trans. Ames Hodges and Mike Taormina (New York: Semiotext(e)).
TP	Deleuze, Gilles, and Guattari, Félix. (1987) *A Thousand Plateaus: Capitalism and Schizophrenia*, trans. Brian Massumi (Minneapolis: University of Minnesota Press).
WP	Deleuze, Gilles, and Guattari, Félix. (1994) *What Is Philosophy?*, trans. Hugh Tomlinson and Graham Burchell (New York: Columbia University Press).

1

The "Epochality" of Deleuzean Thought …

The history of philosophy rather than repeating what a philosopher says, has to say what he must have taken for granted, what he didn't say but is nonetheless present in what he did say.

Gilles Deleuze[1]

The history of philosophy has a doxa. This doxa issues in a characteristic gesture, somewhat ritualized in the way that such doxastic gestures tend invariably to be, which shows itself in the willingness of the historian of philosophy to traffic in commonplaces about the "epochal" qualities of the great philosopher, the possessors of such uniquely distinctive qualities most typically being said to include Descartes, Kant, Hegel, Marx, Nietzsche, and Heidegger. Thus, Descartes is "epochal" because he made Knowledge and Knowing predicates of the *res cogitans*, thereby supplanting *divinitas* as the "holder" of this predicate (here we are told that before Descartes Knowledge was basically a component of theological, as opposed to human, reason); Kant because he provided a reading of the so-called transcendentals—truth, goodness, and beauty (the focus of the three *Critiques*)—that did not invoke a supreme being as the transcendental of these transcendentals; Hegel because he gave us the most profound architectonic of forms, the most subtle structural logic of their modes of change and their interrelationships; Marx because he realized so powerfully that we now had to see the transcendentals as having their basis in a historically determinate social formation—namely, productive labor in capitalism; Nietzsche, because in a way without parallel, he saw everything, including divinity (and the will to truth, goodness, and beauty), as the product of an irreducible power of fabulation; Heidegger because he managed to tell the whole story of Western philosophy in terms of its decisive permeation by a certain myth of the *logos* (and its ancillary mythemes of the original, the identical, and the corresponding); and so forth. It is easy to say, of course, that such gestures of homage are the result of a simplifying propensity, not necessarily misleading or egregiously propagandizing, but simplifying nonetheless. What then are we to make of Foucault's famous tribute to Deleuze, doubtless delivered somewhat tongue in cheek, but now adverted to in just about every discussion of Deleuze's work, "*Mais un jour, peut-être, le siècle deleuzian*"?[2]

Is there any point in proposing the "epochality" of Deleuzean thought, in Foucault's or some other way? And, perhaps more importantly, what would it be to make a proposal of this kind where Deleuze is concerned? Or is any such attempt doomed to have the character of a "phantasmology" (the term is Foucault's), since it rests on the fantasy of a general philosophy of history marked by so-called "epochal" turning points—and, we could go on to say, there is no such thing as a general history of philosophy, because all such histories are founded on some dubious myth of origination, such as that of Plato as the "father" of philosophy (here one recalls Whitehead's dictum that all philosophy is a series of footnotes on Plato)?[3] Furthermore, it could be argued that this general philosophy of history is what it is only because it casts philosophy, problematically, as an attempt to tell again and again a certain kind of story about the world, the subject, and God, so that even those trying to tell a story without this triptych, nonetheless, end up by saving a place for their spectralized presences.[4] These objections to a general philosophy of history do not however pose an insurmountable problem for the proponent of a Deleuzean thought. For it could be argued that the achievement of this thought lies precisely in the break that it makes with the axioms that underlie the "phantasmology" that is this general philosophy of history: Deleuze's thought is a "reversed Platonism" with no need to do philosophy in a way that, say, begins from Plato and culminates in some later figure (e.g., Heidegger) who has to "end" philosophy by destroying the Platonic first principles (Plato as the father-mother who gives birth to abstraction, the transcending of sensuousness) from which philosophy begins (although Heidegger is of course undeniably important for Deleuze). This in fact is the gist of the account of Deleuze's accomplishment given by Foucault in "Theatrum Philosophicum."

Similar sentiments underpin the many other overlapping or parallel depictions of Deleuze's achievement: it is said that he "overturned" Hegel; that he bypassed Sartre and Merleau-Ponty (saying hardly a printed word about them in the process); that in a manner akin to cutting the proverbial Gordian knot he "undid" psychoanalysis and semiology; that even though he had precursors (especially Nietzsche), he was the first to invent a truly "post-dialectical" philosophy; that he was the first to "theorize" a cinema of the sublime; that, motivated by his "reversed Platonism," he produced profoundly original philosophical commentaries on Spinoza, Leibniz, Hume, Kant, Nietzsche, and Bergson; that he wrote innovative literary studies of Proust and Kafka; that he provided an unusual and suggestive interpretation of masochism; that he formulated, in his work on Francis Bacon, an aesthetics that may have been the first such to relate, in terms of a rigorous complementarity, the iterabilities of sense to the plexus of sensation. The list could go on.[5]

The assertion of "epochality" in the history of philosophy, however, cannot rest on the mere assertion of a difference between this or that thinker or this or that movement or system of thought. The occasion or system that produces the putative difference in question has to be accounted for before the import of the latter can be seen, and this is not done when one pays one's respects to Deleuze merely by saying, however sagely or grandiloquently, that he "overturned" Hegel or whatever. Foucault, for one, did a great deal more than this (in "Theatrum Philosophicum"). But what Foucault did not do, and this is a troubling idealism in his otherwise remarkable assessment of Deleuze in this essay, is to show what it is about Deleuzean concepts that gave them their particular affinity for *this* century. For Foucault to tell us, even with the erudition and conceptual acumen so palpably displayed in "Theatrum Philosophicum," that Deleuze, among other things, "reversed" Platonism is not by that very fact to tell us what it is about Deleuzean thought that expresses something different—something critically, indeed radically, different—about that thought and its relation to this century.

To posit a distance between Deleuzean thought and its Platonic or Cartesian or Hegelian counterparts is not by that fact alone to account for the centrality of *that* thought for *this* century. To do this one has, at the very least, to delineate something like the imaginary or the épistémè (the Foucauldian resonance here is certainly not inadvertent) of *le siècle deleuzian*, and then set out those aspects of Deleuzean thought which have a peculiar saliency for this épistémè or imaginary. The thought that is "Deleuzean" has to be read in terms of the épistémè, but, equally, the épistémè has to be approached in terms of the thought. It is this reciprocity and congruence between Deleuzean thought and the imaginary constitutive of his century that will give substance to the claim that there may come a time when the name of Foucault's friend and colleague will function emblematically as one of the names for "our century."[6]

Hegel told the story of philosophy as the story of the emergence of abstraction from the immediacy and concreteness of the sensuous order. Moreover, he told this as a story for an age—the age of which he was a denizen, namely, "modernity"—that was beginning to be synonymous with the exponential proliferation of abstract forms. It is fashionable to depict Deleuze as an anti-Hegelian, and indeed there are statements in his works that lend an air of incontrovertibility to judgments of this kind. But at best this tells only a part of the story. Granted that Deleuze and Guattari's *Capitalisme et schizophrénie* can be viewed as an immense "unwriting" or conceptual unraveling of Hegel's *Phenomenology of Spirit*.[7] To say this, and only this, however, is to overlook the fact that Deleuze is like Hegel (and Spinoza and Leibniz of course) in being one of the great producers of an architectonic for the organization of the sensuous; like them Deleuze undertook this as a "project" of immense conceptual orchestration, one that, by virtue of being conceptual, necessarily involves movement beyond the percepts and affects that constitute the sensuous. In the case of Hegel this movement beyond the sensuous takes one inevitably into the universal, whereas in the case of Deleuze the universal is deliberately bypassed, and abstraction, the movement beyond the sensuous, takes the Deleuzean thinker into the realm of the multiple and the singular.

But what is it about the epoch that favors or calls for an orchestration of the sensuous that involves the multiple and the singular, as opposed to the universal? Here it is important to say something about the image of thought sponsored by our epoch, before trying to connect up this image of thought with Deleuze's philosophy.

This is an age that has witnessed, and ostensibly will go on witnessing—not just in the idioms that go by the names of so-called theoretical formulation, but also in the domains of everyday life—a huge growth of new forms of movement, change, and juxtaposition or adjacency. This development has been accompanied by the emergence of new and very different subjectivities and potentials: a relative short span of time separates, say, Bertrand Russell or T.W. Adorno (designating here not so much individuals as types of consciousness) from Monique Wittig or Hakim Bey (again signifying forms of consciousness), but they are eons apart in terms of their intellectual (and "affective") distance from each other. (The distance of Adorno and Russell from someone like Dennis Rodman or Arnold Schwarzenegger would seem to be more obvious if not impressive; it is hard, for example, to imagine Adorno surfing the internet or the co-author of *Principia Mathematica* wearing a pair of Nike sneakers—something many a sedate and decorous college professor would do today.)

This, moreover, is the time of a rapid and seemingly inexorable development of new forms of knowledge, knowledges that are no longer predicated on principles, amounting to axioms for "right judgment," that invoke notions of the true, the false, the erroneous, and so forth. Instead, these new knowledges point in very self-conscious (the preferred term in some quarters is "self-reflexive") ways to their beginnings in an irreducible fictiveness or fabulation. The emergence of these new knowledges has been accompanied, concomitantly, by the rise of a whole range of sciences, based on the creation of "nonstandard" logics and topologies of change and relation, and typically devised to deal with situations that have the character of the irregular or the arbitrary.

These new logics and topologies concern themselves not only with the structural principles of change and process, but also with surfaces, textures, rhythms, connections, that is, items possessing fractalized forms that can be expressed and analyzed in terms of such notions as that of "strings," "knots," "flows," "labyrinths," and so forth. The "rhizome," probably the best-known figure in the conceptual repertoire developed by Deleuze and Guattari in *Mille plateaux*, has quite obvious affinities with these by now commonplace categorizations of the fractal sciences. The time of "rhizomatic structures" may indeed be the time of an invention of a "new" Baroque, as Deleuze himself has pointed out in his book on Leibniz.[8] This "new" Baroque, and its accompanying burgeoning of "asystemic" but still interrelated forms, has not only coincided with a reconfiguration of the human sensorium and a further and even more extensive elaboration of our sensibilities: just as significantly, the new logics and topologies associated with it are also generating principles of integration that allow radically different mechanisms to function in concert. Computer and cybernetic technologies, the nervous system, commodity production, speech and semiosis—areas before constituted on the basis of divergent and even incommensurate logics and conceptual idioms—are now being orchestrated in terms of a language that renders them "isomorphic," fundamentally congruent.

The "cyberspaces" of the writings of William Gibson, Bruce Sterling, Neal Stephenson, and others represent in many ways a culmination, impressed more and more deeply into our cultures, of these integrations and "concerts." Indeed, "cyberspaces" have striking affinities with "the fold" that Deleuze takes to be the defining feature of the Baroque.[9] (Incidentally, the intellectual career of Michel Serres can be seen as a parallel to that of Deleuze's, inasmuch as it is largely, but of course not entirely, an attempt to speak rigorously of the conceptual dimensions that subtend these new transformations in science and logic.[10])

Along with the shifts and transformations associated with this new historical phase, capitalism itself is being transformed yet again. In its current manifestations capitalism is becoming more abstract, more "diagrammatic," because only in this way can it ensure that every and any kind of production—

even that of a "precapitalist" variety—is mediated by it and placed at the disposal of accumulation. This latest phase of capitalist development has been depicted and analyzed under a variety of by now well-known titles: "advanced capitalism," "late capitalism," "disorganized capitalism," "integrated world capitalism," "globalized capitalism," "post-Fordism," etc. The movement to this current phase, marking the collapse of the previous world economic order, is manifested in several different registers. These include the creation of an international division of labor, the increasingly significant role of transnational corporations in the composition of capital, the rise of an international debt economy, the introduction of flexible manufacturing systems and labor processes, the rapid growth (especially in the economies of the peripheral and semiperipheral nations) of standardized markets and patterns of consumption, the emergence of decentralized and so-called informal economies, the development of complex securities and credit systems, the transformation of the capitalist state, the inauguration of a new semiotics of value, and so forth.[11]

It is now something of a commonplace for economic theorists to argue that this shift to a new paradigm of production and accumulation can be seen as a response to the collapse of the preceding system of capitalist development, a system that had prevailed since 1945. In the account given by Samir Amin, an account whose lineaments are to be found in just about every other narrative given by theorists of the post-war world-system, the post-war system had three focal points: Fordism in the countries of the west, Sovietism in the countries of the eastern bloc, and developmentalism in the so-called third world.[12] The collapse of this world-system in the 1970s produced yet another mutation in capitalism, and the conceptual innovations brought about in *Capitalisme et schizophrénie* can be seen as part of an attempt to think this mutation in terms of a reciprocal movement, the *modus operandi* of which is to imbue thought with life by bringing this mutation—"homeopathically"—into thought. This mutation launches thought, but also, in a kind of ceaseless oscillation, rescues this mutation from a life of the undead (this being capitalism's decisive accomplishment) by bringing thought to it, so that this mutation and all that it involves can then be supplanted by a different and creative life that cannot be mistaken for its shadow, the zombie world of capital. How does the conceptual cartography furnished by *Capitalisme et schizophrénie* accomplish this?

Hypercapitalism—the strategic but still chaotic "response" of capitalism to the collapse of the post-war Keynesian and Fordist world-system—poses, unavoidably for all those who purport to be historical or political materialists, the question of its relation as a phenomenon to the lexicon or axioms that can be said to constitute marxism.[13] How will we know that capitalism in its current manifestations is congruent with the axiomatic that is marxism? This compliance or congruence can only be established through a principle, a second-order principle, which cannot of necessity be "marxist," and this because the applicability of marxism to the domain that is called capitalism (or hypercapitalism in its present manifestation) can only be specified metatheoretically, that is, from beyond the range of the theoretical armature whose name is "marxism." It is this metatheoretical or "transcendental" specification that informs us in virtue of what conditions and axioms is *this* domain (i.e., capitalism) governed by *this* axiomatic (i.e., marxism), and *Capitalisme et schizophrénie* gives us precisely the kind of metatheoretical schema that enables the political materialist to connect up the algorithm that is marxism with the cultural and economic phenomenon that is hypercapitalism.[14]

This metatheoretical schema has at its heart a couple of axes—"deterritorialization" and "reterritorialization"—that enable the authors of *Capitalisme et schizophrénie* to understand the logic of capitalism in terms of two complementary sets of practices. Deterritorialization is the movement that decomposes geographical spaces, individual and collective identities, value systems, etc., while reterritorialization is the counterpart movement that recomposes, often by the most artificial means possible, subjectivities, forms of power, and instruments of submission.

The new sciences and logics of integration referred to above—associated above all with the immense growth (reminding one of the kind of uncontainable, because profoundly rhizomatic, exfoliation depicted in the Amazon jungle of Werner Herzog's *Fitzcarraldo*) of communications and the processing of information—destroy the old ways in which we think, remember, perceive, and imagine, while putting in their place new and very different apparatuses for the understanding, imagination, perception, and memory. And, given the nature of the current phase of capitalist development, all these modes of abstraction and functions of isomorphism are put at the disposal of hypercapitalist production and accumulation. Any movement beyond this logic of capital, as a condition of grasping it in its full comprehensiveness, has to think of all its divergent and multitudinous features in terms of a basic univocity of levels and segments, and it is just this that *Capitalisme et schizophrénie* makes possible.[15] This univocity of strata, also referred to as "the plane of immanence" or "the plane of consistency," is populated by multiplicities, singularities, becomings, and intensities, and the plane of immanence connects all these up with each other.

The conceptual cartography of *Capitalisme et schizophrénie* can also be used as the basis for a materialist political ontology whose intent is the transcoding or rearticulation of potential spaces of opposition to the regimes of hypercapitalism. This is an urgent task, for, if one goes by Samir Amin's account; the emergence of the current world-system has also carried with it the destruction of the two models for socialist thought and practice that have existed up to now, namely, social democracy and Sovietism. Any other form of socialism or communism that can hope to succeed from now on must be based on a model of realization very different from those enjoined by social democracy and soviet state socialism (or state capitalism, as C.L.R. James, Cornelius Castoriadis, and others preferred to call it), and this is where the materialist political ontology of *Capitalisme et schizophrénie* becomes germane. But more about that later.

For now, it need only be noted that the purported epochality of Deleuzean thought rests on its relation to the image of thought generated by, or associated with, the world-system that emerged in the decade after the turning point of 1968—it is its congruence with this image of thought (a "prephilosophical understanding") that enables a Deleuzean thinking to transcode the spaces of the capitalist world-system, a consonance that gives Deleuzean thought its "epochality" and makes possible an "unthinking" or "unwriting" of the codes underwritten and perpetuated by this world order.

The *rhizome* is explicitly invoked in *Mille plateaux* as the image of thought "for" this capitalist world order. In this way the *rhizome* functions as a protocol that relates our thinking to this world, thereby inspiring the creation of concepts that enable one to think of the state in relation to the single world market, these concepts in turn being related by the *rhizome* to the strata of minorities, becomings, incorporealities, "peoples," and so forth. Concepts that, for the political materialist, launch a thought capable of expressing and instantiating the desire to undo this world order.

In *What Is Philosophy?* Deleuze and Guattari use the notion of a "conceptual persona" to designate the figures or embodiments of thought used by philosophers as a figure for the creation or elaboration of concepts, such as the Socrates of Plato or the Dionysus of Nietzsche.[16] The personae enable philosophy or reflection of a more general kind to be viewed as particular ensembles of enunciations or stagings, as a "dramatology" enacted through the performances of the conceptual personae.

Having sought, in the preceding sections, to sketch in an admittedly short-handed way, the image of thought that subtends Deleuzean reflection, it may now be appropriate to view Deleuze himself as a "conceptual persona," one who enables a particular thought to be staged in a way that makes possible the crisscrossing connectedness of all kinds of singularities, singularities that open up into possible worlds. It is as if we have to speak of a Deleuze who says,

> This is the event of the collaborator of Guattari in me, the event of the reader of Nietzsche, Spinoza, Bergson (and so forth) in me, the event of the marxist in me, the event of the friend of Foucault in me, the event of the reader of Kafka and Proust in me, the event of the teacher at Vincennes in me, the event of ill-health in me, and ... and ... and ....

All these in so many kinds of incessantly moving, multiplicably connectable ways. And out of the intersection of these lines of connection, there emerges a highly distinctive narrative that brings into an "agrammatical" adjacency the story of the state-form, the story of every mode of production and accumulation, the story of the relation between speech and affect and sensation, the story of the relation between the verbal and the visual, the story of the forms and modes of thought, and the stories of a great deal else. The intersection of these potentially myriad stories propels another story (a Borgesian "story of everything" somehow made possible by all these other stories working together in a massive pullulating concertedness). This is the story of a human autopoesis, our final "self-making" in a form that, for Deleuze as for Foucault, moves beyond the two—"God" and "Man"—that have so far been tried and found wanting.[17]

The lineaments of this great story, mutually implicated by the other stories of *Capitalisme et schizophrénie* are likely to be very familiar to the student of the writings. These include the proposition, derived from Bergson, that neither matter nor mental states exist as such, but are abstractions from the unceasing flux of experience; the granting of an ontological primacy to events over states and emotions (so that, for example, I do not run away because I am afraid, but rather I am afraid because of (the event of) my running away—but this seems to have been there already in William James); the claim that there are no universals, subjects, individuals, unities, abstractions, etc., but only processes and events of universalization, "subjectification," individuation, unification, etc. (while Deleuze very generously gives Foucault credit for this "discovery," it was really more his (and Guattari's) than anyone else's); the preference for geography over history (although this needs to be qualified, or at least stated more precisely, since it is obvious that great importance is given by Deleuze to all kinds of periodization[18]).

But can we pull the different strands of this great story apart from each other, even if only momentarily, so that, hopefully, it becomes easier for us to form some estimation of the contribution that each of these threads makes to that overarching and agglomerated "story of everything"? I am not sure that this can be done, and even if we approach this undertaking in a spirit of high tentativeness and unremitting provisionality, there is, given the almost profligate immensity of the Deleuzean project, bound to be something arbitrary about such an exercise. There is a seamlessness to the great story of *Capitalisme et schizophrénie*, and it is of course quite literally about everything, as well as pivoting on a highly original conception of philosophy—so (one asks almost despairingly) where in this labyrinthine system does one begin a discussion of it? The *alpha* and the *omega* of this story, as I see it, however, are its elaboration of what Paul Patton has aptly called "an ethos of permanent becoming-revolutionary" and its formulation of an utterly distinctive account of speech and events, both of which are brought together in the unique architectonic or "arrangement" that is *Mille plateaux*, surely Deleuze's (and Guattari's) crowning work.[19]

Right from the beginning Deleuze regarded desire as an inchoate form of thought, so that between desire and concept there is, irreducibly, a whole series of intermediate links: desire (always there in the beginning and present throughout the extent of all the linkages), affects, event-designations ("thisnesses" or "hecceities" in his parlance), word-forms, and of course concepts (or perhaps more appropriately for Deleuze, concept-image-narratives[20]). And each of these communicates with the others in a non-hierarchical way and influences the structures of its counterparts.[21]

This vast and polynucleated semiotic nexus is then linked to the already mentioned "ethos of permanent becoming-revolutionary," an ethos, it could be argued (as indeed nearly every thinker inspired by Deleuze in her or his thinking on politics has been disposed to do), that is the basis for the constitution of a politics not "finally" constrained by the orders of capitalism; a politics still to come, and not predicated on the now-defunct forms of social democracy and sovietism. The supersession of these two previous forms of socialism poses issues not just for practice but also for philosophical reflection. In a thought-provoking assessment of the last writings of Louis Althusser, Antonio Negri has argued that in these writings Althusser was addressing the virtually intractable problem of how it is possible to think of the new (i.e., a situation in which an effective revolutionary practice can be achieved) in the absence of its very conditions of possibility. According to Negri, Althusser was therefore trying to define both the limits of the possible in this context, and also establishing the philosophical conceivability of "the violation of impossibility" that a thinking of revolution necessarily involves in a historical epoch such as this.[22] It seems to me that a similar problematic was also being addressed, albeit in very different terms, by Deleuze (and Guattari), especially in the *Capitalisme et schizophrénie* project.

> Our true changes take place elsewhere—another politics, another time, another individuation.[23]

In his Leibniz book, Deleuze maintains that cultural and social formations are constituted on the basis of accords or "concerts."[24] Deleuzean accords are dynamisms which make possible the grouping into ensembles of whole ranges of events, personages, processes, institutions, movements, and so forth, such that the ensuing assemblage becomes precisely that, an integrated formation. Capitalism, as a globalized axiomatic, is thus an "accord of accords," accords which may be quite heterogeneous when placed alongside each other, but which express the same world, albeit from the point of view of the accord in question. Thus, in Malaysia, for example, the accord (or set of accords) that constitutes the "hi-tech" world to be found in downtown Kuala Lumpur (the location of the world's tallest skyscrapers) and the accord (or set of accords) that constitutes the world of Stone Age production to be found among the tribespeople in the interiors of West Malaysia (Sabah and Sarawak) are not intertranslatable (or not directly or immediately so); but what the accord of accords created by capitalism does, among many other things, is to make it possible for the artifacts produced by the "indigenous" peoples of these interior regions to appear on the tourist markets in downtown Kuala Lumpur, where they are sold alongside Microsoft software, Magnavox camcorders, Macintosh Power Books, and so on. The seemingly disparate and incompatible zones of production and accumulation represented by downtown Kuala Lumpur and the interior regions of Sabah and Sarawak (only about 750 miles apart from each other) are rendered "harmonious" by a higher-level accord or "concert" established by capital, even though the lower-level accords remain (qua lower-level accords) disconnected from each other. Each lower-level accord retains its own "spontaneity" (so to speak), even as it is brought into relationship with other such accords by the meta- or mega-accord that is hypercapitalism. The "concerto grosso" brought about by the meta-accord enables the lower-level accords to remain dissociated from each other while still expressing the same world, the world of the current paradigm of production and accumulation.

Deleuzean accords are formed on the basis of selection criteria, that is, inclusion and exclusion criteria for the implementation of this or that accord; these criteria also determine with which other (possible or actual) accords a particular accord will be congruent (or noncongruent). In the current dispensation, such selection criteria (which may or may not be explicitly stated or upheld) seem to be weakening and in some cases are on the point of disappearing altogether. Since selection criteria tend to function by assigning privileges of hierarchy and order, their loss or attenuation makes dissonances or contradictions difficult or even impossible to resolve and, concomitantly, makes divergences easier to maintain. Events, objects, and personages can now be assigned simultaneously to several divergent and even incompossible series. Thus, to provide a now commonplace example, the "same" sculpture that has a ceremonial function enshrined in myth and tribal tradition can now make its appearance in a metropolitan tourist market next to a Hilton or Hyatt hotel where it appears simply as "native art" or, even more bare-facedly, as "tourist art."[25]

These accords appear to have been quite firmly inserted into the preceding culture, and their dissolution or weakening has precipitated the collapse of a number of once deeply entrenched distinctions; the demarcations between public and private, before and after, inside and outside, and so on, have all become difficult, if not impossible, to uphold in previously customary ways. Accords thus severed from the conditions that guarantee their stability become "impossible," and we may be living in worlds, or speaking languages, that are no longer predicated on any real need to sustain accords or on our *belief* in the need for such accords (this almost certainly has a great deal to do—"symptomatically"—with the recent lucubrations of a "history without a future" and its obverse "future without a history" (Fukuyama and Baudrillard in this regard being two sides of the proverbial same coin) that my colleague Fredric Jameson has dealt with suggestively in several recent essays). These are worlds and languages characterized by sheer variation and multiplicity; worlds and languages that partake of a neo-Baroque more truly Baroque than its predecessor (as Deleuze seems to be indicating).

This state of affairs—that of a "systemic" loss or erosion of "transcendental" accords—impels us in the direction of a politics that is no longer subsumable, in respect of its categories and principles if nothing else, under the paradigms of a liberalism contained within a capitalist matrix or those of social democracy or so-called bureaucratic state socialism. If our criteria of belonging and affiliation are now always going to be subject to a kind of chaotic motion, then our authorities and powers have foisted an enabling lie on us when they denied this "knowledge," and through this occlusion have made possible the invention of nation-states, tribes, clans, political parties, churches, perhaps everything done up to now in the name of community. The serious reader of Deleuze may have the feeling, both dread and exhilarating at the same time, that *that* time—the time up to "now"—has begun inexorably to pass. But we still need our solidarities, now more than ever. They are indispensable for any politics capable of taking us beyond capitalism. These solidarities, however, will be based not on the securing or sustaining of "transcendental" accords—capitalism, that most revolutionary of forces, has moved that possibility into desuetude. Our solidarities will be predicated instead on what the reader of Deleuze will think of as the power of singularity, a power still perhaps in search for its decisive models of realization.

A singularity, on this account, is constituted by the notion that a common or shared property cannot serve as the basis of the individuation of X from all that is *not-X*: if I share the property of *being a reader of Deleuze* with someone else, then that property cannot, in and of itself, serve to individuate either me or that person. A singularity, the *being-X* of X that makes X different from all that is *not-X*, cannot therefore unite X with anything else. Precisely the opposite: X is what it is because it is not united to anything else by virtue of an essence or a common or shared nature. A singularity makes possible the realization of a thing with all its properties, and although this or that commonality may of course pertain to the thing in question, that commonality is indifferent to it qua singularity. So, of course, I will have the property *being a reader of Deleuze* in common with other people, thousands of them in fact. But a singularity is determined only through its relation to the totality of its possibilities, and the totality of possibilities that constitutes me is the totality of an absolute singularity—if another being had each and every one of the possibilities whose totality constituted and thus individuated me, then he or she would perforce be indistinguishable from me. We, he or she and I, would be the same being or person.[26]

Deleuze poses for his reader the question of a politics involving solidarities—that is, the formation of collective subjectivities—based on such absolute singularities. He seems to indicate that only such a politics is capable of disarming the monstrous power that keeps in place those who rule us. To insert this possibility of this politics at the heart of one's production of philosophical concepts, indeed to make the former the enabling possibility of the latter, this is what is at stake when Deleuze and Guattari declare that "before being there is politics" (*Car, avant l'être, il y a la politique*).[27] Is that not, for philosophy if nothing else, an epochal declaration?

2

Deleuze's Three Ontologies

Ontology is the dice throw, the chaosmos from which the cosmos emerges.
                                          Gilles Deleuze, *DR*, p. 199

Leaving aside the perpetually vexed question of what exactly an "ontology" is—is it what we find in more or less the "same" way in (say) Aristotle's *Metaphysics*, or Leibniz's *Monadology*, or Whitehead's *Process and Reality*, and so on?—let's begin by making the bald assertion that Deleuze had (at least) three ontologies (which is not to suggest in any way that these three Deleuzean ontologies may not overlap or somehow permeate each other in this or that way).[1]

Regarding Deleuze's ontologies as just so many "problematics" enables us to say that what is productive in his thought is a weddedness to conceptualization as a *process*, so that the conceptualization of the singular, the multiple, the general, the universal, the individual, the particular, and so on involves the processes or operations of singularization, multiplication, generalization, universalization, individuation, particularization, and so forth. A *problematique* in this sense is not simply a "problem" in the conventional English sense of the term, but also has the semantic resonances that go with notions of the *paradigm*, inasmuch as to identify a specific paradigm is not only to recognize a repertoire of questions associated with the paradigm in question, but also involves acknowledgment of a theoretical template that guides the formulation of answers to the questions deemed salient by this paradigm. "Ontology" in the context of Deleuze's thought has to be approached in a way that also grasps this term in a way that has all the characteristic features of a "problematic."[2]

The first of these Deleuzean ontologies can be associated with *Logique du sens*, *Différence et répétition*, and *Proust et les signes*, in which Deleuze resorted to Stoic conceptions of language to complicate and even overturn the then regnant semiological paradigms. In the *Capitalisme et schizophrénie* project, he (along with Guattari of course) made desire and desiring production the cornerstone of his second ontology. The third Deleuzean ontology is to be found in the books on film. The "filmic" ontology is really about the production of images of thought—the thought of the Gigantic, the Infinitesimal, the Absurd, the Anticipatory, the Nonsensical, and so forth.

We shall begin with a consideration of the "filmic" ontology, and then proceed to consider the "semiotic" ontology, before dealing with the ontology of desiring production. The aim here will be to show that the "filmic" ontology is the one most congruent with the perspective on life and immanence that Deleuze sketched in the last paper written before his death (although admittedly this congruence may have a significance strictly limited to this brief last essay, even if one hopes, as I do, that its purview may be somewhat more extended than this).

How does this "filmic" ontology and the positions on life and immanence limned in Deleuze's last published essay deviate, if at all, from the *Capitalisme et schizophrénie* project? Does the "filmic" ontology adverted to here show a Deleuze more finally indebted to Leibniz's theory of the infinite plenitude of the monads than to Spinoza's theory of the two and only two attributes, of which there can then of course be a potentially infinite number of modes (but these modes are nonetheless confined to being modes of the two Spinozian attributes that are body and mind)? Does this Leibnizian proposition regarding an infinite number of monads not confined to two attributes, based as it is on the Leibnizian "filmic" ontology developed by Deleuze with its notion of an infinite plenitude, enable us to address Alain Badiou's criticism that Deleuze is in the end a thinker of unicity, all appearances to the contrary notwithstanding?[3]

These are some of the questions which may need to be addressed when someone attempts to talk about Deleuzean ontologies. Let's also say—again peremptorily—that none of these ontologies is mutually exclusive: as was said a few moments ago, we can find versions of more than one of these ontologies in one and the same work by Deleuze and Guattari, as hopefully will be indicated below.

The "filmic" ontology, as was said above, is concerned primarily with the production of images of thought—the thought of the Gigantic, the Infinitesimal, the Absurd, the Anticipatory, the Nonsensical, the Intolerable, the Exhausted, and so forth. For Deleuze the image of thought, located as it is on the plane of consistency (the "plane of consistency" being for Deleuze the "space" of all becoming, from which emerges all the potentialities that enable the specific constitution of this or that particular set of forces), is the ontologically prior ground from which the production of concepts takes place. The plane of consistency is the ontologically prior ground from which the production of concepts takes place. Before a concept can be produced, therefore, there has to be as its enabling condition an appropriate image of thought.

For Deleuze, therefore, there is really no such thing as, say, the concept of *foolishness* per se (except as a merely obvious but ultimately trivial item of discourse). Rather, there is *the* event/concept of *a* foolishness whose basis in the plane of immanence is the image of thought provided for the concept in question (and here I'm only giving a few examples by way of illustration): when it comes to providing the image of thought for the concept of foolishness there are such exemplary instances as Dostoevsky's "wise fool" Prince Myshkin in his novel translated as *The Idiot*; or the fool that is Don Quixote in the novel by Cervantes; or the narrator Stultitia (also known as Folly) in Erasmus's *In Praise of Folly*; or the judicious psychopath termed the "rational fool" by Amartya Sen in his famous critique of rational choice theory (Sen shows how this psychopath, simply by conducting himself with a modicum of ostensible prudence, can end up by acting in complete accord with the axioms of rational choice theory[4]), and so on.

Cinema, for Deleuze, is thus an immense machine or regime for the generation or orchestration of such images of thought. Deleuze names this cinematic regime for the generation of images of thought the "crystalline regime."[5]

The crystalline regime is opposed in Deleuze's second *Cinema* book to what he calls "the organic regime."[6] In the organic regime, everything is premised on the notion of judgment—"this is true because it has been shown to be not false," "this is false because it has been shown to be non-identical with the true," and so on. The ruling principle for the organic regime is thus forensic and juridical: "If you are right, and I'm your opponent, then I'm wrong," and vice versa. In the organic regime, therefore, concepts and the truth of their accompanying statements can only be ascertained, or determined for their rightness and wrongness, never created or produced.

The crystalline regime, by contrast, does not oppose the true to the false in this quintessentially dialectical and juridical fashion. Instead, it abolishes this dialectical opposition between the true and the false, and puts in its place the notion of a truth that is created or produced, and produced by a stabilization or arrestation, no matter how short-lived, of what Deleuze, following Nietzsche, calls "the power of the false."[7] This incessant encounter with "the power of the false," and the accompanying need to arrest or transmute this power, even if only momentarily as part of an overall creative process incorporating a vast array of endlessly dynamic transformations that constitutes life for Deleuze, ensues in the potentially unlimited proliferation and contagion of the images of thought that underlie the production of concepts.

Of course a great deal more needs to be said here about the crystalline regime, and its use by Deleuze in his delineation of the plane of consistency or plane of immanence (here "plane of consistency" and "plane of immanence" are used interchangeably, although Deleuze scholars will no doubt rightly question whether these two notions are strictly co-extensive, since the first owes its inspiration to Artaud and the second to Spinoza). For now we only need to note that in the valedictory essay published by Deleuze a few months before his death, "L'immanence: une vie," the notion of life, *a* life, becomes absolutely central for the definition of the plane of immanence. Deleuze goes on to say:

> A life contains only virtuals. It is made up of virtualities, events, singularities … The immanent event is actualized in a state of things and of the lived that make it happen. The plane of immanence is itself actualized in an object and a subject to which it attributes itself. But however inseparable an object and a subject may be from their actualization, the plane of immanence is itself virtual … Events or singularities give to the plane all their virtuality, just as the plane of immanence gives virtual events their full reality.[8]

The image of thought is thus virtual—the Intolerable, qua image of thought, was there before *this* intolerable American president existed, or *that* intolerable colleague existed, and so on. Each image of thought expresses a particular world, in the case of the Intolerable, this is a world in which this intolerable American president exists, or one in which this intolerable colleague exists, and so forth. The notion of expressivity, so crucial for Deleuze ever since his work on Spinoza in the 1960s, brings us to the second or "semiotic" ontology/problematic, although more will have to be said about this first ontology at the end of this essay.

If the notions of the image of thought and that of the plane of immanence or consistency, along with its crucial subtending concept of *life*, are absolutely integral to the previously described Deleuzean ontology, then notions of an *encoding, decoding,* and *recoding* are likewise fundamental to the second or "semiotic" ontology/problematic.

As was pointed out above, Deleuze's opuscule "L'immanence: une vie" is a wondrous effort to cut the Gordian Knot of the transcendental subject and its accompanying object by restructuring this age-old problematic as the matter of a singular life that can bear the weight of posing a question, be it the question of revolution or the question of whether one should read Flaubert's *Salammbô* or not, or whatever. To do this, says Deleuze, one has to deal with such questions at the level of virtuality, since to ask the question of the advisability or otherwise of reading Flaubert's *Salammbô* is already to do something abstracted from all those many and varied impulses and passions that bring me to read this work of Flaubert's or to avoid reading it, as the case may be. In the realm of the virtual, the domain of what Deleuze calls Life, the actual is already being undone by the real but not yet actual event that is active without yet being manifestly or concretely present. This virtual is the *not-yet-coded* always scrambling all the existent codes, so this virtual is already real and active, however without yet being actual, and as such is the only thing capable of overturning the established codes. The virtual, and its encompassing images of thought, is thus an exteriority to the already encoded, and therefore represents a condition of possibility for the constitution of the already encoded, as well as the potentiality for a creative or monstrous transmutation of that which is already encoded, that is, its more or less radical decoding and perhaps subsequent recoding.[9]

Is too much philosophical weight being placed here on this short and densely hermetic essay on life, bare life, clearly written *in extremis* as Deleuze's days were drawing to an end? The reader familiar with Deleuze's *oeuvre* will soon realize that the briefly stated claims being made here about encoding, decoding, and recoding are in fact absolutely central to Deleuze and Guattari's *Capitalisme et schizophrénie* project, where there is of course an extensive treatment of the several regimes of signs involved in the constitution of the potentially myriad apparatuses of encoding, decoding, and recoding, all undertaken in the name of a "schizo" (in the *Anti-Oedipus*) or a "nomadic" (in *Mille plateaux*) scrambling of the existing and State-sanctioned codes. Several of Deleuze's able commentators have dealt with his treatment of the regimes of signs in the kind of detail unavoidably missing here—but those I have read agree, even if only implicitly at times, that the connection between the realm of the virtual and the apparatuses of coding is a paramount concern for Deleuze in his often-detailed discussions of semiosis. To put it briefly: the crux of what I've termed the first Deleuzean ontology/problematic, namely, the image of thought understood as the *not-yet-coded*, is the necessary and prior condition for the endlessly ramified practices of encoding, decoding, and recoding that are the essential basis for this second Deleuzean ontology/problematic.

Deleuzean semiosis is infinite, which is to say that the *not-yet-coded* serves as an exteriority that unendingly solicits or incites the task of coding with its accompanying desire,[10] the basic architecture of which is represented in terms of the famous three syntheses which Deleuze and Guattari outline in *Anti-Oedipus*:

1. the disjunctive synthesis of singularities and chains (*"sort, sort ...."*)/ (either ... or ... or)
2. the conjunctive synthesis of intensities and becomings (so that's what it is (*c'est donc*))
3. the connective synthesis of partial objects and flows (and ... and ...)[11]

Semiosis is thus a process which feeds more and more propositions into the coding machines regulated by these three syntheses, propositions which are then added to the already immense reservoir of those created and sanctioned by the prevailing codes—propositions about hitherto unknown galaxies, hitherto unknown tribes in the Amazon jungle, hitherto unknown forms of psychic excitation or debilitation (e.g., the syndrome known as attention deficit disorder was unknown until fairly recently), hitherto unknown personal histories (e.g., the pedophilia of the famous British disc jockey Sir Jimmy Savile, a friend of Prince Charles and Mrs Thatcher, only came to public attention after his death), and so on to infinity.

From the beginning Deleuze viewed desire as an exteriority to thought, which nonetheless functioned as the enabling basis for all the inchoate forms of thought. Between desire and concept there is for Deleuze a series of intermediate links: desire is always present from the beginning and is active throughout the extent of all the linkages, but there also affects; event-designations (or "haecceities" or "thisnesses" in Deleuze's lexicon); word-forms; and of course concepts (or perhaps more appropriately for Deleuze, concept-narratives or concept-images, which for him amount to pretty much the same thing). Each of these linkages communicates with the others in a strictly non-hierarchical way, and moreover influences in more or less crucial ways the dynamism of its counterpart linkages.

This vast and polynucleated nexus is also linked to what Paul Patton has rightly called an "ethos of permanent becoming-revolutionary."[12] The intertwining of desire and politics in Deleuze and Guattari can be noted with little need for commentary in a brief account like this, except to invoke the famous saying in *Mille plateaux*: "Before Being there is politics" (*Car, avant l'être il ya a la politique*).[13] But what is it to place desire at the heart of the political, which for Deleuze and Guattari also entails the converse, namely, placing the political at the heart of desire?

The insight that the orchestration of affect and desire has now become much more significant for determining lines of affiliation in a contemporary politics is absolutely central to the *Capitalisme et schizophrénie* project, where this theme is dealt with under the heading of a "micropolitics."

For Deleuze and Guattari the orchestration of desire in micropolitics has an oscillating logic, as the desire constrained by the orders of capital is deterritorialized, so that it becomes a desire exterior to capital, and is then reterritorialized or folded back into the capitalist social field. When this happens the liberated desire integrates into itself the flows and components of the socius or social field to form a "desiring machine." The heart of micropolitics is the construction of these new desiring machines as well as the creation of new linkages between desiring machines: without a politics to facilitate this construction there can be no productive desire, only the endless repetition of the nondifferent, as what is repeated is regulated by the "old" logics of identity, equivalence, and intersubstitutability (this of course being the underlying logic of the commodity principle as analyzed by Marx).

In micropolitics the fate of repeating a difference that is only an apparent difference is avoided, and capitalism's negative, wasteful, and ultimately nonproductive repetition, a repetition of nonbeing, is supplanted by the polytopia or heterotopia of a micropolitics that brings together the strata of minorities, becomings, incorporealities, concepts, "peoples," in this way launching a "new" political thought and practice capable of expressing and instantiating a desire to undo the prevailing order.

Micropolitics therefore creates the above-mentioned "ethos of permanent becoming-revolutionary," an ethos not constrained by a politics predicated on the now defunct forms of Soviet bureaucratic socialism and a liberal or scaled-down social democracy. In this ethos, our criteria of belonging and affiliation will always be subject to a kind of chaotic motion, and a new political knowledge is created which dissipates the enabling lie told to us by those who now have political power, with their love for nation-states, tribes, clans, political parties, churches, and perhaps everything done up to now in the name of community. At the same time, this ethos will create new collective solidarities not based on these old "loves."

So why talk about three Deleuzean ontologies/problematic and not, say, one Deleuzean ontology/problematic with the three somewhat distinct strands we have sought to identify? There is of course simply no way of providing a straightforward answer to this question—all one can do is to specify the theoretical impulse behind the decision to say that there are three Deleuzean ontologies/problematics, none of which is ultimately exclusive of the other.

In saying this, one can nonetheless suggest that the lynch-pin of the Deleuzean undertaking is the philosophically elaborated thought of the plane of immanence/plane of consistency with its attendant notion of the image of thought harnessed to a notion of the virtual that in the end relies on the sheer givenness, but also the infinite plenitude, of *a* life. If the foregoing is the first ontology/problematic (with this much attenuated sense of primacy as the "first" ontology), then the second consists of the expressivities or semiotic events that bring the resources of expression to this virtual givenness. The dynamism for the generation of expressivities and their basis in the infinite plenitude of plain life is what Deleuze and Guattari call desiring production, our "third" Deleuzean ontology/problematic—what else is desire but the impetus to say one more time "and … and … and," even when the imperative to call an end to plenitude seems to announce itself? The thought of Deleuze is about plenitude and its allied notion of multiplicity, its elaboration in terms of an uncontainable range of expressivities, and also the dynamism supplied by desiring production which drives all of these in the direction of a new earth and a new people.

3

Was Deleuze a Materialist?

Gilles Deleuze said repeatedly that he was an empiricist, empiricism as we know *being* for Deleuze the one philosophical standpoint that was resolutely non-dialectical and immanentist (thereby avoiding what was for him the whole sad drama of dialectics and transcendence). However, Deleuze never made the same repeated and unambiguous claims about his philosophical relation to materialism. How are we to understand this seeming discrepancy between Deleuze's respective attitudes toward empiricism and materialism? My argument will be that Deleuze, insofar as he was a materialist, was an *anomalous* materialist, and that insofar as he was a monist in the spirit of Spinoza, he was an *anomalous* monist (more will be said later about this term taken from Donald Davidson).

At one level, a very basic level, it is clear that empiricism, in making the philosophical avowal that reality can only be approached through our senses, belongs to the theory of the subject, whereas materialism, in maintaining in its most basic form that only matter exists, belongs to the theory of the object.[1] His distance from the aporiae of a crude materialism notwithstanding, Deleuze's philosophy therefore still seems to be in danger of being undermined by the age-old dichotomy between subject ("subject" being the underlying constitutive basis of our putative empiricism) and object ("object" being the concomitant underlying basis of our presumed materialism).

This essay will attempt to address this question, by arguing that Deleuze's key category of the "event" bridges the ontological gap represented by this seeming dichotomy between the "subject" of empiricism and the "object" of materialism.

The Deleuzean event belongs to neither subject nor object, but places both subject and object in a new assemblage, an assemblage in which the object becomes "evented" (as in "what is the event featuring the object *x*?"); and the subject is rendered "eventive" (as in "what is the event into which the subject S is drawn?").[2] Events in the Deleuzean scheme of things are beyond the age-old philosophical dichotomy of subject and object, and Deleuze's philosophical framework is therefore capable in principle of being both empiricist and materialist (provided "materialism" is defined in such a way that we avoid the absurd position that there is nothing else in the universe apart from "sheer" matter). So much for our preliminary throat clearing. Let's see how this works out in more detail, by looking at the relevant Deleuzean philosophemes.

First, it is implausible to view Deleuze as an unqualified or crude materialist of the kind depicted above. There is an obvious sense in which the naïve or unqualified materialist—that is, the person who insists flatly that matter per se is all there is—cannot be taken to represent a remotely defensible philosophical position. Admittedly, these are deep and murky waters that have been trawled without any decisive outcome by philosophers for centuries; and so it behooves us to concede or acknowledge from the outset that there are physicalist/materialist monisms, which insist, with an undeniable *prima facie* acceptability, that *all* the properties we encounter can in principle be reduced to physical properties or the properties of matter.

But why is this kind of monistic materialism, a rigorous monism, still allegedly unacceptable for some? Aren't all monists (and Deleuze as the follower of Spinoza certainly is a monist) committed to being either materialists or idealists? Let's begin here with the construction of an argument, as a prolepsis to dealing with the questions that are posed, unavoidably, for those who have a philosophical commitment to the rudiments of a monistic materialism.

It is hardly deniable that the moment "materialism" is constituted as part of an intellectual or theoretical field, the moment one *asserts* the thesis or doctrine of materialism (asserting being the *event* of a speech act of course, and thus by its nature non-material), that moment of assertion becomes the instant when one has to produce *axioms* which create a *thinking* about matter, and *that* thinking, and its accompanying axioms, cannot of itself be absolutely and purely material. Which modes of reflection are appropriate to a philosophical understanding of the constitution of matter? How do we identify those categories of thought apposite to any thinking done with regard to matter? Such questions immediately take us beyond an unqualified or knuckle-dragging materialism. Quite simply, as has been pointed out by the students of set theory: while horses are material beings, the *set* of horses is not itself a material being. While a mountain is a material entity, the *concept* of a mountain is not itself material. It is of course not this simple. What if the concept is inextricably bound-up with an image, so that what we really have are concept-images, and images do of course have a material component?[3] To get back to the subject of the Deleuzean event.

Deleuze introduced the notion of the event in his *Logique du sens* to designate the immediate resultant of the interaction of various forces:

> Events are effects (thus, for example, the castration "effect," and the parricide effect …). But insofar as they are tied to effects, they must be tied not only with endogenous causes, but with exogenous causes as well, effective states of affairs, actions really undertaken, and contemplations effectively actualized. (*LS*, p. 210)

As a result of this interaction, one or more immanent changes come into being. Deleuze indicates that his understanding of the event is derived from the Stoic concept of *lekta: lekta* are incorporeal transformations or incorporeal predicate events that hover beyond and above the world of space and time and its objects, but which are susceptible to expression in language, and, as such, they constitute the "sayability" of an event.[4] The product of an amalgam of such forces is the event; the event therefore designates a particular internal dynamic of this amalgam of forces, such as the "effective states of affairs, actions really undertaken, and contemplations effectively actualized" mentioned by Deleuze in the above-quoted passage. It should be stressed that the event is not a specific occurrence or happening, it is not a "thing," but is rather that which is rendered actual in *this* or *that* happening or occurrence. To provide an example.

Bears acquire a thicker winter coat before the onset of cold weather. The Deleuzean (and Stoic) event is not what manifestly occurs (the bear's coat becoming thicker)—the bear's coat, *this* bear's coat, becoming thicker is only an evanescent consequence or expression of the actualization of this event. This event (the becoming thicker of *this* bear's coat) is the resultant of an amalgam of forces (the change from autumn to winter, *this* bear's physiology and genetic make-up, geographic location, the vagaries of microclimate, and so on). So, rather than saying "the bear's coat is becoming thicker" or "the bear's coat has become thicker," both of which imply a modification of the "essence" of the bear, the Stoics/Deleuze prefers that we should say "the coat thickens." The use here of the infinitive "to thicken" enables us to make an event-predication with regard to the/this bear and its coat, one which reflects the dynamism underlying the event's actualization, this predication being an incorporeality distinct from both the coat itself and the thickness itself, but which nevertheless expresses the event's dynamism.

Deleuze's account of the event enables us to dispense with an ontology based on substances and the fixed states or qualities of these substances, and with this the identities based on substance. This ontology has prevailed since the time of Plato, and Deleuze wants to overcome or circumvent this Platonism.[5] What are the defining characteristics of an event?

An event lacks a determinate structure, is without spatio-temporal position, is immaterial and has no beginning or end, has no limits (and by virtue of having no limits connects with every other event). Even an inert object can be an event as long as we can identify it as part of a novel and distinctive process; for example, a dead tree is an inert object, but it becomes "eventive" if, say, during a battle there is a short burst of activity in which a soldier dives behind the dead tree to avoid a sniper's bullet. As I said earlier, an event expresses the internal dynamism of the process in which it is embedded, and this particular dead tree, which is the crucial enabling condition for the survival of that soldier during that battle, is "eventive" precisely because it expresses a key element in the process that incorporates the survival of the soldier, and beyond that, there is the process of the entire battle itself (and beyond that, the all-inclusive war of which the battle is a part, and even further beyond that the absolutely immense grouping of events to which that war and all its antecedent and ramified events belong).

Every event is new and *sui generis*—it cannot be repeated as the self-same event it is. Deleuze of course maintains that all events, any event, will connect up with every other event, in multiply transformative ways, so that they all meet-up in a great and singular event, the One. (It was this Deleuzean insistence on the one event that prompted the egregious Alain Badiou to criticize Deleuze for his alleged "monism,"[6] overlooking Deleuze's insistence that the One is a never more than a coming together of endlessly multiple elements in a totality that can never be halted or fully resolved, a totality that is potentially but not necessarily harmonious.) What does all this portend for our understanding of the subject, that is, the possible place for the subject in this unresolved totality?

A problematic way of posing this question would be to assume that the event is a series or process external to the preconstituted subject. Deleuze sees it quite differently. The event, as a process, is integrated with processes that occur within and between the place(s) of the subject(s). The subject is thus the place or situation where a certain kind of affectivity or intensity occurs—where reading *Recherchés du temps perdu* inaugurates a completely new mode of desire for an unsuspecting reader of Proust; or where the soldier who dives behind the dead tree to avoid being shot by the sniper comes, literally, to be propelled into a completely different subject-forming series once he finds he has avoided the sniper's bullet—reflected in the expressions "If I get out of this alive, this is going to make me into a pacifist," "I'm the luckiest person in the universe" (this said by someone who had hitherto believed that life had always given him the short end of the stick), and so on.

Each event is embedded in a physical series (the sniper and his rifle, the dead tree, the fleeing soldier and the patch of ground he is lying on behind the tree, and so on), a physical series that comes from the outside and forces change (the fleeing soldier must wait behind the tree until the sniper goes away, the sniper must try to find a new vantage point if he is to get a fresh sighting of the soldier hidden behind the tree, the fleeing soldier may radio for back-up from his position behind the tree, and so forth). This physical series—which by the way is precisely how we are to understand Deleuze's materialism, at least in principle—occurs as a powerful and exigent bearing-down of the past and of the future on the present moment.

Deleuze, as we have seen, adheres to the Stoic doctrine that every event is connected up with the realm of expressibility, a realm that is ideal and virtual, which contains all the senses an event can come to possess. Every sense and all prospective levels of intensity hover over the physical events that have the capacity to express them. This is conveyed in the feeling of ambiguity and the sense of something yet to be resolved when one confronts the future of the event. Crucial here are the three syntheses of time that Deleuze develops in his *Difference and Repetition*: (1) what is coming? (Expectation); (2) what am I moving/passing into? (I'm never stuck); and (3) which option should I select? (creating the new).[7]

The subject and the object are not dissolved or done away with in this process of event-constitution, rather both are treated as a blend of forces (without in any way implying a synthesis of elements)—the fleeing soldier in our example is a soldier because he has enlisted in an army, carries a weapon, wears a uniform, etc., he can be said to be fleeing precisely because he moves along a certain trajectory (as Wilfred Bion, the pioneering object-relations psychoanalyst who was a much-decorated veteran of the First World War, once remarked, the difference between cowardice and bravery is the direction in which you run).[8] The fleeing soldier is not an object or substance, but an assemblage consisting of a body (which in turn is a further combination of forces), a body which moves and positions itself in certain ways as it interacts with its environment, which responds in this or that way to ever-developing circumstances, which is positioned with regard to a past that overdetermines the present even as it confronts a future fraught with contingencies of every kind. The soldier-assemblage, qua "object," is the resultant of all these sub-apparatuses coming together, and not just coalescing, but also mutating as a consequence of this coalescence. As "subject," the soldier is not an ego or a defined center of consciousness, this of course being the way the subject is understood in the philosophical tradition. Rather, the soldier qua "subject" is another assemblage, an assemblage in ceaseless interaction with the object-assemblage, so much so that these two assemblages—the subject-assemblage and the object-assemblage—constitute a super-assemblage; and this super-assemblage that constitutes our soldier in turn is in constant interaction with a war assemblage, an army assemblage, an enemy assemblage, a territorial assemblage, a geopolitical assemblage, and so on. All interactions between, and within, such assemblages are "eventive." "Subjects" and "objects" are thus sets of events, in continual interaction with other sets of events.

Deleuze and Guattari call this continual interaction a "machinic process" (*agencement machinique*). The machinic process is a mode of organization that links all kinds of "attractions and repulsions, sympathies, and antipathies, alterations, amalgamations, penetrations, and expressions that affect bodies of all kinds in their relations to one another" (*TP*, p. 90). In the *event*, the material/physical and the nonmaterial therefore comingle in an empiricism without limits.

So, was Deleuze a monistic materialist (in which case the charge leveled at him by Alain Badiou would be justified)? Deleuze was an anomalous monist, if I could borrow a term from Donald Davidson.[9] The Davidsonian theory of anomalous monism has two strands, one which states that such non-material phenomena as concepts and sets constitute events which can be mapped onto physical or material events; and, second, that the non-physical is anomalous; that is, under their non-physicalistic descriptions these non-physical events are not and, indeed, cannot be regulated by strict psychophysical laws. The law of gravity, for instance, would apply to a bear, but it is absurd to say that it applies to the *concept* of a bear. Of course the concept of a bear can be mapped onto a physical bear, and indeed in some appropriate sense something like this has to be the case for it to be the concept of a bear, but there are no psychophysical laws which entail that the concept of a bear is reducible, "without remainder," to this or that material or physical object that is ursine. A more precise and productive way of characterizing the bear, being ursine, and their affiliated concepts, is to say that for Deleuze there is a bear-assemblage, consisting of *this* bear, its habitat, its relationships with other bears, and other species (including *Homo sapiens*), the concept-narrative-image "bear" and its cognates, discourses, and epistemologies having "being a bear" or "bearhood" as their focus, etc., all in a ceaseless interaction with each other. We can of course identify sub-assemblages within this bear-assemblage, such as the discourses and epistemologies or the bear's habitat or the bear itself, but this identification does not turn these into discrete substances possessing their associated subjects and objects. To quote Deleuze and Guattari: "Climate, wind, season, hour are not of another nature than the things, animals, or people that populate them, follow them, sleep and awaken within them" (*TP*, p. 263). There are processes involving standpoints that create assemblages capable of producing objectifications and subjectifications, but about objects and subjects per se we have to accept the Deleuzean injunction of a sober nominalism.

All that has been said here about anomalous monism is perfectly compatible—in axiomatic terms without any accompanying strict verbal equivalence—with Stoic doctrine and its Deleuzean appropriation and reformulation. Anomalous monism is a monism (matter is all there is) which nonetheless allows a dualism of attributes or properties (e.g., Spinoza's thought and extension). Now anomalous monism is not of course without its critics[10], but for now that is another story.

4

Force as a Deleuzean Concept

Deleuze's employment of the concept of force (the same in English and French) can be grasped in terms of two distinctive but somewhat overlapping phases. In the first, associated with the "historical" emphasis on the works on Spinoza and Nietzsche (among others) that marked the earlier part of Deleuze's career, force is understood primarily in terms of its relation to notions of speed and movement. In the case of Spinoza, Deleuze is particularly impressed by Spinoza's philosophical ambition to view all of life as the expression of a fundamental striving or conatus, so that the body becomes an ensemble consisting of those forces which it transmits and those forces which it receives. Spinoza, says Deleuze in *Spinoza: Practical Philosophy* "solicits forces in thought that elude obedience as well as blame, and fashions the image of a life beyond good and evil, a rigorous innocence without merit or culpability" (*SPP*, p. 4). This fundamental insight is carried through in Deleuze's work on Nietzsche, where Nietzsche is depicted as someone who follows faithfully Spinoza's injunction that we think "in terms of speeds and slownesses, of frozen catatonias and accelerated movements, unformed elements, nonsubjectified affects" (*SPP*, p. 129).[1]

In the second phase, associated primarily with Deleuze's collaboration with Guattari, the notion of force is effectively generalized, so that it expresses a power that ranges over the entirety of the social order. Here another set of definitions and principles comes to the forefront, even if the earlier indebtedness to the archive associated with Spinoza and Nietzsche is retained, so that the notion of force as a movement with its characteristic speeds and slownesses is still operative for Deleuze. This time, however, the emphasis is more on a specific effect of force, namely, *puissance* or "strength" (as opposed to *pouvoir* or "coercive power"). Each of these intellectual phases will be considered in turn.[2]

In Spinoza's magnum opus, *Ethics, Demonstrated in Geometrical Order* (1677), each being has an essential and intrinsic disposition to preserve its own being, a tendency Spinoza terms *conatus* (Spinoza (2000), p. 171). For Spinoza, a being's good is that which adds to its capacity to preserve itself, and conversely, the bad is that which militates against this capacity for self-preservation. Each being's desire (*appetitio*) is precisely for that which conduces to its self-preservation.[3] A being's capacity for action increases, accordingly, in proportion to the strength of its *conatus*; and conversely, the weaker its *conatus*, the more diminished is its capacity for action. A being enhances its capacity for action when it actively transmits its force; its capacity for action is reduced when it is the passive recipient of some other being's forces. Pleasure or joy ensue when the capacity for action is enhanced, and pain when it is diminished, so that for Spinoza pain is passion only and not action, whereas joy is both pleasure and action.[4]

Freedom is promoted when one's scope for action is expanded, and this expansion is for Spinoza the outcome of a life led according to reason. In a life guided by reason, especially by knowledge of the third kind, one comes to have knowledge of oneself and of God/Nature. In gaining this knowledge, one's mind, which is part of the infinite mind of God, becomes a part of something eternal. The outcome for this kind of knower is beatitude.[5] Deleuze explains the coincidence of power and action for Spinoza in the following terms:

> All power is inseparable from a capacity for being affected, and this capacity for being affected is constantly and necessarily filled by affections that realize it. The word *potestas* has a legitimate use here ... to *potentia* as essence there corresponds a *potestas* as a capacity for being affected, which capacity is filled by the affections or modes that God produces necessarily, God being unable to undergo action but being the active cause of these affections. (SPP, pp. 97–8)

This distinction between *potentia* and *potestas* (or *puissance* and *pouvoir* respectively, in French) is crucially important for the subsequent thought of Deleuze, and in particular for the formulation of a materialist ontology of constitutive power, this being one of the primary intellectual objectives of Deleuze and Guattari's *Capitalism and Schizophrenia* project. For Spinoza was, in the eyes of Deleuze (and Guattari), the initiator of this ontology's guiding insights and principles. However, the thinker who in their view created the image of thought that made possible the comprehensive amplification of Spinoza's principles into a full-blown ontology of constitutive power was Nietzsche.[6]

Nietzsche is, of course, credited by Deleuze with numerous philosophical accomplishments, but primary among these is Nietzsche's method of dramatizing thought. In this staging of thought or "dramatology," the speed and slowness with which a concept is moved, the dynamism of its spatio-temporal determinations, the intensity with which it interacts with adjacent entities in a system, all become primary. As Deleuze puts it:

> The state of experience is not subjective, at least not necessarily so. Nor is it individual. It is flux, and the interruption of flux and each intensity is necessarily related to another intensity, such that something passes through. This is what underlies all codes, what eludes them, and what the codes seek to translate, convert, and forge anew. But Nietzsche, in this writing on intensities, tells us: do not trade intensities for mere representations. The intensity refers neither to signifieds which would be the representations of things, nor to signifiers which would be the representations of words. (*DI*, p. 257)

The criteria and formal conditions associated with a logic premised on notions of truth and falsity, and indeed of representation generally, constitute a "dogmatic image of thought," and thus for Nietzsche have to be supplanted by a topology in which notions indebted to representation are replaced by such concepts as "the noble and the base, the high and the low," and so forth.[7] Representational thinking is constitutively superintended by the *logos*, and in place of this *logos*-driven thinking Nietzsche advances a conception of sense-based (sense-making) "operators." To quote Deleuze (who at this point is, palpably, a follower of Nietzsche):

> In Nietzsche ... the notion of sense is an instrument of absolute contestation, absolute critique, and also a particular original production: sense is not a reservoir, nor a principle or an origin, nor even an end. It is an "effect," an effect *produced*, and we have to discover its laws of production ... the idea of sense as an effect produced by a certain machinery, as in a physical, optical, sonorous effect, etc. (which is not at all to say that it is a mere appearance) .... An aphorism of Nietzsche's is a machine that produces sense, in a certain order that is specific to thought. Of course, there are other orders, other machineries—for example, all those which Freud discovered, and still more political and practical orders. But we must be the machinists, the "operators" of something. (*DI*, 137, original emphasis)

The pivot of this Nietzschean image of thought, for Deleuze, is the concept of force (*macht*), and in particular Nietzsche's insight that "all reality is already a quantity of force" (*NP*, p. 40).[8] At the same time Nietzsche believes the concept of force "still needs to be *completed*: an *inner* will must be *ascribed* to it, which I designate as 'will to power'" (quoted in *NP*, p. 49, original emphasis). It is at this point that Nietzsche can be said to take to a certain culminating point Spinoza's conception of the *conatus*.

The will to power (*wille zur macht*) and its relation to force can be understood in terms of the following propositions that can be extracted from Deleuze's "argument" set-out in *Nietzsche and Philosophy*.

The essence of a force is its quantitative difference from other forces, and the quality of the force in question is constituted by this quantitative difference, and the will to power is thus the principle of the synthesis of forces: the will to power enables the emergence of this quantitative difference from other forces and the quality that is embodied by each force in this relation (*NP*, p. 50).

Force and will should not be conflated—in Deleuze's words, "force is what can, will to power is what wills" (*La force est ce qui peut, la volonté de puissance est ce qui veut*) (*NP*, p. 50). Moreover, when two forces are alongside each other, one is dominant and the other is the dominated, and the will to power is thus the internal element of the production of force (*NP*, p. 51). Nietzsche understands the will to power in terms of the genealogical element of force. Chance is not eliminated by the will to power, since the will to power would be neither flexible nor open to contingency without chance (*NP*, pp. 52–3). Also, depending on its original quality, a force is either active or reactive, while affirmation and negation are the primary qualities of the will to power (*NP*, pp. 53–4); affirmation is not action per se, but the power of becoming active, it is the personification of becoming active, while negation is not mere reactivity but a becoming reactive (*NP*, p. 54). As a result, to interpret is to determine the force which bestows sense on a thing, while to evaluate is to determine the will to power which bestows value on a thing (*NP*, p. 54).

Reactive forces diminish or annul the power of active forces, and every force which goes to the limit of its ability is active, while those who are weak are separated from what they can accomplish (*NP*, pp. 57–61). All sensibility amounts to a becoming of forces (the will to power is the composite of these forces), and forces can be categorized in the following way: (i) *active force* is the power of acting or commanding; (ii) *reactive force* is the power of being acted upon or obeying; (iii) *developed reactive force* is the power of decomposition, division, and separation; (iv) *active force becoming reactive* is the power of being separated, of undermining itself (*NP*, p. 63).

The eternal return indicates that becoming-reactive is non-being, and it also produces becoming-active by generating becoming: the being of becoming cannot be affirmed fully without also affirming the existence of becoming-active (*NP*, p. 72). The object of philosophy is liberation, but this philosophy is always "untimely," since it requires the abolition of negativity and the dissipative power of non-being, a task that will be coextensive with the emergence of a new kind of being, one beholden to neither of the two previous forms of being, God and Man.[9]

A Deleuzean ontology will extract one fundamental principle from these theses, namely, that desire is a kind of *puissance* and thus necessarily a type of force. With this principle Deleuze and Guattari are in a position to formulate the materialist ontology of political practice associated with their *Capitalism and Schizophrenia* project. In particular, the notion of *judgment*, and the vision of philosophy as the "science of judgment," could now be overthrown in favor of philosophies, political and otherwise, which hinged on conceptions of desire and intensity.

By the time the first volume of the *Capitalism and Schizophrenia* project, *L'Anti-Oedipe*, was published, an intellectual and political context had emerged, in France at any rate, that provided enabling conditions for the emergence of the ontological framework developed by Deleuze and Guattari in *Anti-Oedipus* and the project's second volume, *Mille plateaux*.[10]

In (French) philosophy, the then-regnant structuralist and phenomenological paradigms had largely run their course and reached a point of exhaustion by the late 1960s. Phenomenology never really managed to detach itself from the Cartesian model of subjectivity and self-consciousness, and when it became clear that not even Heidegger, the later Husserl, Merleau-Ponty, and Sartre (to mention only some of the more eminent figures involved in this undertaking) were able to resolve or dissolve the conundrums of transcendental subjectivism, the phenomenological paradigm was increasingly perceived to have struck its equivalent of the proverbial iceberg. Structuralism was able to steer clear of the impasses that afflicted Cartesian subjectivism, but its reliance on Saussure's conception of language required it to posit the linguistic code as something of a transcendental entity in its own right; the code had to be assumed from the outset as a condition for determining meaning. When it became clear that the code could not function as a transcendental principle, and this because it effectively reduced all vehicles of meaning to utterance (images were a particular problem for structuralism because many of their properties could not be accounted for in terms of a model based on utterance), the structuralist paradigm fell into desuetude.[11]

At the same time, conceptions of subjectivity derived from psychoanalysis were found to be problematic. Freud and his more immediate followers viewed the libidinal drives as something that had to be contained or channeled if "civilization" was to be maintained (Freud's *Civilization and Its Discontents*

(1930) is the canonical text here), and although some of Freud's followers did seek alternative metapsychological frameworks for understanding libidinal intensities, those who strayed too far from Freud's original metapsychological principles were soon denounced by the official Freudian establishment. Foremost among these "deviationists" was Wilhelm Reich, whose call for a "liberation" of the libidinal drives exerted a powerful influence on *Anti-Oedipus*, although it has to be acknowledged that *Anti-Oedipus* is only one of a number of contemporary French works that sought a more expansive conception of the libidinal drives, often involving an extension, more or less radically different in relation to the concept's origin, of Freud's notion of a "polymorphous perversity."[12] The late 1960s and 1970s in France represented a conjuncture in which the various post- or neo-Freudianisms were consolidated into a loose-knit movement, and the *Capitalism and Schizophrenia* project partook of this conjuncture, at least insofar as its vigorous polemic against Freudianism is concerned.

Also important for the conjuncture which enabled the *Capitalism and Schizophrenia* project (and its ontology of political practice) to emerge was the social and political constellation associated with what came to be known as "the events of May 1968." Important for the genesis of this constellation was the perceived failure of the Soviet Communist project after that country's brutal invasions of Hungary in 1956 and Czechoslovakia in 1968, along with the disclosures concerning Stalin's show trials and purges provided by Khrushchev at the Twentieth Communist Party Congress in February 1956. Just as significant for the French left intelligentsia of that period (the mid-1950s to the late 1960s) was the winding-down of the Bandung Project so soon after its inception in 1955; with the collapse of the Bandung project any hope that a non-aligned Third World could serve as a repository of emancipatory potential rapidly disappeared.[13] In political life, the post-war Gaullist institutional monopoly had pushed the French version of "representative democracy" into a gradual but seemingly inexorable sclerosis, and the post-war compromise between capital and labor, viewed as the basis of a thirty-year period of prosperity (*les trente glorieuses*) was also beginning to unravel (as it did elsewhere in the advanced industrial countries of the Western world).[14] These developments marked, collectively, the transition of one phase of capitalist development to another, as the French manifestation of the social-democratic form of capitalism mutated into the current globally integrated capitalist dispensation that is in place today. This particular transition is embodied in a number of registers: the emergence of a new subject of labor, the creation of new structures of accumulation, the setting-up of new axes of value, the transformation of the capitalist state, the availability of new forms of opposition and struggle, and so on. These and other parallel developments are taken by Deleuze and Guattari to indicate the need for a new ontology of political practice and constitutive power.[15]

All this amounted to a crisis of utopia for French Marxist and marxisant thought, as the question of the transformations undergone by the regime of accumulation and mode of production became a crucial object of inquiry. In a nutshell, Deleuze and Guattari's analytical treatment of "force" helped them advance a revolutionary conceptualization of the mode of production. Their delineation of the notion of "force" enabled a central focus on the concept of a "machinic process" (*agencement machinique*), which could then be used by them to formulate a full-blown ontology of constitutive power that in turn could underpin a new "theorization" of the mode of production.

The machinic process is a mode of organization that links all kinds of "attractions and repulsions, sympathies, and antipathies, alterations, amalgamations, penetrations, and expressions that affect bodies of all kinds in their relations to one another" (*TP*, p. 90). The modes of production are constituted by these machinic processes (*TP*, p. 435). This is the equivalent of saying that the modes of production, subtended as they are by machinic processes, are expressions of desire, and thus of force (in the sense of *potentia/pouvoir*); the modes of production are the resultant of this infinitely productive desire or force. As Deleuze and Guattari would have it, it is desire, which is always social and collective, that makes the gun into a weapon of war, or sport, or hunting, depending on extant circumstances (*TP*, pp. 89–90). The mode of production is thus on the same level as the other expressions of desire, and it is made up of stratifications, that is, crystallizations or orchestrations of ordered functions which are these very expressions of desire.[16] Here Deleuze and Guattari bring about a reversal of the typical marxist understanding of the mode of production: it is not the mode *per se* that allows production to be carried out (as the traditional account specifies), instead, it is desiring-production itself that makes a particular mode the kind of mode that it is. Deleuze and Guattari's recourse to a practical ontology of desiring-production is thus their way of accounting for the organization of productive desire. All this sounds highly recondite, but the principle framed in this part of the *Capitalism and Schizophrenia* project simply elaborates what Marx himself had said, namely, that society has to exist before capitalist appropriation can take place, so that a society/state with already positioned labor has to exist if the realization of surplus value is to take place. To quote Deleuze and Guattari:

> Marx, the historian, and Childe, the archaeologist, are in agreement on the following point: the archaic imperial State, which steps in to overcode agricultural communities, presupposes at least a certain level of development of these communities' productive forces since there must be a potential surplus capable of constituting a State stock, of supporting a specialized handicrafts class (metallurgy), and of progressively giving rise to public functions. This is why Marx links the archaic State to a certain [precapitalist] "mode of production." (*TP*, p. 428)[17]

Before any surplus value can be realized by capital there is politics, that is, force, and this is why the genealogy of force based on Spinoza and Nietzsche (although Hume and Bergson also figure in this genealogy), constructed in the *Capitalism and Schizophrenia* project, is central and unavoidable.

While capitalism is for Deleuze and Guattari an immense set of apparatuses, operating on a planetary scale, that transcodes all reachable spaces of accumulation, its functioning is due to more than just the operation of forces at the level of organizations and formations. The ontology of constitutive power conceptualizes force or *puissance* not just in regard to its role in creating and consolidating a planetary-wide regime of accumulation. This way of conceptualizing also encompasses two complementary facets: on one hand, the ways in which this *puissance* enables at once the emergence and consolidation of the various forms of collective subjectivity; on the other hand, the ways in which these forms make possible the means for capitalism to fashion the kinds of subjectivity (a "social morphology" in Deleuze's words (*N*, p. 158)) required for the collective functioning.

Deleuze has in several works connected the notion of force with the concept of a singularity, primarily because it takes a libidinal investment, and thus the activation of a force or ensemble of forces, to constitute a singularity.[18] If the universe is composed of absolute singularities, then production, any kind of production, can only take the form of repetition: each singularity, as production unfolds, can only repeat or propagate itself. In production, each singularity can only express its own difference, its distance or proximity, from everything else. Production, on this Deleuzean view, is an unendingly proliferating distribution of all the myriad absolute singularities. Production is necessarily repetition of difference, the difference of each singularity from everything else.

Capitalism, however, also requires the operation of repetition. A capitalist axiomatics, at the same time, can only base itself on notions of identity, equivalence, and intersubstitutivity, as Marx pointed out in his analysis of the logic of the commodity form. This being so, capitalist repetition is perforce repetition of the nondifferent; the different in capitalism can never be more than the mere appearance of difference, because capitalist difference can always be overcome, and returned through the processes of abstract exchange, to what is always the same, the utterly fungible. Capitalism and this is a decisive principle in the *Capitalism and Schizophrenia* project only deterritorializes in order to bring about a more powerful reterritorialization. When capitalism breaches limits it does so only in order to impose its own limits, which it projects as the limits of the universe. The power of repetition in capitalism is therefore entirely negative, wasteful, and lacking in any really productive force. Capitalistic repetition is nonbeing in the manner set out by Spinoza. Any collective subjectivity constituted on the basis of this form of repetition will not be able to advance the cause of emancipation. The challenge, at once philosophical and political, posed by the authors of the *Capitalism and Schizophrenia* project has therefore to do with the supersession of this capitalist repetition by forms of productive repetition that are capable of breaking beyond the limits imposed on emancipation by those who rule us. Only force, that is, politics, which is not the same as violence (at least not necessarily), can accomplish this.

For Deleuze, therefore, the ontology of this anti-capitalist power of constitution must take the form of a genealogy of the concept of force. At any rate, it must begin with this genealogy, since Nietzsche and Spinoza were the great discoverers of the scope and nature of force's "social physics." A genealogy of the "social physics" of force adumbrated by Spinoza and Nietzsche augments, philosophically, the critique of capitalism that lies at the heart of the *Capitalism and Schizophrenia* project; indeed, without the first the latter would be impossible.

5

On Producing the Concept of the Image-Concept

One of the great divisions in the reflection on culture undertaken by the Western philosophical tradition has been the one between the *image* (seen by this tradition as belonging to the realm of experience) and the *concept* (seen as being in the realm of the understanding or reason). This problematic dichotomy reached its culminating point in Kant, who assigned its respective terms to two completely different faculties (although to be precise Kant did not use the term "image," preferring instead to use the term "object of experience")—Kant located the *concept* in the domain of judgment (his first *Critique*), while the image was placed in the domain of taste or opinion (his third *Critique*). My essay will be in three parts.

The first will outline the theory of conceptual production employed in this essay, and it will soon be clear that this theory is indebted to the writings of Gilles Deleuze.

The second will trace the history of this dichotomy, going back to Plato and onwards up to contemporary Anglo-American philosophy, where the *image* continues to be identified with the particular, and the *concept* with the universal (witness the protracted debates on the issue of denotation (image-object) versus connotation (concept) in the tradition that extends from Frege via Russell to Quine). This dichotomy also has a profound resonance in popular culture, instanced in the commonplace distinction, typically to be encountered on television shows with a "pop psychology" component such as Oprah or Dr Phil, between someone's "body image" (basically to do with entirely subjective self-perception, as when I say "I'm really fat" or "My baldness makes me unattractive") and the "bodily concept" (what the consensus of experts such as dieticians and doctors tells us, "objectively," about the body—"if your Body Mass Index is X, then you are 'normal' or 'obese' or 'morbidly obese,' etc.").

The third part of my essay will deal with one very significant attempt to cut the Gordian Knot with regard to this dichotomy, namely, the notion of the *image-concept* in the work of Gilles Deleuze (or where Deleuze is concerned it is perhaps more accurate to say *image-narrative-concept*). The aspects of Deleuze's position to be considered here include his treatment of the notion of involuntary memory (Bergson and Proust influenced this area of Deleuze's work), which seems to be neither fully image nor fully narrative nor fully concept. Also pertinent here is Deleuze's notion of the cinematic image that, like involuntary memory, seems to be image, narrative and concept and yet not fully any one of these at the same time.

But first, in the way of some initial footwork, the question of producing a concept needs to be broached.[1] Deleuze and Guattari are explicit about relating the genesis of a concept to the *event* of its production. To quote at some length a relevant passage from their *WP*:

> The philosopher is the concept's friend; he is the potentiality of the concept. That is, philosophy is not the simple art of forming, inventing, or fabricating concepts, because concepts are not necessarily forms, discoveries, or products. More rigorously, philosophy is the discipline that involves *creating* concepts …. The object of philosophy is to create concepts that are always new …. Concepts are not waiting for us ready-made, like heavenly bodies. There is no heaven for concepts. They must be invented, fabricated, or rather created …. Nietzsche laid down the task of philosophy when he wrote, "[Philosophers] must no longer accept concepts as a gift, nor merely purify and polish them, but first *make* and *create* them, present them and make them convincing. Hitherto one has generally trusted one's concepts as if they were a wonderful dowry from some sort of wonderland," but trust must be replaced by distrust, and philosophers must distrust most those concepts they did create themselves.[2]

If we proceed in accordance with this Deleuzean prescription, we'll need to distinguish adequately between the concepts of a *theory* of X (X could be culture or cinema or religion or whatever), the concepts *intrinsic* to X (i.e., a particular culture or cinema or religion, etc.), and that particular culture or cinema or religion in its barest empirical or material *conditions*.[3] A theory of X is something which is produced or created no less than its putative object X. It is a practice, just as cultures and cinemas are multilinear ensembles of practices. A theory, to be more precise, is a practice of concepts. A theory of culture or cinema is not "about" culture or cinema, but about the concepts that cultures or cinemas happen to generate, concepts that are themselves related in more or less complex ways to other assortments of practice, and so on. A theory, in short, operates on the concepts integral to the practical expression of this or that culture or cinema or religion or politics, and so forth.

A *theory* of culture does not therefore impinge directly on the sheerly empirical phenomena constituting culture (its *bruta facta* so to speak), but on the concepts of culture, which however are no less practical, actual, or effective than culture itself. (This is simply another way of registering in a way that is as unavoidable as it is problematic that scarcely deniable affectivity of "thought" with which the "idealist" philosophical traditions have always been impressed, but which their materialist counterparts have found embarrassing or insusceptible of adequate description and analysis, or else reducible in principle to something more fundamental and compelling, namely, "matter.") Culture's concepts are not given in the assemblages of practices that constitute it, and yet they are culture's concepts, not theories about culture. Every culture or cinema generates for itself its own "thinkability" (and concomitantly its own "unthinkability" as the obverse of this very "thinkability"), and its concepts are constitutive of that "thinkability." Another way of making this point would be to say that a culture or cinema has to secrete its myriad expressivities precisely in order to be able to be what it is, and that its concepts—in ways that are inevitably selective, limiting, and even arbitrary—are the thematizations or representations of these expressivities. Or, more generally, the concepts of a culture (or a cinema) are its expressivities rendered in the form of that culture's (or that cinema's) "thinkability."

Theories of culture (or cinema or politics), by contrast, are theories produced by reflection on the natures, functions, and so forth of these expressivities. They operate on a culture's (or a cinema's) "thinkability." It is fine and salutary to ask the question "What is culture?" but there is another kind of question to be asked as well, in this case "What is (a) theory of (culture)?." Culture itself is an immensely varied and complex practice of signs and images, whose theory philosophers of culture and others must produce, but produce precisely as conceptual practice. No theoretical determination, no matter how subtle or thorough, can on its own constitute the concepts of culture. As indicated, these concepts are expressed in advance and independently of theoretical practice. Theorists, qua theorists, can only traffic in theories of culture (or religion or cinema or politics).

The concepts that theorists deal with can function in more than one field of thought, and even in a single domain it is always possible for a concept to fulfill more than one function. For example, depending on the context, the concept "video image" can function in fields as diverse as cultural studies, forensic criminology, electronics, information science, digital art, advertising theory, and so on. Each variable of thought is of course defined by its own internal variables,

variables which have a complex relation to their external counterparts (such as historical periods, political and social conditions and forces, even the sheer physical state of things). (It is tempting here to understand this complexity in terms that are akin to Althusser's sense of the "overdetermined" relation between formations.) It follows that a concept comes into being or ceases to be effective only when there is a change of function and/or field. Functions for concepts must be created or abolished for them to be generated or eliminated, and new fields must be brought into being in order for concepts to be rendered irrelevant or invalid.

All the above seems like a long-drawn-out clearing of the throat, but I'm not really saying anything really new here—Foucault's *Les mots et les choses* contains a now-famous depiction of visibility that conforms in outline to my somewhat perfunctory accounts of function and field. There Foucault discredits the age-old conception of visibility as something that has its origins in a general/generative source of light which casts itself upon and thereby "illuminates" pre-existing objects. For Foucault, visibility is determined by an apparatus (*dispositif*) that has its own particular way of structuring light, determining the way in which it falls, spreads, and obscures; an apparatus that demarcates the visible from the invisible, in this way bringing into being an entire arrays of objects with this or that mode of visibility as their condition of possibility; a scopic apparatus or regime that also causes objects to be wholly or partially effaced, hidden. Hence even something so taken for granted and innocuous as the very visibility of things is created by an apparatus or regime, in this case a scopic regime, which provides "rules" that govern the very existence and operating conditions of visibility. (And these conditions, as Foucault himself never tired of pointing out, are always "political.") It seems obvious that the concept of the *image-concept* likewise conforms to such "rules" for the generation and perpetuation of concepts.[4]

The intellectual-historical conditions for the production of the (Deleuzean) image-narrative-concept are to be found at the heart of the previous philosophical tradition. According to this tradition, the being of a particular, qua particular, can only be received passively through human intuition—I can have a grasp of a particular only by having an actual experience of the particular in question. Concepts, however, can be employed independently of any actual experience, and do not depend on the passive sensible receptivity of an empirical "given" for their use—in Kant's words, concepts are marked by a productive "spontaneity," in contrast to the non-creative "passivity" of sensible intuitions.[5] Deleuze is certainly not the first philosopher who sought to dismantle this dichotomy between concept and intuition, and it is now something of a commonplace to say that Heidegger is the contemporary philosopher who more than any other elevated this dismantling into the quintessential philosophical "project." But Heidegger's basis for this dismantling is still placed within the confines of a phenomenological ontology, that is, he sought to answer the question "how is receptivity possible?" by resorting to the notion of the pre-givenness of being, and in the process could not account for the productive processes that underlie sensibility itself. For Deleuze, by contrast, the central task of philosophy is precisely the creation of a metaphysics capable of accounting for these productive processes.

The problem with this separation between concept and intuition, or *noesis* and *aisthesis*, is one that has permeated the very core of the philosophical tradition. The age-old distinctions between epistemology and aesthetics, (true) judgment and (mere) taste, all have their basis in this separation. And just as venerable are the attempts to overcome this disconnection, an attempt nowhere no apparent than in Kant's realization that he needed to write a *Critique of Judgement* (to wit, aesthetic judgment) to "complete" the project that began with his *Critique of Pure Reason* (dealing of course with judgment in the domain of truth governed by reason). For Deleuze, the attempts to overcome the dichotomy between (general) concept and (particular) sensible intuition are bound to fail, and this because the principles devised in this philosophical "overcoming" succumb to unavoidable metaphysical illusions. The most common of these illusions involves the use of abstract concepts to group together isolated particulars. These abstract concepts—Being, Unity, Thought, Matter, and so forth—are then inevitably bestowed an a priori ontological superiority denied to the metaphysically inferior particulars, and this because notions like Being and Unity, etc., are simply not "given" in immediate experience, and thus must be positioned as a pure exteriority transcending the contents of immediate experience.[6] There is no way round or out of this predicament as long as the distinction between (transcendent) *noesis* and (transcended) *aisthesis* is retained, and Deleuze opts instead to cut the Gordian Knot by assigning to the concept a totally different function and status.

Rather than giving the abstract concept the policing or custodial role accorded it by the previous philosophical tradition, Deleuze prefers to abandon the tradition's static view of the concept as purely designative, or denominative, or descriptive, and instead views the concept as active and creative. A concept for Deleuze (and Guattari) has three intertwined components: a "possible world, existing face, and real language or speech."[7] A field of experience on their view is always related to a simple "there is." Hence, if I experience fear now that the swine flu has reached the place where I live (Blacksburg, Virginia), then it is a condition of having this experience that there is such a thing as the swine flu, that there is a place (Blacksburg) which happens to be my place of residence, and so forth. But this world, the world that *is*, is always in a position to be interrupted and transformed—someone who gazes at it with a look of fear opens up the possibility of a frightening world, a look of fascination opens up the possibility of a fascinating world, a look of bewilderment opens up the possibility of a bewildering world, and so on. Thus the frightening world in which the swine flu comes to Blacksburg can be transformed into a world of hope when I find out that there is an ample supply of flu vaccine at the local hospital, that the known cases of swine flu in Blacksburg and the surrounding towns have been quarantined, and so on, so that I now gaze on the world with a look of hope. Likewise, Tibet is a possible world (it also happens of course to be a part of the actual world), one that becomes real when Tibetan is spoken or Tibet is mentioned within a given realm of experience (a high school geography lesson, a speech by the Dalai Lama, etc.). A possible world is expressed by a face that gazes on a situation (with a look of fear, or fascination, hope, or bewilderment, or whatever), and it takes shape in a language that makes it real (in the way that "Tibet" is made real by those who speak Tibetan or when it is spoken about in a given domain of experience).

A concept also has a relationship to other concepts by virtue of the shared problems addressed by the concepts in question—hence the concepts "hunger" and "poverty" are related to each other in a "problematics" constituted by the need to alleviate famine in a poor country, but have no such connection in a domain of experience where a Wall Street investment banker says "I'm really hungry" as he opens the door to a Michelin three-star restaurant in New York city where the cheapest entrée costs seventy dollars (in this latter situation there would be a completely different "problematic," namely, "I'm feeling hungry, but I'm looking forward to a splendid feast prepared by a celebrity chef," as opposed to the speech forms inherent in the former "problematics," whose typical mode of expression would be "I'm starving, but there's not even a bowl of gruel to be had"). Concepts also relate to each other by having similar components:

> Concepts, which have only consistency or intensive ordinates outside of any coordinates, freely enter into relationships of nondiscursive resonance—either because the components of one become components with other heterogeneous components or because there is no difference of scale between them at any level.

Concepts are centers of vibrations, each in itself and everyone in relation to all the others. This is why they all resonate rather than cohere or correspond with each other.[8]

For example, the concepts "being a sumo wrestler" and "being a whale" could have the element or component "being gargantuan" in common, although of course "being a sumo wrestler" and "being a whale" may have little else in common (since as far as we know, whales don't wrestle and sumo wrestlers unaided by oxygen tanks aren't able to spend several hours underwater without surfacing for air, etc.). There is thus no logically ordained relation between concepts. Hence, while "This is a square circle" expresses a contradiction, this particular contradiction is manifested only when "square" and "circle" come to be related to each other in the same proposition, whereas the proposition "In Kandinsky's painting *Bright Lucidity* a square is painted next to a circle" is certainly not contradictory. There is nothing intrinsic to "square" and "circle," as concepts, which requires them to resonate, or which prevents them from resonating, with each other, as they do in the case of Kandinsky's *Bright Lucidity*. For this reason Deleuze insists that relationships between concepts are constitutively "agrammatical."

The claim that concepts relate to each other, or that this or that component of a concept relates to the components of other concepts, exclusively in terms of their intensive vibrations and not at the level of logical or grammatical connectivity, is precisely what enables Deleuze to identify the concept with the image. Identifying a situation, typically to be seen in the films of Sergei Eisenstein, where there is a movement from image to concept and concept to image, Deleuze says there is a third case, one in which there is an identity of concept and image:

> The concept is in itself in the image, and the image is for itself in the concept. This is no longer organic and pathetic but dramatic, pragmatic, praxis, or action-thought. This action-thought indicates *the relation between man and the world*, between man and nature, the sensory-motor unity, but by raising it to a supreme power ("monism"). Cinema seems to have a real vocation in this respect .... Hitchcock's cinema ... goes beyond the action-image towards the "mental relations" which frame it and constitute its linkage, but at the same time returns to the image in accordance with "natural relations" which make up a framework. From the image to the relation, and from the relation to the image: all the functions of thought are included in this circuit .... This is definitely not a dialectic, it is a logic of relations.[9]

Deleuze gives an example of how this circuit between "mental relations"- "natural relations" and the image works—violence, he says, is "of the image and its vibrations" (p. 164), and not "that of the represented" (p. 164), and a concept such as "grandeur" can only be expressed by "composition" and not "a pure and simple inflation of the represented," since in the latter instance "there is no cerebral stimulation or birth of thought" (*TI*, p. 165). The project embarked upon here by Deleuze is ambitious but not altogether novel (Deleuze clearly views Artaud as a precursor in this enterprise), namely, "a possibility of thinking in cinema through cinema" (*TI*, p. 165):

> Artaud ... says specifically that cinema must avoid two pitfalls, abstract experimental cinema, which was developing at the time, and commercial figurative cinema, which Hollywood was imposing. He says that cinema is a matter of neuro-physiological vibrations, and that the image must produce a shock, a nerve-wave which gives rise to thought, "for thought is a matron which has not always existed." Thought has no other reason to function than its own birth, always the repetition of its own birth, secret and profound. He says that *the image thus has as object the functioning of thought, and that the functioning of thought is also the real subject which brings us back to the images.* (*TI*, 165, emphases mine)

While the object of the image is the functioning of thought, in this Artaudian account followed closely by Deleuze, it has to be noted that the thought in question here is not a "thought of the whole," but rather of a "figure of nothingness," a "hole in appearance" (*TI*, p. 167). Cinema, on this view, is concerned "not with the power of returning to images, and linking them according to the demands of an internal monologue and the rhythm of metaphors, but of 'un-linking' them, according to multiple voices, internal dialogues, always a voice in another voice" (*TI*, p. 167). This (cinematic) thought "can only think one thing, *the fact that that we are not yet thinking*, the powerlessness to think the whole and to think oneself, thought which is always fossilized, dislocated, collapsed" (*TI*, p. 167, Deleuze's emphases).

Drawing on the work of Maurice Blanchot, Deleuze poses the question of how the movement from this "I-am-not-yet-thinking-is-all-I-can-think" to the "I-am-forced to-think (and will attempt (real) thought because I'm forced to think)" is possible. His answer accords with Blanchot's, namely, our ability to think hinges decisively "on the one hand [on] the presence of an unthinkable in thought, which would be both its source and barrier; on the other hand [on] the presence to infinity of another thinker in the thinker, who shatters every monologue of a thinking self" (*TI*, p. 168). In cinema (as in philosophy and literature—Deleuze is explicit about this), thought, which is inseparable from the image, "as soon as it takes on its aberration of movement, carries out a *suspension of the world* or affects the visible with a *disturbance*, which, far from making thought visible ... are on the contrary directed to what does not let itself be thought in thought, and equally to what does not let itself be seen in vision" (*TI*, p. 168, Deleuze's emphases).[10]

The metaphysical context for the declarations made above take us well beyond cinema. In an astonishing paragraph, with its echoes of Nietzsche and the Adorno of *Minima Moralia*, Deleuze dramatizes this contemporary metaphysical condition:

> The modern fact is that we no longer believe in this world. We do not even believe in the events which happen to us, love, death, as if they only half concerned us. It is not we who make cinema; it is the world which looks to us like a bad film .... The link between man and the world is broken. Henceforth, this link must become an object of belief: it is the impossible which can only be restored within a faith. Belief is no longer addressed to a different or transformed world. Man is in the world as if in a pure optical and sound situation. The reaction of which man has been dispossessed can be replaced only by belief. Only belief in the world can reconnect man to what he sees and hears. The cinema must film, not the world, but belief in this world, our only link .... Whether we are Christians or atheists, in our universal schizophrenia, *we need reasons to believe in this world*. It is a whole transformation of belief. It was already a great turning-point in philosophy, from Pascal to Nietzsche: to replace the model of knowledge with belief. But belief replaces knowledge only when it becomes belief in this world, as it is. (*TI*, p. 172, Deleuze's emphases).

The function of the image-narrative-concept is thus to restore this now-lost link between us and the world. The claim that we are "in the world as if in a pure optical and sound situation" has undeniable resonances with the work of Baudrillard after the Gulf War, or the worlds of some of Borges's fables, but for Deleuze there can be no (restored but transformed) linkage with the world if we had no alternative but to dwell in a world consisting exclusively of optical or auditory intuitions or experiences (i.e., pure images)—this world would be little different from a purely hallucinatory universe.

What the image-concept accomplishes, in its ability to disturb or suspend this purely optical and auditory world, is precisely to reconnect that which we see and hear with its exteriority, its "excess," an "excess" that is immanent to that which we see and hear, but which at the same time is capable of taking us to the level of belief (i.e., the concept with its encapsulated narrative, the narrative which establishes this belief). It should be made clear that Deleuze accepts that there are many types of images, concepts, and narratives of a kind which do not require or presuppose any linkage with each other. But what Deleuze does, in his delineation of the image-narrative-concept, is to provide an elaborate metaphysical circuitry for establishing this connection between belief and world on an entirely new basis, but also in the process, to dismantle the age-old separation between *noesis* and *aisthesis*, concept and sensible intuition. Cutting this Gordian Knot is no small philosophical accomplishment, even if some of us may cavil at some of the metaphysical principles adverted to by Deleuze in this undertaking.[11]

6

"A Question of an Axiomatic of Desires": The Deleuzean Imagination of Geoliterature

It is a question of a more luminous life which, on the edge of independence and with the aid of its appeal, will be made imminent, dazzling us by the rapidity of its comprehension of things and of beings. It is a question of an axiomatic of desires, of being luxuriously swathed in the drizzle of their satisfactions.
Tristan Tzara, Noontimes Gained

She was off like a bird, bullet, or arrow, impelled by what desire, shot by whom, at what directed, who could say? What? What?
Virginia Woolf, To the Lighthouse

Gilles Deleuze, in his interview-essay translated as "On the Superiority of Anglo-American Literature" (1987), advances a number of interesting and perhaps remarkable proposition contrasting French and "Anglo-American" literature, perhaps none more intriguing than the claim that in the end the superiority of the latter over the former arises from Anglo-American literature's elective affinity with three philosophical movements: British empiricism, Spinozism, and Stoicism. In this essay I shall outline the main features of this interview-essay, and then focus on the constitutive affinity that Deleuze takes to exist between Anglo-American literature and the three philosophical movements, an affinity that (for Deleuze) exists because the exemplary representatives of Anglo-American literature are possessed by the insight, which is all the more effective for not being explicitly entertained or promulgated, that the book is an assemblage, and that one is a writer precisely because one invents assemblages (of a particular and *qu*ite specific kind).[1]

The Deleuzean Anglo-American "canon" includes such seemingly diverse figures as Charlotte and Emily Brontë, Hardy, Melville, Stevenson, Whitman, Lewis Carroll, Henry James, Joyce, Virginia Woolf, Faulkner, Thomas Wolfe, D.H. Lawrence, T.E. Lawrence, Malcolm Lowry, Lovecraft, Fitzgerald, Henry Miller, Beckett, Wilfred Thesiger, Edmund Carpenter, Arthur Miller, Burroughs, and Kerouac. At the same time, Deleuze makes it clear that the propensity to use the book in order to invent assemblages is not confined to those who happen to write in English (albeit in certain ways and in certain registers). A cursory look at his texts will reveal: (i) that the Bible, "the first novel," is regarded by Deleuze as something of a prototypical "Anglo-American" work; and (ii) that other non-anglophone writers, including several who happen to be French, also partake of this defining propensity, so that Lautréamont, Hölderlin, Ghérasim Luca, Artaud, Genet, François Villon, Gombrowicz, and Tournier all feature in what can be described as an "honorary" Anglo-American canon.[2] So, how is the distinction between these two kinds of literatures to be marked? The aim, never declared as such, is obviously to overturn the tradition associated with Saint-Beuve, Taine and Lanson, with its gridded systems of literary classification (a kind of *anatomie comparée* in Saint-Beuve's parlance, or "tree-system" in Deleuze and Guattari's) intended to identify the "spirit" of a pedagogically useful national literary tradition. Deleuze's efforts to motivate an Anglo-American literature can thus be seen as something of a *Contre Saint-Beuve Mark II*, that is, as an attempt to bypass a monumentalized "French Literature" confected by Saint-Beuve and his successors, by adverting to an assortment of American and English novelists and poets (as well as a few German and renegade French writers) who are taken by Deleuze to constitute a counter-tradition whose emblematic form is "the rhizome" and not the "tree-image" or "tree-system." We don't need to negotiate this "French literature," Deleuze seems to be saying, because we can have Hardy, Lawrence, Virginia Woolf, and so on, in the same way in which, philosophically, he has constructed an assemblage consisting of the Stoics, Scotus, Spinoza, Hume, Nietzsche, and Bergson to show that there is an alternative to the French tradition ruled by the impression that everything philosophically worthwhile somehow has to involve the *cogito* and that "philosophically" everything has to go through Hegel and thus to involve dialectics.[3] The differences between Anglo-American and French literature as these are characterized by Deleuze can be presented schematically in the following terms:[4]

Obviously, and this reiterates the point made in the paragraph at the top of this table, the differences between "French" and "Anglo-American" literature are somewhat stylized on this rendering, since, given Deleuze's criteria, Trollope

A Question of an Axiomatic of Desires

"French Literature"	"Anglo-American Literature"
"poverty of the imaginary and the symbolic, the real always being out off until tomorrow"	line of flight
kings: land, inheritance, marriages, lawsuits, ruses, cheating	kings: movements of deterritorialization, wanderings, renunciations, betrayals, passing by at breakneck speed
invents the bourgeois apparatus of power capable of blocking the English, calling them to account	unleashes the flood of capitalism
voyage	flight
interiority	relationship with the outside
seeks beginning or end as point of origin, point of anchor	the English zero is always in the middle
Trees	crabgrass
too human: person, subject	collection, packet, bloc of sensations
gods: fixed attributes, properties, functions, territories, codes, rails, boundaries	daemons: jump across intervals
trickery, trickster (plagiarisms)	betrayal, traitor (creative theft)
Secrecy	clandestiny
Oedipus	Cain, Jonah
...	Old Testament
Old World, East coast of America	New World, West coast of America, Indians
priest, soothsayer, statesman, courtier, characters in French novels	experimenter, man of war (not marshal or general)
domesticity	the Anomalous, the outsider, terror
"Madam Bovary, c'est moi"	becoming-woman
interpretation	experimentation
phantasms, the survey	programmes
life is reduced to the personal: personal conflicts, perfecting of perfectings, neurotic toadying, narcissistic tribunals	strict impersonality, the personal is an empty category
history, the chronicle	geography, the map
too concerned with past and future, therefore does not know how to become	knows how to become
filiation	alliance
"future of the revolution"	"revolutionary becoming"
"salvation through art"	"salvation in life"

or Walter Scott clearly have more in common with Zola or Anatole France, and would therefore presumably qualify as "French," just as, conversely, the "deviant" Frenchmen Artaud and Genet are regarded by Deleuze as being in principle more "Anglo-American" than "French."[5] The terms "Anglo-American" and "French" are thus *façons de parler*, and derive their sense and their saliency from the ability of the former, and the complementary inability of the latter, to invent the appropriate assemblages. If it is their inexhaustible capacity to invent assemblages—assemblages that are, among other things, "philosophical," but also inextricably ethical and political where Deleuze is concerned—that marks the "Anglo-Americans" and sets them apart from the "French," then Deleuze's grouping of these two dozen or so figures as exemplars of an Anglo-American writing has itself to be viewed as an assemblage, that is, as a constellation which allows "populations, multiplicities, territories, becomings, affects, events" to be brought into conjunctive relationships with each other (*D*, p. 51).[6] "Anglo-American literature" is in effect the assemblage constructed by Deleuze on behalf of Virginia Woolf, Hardy, Faulkner, et al., or more precisely, it is the assemblage that is generated when a "Woolf-assemblage," a "Hardy-assemblage," a "Faulkner-assemblage," etc., is "plugged into" (*être branché*, one of Deleuze's favorite images) a specifically philosophical assemblage, in this case an irreducibly ethical and political assemblage whose lineaments have been traced in now well-known ways by Deleuze (and Guattari). But what is this assemblage whose name is "Anglo-American literature"? What kind of assemblage is a literature whose books constellate "populations, multiplicities, territories, becomings, affects, events" into an ensemble plugged into the three primary components of this philosophical assemblage (British Empiricism, Spinozism, and Stoicism)? What kind of event is the event of "writing" such a constellation, of moving along such a line? Is this the veritable reinvention of the concept of a literary tradition?

An assemblage, according to Deleuze (*D*, p. 69), is

> a multiplicity which is made up of many heterogeneous terms and which establishes liaisons, relations between them, across ages, sexes and reigns—different natures. Thus, the assemblage's only unity is that of co-functioning: it is a symbiosis, a "sympathy." It is never filiations which are important, but alliances, alloys; these are not successions, lines of descent, but contagions, epidemics, the wind.

Where the book, *qua* machinic assemblage is concerned, one side of the assemblage faces what Deleuze and Guattari call "the strata," that is, a plethora of codes and milieux characterized above all by a ceaseless mobility (*TP*, p. 502).

The other side of the assemblage faces "the body without organs," that is, what is fundamentally an agglomeration of part-objects that interrupts the functioning of the three great strata (the organism (*l'organisme*), signifiability (*la signifiance*), and subjectification (*la subjectivation*)) as organizing principles. In *A Thousand Plateaus* Deleuze and Guattari say that the book possesses several bodies without organs, "depending on the nature of the lines considered, their particular grade or density, and the possibility of their converging on a 'plane of consistency' assuring their selection" (*TP*, p. 4). The upshot of the functioning of the bodies without organs is the injunction that writing thus be quantified (*quantifier l'écriture*). This injunction carries with it the following implications which are explicitly drawn by Deleuze and Guattari:

There is no difference between what a book talks about and how it is made. Therefore a book also has no object. As an assemblage, a book has only itself, in connection with other assemblages and in relation to other bodies without organs. We will never ask what a book means, as a signified or signifier; we will not look for anything to understand in it. We will ask what it functions with, in connection with what other things it does or does not transmit intensities, in what other multiplicities its own are inserted and metamorphosed, and with what bodies without organs it makes its own converge. A book exists only through the outside and on the outside. A book itself is a little machine; what is the relation (also measurable) of this literary machine to a war machine, love machine, revolutionary machine, etc.—and an *abstract machine* that sweeps them along? (*TP*, p. 4. Emphasis as in original.)

Several examples are provided in *A Thousand* Plateaus of the other "machines" literary works are plugged into: Kleist and Kafka insert themselves into "a mad war machine" and "bureaucratic machine" respectively (*TP*, p. 4); Woolf (in *The Waves*) a "wave machine" (*TP*, p. 252); Ken Kesey a "fog machine" (*TP*, p. 520 n. 18); Charlotte Brönte a "wind machine" (*TP*, p. 261[7]); Melville a "delirious machine," and T.E. Lawrence a "machine for manufacturing giants."[8] Writing has perforce to do with something other than itself, it measures this exteriority by surveying and mapping it, including domains that are yet to come.[9] Writing, in other words, has to do with the creation of worlds that are specified by the assemblages the writer enters into, even as he or she is invented by still other assemblages. The insertion into an assemblage thus constitutes a kind of therapy, a proposition that is integral to several of the essays in Deleuze's late work *Essays Clinical and Critical*.

An assemblage has two components. One is a state of things and bodies, which commingle and transmit affects to each other, in the way that, for instance, the prison is an assemblage because cells and dungeons and the bodies of those made prisoners constitute each other affectively. The other component consists of utterances and regimes of utterances. Regimes of utterances in turn comprise "two non-parallel formalizations," namely, *Sentences* or forms of content (*formalisation de contenu*) and *Figures* or forms of expression (*formalisation d'expression*), the former being attributes of bodies, the latter constituting the "expressed" of the utterance.[10] The distinction between *Sentence* and *Figure* is adapted from the linguist Louis Hjelmslev, and it and its accompanying notions are used by Deleuze (and Guattari) to abolish the traditional three-decker division between object ("the world"), representation ("the book"), and subjectivity ("the author"), this triadic schema viewing the book as the indispensable mediating link between the external world and the internal world of the author.

In place of this triptych, the authors of *A Thousand Plateaus* propose the assemblage as an organizing device which links sets of multiplicities extracted from each of these three orders. The upshot is that a book is always written from and through its outside; it is defined by this "outside" and not by the figure of the author (its putative "subject") or that of the world (its equally specious "object"). This outside is a multiplicity, and into it is plugged a collective assemblage of enunciation and a machinic assemblage of desire, each permeating the other. The function of the book is thus to assemble with this heterogeneous outside, to move "rhizomatically," and not to represent "the" world. Deleuze believes that Anglo-American literature exemplifies this "rhizomatic" principle, it knows "how to move between things, establish a logic of the AND, overthrow ontology, do away with foundations, nullify endings and beginnings. They know how to practice pragmatics" (*D*, pp. 23–5).

Although he is not mentioned by Deleuze and Guattari, the target of the barely suppressed polemics of this passage, with its insistence on the centrality of the "outside" of the text, has to be Derrida, whose famous (some would say "notorious") claim in *De la grammatologie* that "there is nothing outside of the text" (*il n'y a pas de hors-texte*) crisply encapsulates the notions of intertextuality Deleuze and Guattari are keen to repudiate.[11] While the proponents of intertextuality (an admittedly rather amorphous term encompassing such diverse but sometimes overlapping items as the displacement of "meaning," the "infinite play of semiosis," the heterogeneity of the text and its contexts of "origin," the determination of a discourse by other discourses, a text's "influences," the text's constitutive "undecidability" as it confronts its readers, the circulation of ideology, and so forth) make some claims in the course of formulating their positions that would be acceptable in principle to Deleuze, such as the Tel Quel's group's emphasis on the "death" of the subject, their dependence in the end on an "ontology" of the signifier and signified, with the correlative assertion of a fundamental disruption of the relation between signifier and signified, is ultimately incompatible with the "pragmatics" of writing that Deleuze is advocating.

Deleuze is certainly not against the notion of a text having its organizing principles controverted or dismantled, but the qualified objection he has to structuralism—that it is necessarily "a system of points and positions"—is one that is also applicable to Derrida and other poststructuralists, who want to insist on the irremediable "instability" and "decenteredness" of this system, but who have to retain it precisely in order: (i) to affirm that it is marked by these characteristics; and (ii) to demonstrate the system's "aporetic" qualities by working rigorously within it, by tracking down the points and the ways in which the "structurality" of its structure becomes so attenuated or fraught that it can be seen to be less than that.[12] For Deleuze, the text's instability comes not so much from the absence of a semiotic Archimedean point intended to guarantee or establish a determinate and monocentric meaning (the fantasy promulgated by the "logocentrism" undermined by Derrida and his followers), but from the "power of the false," a Nietzschean conception Deleuze uses as the basis for the account of simulation he developed in *Logique du sens*. According to Deleuze, the purported "essence" of "the same" and "the similar" can only be *simulated*, and so there is no essential congruence between the copy and its "original," with the "anarchic" and "nomadic" consequence that the book or work is a non-hierarchized "condensation of coexistences and a simultaneity of events." The simulacrum preempts the participation of the ostensible replica in its "origin," it dissolves all foundations, and it "assures a universal breakdown (*effondrement*), but as a joyful and positive event, as an un-founding (*effondement*)" (*LS*, pp. 262–3).[13] Deleuze then goes on to say: "That the Same and the Similar may be simulated does not mean that they are appearances or illusions. Simulation designates the power of producing an *effect*" (*LS*, p. 263, emphasis as in original). The Deleuzean book, in short, is always and unavoidably a series of effects generated by the "power of the false," a power that functions as the book's "outside" in order to overwhelm the text's aspirations to fixity and hierarchy.

Derrida does of course acknowledge the force of the Nietzschean *Pseudos* when he makes his well-known distinction, in "Structure, Sign, and Play in the Discourse of the Human Sciences," between two fundamental "interpretations of interpretation"; one "dreaming" of "deciphering a truth or an origin that escapes play and the order of the sign," and another, "the Nietzschean," in his words, which "is no longer turned toward the origin," and "affirms play and tries to pass beyond man and humanism" (1978, pp. 292–3). But Derrida prefers not to choose between these two approaches, on the grounds that to "choose" today is "trivial" in any case, and also because any such "choice" would be nugatory as long as we do not determine what precisely the "differenceness" *is* in the "irreducible difference" between these two approaches. Deleuze is not detained by such reticences. His espousal of the power of *Pseudos* is positive rather than optative, and he gives an account of it that differs significantly from Derrida's. Where Derrida views this power as a decomposing principle or propensity lodged inextricably in the text's structure, Deleuze, as several key passages from *Logique du sens* make clear, regards the power of *Pseudos* primarily as the power to create effects. In other words, Deleuze's espousal of the Nietzschean *Pseudos* takes the form of the positing of a *vitality* or *vitalism* of the text or book, and it is this vitality or vitalism, drawn from the text's "outside"—because for Deleuze the power of simulation is the *sine qua non* of the text's emergence, its enabling anteriority/exteriority, so to speak, and thus one it cannot create for itself even as it transmits its force—that undermines the text's "foundations." Where the book is concerned, there can for Deleuze only be inventing and assembling, never interpretation. If Deleuze is a "poststructuralist" (a term whose provenance is American, not French!), then it has to be acknowledged that his "poststructuralism" is as much Bergsonian as it is Nietzschean, and that it is this unquenchable vitalism of the text that sets him fundamentally apart from Derrida, whose approach does not require him to say anything about the power which possesses the book and its writer so that they can affect or be affected by other assemblages.[14] But what is this power, derived as it is from *Pseudos*, of invention and assembling?

According to Deleuze (and Guattari), the writer is responsible to this power, which also happens to be the source of his or her becoming-other.

> If the writer is a sorcerer, it is because writing is a becoming, writing is traversed by strange becomings that are not becomings-writer, but becomings-rat, becomings-insect, becomings-wolf, etc … Writers are sorcerers because they experience the animal as the only population before which they are responsible in principle. The German preromantic Karl Philipp Moritz feels responsible not only for the calves that die but before the calves that die and give him the incredible feeling of an unknown Nature—*affect*. For the affect is not a personal feeling, nor is it a characteristic, it is the effectuation of a power of the pack that throws the self into upheaval and makes it reel. Who has not known the violence of these animal sequences, which uproot one from humanity, if only

for an instant, making one scrape at one's bread like a rodent or giving one the yellow eyes of a feline? A fearsome involution calling us towards unheard-of becomings.[15]

The book belongs to an order in which utterances and bodies commingle to bring about unanticipated "becomings-other." The vitalism which subtends Deleuze's account of how this traffic between bodies and utterances occurs is also the basis for his treatment of the so-called problematic of dualisms. Deleuze maintains that it is a question not simply of undermining the hold of dualisms, but of getting language per se to flow between the terms of dualisms (he calls this the invention of "stammering"), and that it is this flow or stammering, "the AND," which constitutes the multiplicity that transposes the terms of a dualism into a completely new infrastructure of relationships, not just semiotic and syntactic, but also assemblages that, in the manner identified by Spinoza, transmit affects and other "powers of the body." The "AND" between the two terms of the dualism "is neither the one nor the other, nor the one which becomes the other," but a line of flight "which passes between the two terms … the narrow stream which belongs to neither one nor to the other, but draws both into a non-parallel evolution, into a heterochronous becoming."[16] The objective is to avoid retaining the structure of the dialectic, a structure that, ostensibly, is kept in place even by those who try to undermine it by bringing out the suppressed "undifferentiatedness" that is lodged in the "difference" between the two terms that are (dialectically) counterposed—this being the Heideggerian heart of Derrida's strategy for dealing "deconstructively" with the dialectic of identity-and-difference.[17]

It has already been noted that the concept of a "simulation-effect" is one of the decisive features of the conceptual armature developed in *Logique du sens*. The simulacrum sets things in motion, because if each "copy" is the "original" of itself (the theme of the famous first appendix in *Logique du sens* that seeks a "reversal" of Platonism), then repetition of this or that "copy" can only be repetition of difference (the primary theme in *Différence et répétition*), each and every time necessarily (hence the convergence of the respective thematics of *Différence et répétition* and *Logique du sens*). Since variation is the defining feature of repetition, every repetition carries with it possibilities for the emergence of new lines of flight and becomings-other, and thus for the creation of new assemblages. Every repetition, therefore, is an event or "incorporeal transformation" that contains within it the "components of passage" that will set up a new line of flight and the possible emergence of a new assemblage: repetition provides the conceptual ground or axiomatics for the emission of singularities or *haecceities* ("thisnesses"), and assemblages are the systems which transmit and receive intensities and *haecceities*.[18] If the book is an assemblage and the writer an inventor of assemblages, then the questions of what it is that the book receives and transmits, and what it is that the writer does in the course of inventing assemblages, becomes important for Deleuze.

Deleuze insists that there is no significant difference between painting, music, and writing, and says in an important passage in the "Anglo-American Literature" interview-essay that "these activities are differentiated from one another by their respective substances, codes, and territorialities, but not by the abstract line they trace, which shoots between them and carries them towards a common fate" (*D*, p. 74). Deleuze maintains that the painter, musician, and writer can each produce philosophy when they find an "outside" to painting, music, and writing, when "the melodic line draws along the sound, or the pure traced line colour, or the written line the articulated voice." There is thus no real need for philosophy: for Deleuze, "it is necessarily produced where each activity gives rise to its line of deterritorialization," and philosophers themselves necessarily produce their work from the outside. Deleuze goes on to say: "Writing is very simple … [I]t is becoming, becoming something other than a writer, since what one is becoming at the same time becomes other than writing. Not every becoming passes through writing, but everything which becomes is an object of writing, painting or music. Everything which becomes is a pure line which ceases to represent whatever it may be." In other words, since writing (both "philosophical" and "novelistic"), painting, and music involve the creation of lines of flight first and foremost, and cease to traffic in representations by virtue of this creation of a becoming-other, what is crucial for them all is this becoming-other, the "delirium" that constitutes an "outside" for philosophy, literature, painting, and music.[19]

There is of course for Deleuze a crucially important difference between the characters or aesthetic figures that the novelist creates and the conceptual personae who are the subject of the philosopher's thinking and writing, namely, that conceptual personae "are the powers of concepts" while aesthetic figures are "the powers of affects and percepts" (*WP*, p. 65). That is to say, concepts are effective by virtue of being images of "Thought-Being," while aesthetic figures do so by being images of "a Universe," so that philosophy is "the [constitution] of immanence or concepts" while literature is the "constellation of a universe of affects and percepts."[20] At the same time, Deleuze and Guattari allow the possibility of a crossing-over of these two forms into each other "in a becoming that sweeps them both up in an intensity which co-determines them" (p. 66).

As examples Deleuze and Guattari point out that Kierkegaard uses the operatic character Don Juan as a conceptual persona, and that Nietzsche's conceptual persona Zarathustra has become an exemplary figure in music and theatre, so that "it is as if between them, not only alliances but also branchings and substitutions take place" (p. 66). They also refer to Michel Guerin's *La terreur et la pitié* and credit him with being the foremost discoverer of the role of conceptual personae in philosophy by using them within a "logodrama" or "figurology" that imbues thought with affect, so that "the concept as such can be concept of the affect, just as the affect can be affect of the concept" (p. 66). The "planes" from which art is composed and from which philosophy is written can permeate each other, and entities from the one "plane" can move on to the other.

Philosophical innovation occurs when a thinker creates a new image of thought, and produces a new "plane" (the "plane of immanence") for the writing of philosophy. But this philosophical "plane" can also be occupied by poetic, novelistic, pictorial, or musical figures. For Deleuze (and Guattari) the opposite is also true: philosophical figures can also be transported on to the artist's "plane of composition." To quote them:

> These thinkers are also "half" philosophers but also much more than philosophers. But they are not sages. There is such force in those unhinged works of Hölderlin, Kleist, Rimbaud, Mallarmé, Kafka, Michaux, Pessoa, Artaud, and many English and American novelists, from Melville to Lawrence or Miller, in which the reader discovers admiringly that they have written the novel of Spinozism. To the sure, they do not produce a synthesis of art and philosophy. They branch out and do not stop branching out. They are hybrid geniuses who neither erase nor cover over differences in kind but, on the contrary, use all the resources of their "athleticism" to install themselves with this very difference, like acrobats torn apart in a perpetual show of strength. (*WP*, pp. 66–7)

And if Melville, Lawrence, Miller, and others (e.g., such exponents of "Anglo-American literature" in the expanded sense as Artaud) can invent assemblages that are plugged into the assemblage that is Spinozism to form a "co-determining intensity," they can also invent functionally similar "branching-out" assemblages that plug into the assemblages that are British empiricism and Stoicism.[21] Why write about British empiricism? Why write about Spinozism? Why write about Stoicism?, ask Claire Parnet/Deleuze each time in the "Anglo-American Literature" essay before providing the lineaments of an answer.

Deleuze's answer to the first of these questions is succinct—"Because empiricism is like the English novel. It is a case of philosophizing as a novelist, of being a novelist in philosophy" (p. 54). The primary philosopheme taken by Deleuze to mark British empiricism is the procedure or "function"—never "principle," for Deleuze insists that empiricism does violence to *all* principles—that all relations are external, and that terms and relations constitute all that there is. This extraordinary "function" carries with it the implication that a relation can change without affecting its terms (something that Hegel and his followers would regard as incongruous), so that relations always exist "in the middle"—a change in the relation, say, moving a glass off the table, does not alter the terms in this relation, the glass or the table. "If one takes this exteriority of relations as a conducting wire or as a line," Deleuze goes on to say, "one sees a very strange world unfold, fragment by fragment: a Harlequin's jacket or patchwork, made up of solid parts and voids, blocs and ruptures, attractions and divisions, nuances and bluntnesses, conjunctions and separations, alternations and interweavings, additions which never reach a total and subtractions whose remainder is never fixed" (p. 55). Empiricism, in short, is able to substitute the AND for IS, the AND being the path which underlies all relations, and in this way empiricism creates yet another remarkable function: "a multiplicity which constantly inhabits each thing" (p. 57). Hence to write like Lawrence or Woolf or Miller is already to write as an empiricist, and in his early *Empiricism and Subjectivity*, Deleuze identifies several features of Hume's empiricism that will later appear, whether explicitly or implicitly, in his account of the assemblage that is "Anglo-American literature."

These include relations are external and irreducible to their terms (p. 123); "we should not ask what principles are, but rather what they do" (pp. 132–3)[22]; "the subject is constituted by means of principles and ... is grounded in the fancy (*fantasie*)" (p. 127); the mind is a collection of impressions (p. 132); the understanding is grounded in the imagination (p. 127); "the exception is a natural thing" (p. 56); the passions transcend the mind (p. 63); the given is the product of the powers of nature (p. 109); and "subjectivity" is a process (p. 113). These formulations embody "territorialities" that furnish the ground for concepts, and their agglomeration ensues in a "Hume-assemblage" with its constituting emphasis on the anomalous and the exceptional, as well as on multiplicities—multiplicities generated by the substitution of AND for IS necessitated by the externality of relations—that inhabit all beings. Empiricism corrupts and undermines Being, and puts experimentation and blocs of becoming in its place. It renders these in the form of concepts, but their functions can also be expressed through affects and percepts, which in Deleuze's eyes is how the great American and English novelists come to "write" their versions of this empiricism.

From Spinoza the Deleuze of the "Anglo-American Literature" essay derives a similar emphasis on the AND, and in doing this characterizes the "Spinoza-assemblage" in terms of the injunction "to make the body a power which is not reducible to the organism, to make thought a power which is not reducible to consciousness" (p. 62). The components of this kinetic assemblage include "soul and body, relationships and encounters, powers to be affected, affects which realize this power, sadness and joy which qualify these affects," so that Deleuze's Spinoza, unexpectedly but not implausibly, is somehow a bastard ancestor of the bastard Kerouac, someone for whom "the soul is neither above nor inside, it is 'with', it is on the road, exposed to all contacts, encounters, in the company of those who follow the same way, 'feel with them, seize the vibration of their soul and their body as they pass', the opposite of a morality of salvation, teaching the soul to live its life, not to save it" (p. 62). So, like the "Hume-assemblage," the "Spinoza-assemblage" is one whose *raison d'etre* is an unceasing experimentation.[23] Like Spinoza and Hume, the Stoics found ways of getting rid of the indicative IS, by substituting for it any verb of the infinitive form that emerges from a state of things ("to flee," "to arrive," "to stop," etc.), these verbs in turn designating events ("Caesar arriving," "Deleuze writing," etc.). This in turn is tied to an ethics/politics, because making an event—however small—is the most delicate thing in the world: the opposite of making a drama or making a story. Loving those who are like this: when they enter a room they are not persons, characters, or subjects, but an atmospheric variation, a change of hue, an imperceptible molecule, a discrete population, a fog or cloud of droplets. Everything has really changed. Great events, too, are made in this way: battle, revolution, life and death ... True Entities are events, not concepts. It is not easy to think in terms of the event. All the harder since thought itself then becomes an event. Scarcely any other than the Stoics and the English have thought in this way (*D*, p. 66).

> The Deleuzean philosophical counter-tradition is formed from a concatenation of the Stoic, Spinozan, and Humean, as well as the Scotist, Nietzschean, and Bergsonian assemblages (Leibniz becomes important for Deleuze later on), each with its history of the clandestinies of becoming, all coming together to constitute an alternative to the history of Being that extends in a meandering trajectory from Plato and Hegel to the present, a tradition in which Heidegger and Derrida have to be included as dissident members.[24] Anglo-American literature for Deleuze is distinctive precisely because its exemplary writings can be "mapped" on to these assemblages and not any other (such as the Platonic-Hegelian). The determining criterion or set of criteria for what constitutes "Anglo-American literature" is thus an ensemble of philosophemes, albeit with the significant proviso that for Deleuze (and Guattari) this philosophy is always

one based on the proposition that philosophy is necessarily constituted from its "outside," from the event, *this* event, which it then has to construct from affects and percepts, though never as a drama or story. And not just any philosophy, and therefore necessarily by implication not just any literature: where Deleuze is concerned, only the Stoic-Scotist-Spinozan-Leibnizean-Humean-Nietzschean-Bergsonian "super-assemblage" qualifies as this thinking of the "outside," this thinking with affects and percepts. Thus Hermann Broch, whose *Der Tod des Virgil* is surely one of the great novels of the Hegelian assemblage—"Nothing unreal will survive," declares Broch's protagonist Virgil, using "real" very much in the sense of "actual" in Hegel's famous aphorism "What is rational is actual and what is actual is rational"—is not likely to have a place in Deleuze's Anglo-American literary canon, and this not because it is "German" (for as we have seen Kleist and Kafka are grouped by Deleuze with the great Anglo-Americans), but precisely because it is not a book that can be plugged into the Stoic-Scotist-Spinozan-Leibnizean-Humean-Nietzschean-Bergsonian "super-assemblage." In fact, given Deleuze's literary and philosophical criteriology, *Der Tod des Virgil* is perhaps more appropriately to be categorized as a novel whose basic affinity is with the assemblage that is "French literature."

But why, in this case, is there no Anglo-American philosophical tradition that parallels its extraordinary literary counterpart? Deleuze and Guattari have noted that American philosophy departments are dominated by the study of logic, with phenomenology as a small adjunct, and those of us who have studied in philosophy departments in either Britain or the United States will know that Hume, for instance, is never studied in a way that accords with Deleuze's understanding of him, namely, as one of the great exponents of constructivism in philosophy.[25] Instead, in the version of the history of philosophy typically promulgated in British and American philosophy departments, Hume is depicted as someone with an abiding interest in something called "sense-data" and is lumped by virtue of this interest with Locke and Berkeley as "British empiricists," who in turn are pitted against a "Rationalist" tradition whose primary exemplars are Descartes, Spinoza, and Leibniz, so that in the end a Strawsonian or Bennettian Kant can be viewed as the towering figure who brings about a *rapprochement* between these two contending traditions. The nineteenth century is omitted, or rather is given over to "Continental Philosophy" because *that* is where Fichte, Hegel, Schelling, Kierkegaard, Schopenhauer, and Nietzsche are deemed to belong, while the history of ("real") philosophy resumes early in the twentieth century with Frege and Russell, before going through Wittgenstein and Austin in order to end up with Quine and Davidson (and with this terminus the student has been brought "up-to-date"). It would never occur to anyone schooled in this tradition to regard Hume and Spinoza as two philosophical allies in the way proposed by Deleuze, and to have them aligned with Nietzsche against "the rest" (with Leibniz as a possible exception for the later Deleuze). Given this syllabus, and all the "arborescent" assessments normatively built into it, it is hardly likely that anyone thinking along its lines will be able to conceive of an Anglo-American philosophical tradition capable of serving as an appropriate complement to the Anglo-American literary tradition identified by Deleuze (and Guattari). If anything, the literary complement of this overwhelmingly "arborescent" Anglo-American philosophical tradition in Deleuze's scheme of things is quite likely to be "French Literature"! If the Anglo-Americans write in affects and percepts in order to form multiplicities, then only a philosophy whose basic tenor is "constructivist" will accord with the decidedly modernist writers assigned by Deleuze to this counter-tradition.

In the "Geophilosophy" chapter of *What Is Philosophy?* Deleuze and Guattari maintain that philosophy has known three major "reterritorializations," each with its associated modalities: on the Greeks in the past (Hegel and Heidegger being the preeminent figures of this "reterritorialization"[26]); on the democratic State in the present, so that philosophy comes to be marked by national characteristics ("German philosophy," "French philosophy," "English philosophy," etc., with the *cogito* being used as the primary instrument for accomplishing this "national" conquest of the plane of immanence (pp. 102–11)); and "on the new people and earth in the future" (p. 110). This future constitutes the "moment" for the geophilosophy proposed by Deleuze and Guattari.

The reterritorialization of philosophy is also the occasion for conceptual renovation. The first of the two reterritorializations mentioned above—the Greeks and democratic State—do not provide adequate conditions for the creation of concepts. The first because for this reterritorialization to be more than just a vapidly nostalgic longing for the Greeks, the Greeks will have to be reterritorialized on us even as philosophy is reterritorialized on them (Deleuze and Guattari, with Heidegger's egregious identification of the Greek *polis* with the Nazi *gleichschaltuung* in mind, his rejoining of the Greeks through the Germans, quote Nietzsche who asked if there was "anything worse … than to find oneself facing a German when one was expecting a Greek?" (p. 108)).

The reterritorialization of philosophy on the modern State will not work either. The modern State is a seamlessly incorporated element in the history of capitalism, and thus prevents both the liberation of subjugated peoples and the emergence of concepts: it, and that means "we," cannot create and it/we "lack resistance to the present" (p. 108). So, the generation of new concepts has to await a philosophical reterritorialization of the future, for a new earth and a people who are yet to come, who will provide philosophy and politics with the "correlate of creation," the wherewithal for a becoming-other, that is presently lacking.

If philosophy and art converge in the project of beckoning this new earth and new people, then

> the race summoned forth by art or philosophy is not the one that claims to be pure but rather an oppressed, bastard, lower, anarchical, nomadic, and irremediably minor race—the very ones that Kant excluded from the paths of the new Critique. Artaud said: to write *for* the illiterate—to speak for the aphasic, to think for the acephalous. But what does "for" mean? It is not "for their benefit," or yet "in their place." It is "before." It is a question of becoming. (p. 109)

For Deleuze and Guattari it is not a matter of the thinker "doing something for" the illiterate, etc., but rather it is that the thinker becomes illiterate, becomes Indian, becomes rat, so that the illiterate, the Indian, the rat, can become something else: "The agony of a rat or the slaughter of a calf remain present in thought not through pity but as the zone of exchange between man and animal in which something of one passes into the other. This is the constitutive relationship of philosophy with nonphilosophy" (p. 109). Becoming is two-way, which is not to say that it is reciprocal or involves the exchange of attributes. It is this double becoming which brings forth the new earth and the people who are to come: "The philosopher must become nonphilosopher so that nonphilosophy becomes the earth and people of philosophy," so that the people constitute the thinker's becoming-other by virtue of their becoming-people, even as the thinker is internal to the people as part of their becoming (p. 109).

In this deterritorialization-reterritorialization of the double becoming between people and art/philosophy, neither the artist nor the philosopher is capable as such of creating the new people. Art and philosophy can only "summon" the new people in their becoming-other, and share in the same resistance "to death, to servitude, to the intolerable, to shame, and to the present" (p. 110). Deleuze and Guattari link the creation embodied in "pure becomings" and "pure events" on the plane of immanence to this fundamental resistance, and then pose the question of this resistance at the level of thought: thinking is experimentation above all, and experimentation is always a "becoming-other" that makes greater demands on us than the appearance of truth itself. This is the line on which a thinking based on the anomalous, experimentation, manifests itself, and it is from this experimentation that the new earth and the new people emerge from under the shadow of the Greeks and States.[27] Philosophy, geophilosophy in this case, takes experimentation into the domain of concepts, and literature into that of affects and percepts. It follows from this that geophilosophy ("concepts") will have its complement in a geoliterature ("percepts" and "affects"). But is Anglo-American literature this geoliterature? If geophilosophy emerges from a new reterritorialization on the future, then does it not follow that Anglo-American literature will itself have to undergo a similar reterritorialization on the future in order to become geoliterature? Or is Anglo-American literature already reterritorialized on the future in such a way that it is capable of functioning as the equivalent of a geoliterature, it is the latter in all but name?

This is the age of national philosophies which perforce also partake of "the modern" and its appurtenances. Deleuze and Guattari believe that it is the mark of the philosophical "modern" to possess the concept but to have lost cogniscence of the plane of immanence. (It's possible therefore to understand the two volumes of *Capitalism and Schizophrenia* as an immense orchestration or collocation of concepts intended to reclaim the plane of immanence for philosophy, their "postmodernity," so to speak.) There is a French philosophy that creates its personae who manage concepts by submitting them to the exigencies of "epistemology," whose basic function is the reterritorialization of consciousness; a German philosophy whose personae have retained the absolute but who, unlike the French, deterritorialize consciousness in order to find absolute foundations for philosophy, which in turn is viewed as the science of consciousness. Deleuze and Guattari's description of English philosophy shows their profound affinity for it and needs to be quoted in full because it defies summary:

> The English are precisely those nomads who treat the plane of immanence as a movable and moving ground, a field of radical experience, an archipelagian world where they are happy to pitch their tents from island to island and over the sea. The English nomadize over the old Greek earth, broken up, fractalized, and extended to the entire universe. We cannot even say that they have concepts like the French and Germans; but they acquire them, they only believe in what is acquired—not because everything comes from the senses but because a concept is acquired by inhabiting, by pitching one's tent, by contracting a habit. In the trinity Founding-Building-Inhabiting, the French build and the Germans lay foundations, but the English inhabit. For them a tent is all that is needed. (p. 105)

Clearly inspired by the account of *habit* given by C.S. Pierce, Deleuze and Guattari transpose the lineaments of the Piercean account into an ethnology of "the English":

> They develop an extraordinary conception of habit: habits are taken on by contemplating and by contracting that which is contemplated. Habit is creative. The plant contemplates water, earth, nitrogen, carbon, chlorides, and sulphates, and it contracts them in order to acquire its own concept and fill itself with it ["enjoyment"—Deleuze and Guattari use the English word in the original]. The concept is a habit acquired by contemplating the elements from which we come (hence the very special Greekness of English philosophy, its empirical neo-Platonism). We are all contemplations, and therefore habits. *I* is a habit. Wherever there are habits there are concepts, and habits are developed and given up on the plane of immanence of radical experience: they are "conventions." That is why English philosophy is a free and wild (*sauvage*) creation of concepts. (p. 105)

The reader of this passage quickly realizes that the authors of *Capitalism and Schizophrenia* are thus to be reckoned "English philosophers" (they are hardly French and not remotely German!), and that the perspective of geophilosophy is attained largely through the generalization, their generalization, of the *modus operandi* of English philosophy.[28] Of all the national philosophies of the "imagined community" type, the English alone has not abandoned the plane of immanence that geophilosophy seeks to restore in the name of a new earth and a people yet to come, an ethical and political "project" it will moreover undertake through "a free and wild creation of concepts."

This provides a clue as to how one can extract "geoliterature" from the lineaments of Anglo-American literature. We simply try to generalize the latter's way of creating and organizing percepts and affects, since, as we have seen, Anglo-American literature derives its primary features from its capacity to be plugged into the conceptual reticle of Hume-Spinoza-Stoic philosophical assemblage: what this assemblage renders in terms of concepts, Anglo-American literature transposes into percepts and affects. Both summon, in their respective modes, the new earth and the new people in ways not possible for the national philosophies (although English philosophy expresses this summons inchoately) and their precursor transcendental philosophies, and of course French literature (although Anglo-American literature anticipates geoliterature).

But how can the assemblage that is Anglo-American literature undergo this generalization into geoliterature when, with a few exceptions (Kleist, Hölderlin, Charlotte and Emily Brontë, Robert Louis Stevenson, and mystery- and travel-writers like Lovecraft and Thesiger), the novelists in Deleuze's "canon" are so emphatically modernist? Will a certain parochialism—geoliterature as hinted at here seems suspiciously like a repristinated modernism—stand in the way of this generalizability? I do not see why it should. If the primary desideratum determining what geophilosophy is is the reclaiming of the plane of immanence for the creation of new concepts (what Deleuze elsewhere calls "experimentation") in the name of a new earth and a new people, then, the risk of some simplification notwithstanding, it could be argued that any literature will in principle qualify as "geoliterature" so long as it can be plugged into the adjacent geophilosophical assemblage, that is, provided it creates affects and percepts capable of functioning as the necessary correlate to geophilosophy's concepts. So, why not Garcia Márquez or Julio Cortázar or Salman Rushdie or anyone similar bypassed in the initial Deleuzean specification of the Anglo-American literary *Nachlass*, such as the overlooked Victorian poet-physician Thomas Lovell Beddoes (who significantly influenced Beckett)? Does a writer "write with a view to an unborn people that doesn't yet have a language?" asks Deleuze, and he certainly should not object to the inclusion in geoliterature's wayward "canon" of anyone who wrote in this vein, and in the name of the ethical and political project that for Deleuze is the writer's (as opposed to the author's) reason for becoming.[29] To ask what such an ambition might mean is to have begun to imagine what the possible contours of a geoliterature might be. But are Garcia Márquez, Cortázar, Rushdie, Vargas Llosa, and others like them sufficiently "exhausted" or "sparse" (in the way that Beckett and Kafka obviously are for Deleuze) to belong plausibly to a geoliterature constructed according to broadly Deleuzean specifications?

Deleuze, albeit with some exceptions (Melville and Henry James are hardly "sparse" and "exhausted"!), is palpably wedded to authors firmly lodged in the experimentally minimalist wing of modernism, and it will be hard for many of his commentators to see how the exponents of a literary "magical realism" (say), whose works are typically marked (some would say "trademarked") by a well-known narrative exuberance and prolixity, can be accommodated within the purview of a literary movement or tradition established on the basis of recognizably Deleuzean "axioms." Nevertheless, I think a case of sorts can be made for the inclusion of Garcia Márquez, et al., in the "canon" of such a geoliterature.

Making a case for including authors such as Garcia Márquez and Rushdie in a "Deleuzean" "geoliterature" will require the bringing together of two different but related and overlapping Deleuzean theoretical accomplishments. One is the axiomatics for organizing the sensuous created by Deleuze (and Guattari) in *Capitalism and Schizophrenia*: the sensuous being of course the domain that Deleuze and Guattari take to be embodied in percepts and affects and constituted by desire. This axiomatics—whose architectonic heart is adumbrated in the two volumes of *Capitalism and Schizophrenia*, although it is "complicated" in later works, primarily *Le Pli*—has the scope of an immense *conceptual* orchestration of the domain of the sensuous.[30] This axiomatics of desire, or appropriate segments of it, underlie Deleuze (and Guattari's) work on literary figures such as Kafka, on cinema, on artists like Francis Bacon, on semiosis (in the Piercean as opposed to the Saussurean register), on music, on the history of philosophy, and so forth. The second area of accomplishment is the extraordinary theory of images developed by Deleuze in the two *Cinema* books. It is striking that in both these areas Deleuze evinces a powerful interest in the capacity of the text and the image to proliferate and multiply, to fold, unfold, and fold again, even to infinity.[31] It is as if Deleuze, his fondness for Beckett notwithstanding, is compelled to eschew a Beckettian ascesis of the text in his own textual production, and that, moreover, he explicitly acknowledges the force of this irresistible semiotic and graphic mobility in his treatment of cinematic conceptual production, even if his own preference in literature happens in the main to be for this or that version of a modernist minimalism.

One thinks here immediately of the brilliantly suggestive discussion of the *oeuvre* of Werner Herzog in the first *Cinema* book (*MI*, pp. 184-6). In this remarkable disquisition on Herzog, Deleuze declares that Herzog is a "metaphysician" who deals in forms and conceptions ("the Large" and "the Small") that "designate Visions which deserve even more to be called Ideas."[32] Herzog's films are populated by visionaries and dreamers who are larger than life, who inhabit an environment that is itself larger than life, and who are fated or doomed to find an action or mode of being commensurate with this largeness. This metaphysical structure conduces to the hypnotic and hallucinatory qualities which mark Herzog's films: the latter are displayed when the hopelessly visionary protagonist soars over a necessarily bounded nature, and the former when this protagonist comes up against the limits of an unrelenting nature. The "action" of the Herzogian film involves a modulation of the landscapes and the actions, in the process "realizing" the Large as a pure Idea. Herzog treats the Small in a similarly metaphysical way: the dwarves and weaklings who populate his films unavoidably bring nature down to their scale and thereby enfeeble it. But they transcend this diminished nature through "vast hallucinatory visions of flight, ascent, or passage, like the red skier in mid-jump in *Land of Silence and Darkness* or the three great dreams of landscapes in *The Enigma of Kaspar Hauser*" (p. 186). The Large and the Small therefore modulate each other as well, since the counterpart of the red skier (who transmutes the Small into the Large) is Fitzcarraldo whose gigantic vision of a shrine to Verdi in the Amazon jungle culminates in a tawdry performance by a bedraggled troupe of singers in front of a small audience (the transmutation of the Large into the Small).

A similar hallucinatory quality pervades literary magical realism, with its well-known propensities for disjointed temporalities, the "exchange of qualities" between the dead and the living, the haphazard merging of personas, as well as the by-now hackneyed piquancy of musicians who can play their instruments simply by placing the mouthpieces against their necks and moving their throat muscles, animals who can count and talk, and so on. But more significantly, the metaphysically prescient modulation between the Large and the Small which Deleuze finds in Herzog is, for instance, also to be found in a novel like Rushdie's *Midnight's Children*. Rushdie's main protagonist, Saleem Sinai, through sheer inadvertence, has a biography that is virtually coextensive with the history of post-independence India (the instantiation of the Idea of the Large, in Deleuzean terms). At the same time Saleem has a preternatural sense of smell, one so acute that he achieves preeminence in his career—pickle-making—because he can identify with his nose, in a kind of miraculating interchangeability of the senses, flavors that are indiscernible to others (the manifestation of the Idea of the Small). Moreover, Saleem's unique and distinctive nasal passages also allow his sense of smell to serve as a conduit for memories and ideas—he smells out the past and his thinking is a veritable sniffing out … He does metaphysics through the nose. And Saleem is possessed by an extraordinary desire: to be something like an Indian Everyman by savoring, and not banishing as intrinsically alien, the experiences of everyone he comes across. The desire in this case is not the aggrandizing desire to be "all," but the very Deleuzean quest to have as many facets of the multiple refracted into interstices of one's being.

This convergence, if that is the way to describe it from my admittedly brief sketch, between the film-maker Herzog and the novelist Rushdie should not be surprising, given Deleuze's several statements to the effect that both the great film-makers and the primary novelists of the "Anglo-American" tradition have always been philosophers. In which case, the power of Hume, Spinoza, and Bergson as creators of concepts, as inaugurators of the philosophical "super-assemblage" delineated by Deleuze, is a power that can be manifested in film and novel alike. This power is the basis of a geoliterature that will, at any rate where its axioms are concerned, be an amplification of the "Anglo-American" literature that Deleuze uses as the primary instrument for the reinvention of the concept of a literary tradition.

7

"Existing Not as a Subject but as a Work of Art"—The Task of Ethics? or Aesthetics?

> *It's to do with abolishing ways of existing or, as Nietzsche put it, inventing new possibilities of life. Existing not as a subject but as a work of art—and this last phase presents thought as artistry.*
>
> Gilles Deleuze[1]

Deleuze endorsed repeatedly the well-known conviction of Michel Foucault and Nietzsche that life had to be lived as a work of art. This raises the question whether the terms under which a life is led properly belong to ethics (this of course being the traditional or consensual position taken when it comes to answering the question "how should I lead my life?"). But to suggest that life be led as a work of art implies, palpably, that it is aesthetics, and not ethics, which superintends the question "how should I lead my life?." At one level the answer to this question can only be sheerly commonplace and quite worn-out: of course the answer given depends on how "ethics" and "aesthetics" are defined! But at another level it certainly isn't trivial. If Deleuze had an ethics, then what kind of ethics is it, and is this an ethics with a depth and scope capable of superintending the question "how should I lead my life?." Or would this task be left to an aesthetics, and if so, what kind of aesthetics did Deleuze have? Or are ethics and aesthetics related in such a way in Deleuze's thought that it is *both* ethics and aesthetics which oversee the terms of the question "how should I lead my life?." If this is the case, then how does Deleuze conceive of the relation between ethics and aesthetics, and how do they function conjointly when dealing with the question of leading one's life as a work of art?

Deleuze, while making a clear distinction between "ethics" and "morality," never in my view made really precise the difference between "ethics" and "aesthetics" when it came to defining the notion of a "style of life" (*un style de vie*) or "life as a work of art" (*la vie comme oeuvre d'art*).[2] The nearest he came to it was in an interview with Foucault's biographer Didier Eribon which dealt with Deleuze's book on Foucault, where it emerges during the course of the interview that while "ethics" has to do with "a set of optional rules that assess what we do, what we say, in relation to the ways of existing involved," aesthetics by contrast has to do with "a style of life, not anything at all personal, but inventing a possibility of life, a way of existing." In a word: ethics centers on *assessing* a way of existing, while aesthetics focuses on *inventing* a way of existing.[3] But this proposal begs as many questions as it is likely to answer, since the weight of Deleuze's distinction now hinges on the relationship between assessment and invention when it comes to specifying the terms under which a life is led. We need therefore to begin by finding an adequate and principled basis for establishing the demarcation between "ethics" and "aesthetics," otherwise there will be no good grounds for maintaining the distinction between "assessing a way of life" and "inventing a way of life" in the way that Deleuze seems to make it—someone with contrarian inclinations could come along and insist that ethics alone is capable of sustaining both assessment and invention, another potential contrarian that it is aesthetics instead which can do this on its own without any need for a recourse to ethics. Consequently, the follower of Deleuze who insists that, contrary to the suggestions of these two hypothetical contrarians, the assessment of a life lies with ethics, and the invention of a life with aesthetics, has then to show *ab initio* that there is a fundamental distinction to be made between ethics and aesthetics, the essential nature of which requires that assessment and invention be assigned to the realms of ethics and aesthetics, respectively. There has, in other words, to be something intrinsic to ethics and aesthetics which warrants the assigning of the assessment of the terms by which a life is led to ethics, and the invention of a life to aesthetics, in the way proposed by Deleuze.

While the distinction between ethics and aesthetics goes all the way back to the pre-Socratics, it was Kant who first made a rigorous division between these two domains, when he made his vitally important critical redaction of a previous form of philosophic reflection based on the so-called medieval transcendentals of truth (knowledge), beauty (aesthetics), and goodness (ethics). Both Foucault and Deleuze, in our view, adhere to, but also advance and modify significantly, the important separation embodied in Kant's second and third *Critiques* between ethics and aesthetics, respectively (and also between these theoretical domains and that of knowledge or epistemology, the latter being of course the focus of Kant's first *Critique*). But first we need to ask the question of the sense in which Deleuze could have been said to have an ethics—he was one of the truly great philosophical followers of Nietzsche, and the latter's relentless undermining of any philosophical basis from which a putative project of assessment or evaluation can be undertaken raises the question whether ethics can exist as anything more significant than a mere *façon de parler* for Nietzsche and his epigoni (including Deleuze).

Those who propose that Deleuze (and of course Guattari) had an ethics include Michel Foucault, who in his famous foreword to *Anti-Oedipus* declared that

> *Anti-Oedipus* (may its authors forgive me) is a book of ethics, the first book of ethics to be written in France in quite a long time (perhaps that explains why its success was not limited to a particular "readership": being anti-oedipal has become a life style, a way of thinking and living).[4]

More recently Daniel W. Smith has argued that Deleuze and Guattari are the exponents of an "immanent ethics," one which has two primary features (to quote Smith):

> It focuses on the differences between modes of existence, in terms of their immanent capabilities or power (active versus reactive, in Nietzsche; active versus passive, in Spinoza), and it poses, as one of its fundamental problems, the urge toward transcendence that effectively "perverts" desire, to the point where we can actually desire our own repression, a separation from our own capacities and powers.[5]

My aim here is not to take issue with Smith (or indeed Foucault). Smith, who has been a consistently superior interpreter and translator of Deleuze, shows us what it is in Deleuze's thinking that warrants the characterization of appropriate aspects of it as an "immanent ethics." Smith succeeds in this demonstration, that is, he shows convincingly how Deleuze adheres to the positions of Spinoza and Nietzsche on the passions, as well as maintaining that an ethics which eschews immanence invariably sunders us from our powers and capacities.[6]

Deleuze was of course a sympathetic and innovative reader of Foucault, and the primary aim of this essay is to show how Foucault's delineation of an "aesthetics of existence" or a "stylistics of being" is fundamentally in accord with the Deleuzean point of view, and to draw some conclusions from this for understanding Deleuze (and Guattari). Along the way we'll need to deal with the Kantian diremption between aesthetics and ethics, expressed by

Kant in terms of his baroque theory of the faculties, a theory which happens to be dispensable in its entirety when viewed from a Deleuzean point of view, as we shall shortly see. Also to be discussed is the plausibility or otherwise of Foucault's characterization of an "aesthetics of existence" or "stylistics of being," and by extension the compatibility or otherwise of this "aesthetics" or "stylistics" with those propositions of Deleuze which deal with the passions, their enabling conditions, and the assemblages within which they are positioned.

The Kantian partitioning between ethics and aesthetics is judged to be problematic, and inherently so, by Deleuze in his commentary on Kant, since this distinction was required by Kant to address problems posed at quite another level by his multipart philosophical architectonic. For Kant, the fundamental difference between truth (i.e., theoretical judgment or knowledge) and goodness (i.e., practical judgment or ethics) is that while both define an "interest of reason," the former nonetheless defines a "speculative reason" while the latter is associated with a "practical reason." Truth and goodness are quite different with regard to their respective faculties, even though both serve a "legislative" function when it comes to their respective deployments of reason.[7] By contrast, the faculty of feeling (the domain of aesthetics) is not legislative—it has no objects over which it legislates. To quote Deleuze:

> Kant therefore refuses to use the word "autonomy" for the faculty of feeling in its higher form: powerless to legislate over objects, judgement can be only *heautonomous*, that is, it legislates over itself …. The faculty of feeling has no *domain* (neither phenomena nor things in themselves); it does not express the conditions to which a kind of objects (sic) must be subject, but solely the subjective conditions for the exercise of the faculties. (Deleuze, *KCP*, p. 48, italics as in original)

Deleuze goes on to say:

> In the *Critique of Judgement* [which deals with the faculty of feeling] the imagination does not take on a legislative function on its own account. But it frees itself, so that all the faculties together enter into a free accord. Thus the first two Critiques set out a relationship between the faculties which is determined by one of them; the last Critique uncovers a deeper free and indeterminate accord of the faculties as the condition of the possibility of every determinate relationship. (Deleuze, *KCP*, p. 68)

In other words: the *Critique of Judgement*, whose focal point is the aesthetic realm, is used by Kant to resolve the problem, necessarily unique and internal to his recondite system, of the relation of the three faculties to each other. Kant, according to Deleuze and numerous other commentators, wanted to extricate purpose from any theological determination, and correlatively, to provide theology itself with an ultimate human ground. Theological principles could therefore only be postulated in the mode of an "as if" since any putatively fuller theological conceptions were sequestered in the noumenal realm unattainable to human beings. The task of the third *Critique* was to realize this goal, by showing that the accord of the faculties is not subject to a more profound or overarching meta-accord—classically provided by a theologically sustained "transcendental of transcendentals" which for Kant had necessarily to be lodged in the noumenal domain—than the one provided by the "common sense" (*sensus communis*) of aesthetic taste, that is, "*human* practical activity" (Deleuze *KCP*, p. 69, italics as in original).

For all the occasional amusement that Nietzsche enjoyed at Kant's expense, the revolutionary turn to perspectivalism associated with Nietzsche was in truth made possible, philosophically, by Kant's seemingly much less radical "detranscendentalization" of the aesthetic (and also of the complementary metaphysical bases of truth/knowledge and goodness/ethics). After Kant, the classical notions of truth, goodness, and beauty were severed decisively from any such infinitizing meta-accords, these being banished by Kant to the noumenal realm beyond the reach of knowledge as opposed to the exigencies of mere postulation, the latter being of course the only option now open to the schemas of theology and any forms of thought having theology as their ultimate basis. Freed now from the tutelage of any such infinitizing meta-accords, truth, goodness, and beauty could finally be opened up to the kind of strictly immanentist genealogy proposed by Nietzsche and subsequently extended by Foucault and taken up by Deleuze.

As a consequence, ethics and aesthetics could be served by entirely separate though sometimes overlapping presuppositional frameworks, each constituted by their own specific accords, or by some alternative though not necessarily "superior" accord, capable of subsuming one or the other, or even both, of them. It now became possible, in principle, to subsume ethics under aesthetics. There are at least two roads to this subsumption of the ethical by the aesthetic, and both are compatible with a Deleuzean philosophical perspective. One route is provided by Nietzsche (as interpreted by Deleuze himself in several texts); the other derives from Foucault's depiction of the Greek and Roman "care of self" (although of course Foucault's genealogy of this "care of self" was inspired in large part by Nietzsche's conception of life as a ceaseless dynamism or *energeia*, and by the latter's identification of life with the imperative invention of new styles of existence).

Deleuze's estimation of Foucault's indebtedness to Nietzsche on the question of our positioning with regard to power is worth quoting at length:

> [Are] we condemned to conversing with Power, irrespective of whether we're wielding it or being subjected to it? [Foucault] confronts the question in one of his most violent texts, one of the funniest too, on "infamous men." And it takes him time to come up with an answer. Crossing the line of force, going beyond power, involves as it were bending force, making it impinge on itself rather than on other forces: a "fold," in Foucault's terms. Force playing on itself. It's a question of "doubling" the play of forces. Of a self-relation that allows us to resist, to elude power, to turn life or death against power. This, according to Foucault, is something the Greeks invented. It's no longer a matter of determinate forms, as with knowledge, or of constraining rules, as with power: it's a matter of optional rules that make existence a work of art, rules at once ethical and aesthetic that constitute ways of existing or styles of life (including even suicide). It's what Nietzsche discovered as the will to power operating artistically, inventing new "possibilities of life." One should, for all sorts of reasons, avoid all talk of a return to the subject, because these processes of subjectification vary enormously from one period to another and operate through very disparate rules. (Deleuze, *N*, p. 98)

"Rules at once ethical and aesthetic" is the phrase used by Deleuze in this passage, and yet we know from his previous formulations that this can't really be so: according to these other Deleuzean formulations, "constraining" rules have to with morality, rules of "assessment" with ethics, while "enabling" rules belong to the aesthetic sphere. Given this compartmentalization, how can the same rule be both ethical and aesthetic? Or is Deleuze, rather, proposing that rules drawn from both the ethical and the aesthetic domains are required if new "possibilities of life" are to be invented (these "new possibilities" being of course a requisite for making one's life a work of art)? The latter option is certainly the much more plausible alternative, in which case there remains the business of sorting out the respective parts played by ethical and aesthetic rules when it comes to outlining the sense in which for Deleuze we are capable of "existing not as a subject but as a work of art." Further helpful elaboration where this issue is concerned is provided in the same interview that Deleuze had with Didier Eribon:

> Subjectification isn't even anything to do with a "person": it's a specific or collective individuation relating to an event (a time of day, a river, a wind, a life ...). It's a mode of intensity, not a personal subject. It's a specific dimension with without which we can't go beyond knowledge or resist power. Foucault goes on to analyze Greek and Christian ways of existing, how they enter into

forms of knowledge, how they make compromises with power. Foucault, true to his method, isn't basically interested in returning to the Greeks, but in us today: what are our ways of existing, our possibilities of life or our processes of subjectification; are there ways for us to constitute ourselves as a "self," and (as Nietzsche would put it) sufficiently "artistic" ways, beyond knowledge and power? And are we up to it, because in a way it's a matter of life and death? (Deleuze, *N*, pp. 98–9)

For Deleuze, as with the later Foucault, it is therefore a question of finding possibilities of life which "go beyond knowledge" and enable a "resistance to power," that is, finding ways to constitute life in a "sufficiently artistic way." The emphasis in this declaration is clearly on the aesthetic, since if anything for Foucault and Deleuze the power of invention resides in the "creative" aesthetic and not the "evaluative" ethical. This is not to suggest that the ethical is superfluous. Quite obviously, a way of life has to be scrutinized, and scrutinized rigorously, as a condition of shaping one's life as a work of art, which means that ethics (i.e., the set of practices and precepts which makes this scrutiny or evaluation possible) is indispensable for this process of aesthetic life-shaping. But there is another angle to this story which needs to be taken into account.

Deleuze, in his intellectual portrait of Foucault, makes an important distinction between "subject-type individuations" and "event-type individuations." Only the former require a subject, the latter, by contrast, are subjectless, the implication here being that only individuations requiring a subject can be assessed from an ethical point of view. To quote Deleuze:

> There are also event-type individuations where there's no subject: a wind, an atmosphere a time of day, a battle ... One can't assume that a life, or a work of art, is individuated as a subject; quite the reverse. Take Foucault himself: you weren't aware of him as a person exactly. Even in trivial situations, say when he came into a room, it was more like a changed atmosphere, a sort of event, an electric or magnetic field or something. That didn't in the least rule out warmth or make you feel uncomfortable, but it wasn't like a person. It was a set of intensities. (Deleuze, *N*, p. 115)

The "Foucault" just portrayed by Deleuze is subjectless ("you weren't aware of him as a person exactly"), and as an amalgam of intensities and nothing more, when individuated as the event that is "Foucault," is surely quite beyond assessment in terms of the ethical.

Deleuze, in the same text on Foucault, provides yet another basis for conceptualizing the respective contributions of the ethical and the aesthetic to the processes involved in shaping one's life. It lies in the interesting distinction that Foucault made between love and passion in a conversation with the German film director Werner Schroeter.[8] Deleuze says of Foucault's distinction:

> The distinction is nothing to do with constancy or inconstancy. Nor is it one between homosexuality and heterosexuality, though that's discussed in the text. It's a distinction between two kinds of individuation: one, love, through persons, and the other through intensity, as though passion dissolved persons not into something undifferentiated but into a field of various persisting and mutually interdependent intensities ("a constantly shifting state, but not tending toward any given point, with strong phases and weak phases, phases when it becomes incandescent and everything wavers for an unstable moment we cling to for obscure reasons, perhaps through inertia; it seeks, ultimately, to persist and to disappear ... being oneself no longer makes any sense ... "). Love's a state of, and a relation between, persons, subjects. But passion is a subpersonal event that may last as long as a lifetime ("I've been living for eighteen years in a state of passion about someone, for someone"), a field of intensities that individuates independently of any subject. Tristan and Isolde, that may be love. But someone, referring to this Foucault text, said to me: Catherine and Heathcliff, in *Wuthering Heights*, is passion, pure passion, not love. A fearsome kinship of souls, in fact, something not altogether human (who is he? A wolf ...). It's very difficult to express, to convey—a new distinction between affective states. (Deleuze, *N*, p. 116)

That is to say, individuation through love is susceptible in principle to being evaluated in ethical terms, whereas passion, as a field of uncontrollably oscillating intensities, can only be assessed aesthetically. This alignment love-ethics/passion-aesthetics can be expanded further, since it is obvious that for Deleuze (and Foucault) the fundamental operative register for ethics is an evaluative scheme shaped by desiderata based on prudence, whereas the accompanying active principle for aesthetics is transgression (i.e., love-ethics [prudence]/passion-aesthetics [transgression]).[9] The complication arising at this point is that while transgression involves, *per definiens*, the violation of a prohibition, and hence is to this extent incompatible with the requirements of morality, it is not obvious that transgression is in all cases incompatible with the requirements of *prudentia* (i.e., ethics, as defined by Deleuze, if we permit the accompanying slightly Aristotelian gloss). For some transgressions, or what appear initially to be transgressions, *can* be prudential: assassinating a ruler in the very early stages of what is seemingly an emerging reign of tyranny, for example.

The affinity between Catherine and Heathcliff is passional, and in its climacteric ravishingly so, hence it is certainly not guided by any of the requirements of *prudentia*, and Heathcliff's consistently sadistic behavior toward those around him (albeit driven and intensified by the shattering realization of Catherine's ultimate unattainability) is impossible to characterize as moral or even ethical by any standards reasonably to be associated with the term "ethical," let alone "moral." Deleuze is right—the passional event that is "Heathcliff and Catherine" is profoundly constitutive of an aesthetics or stylistics of existence and hence is "para-ethical." "Heathcliff and Catherine" as an event partook of an art of life in the manner of some of the Greek and Roman personages who fascinated Foucault toward the end of his life, and the reader of *Wuthering Heights* knows that there is no schema of evaluation (the requisite hallmark of ethics) within which the event of "Heathcliff and Catherine" can be contained in order to make it explicable and seemingly rational. (As the third-rate literary critic would say, that is the "beauty" of the story, and for once this untalented critic may be right.)

But what of Tristan and Isolde, whose affinity for each other according to Deleuze is in the register of love, and "courtly" love at that, and thus can presumably be subsumed under something like an ethics (with its forms of evaluation based on something approximating to *prudentia*?).[10] Courtly love (*amour courtois*) permitted the expression of passion, but any such passion had to be disciplined or chastened by the requirements of chivalry or nobility, and above all tempered by the ideals of refinement ("courtliness") expected of a member of a royal court.[11] It is simply impossible to view the vulpine Heathcliff (to recall Deleuze's invocation of this particular becoming-wolf) as an exemplar of *amour courtois*. At the same time, the essential ingredient of *amour courtois*, namely, courtly refinement, makes it an ideal that only a few can pursue and attain. In this respect *amour courtois* has an undeniable kinship with stoic ethics. Foucault characterizes stoic ethics in the following terms:

> The reason I think, that the principal aim, the principal target of this kind was an aesthetic one. First, this kind of ethics was only a problem of personal choice. Second, it was reserved for a few people in the population; it was not a question of giving a pattern of behavior for everybody. It was a personal choice for a small elite. The reason for making this choice was the will to live a beautiful life, and to leave to others memories of a beautiful existence. I don't think that we can say that this kind of ethics was an attempt to normalize the population.[12]

The "art of life" embodied in stoic ethics according to Foucault (and *amour courtois* according to us) required the cultivation of a *tekhnē tou biou* in which establishing a scrupulous control over the self was central to its attainment.[13] To quote Foucault on this cultivation of self required by Greek ethics:

The Greeks problematized their freedom, and the freedom of the individual, as an ethical problem. But ethical in the sense in which the Greeks understood it: *ēthos* was a way of being and of behavior. It was a mode of being for the subject, along with a certain way of acting, a way visible to others. A person's *ēthos* was evident in his clothing, appearance, gait, in the calm with which he responded to every event, and so on. For the Greeks, this was the concrete form of freedom; this was the way they problematized their freedom. A man possessed of a splendid *ēthos* who could be admired and put forward as an example, was someone who practiced freedom in a certain way .... [E]xtensive work by the self on the self is required for this practice of freedom to take shape in an *ēthos* that is good, beautiful, honorable, estimable, memorable, and exemplary.[14]

It is hard to deny that in this account of the *ēthos* of the exemplary Greek male of antiquity, a certain cultivation of style, a turning of one's life into a work of art, becomes pivotal—giving visible form in one's personal bearing to the qualities listed by Foucault ("good, beautiful, honorable, estimable, memorable, and exemplary") are very much the defining feature of this Greek *ēthos* (and in our submission, the *ēthos* of the medieval *amour courtois*).[15] But is this *ēthos* of nobility and chivalry, which bears all the marks of the ethical, justifiably to be regarded as "aesthetic" in its key dimensions?

Clearly "style" per se is not the issue here. The consummately excellent Greek male of antiquity is obviously the practitioner of a certain kind of stylistics of existence, and yet the core of this stylistics in the Greek case is a steady and concerted disciplining of the passions. Where does this leave the Deleuzean notion of an individuation based on intensities (the ostensible province of aesthetics, understood in terms of the becoming-wolf of Heathcliff and Deleuze's own encounters with Foucault) as opposed to individuations hinging on a subject or person (the seeming domain of ethics with its emphasis on a regulation of intensities)?

This issue is ultimately irresolvable. Deleuze's distinction between these two kinds of individuation is probably best regarded as a proposal with a heuristic intent. The Kantian separation between ethics and aesthetics is untenable, designed as it was to resolve a problematic specific to the internally disjointed philosophical system of the sage of Königsberg, and the evident inability of Deleuze (and Foucault) to separate the ethical from the aesthetic, except on an ad hoc basis, should consign this demarcation to desuetude. This collapse of the distinction between the ethical and the aesthetic should pave the way for a conceptual possibility that is more Deleuzean than any attempt to differentiate between the ethical and the aesthetic within the seeming residues of the Kantian system. The primary issue here, to pursue this possible Deleuzean insight, admittedly one inspired by Spinoza and Deleuze, is the balance of forces between those that are active and those that are reactive, and how these configurations of forces enable life.

In his last published essay Deleuze provided a lapidary formulation of what is at stake here:

> We will say of pure immanence that it is A LIFE, and nothing else. It is not immanence to life, but the immanent that is in nothing is itself a life. A life is the immanence of immanence, absolute immanence: it is complete power, complete bliss. It is to the degree that he goes beyond the aporias of the subject and the object that Johann Fichte, in his last philosophy, presents the transcendental field as a life, no longer dependent on a Being or submitted to an Act—it is an absolute immediate consciousness whose very activity no longer refers to a being but is ceaselessly posed in a life.[16]

The "old" demarcation between ethics and aesthetics rested on the "old" philosophy which traded on the distinction between Being and Act. In his last philosophical statement Deleuze therefore pointed to a way of moving beyond both these distinctions—life, with its associated philosophic *a prioriae*, for him supplants the distinction between ethics (the correlative of Being) and aesthetics (the correlative of Act). Only in this way can life be lived as a work of art, that is, something at once powerful and blissful.

8

The Socius and Life

Traditional philosophy relied overwhelmingly on the operation of transcendental principles which were required by this philosophy to make knowledge claims possible, as well as judgments about morality and beauty. To be brief: a particular judgment regarding knowledge, goodness, or beauty cannot provide or certify its own conditions of possibility—these conditions of possibility are exterior to the judgment itself. Hence the assertion "The Mona Lisa is a work of beauty" has as its condition of possibility this or that conception of beauty which is the basis for the making of this assertion, a conception—one that is in effect an accompanying and underlying condition of possibility—which has to be given in advance of the specific claim regarding the Mona Lisa.[1]

There are also transcendental principles, perhaps less widely acknowledged than the ones that underlie the epistemology and aesthetics of traditional philosophy, which in turn lie beneath the constitution of the social order. These principles are embodied in what Deleuze and Guattari call the socius.[2] As just mentioned, the well-known philosophical counter-tradition inaugurated by Nietzsche, and continued by Heidegger, undertook a dismantling of the transcendental basis of traditional philosophy, and the work of Deleuze (and Guattari) is to be located in this counter-tradition. Hence, for Nietzsche, once transcendental principles are relinquished, there is in principle no way to make an absolute distinction between "A knows X" and "X is the lie that A happens to believe in." In their reflection on the socius, conducted as part of the *Capitalism and Schizophrenia* project, Deleuze and Guattari seek what amounts to a comprehensive undoing of the transcendental principles that underlie the constitution of the social order. An example of such a transcendental sociopolitical principle would be an affirmation like "freedom is the essential condition for the constitution of the commonwealth"—the "freedom" that is the basis of the commonwealth's constitution cannot be bestowed *after* the constitution of the commonwealth, since this freedom has to be in place before the commonwealth can be constituted. Or so traditional transcendental arguments of this kind go. The difference between a traditional transcendental argument of this kind, and one of the Deleuzean variety, is that the traditional kind of transcendental argument depends fundamentally on the notion of representation—"freedom" has to be represented, or brought to representation, in advance of this concept's deployment in such claims as "freedom is the essential condition for the constitution of the commonwealth." Hence an ideal essence, in this case the ideal essence of "freedom," becomes the basis of thought and being whenever one reflects on the nature of truth or the ideal form of political organization.

In the Deleuzean version of transcendentalism, by contrast, the transcendental field consists of vitalities and intensive singularities, and not abstract essences—these vitalities and singularities constituting a virtuality which transcends actuality because they provide eternal potentialities which are the basis of any transformation of the actual.

In *Anti-Oedipus*, the socius is said to be necessary because desiring production is coterminous with social production and reproduction, and for the latter to take place desire has to be coded and recoded, so that subjects can be "prepared" for their social roles and functions. The socius is the terrain of this coding and recoding. This decoding and recoding of desire so that subjects can undertake their roles in social and political systems has undeniable affinities with Althusserian conceptions of the functioning of ideology, and especially Althusser's notion of interpellation, with the significant difference that Althusser was not really prepared to deal with the subject of desire in case this opened up the can of worms that Althusser and his followers had consistently excoriated as "humanism." This of course was a huge lacuna in the Althusserian scheme of things, because interpellation necessarily presupposes a place in an ideological structure from which political action becomes possible and active, and as well as the possibility of movements between such structures, which the early Althusser tried to accommodate with his notion of a "form of transition" from one structure to another. But Althusser never dealt with the problem of the forces and distributions, lodged in one of his "forms of transition," which necessarily attend the emergence of a new structure, and thus could give no satisfactory account of the places within emergent structures which enable innovative forms of social and political agency. Althusser's followers (I am talking here about followers as opposed to those disciples who may have remained oblivious of this problem) had to contend with this very significant difficulty—Althusser's student Foucault did this to some extent by talking of "practices of subjectivation," and Deleuze and Guattari's notion of a "desiring production" can be said to do the work that the Althusserian subject of interpellation could not do in making possible political and social innovation and novelty.

Deleuze recognized this problem in his schematic overview of structuralism, titled in French "À quoi reconnaît-on le structuralisme?," when in a footnote in that 1972 essay he notes approvingly that Foucault did recognize the difficulty posed by structural mutation, when he said that "[this profound breach in the expanse of continuities], though it must be analyzed, and minutely so, cannot be 'explained' or even summed up in a single word. It is a radical event that is distributed across the entire visible surface of knowledge, and whose signs, shocks, and effects, it is possible to follow step by step."[3] Deleuze, first by himself, and later in conjunction with Guattari, pushed the question of the enabling conditions for this radical event that Althusser could not account for (though in a few tantalizing essays in the periods of lucidity he enjoyed before his death Althusser did come up with the notion of an "aleatory materialism" that sought to register the outlines of this radical event).[4] Deleuze's answer to this question was of course "desiring production," with the socius as the empirico-transcendental context in which desiring production takes place.

For Deleuze (and Guattari), therefore, a way had therefore to be found which allowed structure and form to be reconciled with the novelty and spontaneity of the event. This issue has been the basis of a long-standing debate in the philosophy of the social sciences concerning the relation between structure and agency, or act and being. The proposed solutions for this conundrum have been several. We have mentioned Althusser's notion of the contingent or aleatory event, which he derived from Machiavelli; and then there is Raymond Williams's appeal to "lived experience" as his way of breaking this seeming impasse between impersonal structure and the agency of individual subjects.[5] One could also mention Alain Badiou's appeal to the response of "evental fidelity" that the political subject is called upon to make when confronted with the structural breaks that occur when a decisive political transition is in the offing.[6]

Deleuze's proposal here is seemingly quite simple—there is something elemental, absolutely irreducible, which he calls life (*vie* in French), that subsequent thinkers such as Agamben and Roberto Esposito have in turn called "bios" in their characterizations of the biopolitical.

The appeal to something sheerly irreducible creates potentially as many problems as the ones it is intended to solve. As we know from the writings of Derrida and his epigoni, the appeal to something that is taken to be constitutively fundamental is always parasitic on that which Derrida calls the "supplement," meaning that what is regarded as "fundamental" is, in the end, necessarily and unavoidably derivative. How does Deleuze resolve this difficulty when he makes his appeal to *la vie*?

Deleuze's very short essay "L'immanence: une vie" hinges on the fundamental distinction between the possible and the virtual that has in various parts of his *oeuvre* appeared to be theoretically significant for Deleuze. In this essay this distinction becomes the basis for a politics. Basically, Deleuze wants to say that there are two ways of posing any question, one in terms of possibility, the other in terms of the notion of the virtual. To give an example (mine, not Deleuze's). "Is a revolution possible?" poses a question that can only be answered in terms that view the possibility of revolution as a prolepsis to its actualization. So, "Is a revolution possible?" is just another way of asking the question "How can the revolution become actual?." But once the question of revolution comes to be posed in terms of the question "How can the revolution become actual?," it ceases to be a revolutionary question for Deleuze. Why is this so? The answer is that to ask "How can the revolution become actual?" is simply another way of asking, given the present situation and its constraints, how can the revolution be started, how can it be placed as a viable option before the citizens of a country, and so forth? And the answer, for Deleuze, will already depend on something transcendental, in that *this* way of asking this question will presume a pregiven subject for whom it makes sense to pose the question "How can the revolution become actual?," and an object that can be designated as this revolution that the subject in question, if not all political subjects, will find desirable.

But herein lies the problem that exercised Deleuze from his first book on Hume to this last essay, namely, this pregiven subject is going to have to be a transcendental subject of consciousness and thus is always an abstract subject-in-general. The question "How can the revolution become actual?" if asked in relation to such a subject necessarily begs the question "all subjects?" and if not all subjects, then "which specific subject (or subjects)?," and then one unavoidably succumbs to the shallow empiricism which answers the question by providing a list of people who would probably welcome the revolution or not as the case may be (is this *my* revolution?, in the words of the song by The Who)— my uncle Frederick, but not my aunt Elizabeth, my cousin Suzanne, but not my grandfather Eric, and so on. Or more generally, one commits the banal idiocy of saying that a revolution will be welcomed by most of the people of Rwanda and Burkina Faso but not by the people of the United States. The same goes with the object "revolution"—it simply invites the question "what revolution?," and the endless and inconclusive attempts to answer this question culminate in an Alice in Wonderland world where someone's hallucination happens to be another's reality and vice versa.

"L'immanence: une vie" is a wondrous effort to cut this Gordian Knot of the transcendental subject and its accompanying object by posing it as question of the singular life that can bear the weight of posing a question, be it the question of revolution or the question of whether one should read Charles Dickens or not. To do this, says Deleuze, one has to deal with such questions at the level of virtuality, since to ask the question of reading Dickens is already abstracted from all those impulses and passions that bring me to read Dickens or to avoid reading him, as the case may be. In the realm of the virtual, the realm of what Deleuze calls Life, the actual is already being undone by the real but not yet actual revolution that is active without yet being manifestly present. This virtual is the not-yet -encoded already scrambling all the existent codes, so it is already real and active, without yet being actual, and as such is the only thing capable of overturning the established codes of the socius. This sounds like a minor victory, or even an ersatz triumph, but most assuredly it is not—what Deleuze is saying is that when the visible and presently actual annuls the revolutionary event, we have to look to its life, its bare life, as something real and active that for now is somehow being kept at bay or being postponed by forces that are counter-revolutionary (and these forces may or may not be visible to us).

What comes next? In one of the sayings of George W. Bush, who probably knows very little about revolutionary praxis, but who somehow stumbled on its great secret when he said in New Orleans just after Hurricane Katrina: "We're gonna clean all this mess up."[7] *That's* where we begin.

9

"1000 Political Subjects ..."

Is it possible for a compatibility to exist between Althusser's well-known doctrine of the interpellation of the subject by the ideological apparatuses of the state and the theses regarding the assemblages of the State propounded by Deleuze and Guattari in *Mille plateaux*?[1] Is there, more generally, a recognizable political subject whose ontological shape and character is limned in *Mille plateaux*, even as it is "undone" by Deleuze and Guattari? And is there a fundamental connection between this subject and the traditional metaphysical-epistemological subject that is also unraveled in *Mille plateaux*? At first sight, the likely answers to these questions are probably going to be negative, although our "no" will almost certainly have to be somewhat less emphatic where the second and third questions are concerned.

There are only a couple of references to Althusser in *Mille plateaux*, but what is there indicates explicitly that Deleuze and Guattari consider Althusser's notion of the constitution of social individuals as subjects to be profoundly mistaken. To quote Deleuze and Guattari:

> Neither is it a question of a movement characteristic of ideology, as Althusser says: subjectification as a regime of signs or a form of expression is tied to an assemblage, in other words, an organization of power that is already fully functioning in the economy, rather than superposing itself upon contents or relations between contents determined as real in the last instance. Capital is a point of subjectification par excellence. (*TP*, p. 130)

Deleuze and Guattari's rejection of the concept of ideology clearly stems from their conviction that the Althusserian conception of ideology relies on the discredited base-superstructure distinction. As they see it, subjectification is constituted by an assemblage or "organization of power" that already functions in the economic "base," and so cannot be seen as the outcome or resultant of processes located purely at the "superstructural" level, which of course for Althusser is determined "in the last instance" by the economic "base." And yet, and yet .... It is by no means obvious that Althusser is as wedded to the base-superstructure distinction in the way ostensibly presumed by Deleuze and Guattari. It could after all be argued that Althusser's treatment of ideology, resting as it does on the crucial proposition of an "overdetermination" of all the apparatuses, is intended precisely to obviate any reliance on the unacceptable "base-superstructure" distinction.[2] What if we accept, for the purposes of argument at any rate, that the notion of an interpellation can be detached from any unacceptable reliance on the "base-superstructure" distinction (postponing for the time being judgment on Althusser's putative weddedness to this distinction), so that an interpellation could in principle be said to take place as long as some kind of apparatus or agency constituted by the appropriate disposition of power provides enabling conditions for its occurrence? If this much is acknowledged or conceded, then it may be possible to say that subjects could be interpellated by State assemblages of the kind identified and described by Deleuze and Guattari in *Mille plateaux*. A great deal will hinge on the interpretation placed on the notion of such an interpellation, and how we specify the stakes that are at issue in retaining this Althusserian notion. At any rate, there is here the core of a hypothesis that is worth examining as a prolepsis to the question of the kind of political subject, with its allied account of political sovereignty, to be found in *Mille plateaux* and other associated writings by Deleuze and Guattari, whether authored individually or conjointly (or with other authors in the case of Guattari).

There is a conventional wisdom in the history of philosophy regarding the more or less intrinsic connection between the metaphysical-epistemological project that seeks an absolute ground for thought or reason, and the philosophico-political project of finding a ground in reason for the *modus operandi* of a moral and political subject. According to the lineaments of this well-seasoned narrative, the essential congruence between the rational subject of thought and the complementary subject of morality and politics was posited by Plato and Aristotle, and this unity between the two kinds of subject then found its suitably differentiated way into the thought of Hobbes, Locke, Spinoza, Leibniz, Hume, Kant, and Hegel (among many others). The core of this narrative is expressed by the somewhat Kantian proposition, characteristic of the Enlightenment in general, that reason provides the vital and indispensable criterion by which all judgments concerning belief, morality, politics, and art are to be appraised; so that reason is the faculty that defines and regulates the thinking being's activity, while this activity is in turn the essential means for reason's deployment in any thinking about the world, for the thinking being's capacity to describe and explain the world in ways that accord fundamentally with reason's precepts, and this precisely because reason is the irreducibly prior and enabling condition of any use of this capacity. Reason, in other words, constitutes the thinking being, and the activity of this being in turn enables reason to unfold dynamically (to provide a somewhat Hegelian gloss on this initially Kantian proposition). In the topography of this unfolding of reason, both thought and politics find their foundation.[3]

The philosophical tradition provides another way of delineating this connection between the subject of thought and the political subject, one that also derives its focal point from Kant. Using the distinction between a *subjectum* (i.e., the thing that serves as the bearer *of* something, be it consciousness or some other property of the individual) and a *subjectus* (i.e., the thing that is subjected *to* something else), the tradition has included among its repertoire of concepts a figure of thought taken from medieval philosophy that hinges on the relation between the *subjectum* and the *subjectus*. Etienne Balibar, in his fascinating essay "Citizen Subject," uses this distinction to urge that we not identify Descartes's thinking thing (*res cogitans*) with the transcendental subject of thought that very quickly became an ineliminable feature of modern epistemology. Nothing could be further from the truth, says Balibar, because the human being is for Descartes the unity of a soul and a body, and this unity, which marks the essence of the human being, cannot be represented in terms of the *subjectum* (presumably because the *subjectum*, qua intellectual simple nature, can exist logically without requiring the presupposition of a unity between soul and body).[4] As the unity of a soul and a body, the human individual is not a mere intellectual simple nature, *a subjectum*, but is, rather, a subject in another quite different sense. In this other different sense, the human individual is a subject transitively related to an other, a "something else," and for Descartes this "something else" is precisely the divine sovereignty. In other words, for Descartes the human individual is really a *subjectus*, and never the *subjectum* of modern epistemology (which in any case owes its discovery to Locke and not to Descartes). For Balibar, therefore, it is important to remember that Descartes, who in many ways is really a late scholastic philosopher, was profoundly engaged with a range of issues that had been central for medieval philosophy, in this particular case the question of the relation of lesser beings to the supreme being, a question which both Descartes and the medieval philosophers broached, albeit in differing ways, under the rubric of the divine sovereignty.

The Cartesian subject is thus a *subjectus*, one who submits, and this in at least two ways that were significant for both Descartes and medieval political theology: (i) the subject submits to the Sovereign who is the Lord God; and (ii) the subject also yields to the earthly authority of the prince who is God's representative on earth. As Descartes put it in his letter to Mersenne (April 15, 1630): "Do not hesitate I tell you, to avow and proclaim everywhere, that it is God who has established the laws of nature, as a King establishes laws in his Kingdom."[5] From this passage, and from his other writings, it is clear that the notion of sovereignty was at once political *and* theological for Descartes, as it had been for the earlier scholastic philosophers. This is not the place for a detailed discussion of Balibar's argument, which in addition to being a little sketchy is also not entirely new—Leibniz, Arnauld, and Malebranche had long ago viewed Descartes, roughly their contemporary, as a follower in the footsteps of Augustine who found philosophy's *raison d'être* in the soul's contemplation of its relation to God, and who therefore took the dependence of lesser beings on the supreme eminence as philosophy's primary concern.[6] But if Locke is the inventor of the modern concept of the self, who then is the real author of the fully fledged concept of the transcendental subject, if Balibar is right to insist that it is not Descartes?

The true culprit here, says Balibar, is not Descartes, but Kant, who needed the concept of the transcendental subject to account for the "synthetic unity" that provides the necessary conditions for objective experience. Kant chose to foist onto Descartes something that was really his own "discovery," and with Heidegger as his more than willing subsequent accomplice in this dubious undertaking, the outcome of this grievous misattribution has been momentous for our understanding (or lack thereof) of the course taken by the history of philosophy.[7] Kant however was about more than just the "discovery" of the transcendental subject. The Kantian subject had also to prescribe duties for itself in the name of the categorical imperative, and in so doing carve out a realm of freedom in nature that would enable this subject to free itself from a "self-inflicted tutelage" that arises when we can't make judgments without the supervision of an other, and this of course includes the tutelage of the King. The condition for realizing any such ideal on the part of the enlightened subject is the ability to submit to nothing but the rule of reason in making judgments, and so to be free from the power of the despot when making one's judgments entails a critical repositioning of the place from which sovereignty is exercised: no more is this place the body of the King, since for Kant this "tutelage" is stoppable only if the subject is able to owe its allegiance to a republican polity constituted by the rule of reason and nothing but the rule of reason. Whatever criticism Balibar levels at Kant for the (supposed) historical mistake he made with regard to Descartes, the philosopher from East Prussia nonetheless emerges as a very considerable figure in Balibar's account. For Kant also created the concept of a certain kind of practical subject, one who operates in the realm of freedom, and this practical subject, whose telos is the ultimate abolition of any kind of "self-inflicted tutelage," had to destroy the "subject" of the King (i.e., the *subjectus* of Descartes and medieval political theology) in order to become a "self-legislating" rational being. Kant's therefore simultaneously created the transcendental subject (i.e., the *subjectum* of modern epistemology) and discredited philosophically the *subjectus* of the previous philosophical and political dispensation.

The real philosophical adversary of Kant is Hobbes. Hobbes stated the crux of the principle of sovereignty when he asserted that if the sovereign is the origin of law, then no law can bind the sovereign, and thus the State. The only basis for the functioning of the State is the decree of the sovereign, and force is effectively the determinant of the relation that the sovereign has to his subjects, or to other sovereigns. The sovereign does not derive his authority from the State, since the State only exists by virtue of the insuperable authority that emanates from the sovereign. The sovereign is necessarily the animating principle underlying all authority, and hence a subject's refusal of the authority of the sovereign is the subject's refusal of its own authority, and thus of itself. As Hobbes puts it, the sovereign is "the Publique Soule, giving Life and Motion to the Commonwealth."[8] The subject's authority, provided it is not usurped or feigned, can only be the authority of the sovereign, and a subject's disowning of the sovereign's authority is thus necessarily a nullification of the very ground of the subject's own authority.[9] The unavoidable concomitant of this position on the character of sovereignty is that the State can have only one sovereign, who therefore represents all the people (so that his acts are willy-nilly their acts as well), and all associations within the commonwealth are based on the principle of the State and the sovereign who gives the State its *raison d'etre*.[10] Against Hobbes, Kant asserts that "the people too have inalienable rights against the head of state .... For to assume that the head of state can neither make mistakes nor be ignorant of anything would be to imply that he receives divine inspiration and is more than a human being."[11]

The concomitant of Kant's philosophical evisceration of the "subject" of the King was thus the political emergence of the republican citizen who from 1789 onwards would supplant the subject/*subjectus* of the previous epoch. In the process, Descartes's philosophical world of subjects who submit to the laws of God and King was dislodged by Kant's world of "self-legislating" rational subjects who engage in this legislation precisely by adverting to the notions of right and duty. This new subject is the embodiment of right and of the operation of practical reason (right being for Kant the outcome that can be guaranteed only by the proper use of practical reason), and furthermore the subject is considered a citizen to the extent he or she embodies the general will, in which case the only laws worthy of the name are those framed to reflect "the united will of the whole nation."[12] Sovereignty is thus glossed by Kant through a recasting of the Rousseauan social contract. Laws are rationally promulgated only when they exemplify the general will, and this exemplification of the general will is possible only if there is a perfectly just civil constitution. The outcome, as the philosophy textbooks tell us, was a crucial separation of the earthly from the heavenly city. However, if Kant is the inaugurator of the Citizen Subject, then for Balibar Michel Foucault is the great theorist of the transition from the world of kingly and divine sovereignty to the world of rights and duties determined by the State and its apparatuses, and Balibar concludes his essay with the following observation: "As to whether this figure [the Citizen Subject] like a face of sand at the edge of the sea, is about to be effaced with the next great sea change, that is another question. Perhaps it is nothing more than Foucault's own utopia, a necessary support for that utopia's facticity."[13] I would like now to address the Foucauldian question left by Balibar for future consideration, and pose the question of the current destination or fate of the Citizen Subject. To do this we have to look again at Kant.

The reason that constitutes the subject is perforce a Transcendental Reason. The Kantian inflection here is not accidental, because the reason that grounds the subject is not a reason that can be specified within the terms of the activity of the subject: this reason is the basis of this subject's very possibility *qua* subject, and by virtue of that, reason is necessarily exterior to the subject. Reason in this kind of employment is thus the activity of a single and universal quintessence whose object is reason itself, so that reason has necessarily to seek its ground within itself, as Hegel noted.[14] Reason, by virtue of its self-grounding, is perforce the writing of the Absolute.[15] The subject's ground, which has to reside in Reason itself, is therefore entirely and properly metaphysical, and any crisis of Transcendental Reason unavoidably becomes a philosophical crisis of the subject. Kant himself was the first to realize this, although it was left to his philosophical successors in the movement known as "early Romanticism" (*Frühromantik*) to make the acknowledgment of this crisis of Transcendental Reason into a starting point for philosophical reflection.

With Nietzsche however the hitherto radical figure of the transcendental subject is propelled into a crisis, and with this crisis the fundamental convergence between the metaphysical-epistemological subject and the philosophico-political subject is denied plausibility. We all know from the basic textbooks in the history of philosophy that reason, insofar as it operates on both the understanding and the will, is placed by Nietzsche entirely within the ambit of the *wille zur macht*, so that power/desire becomes the enabling basis of any epistemological or moral and political subject, thereby irretrievably undermining or dislocating both kinds of subject. As a result of the intervention represented by Nietzsche, truth, goodness, and beauty, that is, the guiding transcendental notions for the constitution of this epistemological and moral and political subject, are henceforth to be regarded merely as the functions and ciphers of this supervening will to power. The same conventional wisdom also assures us that Marx and Freud likewise "undid" the two kinds of subject and thus undermined even further any basis for their essential congruence. The constellation formed by Nietzsche, Marx, and Freud (and their successors) shows both the transcendental subject and the ethico-political subject of action to be mere conceptual functions, lacking any substantial being (Kant of course having already argued in the *Critique of Pure Reason* that the subject of thought is not a substance).

This hackneyed narrative about the collective impact of the great "masters of suspicion" is fine as it goes; what is far more interesting, however, is the story of what had to come after Nietzsche, Marx, and Freud, of what it is that was going to be done with the ruins of the epistemological and moral and political subject who ostensibly had reigned from Plato to Hegel before receiving its quietus in the latter part of the nineteenth century. It is interesting that Balibar, who is as resolute a marxist as anyone could be in these supposedly post-marxist days, appears not to take on board Marx's critique of bourgeois democracy in "Citizen Subject," but instead regards Foucault as the thinker who more than any other registered the crisis of this Subject. Be that as it may, it is hard to deny that the transcendental subject of modern epistemology suffered calamitously at the hands of Nietzsche (and Heidegger after Nietzsche), and that political and philosophical developments in the twentieth century cast the Citizen Subject adrift in a rickety lifeboat headed in the direction of the treacherous reefs mapped by Foucault.

But can the course of this stricken lifeboat be altered, and the functions and modes of expression typically associated with the Citizen Subject be reconstituted in some more productive way, so that this Subject, or its successor (but who would that putative successor be?), would be able to meet the political and philosophical demands generated by the presently emerging conjuncture? Here one senses a certain ambivalence at the end of Balibar's essay, a wish that Foucault was perhaps not going to be right when it came to a final reckoning of the fate of the Citizen Subject, and that new and better times will somehow come to await a radically transformed Citizen Subject. But what could the shape and character of this new life for the Citizen Subject be? Balibar has an emphatic proposal: the Citizen Subject will live only by becoming a revolutionary actor.

I want to take Balibar's proposal as the starting point for the discussion that will occupy the rest of this essay. There is also the question of the theoretical "space" that used to be occupied by the transcendental subject of epistemology. While we may not quarrel with Balibar's suggestion that the Citizen Subject supplanted the *subjectus* who owed its fealty to the sovereign monarch and sovereign deity, it has also to be acknowledged, and Balibar himself is certainly aware of this, that Kant placed under the category of *Right* not merely action, but also knowledge: the Kantian subject is both the Citizen Subject who acts and the epistemological subject who reflects in accordance with the principles of Reason. This subject may have been displaced or finally extinguished in the latter part of the twentieth century, but the question of the "right use" of Reason remains, or at any rate, the question of the place of a hoped-for right use of Reason still poses itself. This question is therefore one that demands to be addressed.

Whatever Foucault may have said about the supersession of the post-classical *épistémè*, and the death of Man-Citizen that accompanied this supersession (I take Foucault's Man-Citizen to be coextensive with Balibar's Citizen Subject), it is obvious here that the subsequent mutation of classical liberalism into a globalizing neoliberalism and the disappearance of socialism to form the basis of a new conjuncture—a conjuncture which some have called the "post-political" politics of the time after 1968—represents an added inconvenience for the already punishing and wobbly trajectory taken by this Citizen Subject or Man-Citizen. The culmination of this trajectory in the "post-political" politics of the last few decades seems at one and the same time to reduce the weight of the critique represented by Nietzsche, Marx, and Freud (the subject's apparent superfluity in this "post-political" dispensation undermines the very need for its critique; with the effacement of the object of critique, critique also finds itself fading into nothingness), while at the same time making more urgent the question of the ontological status of the subject of this "post-political" politics (is it still some kind of vestigially effective subject, a barely breathing remnant of the Man-Citizen of Foucault's modern *épistémè* or Balibar's Citizen Subject of the time after 1789?); and if so, what powers (if any) reside in this brute remnant, or are we left today with nothing for the metaphysical constitution of the possibility of politics but the sheer acknowledgment of the power of the body, the power of bare life (as proposed by the thinkers of the "inoperative" community and the community to come), or the appeal to some kind of undeconstructable justice coming from the outside of any totality (as proposed by Derrida and his epigoni), etc.?

We don't have to hear too much along these lines in order to recognize that the practices and orders of thought associated with the "societies of control" delineated by Deleuze, and those of the domain of the biopolitical identified by Foucault, but also developed by Agamben and Hardt and Negri (Hardt and Negri however taking the biopolitical in a very different direction from Agamben), each derives their saliency from this "post-political" conjuncture. Also important here is the attempt by Gayatri Chakravorty Spivak to outline a form of constitutionalism that is not indebted to the metaphysics of classical (and therefore definitively Western) political sovereignty. The centrality of the problematic of the "post-political" for any putative project of liberation, and marxism is such a project if it is anything, can therefore hardly be gainsaid—this problematic is no merely tangential *l'effet Foucault*!

What kind of political subject, if any, can continue to exist in the conjuncture of a "post-political" politics, and has this subject to possess an intrinsic and defining connection to the political sovereignty that grounded the classical Citizen Subject?

Deleuze and Guattari, using the writings of Georges Dumézil as their initial template, provide a fascinating narrative when addressing the question of political sovereignty in the plateau titled "Treatise on Nomadology."[16] Invoking Dumézil's dualism of the shaman-king and the priest-jurist, Deleuze and Guattari go on to say:

> Undoubtedly, these two poles stand in opposition term by term, as the obscure and the clear, the violent and the calm, the quick and the weighty, the terrifying and the regulated, the "bond" and the "pact," etc. But their opposition is only relative; they function as a pair, in alternation, as though they expressed a division of the One or constituted in themselves a sovereign unity. "At once antithetical and complementary, necessary to one another and consequently without hostility, lacking a mythology of conflict: each specification at any one level automatically calls forth a homologous specification on another. The two together exhaust the field of the function." They are the principal elements of a State apparatus that proceeds by a One-Two, distributes binary distinctions,

and forms a milieu of interiority. It is a double articulation that makes the State apparatus into a *stratum*.[17]

Deleuze and Guattari take Dumézil's personifications, at once complementary and mutually reinforcing, of the magician-king and the jurist-priest to constitute the two-pronged function of the State. They also follow Dumézil in opposing to this State apparatus, and thus the figures of the magician-king and the jurist-priest, the counter-force represented by the war machine. The respective properties possessed by the State apparatus and the war machine can be tabulated in the following manner:[18]

State Apparatus	**War Machine**
Sovereignty (*pouvoir*)	power (*puissance*)
Law	event
fixity of Being	ontological innovation
gravity	celerity
the public	secrecy
binary distributions	multiple becoming
permanence	evanescence
conservation	power of metamorphosis
milieu of interiority	milieu of exteriority
internal, biunivocal relations	external relation
polis	*nomos*
semiology	strategy, pragmatics
"striated" space	"smooth" space
coding/decoding	territorialization/deterritorialization
king, jurist	warrior, prophet
concentration	dispersion
strategies of exclusion	resistance, openness
"arborescent"	"rhizomatic"
hierarchical	non-hierarchical
identity	transformation
individuality	singularity
false plenitude, empty repetition	facing the void
delimitation	immeasurability
Goethe, Hegel	Kleist, Artaud
organs of power	packs, bands

theorems	problematics
formal concentration of power	solidarity
religion	offenses against gods and priests
harmony	rhythm
architecture, cooking	music, drugs
history	geography
measured time (*chronos*)	indefinite time of event (*Aeon*)
Egyptian state	Moses
Man	"becoming-woman"

Deleuze and Guattari caution against viewing the opposition between the State apparatus and the war machine in strict binary terms:

> The problem is that the exteriority of the war machine in relation to the State apparatus is everywhere apparent but remains difficult to conceptualize. It is not enough to affirm that the war machine is external to the apparatus ... What complicates everything is that this extrinsic power of the war machine tends, under certain circumstances, to become confused with one of the two heads of the State apparatus. Sometimes it is confused with the magic violence of the State, at other times with the State's military institution .... So there is a great danger of identifying the structural relation between the two poles of political sovereignty, and the dynamic interrelation of these two poles, with the power of war .... [W]henever the irruption of war power is confused with the line of state domination, everything gets muddled; the war machine can then be understood only through the categories of the negative, since nothing is left that remains outside the State. But, returned to its milieu of exteriority, the war machine is seen to be of another species, of another nature, of another origin. (*TP*, p. 355)

Returning to the question of Althusserian interpellation, it seems plausible, if not obvious, to say that any neo-Althusserian wishing to retain the notion of such an interpellation, while adhering to Deleuze and Guattari's conception of political sovereignty, will have to accept that any such interpellation at the hands of the State apparatus will necessarily be according to "theorems" derived from the twin poles of its political sovereignty, to wit, the shaman-king and the jurist-priest. For Deleuze and Guattari, the Law of the State is despotic and priestly in its most fundamental impulses, and anything like an interpellation (admittedly not a notion Deleuze and Guattari would want to use) is perforce conducted in congruence with those "theorems" sanctioned by the State's despotic and sacerdotal orders, these sacred or quasi-sacred orders persisting even when the polity in question is a liberal democracy with an accompanying normativity ostensibly resting on entirely secular premises.[19] Ethico-political subjects interpellated in this way will therefore be caught up in a transcendental validation of their subjectivities—legitimation at the hands of the State for Deleuze and Guattari always places the subject at the mercy of an *arché* or founding principle that requires the citizen to be created in the image of the State's figures of sovereignty, in this case the overarching despot and priest. The outcome, for Deleuze and Guattari, will in any case be a thousand little despots, a thousand little priests, all defined as model Citizen Subjects.

The State, on this account, is the product of thought, in this case a thinking which is inextricably linked to a desire that for Deleuze and Guattari is ubiquitous and endlessly productive:

> Everything is production: *production of productions*, of actions and of passions; *production of recording processes*, of distributions and of co-ordinates that serve as points of reference; *production of consumptions*, of sensual pleasures, of anxieties, and of pains. Everything is production, since the recording processes are immediately consumed, immediately consummated, and these consumptions directly reproduced. (*AO*, p. 4, original italics)

The implications of this position are profound and radical, and they point, among other things, to a significant difference between a standard and almost normative reading of Foucault and the authors of *Capitalisme et schizophrénie*. Deleuze and Guattari clearly accord great importance to "desiring production" (as indicated by the above passage). But this undeniable saliency of "desiring production" does not translate into the primacy of the modes of production as such, which is what one would expect of a more conventional marxist or marxisant thinking. Instead Deleuze and Guattari bestow this primacy on the so-called machinic processes, that is, the modes of organization that link all kinds of "attractions and repulsions, sympathies and antipathies, alterations, amalgamations, penetrations, and expressions that affect bodies of all kinds in their relations to one another."[20] The modes of production depend on these machinic processes for their constitution.[21] The upshot is that the modes of production are always themselves the product or derivation of a ceaselessly generative desire: what enables each mode to be constituted is an always specific, indeed aleatory, aggregation of mutually permeating desires, forces, and powers. The organization of productive desire gives the mode of production its enabling conditions, and not vice versa, as is the case in some of the more typical marxisms. In arriving at this formulation, though, Deleuze and Guattari are very much in line with what Marx himself said about the necessity for society to exist before capitalism can emerge in anything like a fully fledged form: a society-state with prexisting surpluses has already to exist if the (capitalist) extraction of surplus-value is to take place. To quote Deleuze and Guattari:

> Marx, the historian, and Childe, the archaeologist, are in agreement on the following point: the archaic imperial State, which steps in to overcode agricultural communities, presupposes at least a certain level of development of these communities' productive forces since there must be a potential surplus capable of constituting a State stock, of supporting a specialized handicrafts class (metallurgy), and of progressively giving rise to public functions. This is why Marx links the archaic State to a certain [precapitalist] "mode of production." (*TP*, p. 428)

The state, in other words, gives capital its "models of realization."[22] But the state that provides capital with the models it needs in order to be effectuated is already functioning even before it manifests itself as a concretely visible apparatus. The state, in this case the Palaeolithic state, destroys or neutralizes the hunter-gatherer societies that it came to supersede, but before this happens there has to be a necessary point of convergence between the State and the hunter-gatherer troupes. This point of convergence, which the troupes ward off and anticipate at the same time, designates a situation or space in which—"simultaneously"—the existing hunter-gatherer formations are dismantled and their successor state-formations put in place. In the words of Deleuze and Guattari, the two sets of formations unfold "simultaneously in an 'archaeological', micropolitical, micrological, molecular field."[23]

The state, on this view, achieves its "actuality" through a complex and uneven process that involves the arresting or caging of non-state formations, so that both state and non-state formations exist in a field of perpetual interaction. This interactive field, in the parlance of Deleuze and Guattari, is irreducibly "micropolitical" or "molecular," and so state-formations, which for them are of course quintessentially "macropolitical" or "molar," are not positioned in a field that has already been transformed by the state apparatuses or their prototypes into something that is (now) exclusively "macropolitical" or "molar." It is virtually an axiom for Deleuze and Guattari that before, and alongside, the macropolitical there is always the micropolitical. The state has perforce to interact with the micropolitical. This is at odds with a certain interpretation of Foucault (here regarded as the exemplary philosopher of the micropolitical) which views micropolitics to be a relatively new "development" arising more or less strictly in response to forms of power, pre-eminently "biopower," that did not exist before the onset of the most recent phases of modernity. While it is not quite clear whether Foucault himself should be saddled with this view, it remains the case that for Deleuze and Guattari the state apparatuses always emerge in a "molecularized" field that the state never entirely contains or neutralizes. The appearance of the state cannot therefore be the outcome of its own efficacy, of any inherent propensity on its part to generate its own enabling conditions. Whatever its powers, autogeny is beyond the power of the state to accomplish. Micropolitics has therefore always been antique in its provenance, and the state came about as an invention designed to arrest these micropolitical forces. Moreover, as an invention, the state had necessarily to be "thought" before it could begin to be efficacious in any social and political field.[24] But the state has to deny this irremovable factitiousness of its "origins," and present itself precisely as its "opposite," that is, as an unthought (at any rate where "origins" are concerned): "Only thought is capable of inventing the fiction of a State that is universal by right, of elevating the State to the level of de jure universality" (*TP*, p. 375).

Thought confers on the state its character of a singular and universal form, the fullest expression of the rational-reasonable (*le rationnel-raisonnable*). The foremost exponent of this "thought" behind the genesis of the state is of course Hegel, who explicitly views the state as the embodiment of the universal, as the realization of reason, and thus as the spiritual community that incorporates all individuals within itself. Against this view, which derives the state from the rational-reasonable, Deleuze and Guattari hold that it is the rational-reasonable itself that is derived from the state. The state provides the formal conditions for the enactment of the rational-reasonable,[25] and thought (as the primary instantiation of the rational-reasonable) in turn necessarily confers on the state its "reason" (*lui donner, necessairement "raison"*).[26] Reason or thought becomes the province of the state on this Hegelian (or quasi-Hegelian) view, and Deleuze and Guattari therefore propose a wresting of thought from the state and a complementary returning of the state to thought, in the form of an acknowledgment of the state's irreducible fictiveness.[27]

The archaic state that arose from a recoding of the primitive territorial codes of the hunter-gatherer troupes instituted an organized production associated with the creation of "a particular kind of property, money, public works …."[28] But this archaic state was not able to prevent a substantial quantity of "decoded flows" from escaping:

> The State does not create large-scale works without a flow of independent labor escaping its bureaucracy (notably in the mines and in metallurgy). It does not create the monetary form of the tax without flows of money escaping, and nourishing or bringing into being other powers (notably in commerce and banking). And above all it does not create a system of public property without a flow of private appropriation growing up beside it, then beginning to pass beyond its grasp; this private property does not itself issue from the archaic system but is constituted on the margins, all the more necessarily and inevitably, slipping through the net of overcoding. (*TP*, p. 449)

This epochal transformation confronted the succeeding state apparatuses with a new task. Where the previous state-form had to overcode the already coded flows of the hunter-gatherer groups, the new state apparatuses had to organize conjunctions of the decoded flows that had been escaping their archaic predecessor. These became the apparatuses of a polynucleated and more complex kind of state. But even here the state could not prevent decoded flows from escaping (yet again), and the most recent versions of these flows attained an "abstract," "generalized" conjunction which overturned their adjacent state apparatuses and created capitalism "at a single stroke."[29] Capital thus represents a new and decisive threshold for the proliferation of flows, and, in the words of Deleuze and Guattari, this "force of deterritorialization infinitely [surpasses] the deterritorialization proper to the State."[30] But capital's superiority in this regard does not spell the end of the state. Instead the state underwent a further mutation, and the modern nation-state was born.

The relation between the state and capital is thus one of reciprocity. Capitalism is an "independent, worldwide axiomatic that is like a single City, megalopolis, or 'megamachine' of which the States are parts, or neighborhoods."[31] The state-form is not totally displaced by the "worldwide, ecumenical organization" of capital, but it has, in its modern manifestation, become a "model of realization" for capital. As such, it is the function of each state today to "[group] together and [combine] several sectors, according to its resources, population, wealth, industrial capacity, etc." (*TP*, p. 454). Under capitalism, the state serves "to moderate the superior deterritorialization of capital and to provide the latter with compensatory reterritorializations" (*TP*, p. 455). The state becomes a field for the effectuation of capital, and it does this by reharnessing and reorganizing flows which capital brings together and decomposes.[32] Capitalism will even organize and sustain states that are not viable, for its own purposes, primarily by crushing minorities through integration and extermination.[33] The primacy of capital manifests itself at the highest level of abstraction: capital is an international organization that can organize with a prodigious resourcefulness the various state formations in ways that ensure their fundamental "isomorphy" (which is not to be confused with "homogeneity" in Deleuze and Guattari's scheme).

International capitalism is capable of bringing about the "isomorphy" of very diverse forms and their attendant forces. In his Leibniz book, Deleuze maintains that cultural and social formations are constituted on the basis of "concerts" or "accords."[34] These "accords" are organizing principles which make possible the grouping into particular configurations of whole ranges of events, personages, processes, institutions, movements, and so forth, such that the resulting configurations become integrated formations. As a set of accords or axioms governing the accords that regulate the operations of the various components of an immensely powerful and comprehensive system of accumulation, capital is situated at the crossing point of all kinds of formations, and thus has the capacity to integrate and recompose capitalist and noncapitalist sectors or modes of production.[35] Capital, the "accord of accords" par excellence, can bring together heterogeneous phenomena, and make them express the same world, that of capitalist accumulation. Thus, in Malaysia, for example, the accord (or set of accords) the "hi-tech" world of downtown Kuala Lumpur (the location of the world's tallest skyscraper at its time of construction), and the accord (or set of accords) that constitutes the world of Stone Age production to be found among the tribespeople in the interiors of west Malaysia (Sabah and Sarawak) are not inter-translatable (or not directly or immediately so); but what the "accord of accords" created by capitalism does, among a myriad other things, is to make it possible for the artifacts produced by the "indigenous" peoples of these interior regions to appear on the tourist markets in downtown Kuala Lumpur, where they are sold alongside Microsoft software, Magnavox camcorders, Macintosh Power Books, and so on. The disparate and seemingly incompatible spheres of production and accumulation represented by downtown Kuala Lumpur and the interior regions of Sabah and Sarawak (which are only about 750 miles away from Kuala Lumpur) are rendered "harmonious" by a higher-level accord or concert established by capital, even though the lower-level accords remain (qua lower-level accords) disconnected from each other. Each lower-level accord retains its own distinctive productive mode and its associated social relations of production, even as it is brought into relationship with other quite different modes and social relations of production (each of course with their own governing ground-level accords) by the meta- or mega-accord that is capitalism in its current world-integrated phase. The "concerto grosso" brought about by this prodigiously expansive capitalist accord of accords enables the lower-level accords to remain dissociated from each other while still expressing the same world, the world of the current paradigm of accumulation. In a country like Malaysia, and indeed anywhere else in the world, every kind of production can thus be incorporated by the capitalist algorithm and made to yield a surplus value.

This development has effectively dismantled the intellectual terms of the age-old debate about "precapitalist" modes of production and their relation to a successor capitalism. This debate was concerned, in the main, with the putative "laws" that underlay the supersession of the "precapitalist" modes by their capitalist successors, but the question of this supersession has become moot in the current phase of accumulation: as the case of Malaysia illustrates, the "precapitalist" modes can continue to exist in precisely that form, but are inserted at the same time into a complex and dynamic network that includes, in the spirit of a vast and saturating ecumenism, all the various modes of production, "precapitalist" and capitalist alike, so that they function in concert with each other, in this way promoting of course the realization of even greater surplus-values.[36]

Accords are constituted by selection criteria, which specify what is to be included or excluded by the terms of the accord in question. These criteria also determine with which other possible or actual accords a particular accord will be consonant (or dissonant). The criteria that constitute accords are usually defined and described by narratives governed by a certain normative vision of truth, goodness, and beauty (reminiscent of the so-called medieval transcendentals, albeit translated where necessary into the appropriate contemporary vernacular). A less portentous way of making this point would be to say that accords are inherently axiological, value-laden. What seems to be happening today, and this is a generalization that is tendentious, is that these superposed narratives and the selection criteria they sanction, criteria which may or may not be explicitly formulated or entertained, are being weakened or qualified in ways that deprive them of their force. Such selection criteria tend to function by assigning privileges of rank and order to the objects they subsume ("Le Pen is more French than Zidane," "One cannot be a good American and a Communist," "Turks are not Europeans," etc.). The loss or attenuation of the customary force of such accords makes dissonances and contradictions difficult or even impossible to resolve, and, correlatively, makes divergences easier to affirm. Events, objects, and personages can now be assigned to several divergent and even incompossible series, a phenomenon spectacularly demonstrated by Lautréamont's uncannily surrealistic definition of reality as "the chance encounter between a sewing-machine and an umbrella on a dissecting-table."

Such a Lautréamontean, culturally sanctioned disposition in the present day, conducing as it does to a traffic in all kinds of incompossibilites and divergences, is becoming increasingly commonplace. As each of us takes the opportunity to negotiate for the fifteenth or hundredth or whatever time, the several historical avant-gardes, the writings of Borges, cyberpunk, and so forth, we become familiarized with the propensities of a Lautréamontean consciousness in ways not available to a learned and cosmopolitan person living as recently as fifty years ago. Thus, for instance, we have a whole genre ("magical realism") predicated on the logic of incompossibility (something can be a bird and Simon Bolivar at the same time, and even more "implausibly," at the same point in space); there is a new technological form based on the same logic (such as the morphing that Michael Jackson undergoes in his video *Thriller*); as well as entire schools of music which use tones in series that escape or block any kind of resolution by the diatonic scale (as in the work of John Cage or Toru Takemitsu or free improvisational jazz).[37] Such examples can be multiplied according to one's taste.

This pervasive weakening of the force of these "transcendental" accords, and of the narratives and images which sustain them, may be associated with the collapse of a number of once widely entrenched distinctions: the boundaries between public and private, inside and outside, before and after, political left and political right, and so on have all become difficult, if not impossible, to uphold. In the process, however, accords thus detached from the narratives and other conditions capable of guaranteeing their stability likewise become "impossible." We may be living in worlds that are no longer predicated on any real need to secure and maintain accords, worlds characterized by sheer variation and multiplicity (but still functioning according to an axiomatics— i.e., capital—that ensures their fundamental isomorphism in the face of this uncontainable diversity), worlds that partake of a neo-Baroque perhaps more "truly" Baroque than its predecessor, as Deleuze has maintained in his book on Leibniz. Or rather, these are worlds in which the work of accords is now done emblematically and allegorically, so that there is no real accord for what it is that, say, constitutes "Englishness" (or perhaps more accurately, there is now the realization that our accords determining what it is that constitutes "Englishness" rest on an ineliminable fictiveness, so that these accords lack any kind of transcendental legitimation): in the absence of anything approximating to a transcendental back-stopping, "being English" can only be designated ascriptively or emblematically, that is, non-absolutely, as when Queen Elizabeth

II (who had as much claim to be regarded as German as English) is so easily allowed to "count" as "English," while supporters of the late Enoch Powell, an Anglophone and intellectually upscale version of Jean-Marie Le Pen, were able nastily to cavil over whether a London-born son or daughter of a Jamaican immigrant could justifiably be regarded as "English."

The ascriptive or emblematic imputation of "Englishness" would allow it to be placed into at least a couple of divergent series. There would be Enoch Powell's grimly robust and settled series, which would effectively confine "Englishness" to him and his benighted ilk, but other more expansive series would include London-born children of Jamaican immigrants, the half-American Winston Churchill, the Somali-born Mohamed "Mo" Farah who is Britain's greatest long-distance runner ever, and so on. Crucial to this more ascriptive way of assigning or determining identities is the abandonment of the concept in favor of description (a move delineated by Deleuze in his Leibniz book). Typically, the specification of an identity requires that the identity under consideration be determinate in regard to a concept ("being a communist," "being Irish," "being an economist," or whatever), a concept whose range of applicability is regulated by certain criteria of belonging. These criteria are motivated and underpinned by accords of the kind described above, and the breakdown of these accords means that the concepts they support and organize can be replaced by descriptions. Hence, for example, in place of the concept "being an English person" one could have the descriptions "Queen Elizabeth II conducting herself as an English woman," "'Mo' Farah is the Somali-born runner who represents England," "the Japanese-born anglophone novelist Kazuo Ishiguro," and so forth. Such descriptions, as opposed to the concept "being English" or "being British," would allow "Englishness/Britishness" to be used ascriptively or emblematically, so that "it" could be placed, depending on the particular instances involved, in two or more divergent series. This substitution in principle of the description for the concept would not be an inappropriate way of acknowledging the emergence of a new intellectual and cultural condition (we could call it the time after the end of the Empire, which is "our time" undeniably) in which it has become more difficult than ever to claim that there really are "transcendental" accords which subtend this or that way of designating "Englishness."

The worlds opened up by *Capitalisme et schizophrénie* are worlds whose accords are characterized in very decisive ways by the kinds allegorizing and emblematizing propensities just described. These are worlds marked by the "systemic" loss of transcendental accords; they are worlds that are perhaps seeing the exponential growth of the capacity to accommodate what Deleuze and Guattari call "the anomalous" (*l'anomal*). The anomalous, in their view,

> has nothing to do with the preferred, domestic, psychoanalytic individual. Nor is the anomalous the bearer of a species presenting specific or generic characteristics in their purest state; nor is it a model or unique specimen; nor is it the perfection of a type incarnate; nor is it the eminent term of a series; nor is it the basis of an absolutely harmonious correspondence. The anomalous is neither an individual nor a species; it only has affects, it has neither familiar nor subjectified feelings, nor specific or significant characteristics. (*TP*, p. 244)

The realm of the anomalous, for Deleuze and Guattari, lies between the domain of "substantial forms" and that of "determined subjects"; it constitutes "a natural play full of haecceities, degrees, intensities, events, and accidents that compose individuations totally different from those of the well-formed subjects that receive them."[38] The upshot is that each individual is a potentially infinite multiplicity, the product of a phantasmagorical movement between an inside and an outside.[39]

All this amounts to the lineaments of a new and interesting theory of the place of the "subject" in the cultures of contemporary capitalism. *Capitalisme et schizophrénie* approaches this theory of the "subject" via a theory of singularity—"singularity" being the category that more than any other goes beyond the "collective" versus "individual" dichotomy that is essential to the Hobbes-Rousseau-Hegel tradition of reflection on the state or sovereign. This account of singularity, and here I have to be very brief and schematic, can in turn be connected up with the theory of simulation given in Deleuze's *Logique du sens* and *Différence et répétition*, since for Deleuze simulation (or the simulacrum) is the basis of singularity.[40]

In a universe of absolute singularities, production can only take the form of singularity: each singularity, in the course of production, can only repeat or proliferate itself. In production each simulacrum can only affirm its own difference, its distanciation from everything else. Production, on this account, is a ceaselessly proliferative distribution of all the various absolute singularities. Production, in Deleuze's nomenclature, is always repetition of difference, the difference of each thing from every other thing. Capitalism, though, also embodies a principle of repetition. The axiomatic system that is capitalism is one predicated on identity, equivalence, and intersubstitutivity (this of course being the logic of the commodity form as analyzed by Marx). In which case, repetition in capitalism is always repetition of the nondifferent; or, rather, the different in capitalism is always only an apparent different, because it can be overcome and "returned," through the process of abstract exchange, to that which is essentially the same, the always fungible. Capitalism, as *Capitalisme et schizophrénie* indicates, effects an immense series of transformations ("deterritorializations") only to make possible more powerful recuperations and retrenchments: it breaches limits only in order to impose its own limits, which it "mistakenly" takes to be coextensive with those of the universe.[41] The power of repetition in capitalism is therefore negative, wasteful, ultimately nonproductive. Capitalistic repetition can therefore be said to be nonbeing in Spinoza's sense, a conclusion that Deleuze and Guattari, and Negri, do not hesitate to draw.

Capital, in the scheme of *Capitalisme et schizophrénie*, is constitutively unable to sustain a culture of genuine singularities, even though of course it creates the conditions for the emergence of a culture that could, with the requisite transformations, mutate into a culture—a culture that will however necessarily be "post-capitalist"—which has the capacity to produce such singularities.[42] Intrinsic to the notion of a singularity is the principle that a common or shared property cannot serve as the basis of the individuation of X from all that is not-X: if I share the property of being over six feet tall with anyone else, then that property cannot, in and of itself, serve to individuate either me or that person. A singularity, the being-X of that X that makes X different from all that is not-X, cannot therefore unite X with anything else. Precisely the opposite: X is a singularity because it is not united to anything else by virtue of an essence or a common or shared nature. A singularity is a thing with all its properties, and although some commonality may pertain to this thing, that commonality is indifferent to it qua singularity. So, of course, Félix Guattari will have the property "being French" in common with other people, many millions of them in fact. But a singularity is determined only through its relation to the totality of its possibilities, and the totality of possibilities that constitutes Guattari is the totality of an absolute singularity—if another being had each and every one of the possibilities whose totality constituted and thus individuated Guattari, then that being would perforce be indistinguishable from Guattari. This being and Guattari would be the same person.

In a time when "transcendental" accords can no longer really give us our worlds, we have to look for worlds that give us a different basis for the construction of solidarities, worlds in which a new kind of politics can find its *raison d'etre*. This politics will start from the realization that our criteria of belonging are always subject to a kind of chaotic motion, that our cultures have always told us an enabling lie when they denied this, and through this denial have made possible the invention of nation-states, tribes, clans, political parties, churches, perhaps everything done up to now in the name of community. The reader of Deleuze and Guattari may have the feeling, of both dread and exhilaration at the same time, that that time, the time up to "now," has begun inexorably to pass. But we still need our solidarities, now more than ever. They are indispensable for any politics capable of taking us beyond capitalism. These solidarities, however, will be based not on the securing of "transcendental" accords—capitalism, that most revolutionary of forces, has moved that possibility into desuetude. Our solidarities will be predicated instead on what the reader of Deleuze and Guattari will know as the power of singularity, a power still perhaps in search for its appropriate models of realization.[43]

Since this politics still awaits its models of realization, the power of singularity, which despite the absence of these models, is still precisely that, a power, can only manifest itself as the undertaking of a certain risk, the "playing of uncertain games," all the things that conduce to the "revolutionary-becoming" of people who have not yet made the revolution their explicit agenda. What will be the relation of this "revolutionary-becoming" to the project of the state? Can the solidarities associated with these singularities be regimented, and thus neutralized, by the state in ways that preempt insurmountably the prospects of any kind of revolutionary transformation?

The flows of power in the current social and political dispensation are fluid and relatively open, even as they are powerfully managed and contained by the elites who rule us. This development underlies the increasingly widespread perception that governments in the advanced industrial countries wield more and more control despite the simultaneous prevalence of ideologies of deregulation, privatization, and "getting the government off the backs of the people" (the mantra of Ronald Reagan among others). And so it looks increasingly as if the notion of representation which made the previous kind of "citizenship politics" possible has now been supplanted, even as the instruments which underpin it are treated as sacred objects. There is perhaps no better example of this than the American Constitution, traduced by an ever-expanding capitalist depredation even as its traducers profess their undying veneration for this old document.[44] The blocking of any passage through the philosophy and politics of representation underlying such developments will have significant effects not only on our conceptions of citizenship, but also on our related notions of ethnicity, race, patrimony, clan, nation, and sovereignty. These notions have deeply ingrained personal resonances that will continue to be felt despite the criticisms directed by philosophers and theorists at the concept of representation. But if the philosophy of representation no longer works, and its limitations are impossible to conceal, what then should be put in its place? The invention of something different (such as the Deleuzean notion of a political desire or willing based on singularities not regulated by transcendental accords) to put in place of the system of representations that has governed thinking and practice about ethnicity, race, patrimony, clan, nation, and sovereignty—these representations being the cornerstone of the *mentalité* that has prevailed since 1789 or 1492 (used here as emblematic markers)—will have to be an immense collective undertaking, perhaps spanning many generations. The core of this system of representation is its imperative that all are required to "belong" in some way or other to the various collectivities superintended by this system's logic. An enabling political desire will free us from the need to continue to make this a world where all are required to belong to such collectivities.

State power is of course the most significant impediment to the realization of this undertaking. The state identifies, counts, and assigns to its various classificatory systems countless numbers of human beings, all as part of its administrative remit, and the pressing question for the Deleuzean account of political desire is its capacity to mobilize desire in ways that make possible an obviation of state power. The world is changing even as we reflect on it. The collapse of the Soviet Union has been largely instrumental in the emergence of a US hegemony. As a result, the antagonism between capitalism and bureaucratic socialism has been replaced by a range of struggles among competing brands of capitalism (German social market capitalism, the Blairite Third Way, Chinese state capitalism, American free-market capitalism, and so on). Here the outcome is still uncertain, as indicated by the continuing world economic stagnation and the wars being fought by the Bush and Obama administrations and their allies. Despite this uncertainty, there are a number of trends in the international system that appear to be fairly consequential. Preeminent among these is a more active role in this system for regional as well as local states, and these are being accompanied by new structures of cultural identification that are tied to regions or subregions rather than nation-states (such as the various "separatisms" associated with the Basques, Catalonians, Chechnyans, Kurds, Corsicans, Irian Jayanese, Sri Lankan Tamils, Punjabi Sikhs, Kashmiris, Eritreans, or the people of Aceh).[45] One outcome of this development is the increased coexistence of the transnational and the interlocal, with the nation-state having a transformed but still noteworthy function as the apparatus that manages the flows between them. Conceptions of sovereignty and citizenship are being modified in the process, especially since the state-system is deemphasizing govern*ment* in favor of govern*ance* and *meta-governance* as older and more expansive official State institutions are scaled-down or sidelined, and administration increasingly becomes the process of organizing flows between a range of agencies and networks of power and information (viz., governance) and of devising the "axioms" to link together and harmonize all these structures and movements (viz., meta-governance).[46] Conceptions of citizenship, and their attendant forms of political desire and agency, become increasingly flexible and compartmentalized.

The state will only be replaced or restructured slowly. In failed states such as Somalia, for instance, a state-form of some kind will have to be introduced prior to the pursuit of its possible supersession, and this because no viable system for the allocation of resources exists in the Somalias of this world, and the possibility of revolutionary transformation in such countries presupposes the existence of such a system to serve as a conduit for decision-making. A counter-capitalist project of the kind delineated in *Capitalisme et schizophrénie* is not likely to succeed unless the social movements that are its vehicle are able to operate at the level of the nation-state (although they would of course certainly not be confined to working at this level).[47] Of course this counter-project has to be efficacious at other levels if it is to be successful, including the education, taxation, and bureaucratic systems, and also show itself capable of sustaining "a more general vision of the democratization of societies and their political and economic management."[48] But this counter-project is for the less-developed countries at any rate, a project that involves the mobilization of a new and different kind of popular national movement. Here an important distinction between the state apparatus and the nation is to be made, and Samir Amin has plausibly argued that the appropriation of the state apparatus is usually the object of a country's national bourgeoisie (who will reconcile themselves to recompradorization by external capitals as long as it will leave the state apparatus in their hands), while the construction of the project of national liberation involves not only delinking (needed to avert recompradorization) but also the formation of a "popular hegemonic alliance" among the people.[49]

The construction of a comprehensive national popular alliance, functioning autonomously of the state system, will furnish the stimulus for adopting a different kind of allocation strategy, one premised on a (selective) delinking, and embarked upon with the purpose of transmuting the state apparatus (since the state is the institutional assemblage that has final control of the regime of growth, and indeed there can be no properly constituted regime of growth without the involvement of the state). The first priority therefore is a "destatized" collective national liberation project, the success of which will then lead to a reconstitution of the state itself. Most existing proposals for economic and political reform in the less-developed countries view the reform and reconstitution of the state as the principal objective whose attainment will then lead to a whole range of other benefits ("efficient" economic development, protection of human rights, the upholding of democracy, etc.). This is to put the proverbial cart before the horse, since in many less-developed countries the state is merely an instrument at the disposal of the ruling elite (who tend invariably to be the recipients of the substantial personal benefits to be derived from subservience to the Washington Consensus, etc.), and it will be necessary therefore to have an alternative and non–state-oriented base within the less-developed countries in question from which the project of state reform can be initiated and sustained.

I have indicated that *Capitalisme et schizophrénie* is perhaps best viewed as a compendium of political knowledge, "non-molar" and "non-arborescent" in aspiration and putative scope, which furnishes "axioms" for the pursuit of the revolutionary project of surmounting capitalism. Deleuze and Guattari insist that there are no pregiven laws to shape or entail this outcome: only struggle, and failures always accompany successes in struggle, can do this. The only other alternative is acceptance of the current finance-led, equity-based accumulation regime with its concomitant American hegemony and continuing worldwide economic polarization.

10

The Radical Event?

There is an inextricable linkage for Deleuze between visibility or the image and immanence:

> Language has no self-sufficiency …. It follows that language has no significance of its own. It is composed of signs, but signs are inseparable from a whole other element, a non-linguistic element, which could be called "the state of things" or, better yet, "images." As Bergson has convincingly shown, images have an existence independently of us. What I call an "assemblage of utterance" is thus composed of images and signs, moving and circulating in the world.[1]

This linkage required Deleuze to break with the linguistic or semiological paradigm based on the difference between signifier and signified, which always remains mired in the endless pit of representation and is thus never able to extricate itself from the aporiae of representation (this perhaps being the main teaching that Derrida has left us, though it was Deleuze who pushed this line of thought much further than Derrida did).[2] Politics, the politics of the radical event, requires this connection with the visible that the paradigm of representation is constitutively, that is ontologically, unable to do justice to. Representation is thus at once necessary and yet impossible. Deleuze and Guattari of course cut the Gordian Knot when dealing with this impasse.

Deleuze (and Guattari) brought about two decisive revisions in our conceptual templates for characterizing the "sayable" and the "visible" (the nod here is of course to Merleau-Ponty's *Le visible et l'invisible*, where this distinction was first developed in something like a systematic way). Where the sayable is concerned, Deleuze, in nearly every one of his works, whether authored singly or jointly with Guattari, took the position, coincidentally fundamental to what Americans call "poststructuralism," that the putative boundary between "sense" and "nonsense" is irreducibly porous, and that this porosity must therefore be conceptualized as a prior and enabling condition for understanding how language or sayability functions. Language on this Deleuzean view works just as much through the scrambling of codes—this scrambling of codes being the marker par excellence of the above-mentioned porosity—as it does through the stability and regimentation of the codes in question.

Where visibility is concerned, Deleuze built on Foucault's insight in *Les mots et les choses* that visibility or light does not radiate from a pure source which bathes or envelopes an object or set of objects in a virtually instantaneous luminosity. Rather, every event of perception is undergirded by a "scopic regime" or "specular structure," and it is only by virtue of this regime or structure that things become visible to us in the way that they do. All "regimes," scopic and nonscopic alike, are tied to a relation with a structure of representation. To quote Deleuze:

> Foucault defines the Classical Age, which falls between the Renaissance and our modernity, by the notion of representation. The Renaissance still understood Its knowledge as an "interpretation of signs"; the relation of the sign to what it signifies was covered by the rich domain of "similitudes." ... According to Foucault, every thought unfolds in a "characteristic" space. However, in the seventeenth-century, *the space of signs* is tending toward dissolution, giving way to the space of representation which reflects significations and decomposes similitudes, causing a new order of identities and differences to emerge. (*Don Quixote* is precisely the first great work to acknowledge the bankruptcy of signs in favor of a world of representation.) This Order, this form of representation, will be completed by positive orders founded on empirical results: "Natural History," "Theory of Money and Value," "General Grammar." These three orders will produce all kind of resonances among themselves, due to their common membership in the space of representation: "character" is the representation of the individual of nature; "money" the representation of the objects of need; the "name" the representation of language itself.[3]

To circumvent the impasses of representation, Deleuze and Guattari appropriated Hjelmslev's attempt to give a more complex account of sense or meaning than the one made possible by the distinction between the signifier and the signified, the distinction between the signifier and signified not being able to connect up the sayable with the visible.[4]

In a 1972 essay Deleuze noted that Foucault did in fact recognize the difficulty posed by structural mutation, and said that (here I quote Deleuze) "[this profound breach in the expanse of continuities], though it must be analyzed, and minutely so, cannot be 'explained' or even summed up in a single word. It is a radical event that is distributed across the entire visible surface of knowledge, and whose signs, shocks, and effects, it is possible to follow step by step."[5] Deleuze, first by himself, and later in conjunction with Guattari, pushed the question of the enabling conditions for this radical event by resorting to the notion of "desiring production," with the socius as the context in which desiring production took place. This essay will examine Deleuze and Guattari's account of this irruptive and transformative event, especially in relation to their characterization of partial objects, a concept originated by Melanie Klein, but which was pushed in a completely new direction by Deleuze and Guattari.

For Deleuze and Guattari partial objects (and even drives) are not mere structural phenomena or stages on a developmental trajectory, but, as they put it in *A Thousand Plateaus*, "entryways and exits, impasses the [human being] lives out politically, in other words, with all the force of his or her desire" (*TP*, p. 13). Psychoanalysis forces the desire of the patient into a grid that can then be traced by the analyst, whereas this desire needs to be kept away from any pretraced identity or destiny. Hence the criticism made by Deleuze and Guattari of Klein's analytical procedure:

> It is obvious that Melanie Klein has no understanding of the cartography of one of her child patients, Little Richard, and is content to make ready-made tracings—Oedipus, the good daddy, and the bad daddy, the bad mommy and the good mommy—while the child makes a desperate attempt to carry out a performance that the psychoanalyst totally misconstrues. (*TP*, p. 13)

Only by eschewing this pretraced identity or destiny can the patient (and the analyst) engage in an experiment with the real. But to undertake this experimentation with the real it is necessary to treat psychic objects as political options and just as significantly, to refrain from relegating partial objects to a merely secondary or provisional status in relation to whole objects.

Partial objects can be nearly anything—a piece of cake, a piece of underwear, a lock of hair, a freckle, a rock in a pond, and so on. Partial objects are invariably, and here I quote from *A Thousand Plateaus*, "menacing, explosive, bursting, toxic, or poisonous" (*TP*, p. 13), and it is this flexible and plastic quality which makes them inherently political. For parts follow a different and yet specific course when they are detached from a whole or from other parts, or when they are collected into other wholes along with one or more other parts, and so the question of the specific processes that underlie this detachment or reattachment is absolutely crucial: is a particular attachment, detachment or reattachment menacing, reassuring, painful, pleasurable, tranquillizing, alluring, and so on?

What makes it any one (or more) of these things? For Deleuze and Guattari it is absolutely essential that we see these processes and their meanings as inherently political, as phenomena that move people on, or hold them back, in the courses taken by their lives.[6]

A previous conception of the radical event associated it with a certain politics of the revolutionary vanguard—"real" revolutionary change, on this account, only took place when this political vanguard took over the post office or the railway station, or succeeded in storming the parliament or the palace of the president or king. When the revolutionary vanguard failed to take over the railway station or storm the royal palace due in large part to its supposed inability to energize the so-called masses, this failure was invariably attributed to poor organization on the part of the vanguard, or the "retrograde consciousness" of the masses, or the sheer force of the repressive apparatuses at the disposal of the ruling powers (or some combination of all of these). It is now commonplace to acknowledge that Deleuze and Guattari had no truck with this vanguardist conception of radical political transformation, perhaps as a consequence of witnessing this vanguardist failure during the events of the French May 1968. To quote Deleuze:

> May '68 is more of the order of a pure event, free of all normal, or normative causality. Its history is a "series of amplified instabilities and fluctuations." There were a lot of agitations, gesticulations, slogans, idiocies, illusions in '68, but this is not what counts. What counts is what amounted to a visionary phenomenon, as if a society suddenly saw what was intolerable in it and also saw the possibility for something else. It is a collective phenomenon in the form of: "Give me the possible, or else I'll suffocate … " The possible does not pre-exist, it is created by, the event. It is a question of life. The event creates a new existence. It produces a new subjectivity (new relations with the body, with time, sexuality, the immediate surroundings, with culture, work …).
>
> May '68 was not the result of a crisis, nor was it a reaction to a crisis. It is rather the opposite. It is the current crisis, the impasses of the current crisis in France that stem directly from the inability of French society to assimilate May '68.[7]

Again, it is commonplace to acknowledge that this vanguardist conception of the radical event fails because it cannot take into account the complexity and power of the assemblages of desire that are fundamental to the success or the failure of any emancipatory aspiration. Why is this? The failure involved here is not merely political (though it is this undeniably), but also profoundly ontological where Deleuze and Guattari are concerned. The vanguardist conception of the radical political event views the failure or non-appearance of this event as the outcome of one of both of the following: (1) the absence of objective conditions such as the above-mentioned organizational failures on the part of the vanguard; and (2) the absence of subjective conditions such as the overwhelming failure to realize that the misery experienced by many in one's society is due more or less directly to the strategic agency of those who rule us. In a word, this vanguardist conception of political transformation is wedded, irreducibly, to the dialectic of subject and object, the agent and the institution or state apparatus. The vanguardist political code is a counter-code, but it is a code which always places itself in a dialectical opposition to the code of the State, and as such this vanguardist counter-code is not in a position to transform the conditions under which the State functions and from which it receives its raison d'etre. The historical situation which perhaps confirmed this for Deleuze and Guattari was the initially surprising decision of the head of the French communist party at that time, Georges Marchais, to support President de Gaulle in the repression of the student revolution of May 1968—Marchais was worried that the students were taking things too far, and that their attempts to overthrow the French government by insurrectionary means would lead to a situation in which there would be no State for the French communist party to take over if and when it came to power![8] There is a sense in which May '68 is symptomatic of a wider phenomenon, one not confined to France, but extending also to the all the Euro-Atlantic capitalist democracies, namely, the exhaustion of an whole series of names and their accompanying political morphology—the militant, the proletariat, the anti-capitalist vanguard, and so on—that hitherto had embodied the core aspirations of an emancipatory politics.

The pivotal-point for the account of transformation given by Deleuze and Guattari, any kind of transformation not just political transformation, resides in the ability of the transformational event to break, really break, with the actual. They insist repeatedly in their account of the difference between the virtual and the actual that it was the virtual which had the ability to break with the actual, since this break could not be accomplished within the actual itself. What the French Communist Party did in May 1868, therefore, was not to break with the actual, but merely to reshuffle some political furniture within the realm of the actual without rupturing the actual itself from the outside.

To get back to the theory of part objects. The challenge for the supporter of Deleuze and Guattari is to specify how a particular attachment, detachment or reattachment that is menacing, reassuring, painful, pleasurable, tranquillizing, alluring, and so on, these being the defining features of the part-object and its associated drives, can be incorporated into a politics with the power to confront the apparatuses of the State on a significant enough scale. Attachments to part objects and the undoing of these attachments, tend to be ephemeral and limited in scope, with a relatively few exceptions, such as the veneration of a national flag (in the end a flag is, materially, only a piece of cloth, in case anyone needs to be reminded of this), or, to provide another example, there are Catholic shrines in countless villages in Spain and Italy, which seem able to claim the adherence of their devotees year after year or indeed lifetime after lifetime. The line of reflection being pushed here suggests a possible lacuna in the thought of Deleuze and Guattari.

This possible lacuna has to do with the nature and function of the myth, especially political myth. This may seem a strange charge to level at Deleuze and Guattari, especially since *A Thousand Plateaus* does engage seriously with a number of mythemes, for example, the Sorcerer, the shaman, the Priest, the aborigine, the wolf of the steppes, and so on. But if the theory of part-objects is to serve as one of the bases for a conceptualization of the radical event, which is the line of argument being canvassed here, then the drives, the myriad dynamisms associated with Deleuzean desiring-production, have to be assembled in ways that turn a piece of cloth into a flag, an assortment of bone fragments into the relics of an ostensible saint, and so forth. This assembling of the part-object to form a mode of subjectivity possessing a radical and irruptive force, one powerful enough to overturn a political regime or to kick out a ruling elite, is the key function of political myth. This of course was one of the several insights associated with Carl Schmitt.

Schmitt maintained that liberal democracy's insurmountable failure was its weddedness to a conception of electoral representation that would ensue inevitably in the bureaucratic management of voter opinion, in this way banishing any need for political myth, any need for liberal democracy to conceptualize the political in terms that had anything more to do with the mere orchestration of opinion.[9] Schmitt and Robert Michels clearly anticipated the political personae of Karl Rove and Alastair Campbell, who masterminded the political careers of George W Bush and Tony Blair respectively. Many of Schmitt's positions as a political and legal philosopher do not survive real scrutiny, but his assessment of the constitutive weaknesses of liberal democracy has perhaps been vindicated by the course of historical events.

But the challenge, adverted to above, of inserting the part-object into a wider scheme of things without dissolving it in the structure of the actual, so that it can only represent a mere reshuffling of the actual, remains for Deleuze and Guattari. How is this challenge to be met? Deleuze and Guattari, in their account of the conceptual persona—examples being Dostoevsky's Idiot or wise fool, Kierkegaard's Don Juan, Nietzsche's mad man, etc.—give us a philosophical basis for conceptualizing political myth in Deleuzean terms.[10] Some conceptual personae are capable of elevating a fixation on a part-object into what amounts to a universal history. The Nietzschean madman is fixated on the death of God, but Nietzsche used this conceptual persona to delineate the course of an entire trajectory of Western rationality. Likewise Kierkegaard's Don Juan, who is endlessly fixated on the minutiae and trivia of seduction, is used to conceptualize modernity's deracination of the ethical. Is there an equivalent conceptual persona in Deleuze and Guattari when it comes to giving an account of political myth? (Myth being that which generates truth-effects without itself being true or false.) There is, and it lies in their conceptualization of the minoritarian, the figure of the minor-being.

Those who are minoritarian are counted out, analytically and in principle. Conversely, those who are majoritarian are counted in, analytically and in principle (the white Christian heterosexual male being the quintessential majoritarian figure). So, who is counted out, who is analytically minoritarian, in today's liberal democracy? It is not too difficult to make this determination—non-documented immigrants （*les sans papiers*), the culturally excluded aboriginal person in certain societies, the women who set up the peace camp at the Greenham Common nuclear missile base in Mrs. Thatcher's Ukay.[11] The problem of course is to find a politics capable of a real democratic inclusivity sufficient to encompass the analytically minoritarian. But the fundamental political and philosophical impulse is there in Deleuze and Guattari—their geophilosophy calls for the creation of a new people and a new earth. We only (!) need to find a way to invent a politics for this.

11

On Producing (the Concept of) Solidarity

It is virtuality axiomatic for many schools of thought—not all of which are readily to be identified with the marxist tradition—that a project of liberation or emancipation can be advanced only if and when certain substantive forms of social solidarity are able to take root in the society in question. Making this axiomatic claim is easy, what is more difficult is ascertaining how these forms of social solidarity are to be generated and sustained, and, as the corollary of this question, how such forms can be protected in situations in which they are likely to be thwarted or threatened. In dealing with this question we confront (among other things) the well-known dialectic between structure and agency, or being and act—do we need the requisite structures or apparatuses to exist before the bonds of solidarity can come into being, or do agents acting in solidarity have to exist in order to bring these structures and apparatuses into existence? As we know only too well, these chicken-and-egg arguments are not only irresolvable but also completely unproductive, and, besides, the appropriate answer to this kind of question is never one or the other of the chicken or the egg but, quite simply, "both." Moreover, any remotely persuasive answer to this question invariably requires reference to a set of conditions or a state of being antecedent to both structure and agency (or act and being) as a way to account for the operations of structure and agency in their creation of the bonds of social solidarity. Or to use a jargon phrase: recourse has to be made to social ontology if we are to answer the question how structure and agency act conjointly in order to produce social solidarity. Thus, and these are examples of what is meant here by this recourse to "social ontology," Michel Foucault had to resort to the concept of a "practice of subjectivation" in order to account for the way an épistémè actually worked at the level of subjectivity; Raymond Williams coined the expression "structure of feeling" as a way of delineating the more concrete and practical realities of social transformation and stasis; Althusser's late outlining of an "aleatory materialism" mitigated the structuralist over-emphasis evident in his earlier treatment of the ISAs (Ideological State Apparatuses); and Deleuze and Guattari used the concept of a "desiring production" to cut the Gordian Knot of the (irresolvable) dialectic of structure and agency. The aim in all these exemplary instances was to do justice to the intricacies of the processes of agent- and subject-formation, in this way countering any tendency which required too much weight to be placed on the causal significance of the system, apparatus, structure, or formation (as opposed to the agent or subject).

The theory of liberation, in dealing with its objects (which are at once practical *and* theoretical), has to avoid the Scylla of viewing the subject in ways that satisfy a shallow empiricist immediacy as well as the Charybdis of regarding the system or apparatus as being no more than an endlessly awkward abstraction—according to the typical scenario associated with this seeming conundrum, the individual subject, qua subject, is at all times "next to me" in its sheer immediacy (how could it be otherwise?); the system qua system, well, the system is always "too much out-of-the-way where I'm concerned" in its inevitable and perhaps necessarily subtle distanciation (again, how could it be otherwise?). But first a digression on the notion of conceptual production.[1]

Producing a theoretically grounded concept of solidarity requires the producer of this concept to begin by distinguishing adequately between

(i) those concepts that constitute a theory of X, or Y, or Z;
(ii) those concepts that belong to a particular manifestation of X, or Y, or Z and which constitute the "expressivity" of X, or Y, or Z, and which can become the objects described and analyzed by the afore-mentioned theory of X, or Y, or Z. These concepts can appropriately be designated as X^*, or Y^*, or Z^* (the superscripted asterisks indicate that X^*, or Y^*, or Z^* are manifestations of X, or Y, or Z);
(iii) the state or condition that is X, or Y, or Z as such, a condition which overdetermines the expressivities yielded by this state or condition.

In the case of the practices, institutional formations, and strategies associated with the myriad forms of solidarity, the application of (i)–(iii) above would yield the following:

(a) is the *theory* whose object could be any form of consistent mutuality or social support, regardless of the ways in which it is expressed, or the number or nature of the protagonists involved, etc. There can be a theory of the solidarity that binds a band of robbers, just as there can be one of the bonds that may exist between saints and heroes. There can be a theory of the solidarity that united the (estimated) crowd of 2 million people which precipitated the overthrow of the Shah of Iran, as well as one which purports to account for the ties that exist within a cloistered convent of half-a-dozen nuns.

(b) the objects in (a) receive *expression* through the words and texts of a very diverse range of agents and organizations (robbers, saints, heroes, members of parliament, Russian oligarchs, American university sororities and fraternities, a platoon of the Israeli army, a drug cartel in Mexico); the writings of academics, novelists, playwrights (Robert Putnam's *Bowling Alone*, Elias Canetti's *Crowds and Power*, David Riesman's *The Lonely Crowd*, the *Journal of Social Philosophy*, Arthur Miller's *Death of a Salesman*, Jack Kerouac's *The Dharma Bums*, etc.); films (Sam Mendes's *American Beauty*, Oliver Stone's *Platoon*, and so on), all these constituting the expressivities that are, or can be, "theorized" by this or that theory of solidarity (i.e., (a) above).

(c) but the expressivities in (b) have as their basis a diffuse array of material conditions whose overall effect is to overdetermine the expressivities in question. A currently existing conceptualization is always provisional and can therefore be superseded by a newer one: no conceptualization expresses or determines in a way that is completely exhaustive the condition or situation that it brings to expression. An expressivity works by naming things, but the thing named is never the thing itself, but is rather the panoply of effects associated with the thing in question. (This is the basis for the famous Althusserian refrain: "the concept of sugar is not sweet," "the concept of water is not wet," etc.) Spinoza was of course the thinker who first turned this insight ("an expressivity is the effect of a thing") into a philosophical axiom, and Althusser and Deleuze (Deleuze admittedly somewhat later than Althusser) are to be credited with the systematization of this insight. The "thing," in this scheme, is a concrescence of its effects (it is the event of this concrescence), and the effects in question vary with the totality of interactions that have that particular thing as their point of focus.

It should be stressed that the process of experiencing an effect gives rise to an "affect," so that there is here a close causal link between "effect" and "affect." Hence, say, the German shepherd dog used by US army interrogators at the

Abu Ghraib prison is a very different "thing" (especially for an interrogated Iraqi prisoner!) from the pampered pooch owned by a wealthy widow living in a luxury condominium in Miami.[2] The "thing" being an assemblage of effects and affects, and there being in principle a huge variability in the way in which these assemblages can be organized, no expressivity (qua the title of the assemblage in question) can eliminate in advance its competitor names and the assemblages designated by them. For instance, the failures of the US banking system associated with the current economic recession have been placed by business commentators and analysts into a number of such assemblages: these failures have been characterized as "a resultant of an American housing market collapse"/ "an evaporation of liquidity in the US banking system"/ "the American species of crony capitalism at work"/"the bursting of the latest US speculative bubble"/ "the result of inadequate banking regulation"/"the outcome of the greed and venality of financial-institution CEOs"/ and so forth. A theory of the failures of the current US banking system is not therefore about this system per se, but about the *concepts* that are generated by the US economic system and its denizens and even its critics, or indeed by anyone through which the effectivity of this system is bespoken. These concepts are in turn related in a variety of ways to other assemblages of practices. Hence, the concepts generated by the conditions associated with contemporary US capitalism can, in the relevant context, be related by an appropriate theory to the concepts or expressivities associated with the assemblage of practices and strategies identified with "neoliberalism" as an economic doctrine (in the manner formulated by economists such as Robert Brenner or the late Andrew Glyn), or "American culture" (in the way analyzed by Thomas Franks, Naomi Wolf, and others), and so forth. Hence a theory of US capitalism does not bear directly on American capitalist formations as such, but rather on the concepts of this or that manifestation of American capitalism and its associated agents and figures, and these concepts (what we have called "expressivities") are just as actual and effective as the condition or set of conditions that is American capitalism itself.[3]

Theories operate on expressivities, and expressivities in turn are connected with the conditions that enable them. The correlations established between expressivities and their enabling conditions depend for their effectiveness on always specific, because contingently ordained, distributions and orderings of power. Theories are thus the outcome of a productive process, no more or no less than the putative object of this process, the expressivities that mediate the conditions which they express even as they are enabled by the conditions in question. A theory is a practice, just as the conditions mediated by an expressivity are always provisional multilinear assemblages of practices structured by arrangements of income, assets, status, power, and so on. A theory, in short, is a practice of concepts located in a macrosocial field with its own practical possibilities and outcomes from these possibilities.

The concepts associated with solidarity are not given in the ensembles of practices that constitute it, and yet they are solidarity's concepts, not theories about solidarity. Hence the formulations of a Charles Tilly or Roberto Mangabeira Unger constitute a theory "about" this or that form of social solidarity, while the concepts of solidarity are likely to include the concrete notions (which may be inchoate or half-formed) of the shared ownership of property in Amish culture, child-rearing strategies in an Israeli kibbutz, the place of cooperatives in rural Bangladesh, the distribution of alms by the church in medieval England, and so forth, that actually are operative in those particular societies in their specific times.

Every concrete rendering of solidarity generates for itself its own "thinkability" (and concurrently its own "unthinkability" as the obverse of this very thinkability), and this even if this or that condition for the production and maintenance of solidarity is not taken to be such by those whose condition it happens in fact to be. Thus the Bangladeshi smallholder (of today) or the Prussian Junker (in the time of Bismarck) in their respective historical and social conjunctures—the former (say) by joining other smallholders in refusing the exactions of a rich landowner and the latter (say) by swearing that Bismarck is "one of us"—contribute to the thinkability of a particular instantiation of social solidarity, even if the individuals in question are unable explicitly to acknowledge that this refusal of deference (in the case of the Bangladeshi smallholder) or blind adherence to Bismarck (in the case of the Prussian Junker) are precisely the kind of conduct that enables a particular embodiment of social solidarity to remain viable.

It is *this* Bangladeshi smallholder's or *this* Prussian Junker's concepts or expressivities that constitute the thinkability of the condition in which (s)he is inserted, even though (s)he may be unable to perform the requisite operation of transcoding that renders a particular refusal of deference to a wealthy Bangladeshi landowner or routine thinking about Bismarck's supposed virtues into an explicit marker or symptom (in something like the Lacanian sense) of a particular system of social solidarity.

Another way of making this point would be to say that a particular manifestation of social solidarity, like each and every social and cultural condition, has to secrete its multiple expressivities precisely in order to be what it is, and that its concepts—in ways that are inescapably selective, confining, and even arbitrary—are thematizations or representations of these expressivities and their attendant conditions. Or more briefly, that the concepts of a particular form of solidarity are its expressivities limned in the form of that order's thinkability.

Theories of social solidarity, by contrast, are the outcome of a theoretical operation whose object is the natures, functions, and so forth of these expressivities. Theories of social solidarity operate on a particular social order's thinkability, and involve a kind of transcoding. It is possible to ask the question "What is the form of social solidarity operating in this dispensation?" but there is another kind of question, involving quite another kind of theoretical operation, that can be asked as well, in this case: "What is (a) *theory* (of solidarity)?" Social solidarities involve a prodigiously varied and complex practice of signs and images with an accompanying orchestration of affectivity, whose theory thinkers like Margaret Mead or Max Weber must produce, but produce precisely as conceptual practice—in this case a practice that generates, always in a metalanguage, concepts that reflect upon the concepts and expressivities of the denizens of this or that form of social solidarity, expressivities which therefore constitute what is in effect a basal or first-order language that comes subsequently to be transcoded.

No theoretical intervention, no matter how refined or thoroughgoing it may be, can on its own constitute the concepts of this or that solidaristic formation: the concepts of the denizen of solidarity are expressed in advance and independently of the personage, invariably an academic, who reflects on the concepts of those whose situations are typically those of the peasant, billionaire banker, factory worker, home-maker, retiree, refugee or asylum seeker, common criminal, and so on. Theorists and intellectuals, qua theorists and intellectuals, can only traffic in theories of social solidarity (or culture or capitalism or whatever).

The concepts that theorists produce can be operative in more than one field of thought, and even in a single field it is always possible for a concept to fulfill more than one function (an obvious example would be the concept of "value," which features prominently in the discourses associated with economics, sociology, ethics, psychology, and aesthetics). Each domain of thought is defined by its own internal variables, variables that have a complex relation to their counterpart external variables (such as historical epochs, political and social conditions and processes, and even the brute physical character of things).[4] It is an implication of this account of conceptual practice that a concept comes into being or ceases to be operative only when there is a change of function and/or field. Functions for concepts must be created or invalidated for the concepts in question to be generated or abolished, and new fields must be brought into being in order for these concepts to be rendered inapplicable or illegitimate.

Theories operate on expressivities, and expressivities in turn are connected with the conditions that enable them. The correlations established between expressivities and their enabling conditions depend for their effectiveness on always specific, because contingently ordained, distributions and orderings of power. Theories are thus the outcome of a productive process, no more or no less than the putative object of this process, the expressivities that mediate the conditions which they express even as they are enabled by the conditions in question. A theory is a practice, just as the conditions mediated by an expressivity are always provisional multilinear assemblages of practices structured by arrangements of income, assets, status, power, and so on. A theory, in short, is a practice of concepts located in a macrosocial field with its own practical possibilities and outcomes from these possibilities. With these preliminaries on the production of concepts now addressed, our initial subject—the impasse between the individual subject and the system or apparatus—can now be considered.

The proposals for dealing with this impasse have been several and various over many decades. In the remaining part of this essay I'll try to deal with two significant "projects" which seek to find a way out of this seeming deadlock between the ostensible immediacy of the subject and the constitutive non-nearness of the apparatus or system. The first of these can be identified with Raymond Williams, the second with the nomadology of Deleuze and Guattari. Let's deal first with the proposals that we'll identify with the work of Raymond Williams, after which I'll consider the suggestions associated here with Deleuze and Guattari (both "Raymond Williams" and "Deleuze and Guattari" signify in this argument something like a form of consciousness, as opposed to an explicit and individually specifiable intellectual biography with its allied and largely academic formulations).[5]

Raymond Williams—a decade or so ago the name had an immediate and virtually automatic resonance, but I'm not so sure about that these days, this being a time when Williams is more likely to be revered than read—provided a distinctive specification of the basis from which the forms of community and solidarity were to be constructed. Williams's working-class background (his father, a veteran of the First World War, was a railway signalman) led him to conclude, on the basis of his decisive early experiences, that any form of advancement, be it intellectual or material, was doomed to failure if it did not involve the pursuit of a common culture, of the positive commonalities provided by a viable community, as well as a recognition that social equality has to be an inextricable part of any society whose raison d'être is supplied by the principles of justice. As he saw it, once he went to a largely upper-class Cambridge as an undergraduate just before the Second World War, no culture was worth having if it excluded the social world of his working-class parents. Rejecting the notion that education was simply about maintaining "the finest human values" (thereby implying that his parents did not and could not possess these values by virtue of belonging to "the labouring classes"), Williams said of his working-class experience and its connection with the Leavisite phrase "the finest human values":

> It [his early working-class experience] did not tell me that my father and grandfather were ignorant wage-slaves; it did not tell me that the smart, busy, commercial culture was the thing I had to catch up with. I even made a fool of myself, or was made to think so, when after a lecture in which the usual point was made that "neighbour" does not mean what it did to Shakespeare, I said—imagine!—that to me it did. (When my father was dying, this year, one man came in and dug his garden; another loaded and delivered a lorry of sleepers for firewood; another came and chopped the sleepers into blocks; another—I don't know who, it was never said—left a sack of potatoes at the back door; a woman came in and took away a bit of washing).[6]

To capture the motivating impulses that underlay the life of a Welsh working-class community like the one into which he was born in 1922, Williams coined the notion of a "structure of feeling."

> In principle, it seems clear that the ... conventions of any given period are fundamentally related to the *structure of feeling* in that period. I use the phrase structure of feeling because it seems to me more accurate, in this context, than *ideas* or *general life*. All the products of a community in a given period are, we now commonly believe, eventually related, although in practice, and in detail, this is not always easy to see. In the study of a period we may be able to reconstruct, with more or less accuracy, the material life, the general social organisation, and, to a large extent, the dominant ideas. It is not necessary to discuss here which, if any, of these aspects is, in the whole complex, determining; an important institution like the drama will, in all probability, take its colour in varying degrees from them all. But while we may, in the study of a past period, separate out particular aspects of life, and treat them as if they were self-contained, it is obvious that this is only how they were studied, not how they were experienced. We examine each element as a precipitate, but in the living experience of the time every element was in solution, an inescapable part of a complex whole.[7]

Culture, therefore, is a "whole way of life," which is constantly being remade and reappropriated by its citizens, who are at once the agents of change as well as being the recipients of such change. This creativity and agency is indispensable for the constitution of community, and community is more likely to flourish when its guiding principles are grounded in mutual, supportive, and democratic, social relationships. For Williams it was axiomatic that only a democratic socialism could provide these enabling human relationships.

This then is an account of genuine community, which locates the basis of such community in the common-or-garden solidarities of British working-class life in the early to middle decades of the twentieth century. This is not to dismiss Williams (as some commentators have) for his working-class sentimentalism, wooly minded idealism, etc. That Williams was after something much less sedate and provincial than British working-class life of the middle of the last century is evident from the following passage in his manifesto *Towards 2000* (published in 1985):

> It is not some unavoidable real world, with its laws of economy and laws of war, that is now blocking us. It is a set of identifiable processes of *realpolitik* and *force majeure*, of nameable agencies of power and capital, distraction and disinformation, and all these interlocking with the embedded short-term pressures and the interwoven subordinations of an adaptive commonsense. It is not in staring at these blocks that there is any chance of moving past them. They have been named so often that they are not even, for most people, news. The dynamic movement is elsewhere, in the difficult business of gaining confidence in *our own* energies and capacities.
>
> It is only in the shared belief and insistence that there are practical alternatives that the balance of forces and chances begins to alter. Once the inevitabilities are challenged, we begin gathering our resources for a journey of hope. If there are no easy answers there are still available and discoverable hard answers, and it is these that we can now learn to make and share. This has been, from the beginning, the sense and impulse of the long revolution.[8]

There is nothing hazy or slack in the proposals made by Williams in the above passage. Yes, the revolution will be long (some of us who were university students in 1968 did not like hearing that from him, but so far he has turned out to be right on this matter). It is clear that a political pedagogy is an integral part of the long revolution—to quote Williams again, "If there are no easy answers there are still available and discoverable hard answers, and it is these that we can now learn to make and share." How do we identify the "hard answers" which we need "to learn to make and share"? Williams was not a philosopher by training, and the question of the philosophical basis of this political pedagogy is one that he did not address. However, it is one I wish to address in the rest of this essay, using Williams's proposals as a kind of containing framework for my discussion.

The kind of philosophical exploration being proposed here will require consideration of what the jargon calls "social ontology"; that is, it will seek to find "axioms" that furnish the basis of a political pedagogy of the kind proposed by Raymond Williams.[9] Here I have to be brief. Williams invites us to challenge the "inevitabilities," or rather what are perceived to be "inevitabilities." Any alternative to these inevitabilities will have, necessarily and unavoidably, the character of something strikingly novel and even anomalous. Gilles Deleuze and Félix Guattari have a discussion of what they call "the anomalous" (*l'anomal*), and it is to this that I now wish to turn. The anomalous, according to Deleuze and Guattari,

> has nothing to do with the preferred, domestic, psychoanalytic individual. Nor is the anomalous the bearer of a species presenting specific or generic characteristics in their purest state; nor is it a model or unique specimen; nor is it the perfection of a type incarnate; nor is it the eminent term of a series; nor is it the basis of an absolutely harmonious correspondence. The anomalous is neither an individual nor a species; it only has affects, it has neither familiar nor subjectified feelings, nor specific or significant characteristics. (*TP*, p. 244).

The realm of the anomalous, for Deleuze and Guattari, lies between the domain of "substantial forms" and that of "determined subjects"; it constitutes "a natural play full of haecceities, degrees, intensities, events, and accidents that compose individuations totally different from those of the well-formed subjects that receive them" (*TP*, p. 255). In an interview on Foucault and his work, Deleuze refers to this movement between "outside" and "inside" as something which involves "subjectless individuations." The claim that individuations in the realm of the Anomalous are altogether different from the well-formed subjects that are their "containers" implies that each individual is a potentially infinite multiplicity, the product of a phantasmagoric movement between an inside and an outside.[10] These "subjectless individuations" are a defining feature of the Anomalous, which is taken by Deleuze and Guattari to be present wherever "lines of flight" are to be found. The domain of the Anomalous is this coextensive with the countervailing constituent power whose political project is the undermining of capitalism's own constituent power. The implications of this conception of the Anomalous for the constitution of the state are drawn by Deleuze in the following passage from his dialogues with Claire Parnet:

> The State can no longer … rely on the old forms like the police, armies, bureaucracies, collective installations, schools, families … It is not surprising that all kinds of minority questions—linguistic, ethnic, regional, about sex, or youth—resurge not only as archaisms, but in up-to-date revolutionary forms which call once more into question in an entirely immanent manner both the global economy of the machine and the assemblages of national States … Everything is played in uncertain games, "front to front, back to back, back to front." (*D*, p. 147)

All this amounts to the lineaments of a new and interesting theory of the place of the "subject" in the cultures of contemporary capitalism. *Capitalisme et schizophrénie* approaches this theory of the "subject" via a theory of singularity—"singularity" being the category that more than any other goes beyond the "collective" versus "individual" dichotomy that is essential to the Hobbes-Rousseau-Hegel tradition of reflection on the state or sovereign. This account of singularity, and here I have to be very brief and schematic, can in turn be connected up with the theory of simulation given in Deleuze's *Logique du sens* and *Différence et répétition*, since for Deleuze simulation (or the simulacrum) is the basis of singularity.

In a universe of absolute singularities, production can only take the form of singularity: each singularity, in the course of production, can only repeat or proliferate itself. In production each simulacrum can only affirm its own difference, its distanciation from everything else. Production, on this account, is a ceaselessly proliferative distribution of all the various absolute singularities. Production, in Deleuze's nomenclature, is always repetition of difference, the difference of each thing from every other thing. Capitalism, though, also embodies a principle of repetition. The axiomatic system that is capitalism is one predicated on identity, equivalence, and intersubstitutivity (this of course being the logic of the commodity form as analyzed by Marx). In which case, repetition in capitalism is always repetition of the nondifferent; or, rather, the different in capitalism is always only an apparent different, because it can be overcome and "returned," through the process of abstract exchange, to that which is essentially the same, the always fungible. Capitalism, as *Capitalisme et schizophrénie* indicates, effects an immense series of transformations ("deterritorializations") only to make possible more powerful recuperations and retrenchments—the "utopia" of a financier like Bernard Madoff is precisely to live and function like a J.P. Morgan, that is, a nineteenth-century "robber baron." Capital breaches limits only in order to impose its own limits, which it "mistakenly" takes to be coextensive with those of the universe. To quote the authors of *Mille Plateaux*:

> If Marx demonstrated the functioning of capitalism as an axiomatic, it was above all in the famous chapter on the tendency of the rate of profit to fall. Capitalism is indeed an axiomatic, because it has no laws but immanent ones. It would like for us to believe that it confronts the limits of the Universe, the extreme limit of resources and energy. But all it confronts are its own limits (the periodic depreciation of existing capital); all it repels or displaces are its own limits (the formation of new capital, in new industries with a high rate of profit). This is the history of oil and nuclear power. And it does both at once: capitalism confronts its own limits and simultaneously displaces them, setting them down again farther along. (*TP*, p. 463)

The power of repetition in capitalism is therefore negative, wasteful, and ultimately nonproductive. (Capitalistic repetition can therefore be said to be nonbeing in Spinoza's sense, a conclusion that Deleuze and Guattari, and Negri, do not hesitate to draw).

Capital, in the scheme of *Capitalisme et schizophrénie*, is constitutively unable to sustain a culture of genuine singularities, even though of course it creates the conditions for the emergence of a culture that could, with the requisite transformations, mutate into a culture—a culture that will however necessarily be "post-capitalist"—which has the capacity to produce such singularities. The conditions that enable capital to survive are the self-same conditions that generate a countervailing constituent power that brings forth the agents and forces needed to resist it. This constituent power provides a basis for the construction of solidarities, worlds in which a new kind of politics can find its raison d'être. A countervailing constituent power is irreducibly anomalous, a dynamism based on an excess or exteriority, and whose ensuing productivity is defined by neither a foundation nor a pregiven order. It is a power that cannot be reduced to a constitution even while it remains constitutive and therefore enabling.[11]

This will be a politics capable of taking us beyond "actually existing capitalism." This politics still awaits its models of realization—this after all is a "long revolution." But its constituent power remains precisely that, a *power*, and this power conduces to the undertaking of a certain risk, the "playing of uncertain games," which hopefully will amount to the "revolutionary-becoming" of people who have not yet made the revolution their explicit political project.

I view the writings of Raymond Williams and Deleuze and Guattari, despite their very significant theoretical differences, as compendiums of political knowledge, premised on the decisive need for a countervailing power to the current capitalist and liberal-democratic dispensation, a compendium which furnishes "axioms" for the pursuit of this revolutionary project with its accompanying pedagogies. These authors indicate that there are no pregiven laws to shape or entail this outcome: only struggle, and failures always accompany struggle, can do this. The only other alternative is resignation in the face of the current finance-led, equity-dominated capitalist regime with its concomitant American militarism. The choice is stark indeed: either a politics which produces yet more Dick Cheneys and Bernie Madoffs, or one which is capable of producing citizens who strive to emulate Rosa Luxemburg or C.L.R. James. The choice is nothing less than world-historical.

12

What Is Becoming-Animal? The Politics of Deleuze and Guattari's "Strange Notion"

We believe in the existence of very special becomings-animal traversing human beings and sweeping them away, affecting the animal no less than the human.
Deleuze and Guattari, *TP,* p. 237

The concept of "becoming-animal," used by Deleuze and Guattari, is much less controversial than their related concept of "becoming-woman," but its character and status as a philosopheme is just as puzzling to many, even those who are well-disposed to the ideas of Deleuze and Guattari. "Becoming-animal" is part of a constellation of terms—"becoming-molecular," "becoming-imperceptible," "becoming-revolutionary," "becoming minor"—used by Deleuze and Guattari to designate the situation of being analytically, as opposed to numerically, in the minority. Hence, while "becoming-molecular" is analytically minoritarian, its opposite is the already majoritarian "being molar"; "becoming-imperceptible" is counterpoised to the analytically majoritarian "being rendered visible by the regimes of the State"; "becoming-revolutionary" is pitted against the State's desire to leave things fundamentally unchanged; and "becoming minor" is opposed by all the majoritarian orders. Where Deleuze and Guattari are concerned "everyone has to 'become-woman', even women" (*TP*, p. 292). Correlatively, "everyone has to 'become-animal', even animals." But what can possibly be meant by this?

As we just saw, Deleuze and Guattari view the status of animals and women, et alia, as being analytically minoritarian, so that women, even if they were in, say, in an American college sorority, would belong to the analytically minoritarian (the "majority" being constitutively "male, white, bourgeois, and Christian"). This essay will deal with three issues: (i) animals, while they may be male, are hardly "white, bourgeois, and Christian," so in what sense are they analytically minoritarian?; (ii) for Deleuze and Guattari, it is clearly the human *identification* with the animal that is the issue (Freud's wolf-man, Kafka's beetle-man

Gregor Samsa, among others), but what is their theorization of this "deviant" identification? (or is "identification" the right way to go about theorizing the connectivities between animal and human); and (iii) a crucial consideration is their theory of the minority, which is based not on a concept of difference and otherness (this being the core of American identity theory), but on the category of the *Same* ("I want everything to be the Same as me," as opposed to the very different logic of desire involved in the theory of difference; that is, "I must abject you because you can never have anything in common with me").

In what sense are animals analytically minoritarian? Our ingrained propensity is to privilege the human over the nonhuman, to make the human the supreme constitutive norm. As long as this propensity goes unchallenged our species identity will never be called into question, and the prospect of a new earth and a new people, the sine qua non of the earth's decisive liberation, will be kept at bay. To quote Deleuze and Guattari:

> To think is to experiment, but experimentation is always that which is in the process of coming about—the new, remarkable, and interesting …. The new, the interesting, are the actual. The actual is not what we are but, rather, what we become, what we are in the process of becoming—that is to sat, the Other, our becoming-other. (*WP*, pp. 111–12)

To embark on a project of becomings, this is the heart of the project of liberation. The project of becomings will therefore involve becomings that are other than human. These becomings-other overturn the hierarchical orders that stand in the way of liberation, not simply by reversing or inverting the terms of the hierarchy, but instead by promoting and intensifying the passages between the terms of a binary opposition, so that both its poles are annulled. In this way a zone of indiscernibility is created as something novel and transformative emerges. One of these zones of indiscernibility involves a becoming-animal of human beings. To quote Deleuze and Guattari again from *WP*: "We become animal so that the animal also becomes something else. The agony of a rat or the slaughter of a calf remains present in thought not through pity but as the zone of exchange between man and animal in which something of one passes into the other" (p. 109). The human organism, as a result of this exchange, now has the potential to expand its affective capacities, of perceiving and acting in new and unanticipated ways. So much is indicated in this dense and in places bewildering passage from *TP*:

> A becoming-animal always involves a pack, a band, a population, a peopling, in short, a multiplicity. We sorcerers have always known that …. If the writer

is a sorcerer, it is because writing is a becoming, writing is traversed by strange becomings that are not becomings-writer, but becomings-rat, becomings-insect, becomings-wolf, etc. We will have to explain why. Many suicides by writers are explained by these unnatural participations, these unnatural nuptials. Writers are sorcerers because they experience the animal as the only population before which they are responsible in principle. The German preromantic Karl Philipp Moritz feels responsible not for the calves that die but before the calves that die and give him the incredible feeling of an unknown Nature—*affect*? For the affect is not a personal feeling, nor is it a characteristic; it is the effectuation of a power of the pack that throws the self into upheaval and makes it reel. Who has not known the violence of these animal sequences, which uproot one from humanity, if only for an instant, making one scrape at one's bread like a rodent or giving one the yellow eyes of a feline? A fearsome involution calling us toward unheard-of becomings. (pp. 239–40)

At the core of this exchange or passage between the human and the nonhuman is something much more the human identification with the animal, it is, rather, the human's passage into the zone where he or she finds herself in the position of Freud's wolf-man or Kafka's insect-man Gregor Samsa, that is, having no means to enact any kind of absolute boundary between human and animal.

Freud's Wolf-Man and Kafka's Gregor Samsa find themselves trapped in the now commonplace oedipal bind. Gregor's father is sternly authoritarian, and later in the story three anonymous lodgers usurp the position of the Samsa family at the dining table, but only to replicate its authoritarian demeanor toward Gregor. Gregor becomes insect in order to escape this oedipal or familial encoding, to find a new affective or relational network for himself, but his attempt fails because he cannot relinquish his human identity despite his acquisition of an insect body. Deleuze and Guattari reject the usual allegorical or symbolic readings of Kafka's story that are now commonplace, and insist that it is about experimentation, although of course it is a desperate experiment involving a metamorphosis that fails ultimately.

Likewise Freud's Wolf-Man, who has a nightmare in which his bedroom window opens to reveal a tree with six or seven wolves sitting on it, has his dream interpreted by Freud in a way that we now see as conforming to routine psychoanalytic orthodoxy; that is, according to Freud, the Wolf-Man is using his dream as a screen for an unbearable childhood primal scene in which the then toddler sees his parents behaving like terrifyingly unrestrained animals—i.e. having sex doggy-style. Deleuze and Guattari reject this interpretation, as the Wolf-Man himself subsequently did—the Wolf-Man came from a wealthy aristocratic family, and he and his siblings slept in the same room as their nurse, and not near their parents. According to Deleuze and Guattari, the only thing that Freud got right about this dream is that it positions the Wolf-Man's desire in a "wild territory" (*territoire sauvage*). But the "wild territory" in question is not some traumatic scene of parental bestiality that the young child chances upon, but rather the *territoire sauvage* of the steppes, that liminal space between forest and farmland which is the characteristic habitat of the wolf pack.

Deleuze and Guattari distinguish between three types of animals: (i) pets and domesticated creatures (which is what Freud reduces the Wolf-Man's dream to, that is, Daddy and Mummy doing it from behind); (ii) scientific animals (animals that lend themselves to taxonomies and the various forms of more or less controlled behavioral observation); and (iii) group animals (animals which operate in packs or swarms). Eugene Thacker has advanced the helpful suggestion that this threefold division of animals lying at the heart of standard epistemologies of animals and animality—the domestic, scientific, and the untamed—is in turn underpinned by the following four principles: (i) that the animal is an individuated being, (ii) that, conceptually, the individual typically precedes the group, (iii) that the group is essentially an aggregate of individuals, (iv) and, most significantly, if the group does have a "life" of its own, it will be that of the individual writ large, that is, the group is a kind of super-individual. The outcome of these four prejudices (they are little more than that) is that groups can never come to have a life of their own; or, the "life" of a group is always necessarily and strictly congruent with the lives of the individuals belonging to the group. The outcome is that the aggregate comes to have "life" only by ceasing to be a group in any plausible sense of the term. (Eugene Thacker argues convincingly that these prejudices also bedevil the ways we distinguish between ourselves and machines and plants.[1])

But what if animals of the non-domestic and non-scientific kind have a life only to the extent that the very life they have confounds and overturns these four assumptions underpinning the regnant epistemologies or ontologies of animal groups? As Deleuze and Guattari point out, in the end this is a political question as well, since the pack of wolves or flock of geese or swarm of rats occupies a very different political space from the domestic space of the much-loved (because Oedipalized) spaniel or terrier, or the isolated caged rat in a laboratory somewhere, or the ducks or geese cooped in the fenced-in yard of some small farm. There is no real liminality with regard to the space of the household pet or the farmyard animal, as there is with the animal of the forest or the steppes and prairies. This liminal space, the space always open to the seemingly arbitrary or anomalous, is however the space par excellence of the *politics* of the wolf pack, and if one accepts this admittedly stylized characterization of liminal animality, it can be said that the Wolf-Man was trying desperately to flee the suffocating domesticity that was the source of his depressive anxiety, by connecting up (in his dream at any rate) with the terrifying multiplicity constituted by the pack of wolves outside his bedroom window. How does the anxiety-ridden depressive in me join a pack, *that* wolf pack, which represents the possibility of a terrifying break from the stifling Oedipalism of my family relationships? For Deleuze and Guattari, the wolf pack in this dream represents to the Wolf-Man a profoundly abhorrent but nonetheless mesmerizing exteriority (the wolves are perched on a tree outside his bedroom window) with its unacknowledged attendant politics.

The dreamed-about wolves are located in a zone of self-estrangement extraterritorial to the interiority, the bourgeois domestic interiority, which Deleuze and Guattari take to be integral to the Wolf-Man's depression and to Freud's analysis of it. Or in the terminology of Deleuze and Guattari, it may just be that the "cure" for the neurotic Wolf-Man is not a couch-bound understanding of the etiology of his neurosis provided by the Freudian psychoanalyst, but rather a mobilizing of the randomly disconnected schizoid elements in his dream that lie outside the bedroom window and whose "secret" resides with that pack of wolves. To enable the Wolf-Man to get off his analysand's couch (where the Wolf-Man in real life, Sergei Pankejeff—whose depressive father and sister both committed suicide—spent more than six decades being treated by successive generations of psychoanalysts with no apparent relief for his debilitating symptoms); so that, finally and yet potentially catastrophically, Pankejeff could venture the risk of getting off the analyst's couch and taking a walk outside, where the dreaded and terrifying but somehow psychically enabling wolves are hopefully (!) to be found.[2]

This alternative politics, post-bourgeois of course (how could a pack of wolves, even in the dream of a young aristocrat, be "bourgeois"?), is one that is collective and multiple at the same time, provided of course that the notion of the collective is construed not in molar, as opposed to molecular, terms. After all, there can be molarized collectivities (one thinks here of Pol Pot's rural collectives, his masquerade for an agrarian utopia), and flawed but seemingly cogent multiplicities that fail precisely because they happen to be molarized despite their possessing all the appearances of a multiplicity that truly works. But the question of alterity in a political context has to be considered if we are to say something persuasive about this new and very different politics.

I say this because for Deleuze and Guattari the question of an alternative politics can only be the question of a politics of all that is intrinsically minoritarian. Only a politics of the minoritarian (a salutary reminder: a minoritarian politics is not the same as the politics of a *quantitative* minority) can on this account be truly revolutionary.

The analytically minoritarian is also the analytically other or different, and here the remarkable theory of difference associated with Deleuze and Guattari comes into play. The conceptualization of the minority is based not on a concept of difference and otherness (this being the core of American identity theory), but on the category of the *Same* ("I want everything to be the Same as me, and I must abject you because you won't/can't be the same as me"), as opposed to the very different logic of desire involved in the theory of difference (that is, "I must abject you because you are absolutely and qualitatively different from me"). The problem with the identitarian theory of difference being counterpoised here with the account of the Same provided by Deleuze and Guattari is that it is based on the simple operation of negation, negation being construed in a strictly dialectical fashion.

Hegel in the *Science of Logic* (1989) distinguished between two kinds of exteriority to a concept, that is, the insurmountable "barrier (*Schranke*)" and the more permeable "limit (*Grenze*)" and alerted us to the difficulty of providing a specification of a concept in terms of its internal determinations (i.e., within its "limits"). And so, while the presence of a conceptual "barrier" (*Schranke*) between, say, being an Indian and being an Australian and being a German, etc. makes the difference between them relatively easy to specify—according to Hegel, we simply use the operation of negation, hence to be English is not to be French, not to be Nigerian, not to be Cuban, not to be Japanese, etc. But when we seek to grasp the concept "being English" within its limits (in Hegel's admittedly technical sense of "limit") the internal determinations of this concept become much harder to specify. What marks someone as "being English" when there are some many individuals who appear to qualify for this designation? Being born in England? But many well-known English persons were born outside England—of literary figures alone, Rudyard Kipling was born in what is now Pakistan, J.G. Ballard was born in China, Tom Stoppard was born in what was then Czechoslovakia. What about being a subject of the Queen of England? But Australians and New Zealanders are also subjects of the Queen of England. Eating roast beef (the French refer to the English as *les Rosbifs*)? But what the English people who happen to be vegetarians from birth? The distinction between "playing at being English" and "being really

English" becomes impossible to maintain at the level of the limit (*grenze*), and there is ample vindication for Hegel's point that the full set of internal determinations of any concept, when apprehended at its "limit," can only be approached asymptotically—one may be English or Indian or Brazilian, but in an irreducible sense, *no* one is fully and completely English or Indian or Brazilian. One is in effect only "sufficiently" English or Indian or Brazilian, and desire, fantasy, and socially imposed convention have to do the rest, as writers on race, ethnicity, and nationality from different fields and theoretical orientations such as Benedict Anderson, Anthony Appiah, Etienne Balibar, and Slavoj Žižek have been telling us.

The problem with the standard theory of identity and difference is that it conceals this irreducible element of convention and contrivance from us, by allowing us to say of the Other that they are not "us" simply because "they" do not possess the qualities that define "us," whether we happen to be English or French, or whatever, and "they" happen to be Brazilian or Chinese or whatever.

The advantage, indeed the beauty, of the alternative offered by Deleuze and Guattari is that it does not require a concept of difference premised on abjection as its first constructive (destructive?) move. The Frenchman who says to me, however playfully, "*Vous et un Rosbif,*" is abjecting me. For Deleuze and Guattari the first move in determining how you and I stand in relation to each other, based as it is on the notion of the Same or the Common, requires us to work on what you or I have, or do not have, in common. The racist is therefore someone who wants us to be exactly the same as him (since he has made his identity or standpoint analytically majoritarian by the equivalent of an a priori diktat). But even the racist then has to work to convince me that his position or identity is analytically majoritarian. If Jean Marie le Pen declares that the footballer Zinadine Zidane is "not" French, because Zidane is not the "same" as him (le Pen), then abjection is not immediately available to le Pen as a discursive strategy if Zidane, or someone else on his behalf, says to le Pen that since Zidane is French-born, he (Zidane) is the "same" as le Pen. The follower of le Pen has to work to make Zidane analytically minoritarian in order to render himself analytically majoritarian ("I, Pierre Bourgeois, am a pure Frenchman, and you, with that strange name 'Zinadine Zidane', aren't"). Hence we can imagine something like the following exchange taking place (assuming that words rather than fists or knives are used at this point). If the follower of Le Pen, his head crammed with primordial nativist impulses, insists that Zidane can't be French because his parents were born in North Africa, then the riposte open to the supporter of Zidane can easily be "but even Dominique de Villepin and Albert

Camus and Claudia Cardinale were not born in France." In the end of course, such exchanges are likely to come to a futile conclusion, since the position of the racist is always based on the tautology underlying any nativist impulse, namely, "Only someone possessing an 'essence' that is 'French' can possess an 'essence' that is 'French.'" The racist or nativist is typically not bothered by this tautology, which is why reasoning with a racist or nativist is futile from the outset.

The position of Deleuze and Guattari therefore requires a productive and transformative politics to abolish or reduce the effectivity of all analytically majoritarian standpoints, and to have these supplanted by their analytically minoritarian counterparts. But not a supplanting that takes the form of a dialectical overturning—instead, what is required is a passage through the zone of indiscernibility between polar opposites which abolishes the opposites in the process, in the name of something new and unanticipated. Hence the need for a becoming-animal, becoming-woman, becoming mineral, becoming-molecular.

13

The Society of Control and the Managed Citizen

In his brief but prescient essay, "Postscript on Control Societies," Gilles Deleuze suggested that in control societies, as opposed to the disciplinary societies of the previous socio-historical formation brilliantly analyzed by Michel Foucault, capitalism has mutated into a ubiquitous "international ecumenical organization" with the capacity to corral into a single comprehensive system even the most disparate structures (scientific, religious, artistic, play and leisure, etc.) and kinds of being.[1]

In this new epoch, productive labor is dominated by new forms of intellectual production and service provision, which are now able to regulate every sector of social life. Consciousness, the affective and emotional components of human life, and the underlying biological bases of these components, are no longer left to "private" spheres but are instead relentlessly capitalized by this new regime of accumulation.

In this epoch, the boundary between State and Society is effectively abolished: State and Society are now a single universe of interlinked networks, in which all capital can in principle be expressed as social capital. Within this novel context, the production of social cooperation, primarily by the service and information industries, has become crucial for capitalism. Capitalism has to ensure that the forms of social cooperation are under its constant control, and this in turn requires that education, training, the work time-cycle, and so on never really end. The business time-scale is now "24/7" so that the Tokyo stock exchange is running when the one in New York closes, in a ceaseless cycle; training nowadays is "on the job" as opposed to being based on the traditional apprenticeship model (itself a holdover from feudalism); with internet banking and financial services one can conduct financial transactions virtually every minute of the day; and education becomes "continuing education," that is, something that continues throughout life, and is not confined to those aged 6–22. This cultural propensity, whose heart is the computer-driven system of vastly ramified communications networks, is reflected in the current regime of capitalist accumulation, where production has become metaproduction, that is, no longer focused—in the advanced economies at any rate—on the use of raw materials to produce finished goods, but rather on the sale of services (especially in the domain of finance and credit) and the generation of "know how," a kind of theoretical expertise which can be sold to less advanced countries to be turned into finished products.

Social control is no longer left to schools and police forces, but is now a branch of marketing, as even politics has become "retail politics," in which politicians seek frantically for an image of themselves to hawk to the electorate, and public relations consultants are more important to prime ministers and presidents than trustworthy and well-trained civil servants (more will be said about this later). Recording, whether in administration or business, is no longer based on the written document kept in the appropriate box of files, but on bar-coding and other forms of electronic tagging, as well as a myriad number of data-processing instruments.

The implications of the above-mentioned developments for politics are simply momentous, and the ensuing sections will consider them in an American context, the assumption being that the American version of this mode of societal regulation is the one most expressive of the current capitalist system of accumulation. The emphasis will be on the creation of the form of political subjectivity most congruent with the structures and strategies put in place by control societies.

In addition to an economic order (whose governing logic is the macroeconomic relation between investment, production, and accumulation), there is also a political order governed by another quite specific logic of power accumulation or domination, and a domestic order governed by a logic of "human resource" reproduction—this domestic order being the source of economic accumulation as well as of the political accumulation of power.[2] These three orders have been decisively transformed in societies of control.

The reproduction of human resources, anodyne though this phrase may sound, involves at its core the reproduction of subjectivities and identities. Anyone inclined to doubt the necessity of this set of societal operations focused on the reproduction of subjectivities and identities need only consider how the political ascendancy of the Republican Party in the United States is due in large part to a carefully nurtured coalition between pro-business interests and networks of conservative Christian evangelicals.[3] And where the constitution of the subjectivities and identities of conservative American Christian evangelicals is concerned, the convergence of a number of key factors had to be achieved before this group could contribute to this Republican Party ascendancy. These included cultural norms (especially a particular ideology of the nuclear family that would however have been starkly incomprehensible to the first Christians); a moral code with a specific conception of "values" (the anti-abortion, anti-gay rights, pro-death penalty, etc., stance of many conservative American evangelicals); a repertoire of religious doctrines (having primarily to do with what has come to be called "the gospel of success"—i.e., "with Jesus on your side you can become a millionaire, win the lottery, clinch the deal," etc.); access to the media (especially television and the internet); as well as the ability to acquire significant streams of revenue. Hence, if Christians in the United States had been formed in terms of their subjectivity and identity in the way that European Lutherans are, or impoverished Catholics living in a Brazilian favela are, say, then the likelihood of their being professed Christians and supporters of anything like a neo-conservative agenda are slim, if not nonexistent. For any group to be formed into political agents of a distinctive kind (and here American evangelical Christians are no exception), certain "mentalities" have to be cultivated at the expense of others, and certain ideals and conceptions of "truth" and "goodness" have to be promoted while others are not. Only when this was accomplished could an alliance between business interests and conservative Christian evangelicals be brought about on behalf of the Republican Party, and the seemingly counterintuitive alliance between Christianity and a blatantly pro-business ideology be enabled.

After all, it is not immediately obvious why individuals who profess to be Christians should be so accommodating of the Halliburtons and Enrons of this world, or be vociferous enthusiasts for an invasion of Iraq (here it is perhaps notable that both the late John Paul II and his successor Benedict XVI, neither of them renowned for their liberal proclivities, were publicly opposed to the American invasion of Iraq, while the American churches have been noticeably silent on the morality of this invasion). Only when a convergence (or "strategic coupling" in the words of Bob Jessop) between the economic mode of production and the socio-political mode of domination is realized can a situation be brought about in which it is easy for the Enrons and Halliburtons of this world to operate with the consent, explicit or tacit, of the overwhelming majority of American citizens.[4]

An almost-perfect concrete illustration of how this "control society" socio-economic mode of domination operates is provided by the typical campaign pitch of the three-term Republican senator Phil Gramm of Texas, who also ran for president in 1996. Gramm would often challenge his Texan electorate to choose between "pulling the wagon" (i.e., being someone who "worked hard," etc.) and "riding the wagon" (i.e., being someone who milked the welfare system, etc.). The ideological tilt of this challenge is not difficult to discern: most Texan voters would want to see themselves as hard-working pullers of the wagon, and not the shirkers and parasites who sponge off the hard-working souls being psychologically enticed by Gramm into identifying with, and thus voting for him (heaven forbid that Senator Gramm should appear to be anything but a wagon-puller!). The truth of the matter however is the total opposite.[5]

While the "pullers of the wagon" are those who in the main would like to see themselves as "hard-working" Texans, those who are the wagon's "passengers" are much more likely to be the hugely wealthy CEOs of Enron, Halliburton, and WorldCom (i.e., to say, the kind of entrepreneur who typically enjoyed Gramm's unflinching support while he was a politician), and so on, as opposed to the run-of-the-mill welfare scrounger whom Gramm invited his electorate to despise—i.e., someone who, no matter how ingenious they are in their attempts to get a free ride out of the welfare system, will only be able to bilk this system of the tiniest fraction of what a CEO like Bernie Ebbers or the late Ken Lay would have acquired as a result of the fraudulent practices of a WorldCom or Enron.

A mode of societal regulation rendering inevitable and acceptable practices such as the one which gave Phil Gramm an eighteen-year stint in the US Senate merits analysis. An aura of eye-winking acceptability is conferred by this mode of societal regulation on the conduct of politicians like Gramm and business executives like Enron's Ken Lay (at least until Enron's senior executives were caught with their fingers in the proverbial till), as indeed it is with regard to a whole range of business practices. The scandal involving the jailed Republican lobbyist Jack Abramoff is especially revealing in this regard, something borne out by the following snippet from an interview he had with the CBS programme "60 Minutes":[6]

> Stahl (the interviewer): How many congressional offices did you actually own?
> Abramoff: We probably had very strong influence in 100 offices at the time.
> Stahl: Come on.
> Abramoff: No.
> Stahl: A hundred offices?
> Abramoff: In those days, I would view that as a failure. Because that leaves 335

offices that we didn't have strong influence in.

The distinctive phenomenological features of this "control society," and overwhelmingly American (although the massive expenses scandal involving dozens of British MPs must qualify this claim), mode of societal regulation include the following:

(i) an inveterate patriotism, involving the unchallengeable conviction that America's special place in the global order is one that it is absolutely entitled to;

(ii) a disposition to favor "business" solutions over those based on an adequately functioning civil society (or at any rate, the interests of civil society in the United States are presumed by its ruling élite to be absolutely coextensive with those of its corporations);

(iii) appeals to religion, especially those invoking notions of a special providence guiding America and those who pledge their allegiance to it;

(iv) a decided preference for incarceration and execution as the "best" way to deal with social ills;

(v) the equation of wealth with supposed virtue, so that poverty comes to possess a taint of criminality or individual dereliction (given expression in the catchphrase sometimes heard on right-wing talk radio shows: "If you're so smart, and you ain't rich, what's wrong with you?");

(vi) the conviction that the United States gives much, very much, more to the rest of the world than other countries and their citizens give to it ("America, the indispensable nation," in the words of former Secretary of State Madeleine Albright);

(vii) the fantasy, common to both Republican and Democratic politicians and the mass media, that everyone in America is "middle class" or belongs to a "working family" (but never the working class, which cannot be mentioned because that would be to subscribe to "class warfare"). Thus the class origins of income inequities are effaced at a single stroke, since presumably Bill and Melinda Gates and their children somehow constitute a "working family"; and the overwhelmingly African-American janitors at my university are "middle class" (like the Gates family?), even though some of them have to hold two or even three jobs to pay the rent, afford health care and a retirement plan, and provide for their children's educations, etc.;

(viii) low levels of political participation, as witnessed by the fact that over half the citizens do not vote;[7] and

(ix) related ideologically to (vii) is the culturally sanctioned propensity to accept relatively high levels of inequality as the unavoidable consequence of being a "society of opportunity and freedom," "a culture of enterprise and competition," etc.[8]

This mode of societal regulation operates in tandem with its concomitant mode of economic production. Here of course the unavoidable fact is the United States' abandonment of the postwar "compromise" between labor and capital, reflected in such programs as Lyndon Johnson's "Great Society," but swiftly abandoned when the implicit or explicit Keynesianism underpinning that "compromise" unraveled in the early 1970s, as the United States then made a rapid transition from Keynesianism to neoliberalism in accordance with the American ruling élite's preferred way of dealing with the "stagflation" that ensued from the termination of this historic "compromise."

This abandonment of the so-called Keynesian "compromise" became the core of the ensuing neoliberalism, with its emphasis on the market as the unquestioned universal mechanism for dealing with every kind of problem ("market fundamentalism" or "marketolatry"), thereby encompassing the cultural and the social, as much as the financial and entrepreneurial, domains. The theoretical underpinnings of this new regime of accumulation gained widespread credence, and became a conventional wisdom all over the world; the Chile of General Pinochet; the Britain of Thatcher, Major, Blair, Brown, and Cameron; the Italy of Silvio Berlusconi, the France of Nicolas Sarkozy; the Australia of John Howard; the Japan of Junichiro Koizumi and his successors, and international organizations such as the IMF and World Bank, all endorsed this conventional wisdom.

The core of this succeeding regime of accumulation, when adequately described and analyzed, soon expresses the not-so-secret result of this transition to a neoliberal strategy of accumulation. In essence, the power of labor in relation to capital had, for this neoliberal regime of accumulation, to be reduced drastically; and the power of capital, especially the burgeoning forms of financial capital, had to be expanded at the expense of those whose incomes were wage-based.

The most immediate outcome of this shift to a form of accumulation privileging forms of income not based on the wage relation was a growing inequality. In particular, with an increased percentage of managerial remuneration being dispensed in the form of stock options—creating what Gérard Duménil and Dominique Lévy (2004) call "the ownership-management interface"—managers of corporations were given a huge incentive to maximize "stockholder value" at the expense of all other business considerations, such as long-term investment in their enterprises, and so on. However, those workers constrained by the wage relation could not enhance their income in this way. How many stock options can a factory worker making $70,000 a year (which is a respectable wage for "blue collar" jobs, since it is almost one-and-a-half times the current median US income) hold in comparison to an executive who makes $700,000 a year (which is not after all a huge salary for most Fortune 500 American business executives)? The differences between CEO income and the incomes of those relying on waged work is staggering: CEOs have been able to reward themselves with big payments, typically in the form of stock options and other kinds of "partnership income," while in real terms US wages have declined. The result is a new rapprochement between ownership and the upper-tier of the salaried class, with "partnership income" becoming increasingly significant in the composition of the remuneration of this upper echelon of the salaried class who, because the "discipline" of the wage relation has been swept to one side for its members, now have income levels that accelerate much more quickly than those who are paid through wages.

The available data on income differences bears out this observation, with those making over $200,000 a year deriving a greatly increased proportion of their income from capital gains, and the United States now reaching levels of income inequality last seen during the "Gilded Age" of the 1920s and 1930s (see Figure 1):[9]

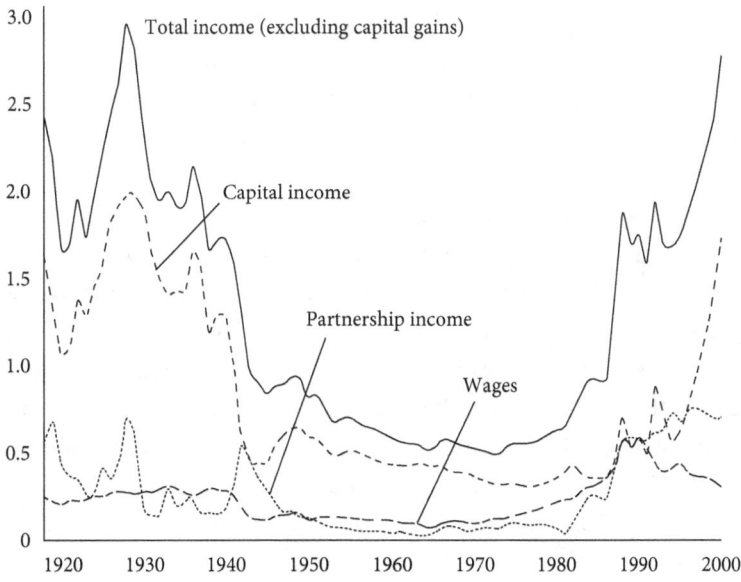

Figure 1 The top 0.01% income share in US total household income (excluding capital gains) and three components, 1918–2000. Source: Duménil and Lévy (2004), p. 109.

The new American plutocracy is now visible even in smaller towns in the United States, especially those just outside the bigger cities in the Sunbelt (Marietta outside Atlanta, Cary near Raleigh, Reston outside Washington DC, and so on), which find themselves dealing with the challenges of "McMansion" construction, when perfectly inhabitable older properties are torn down to make way for fake mansions with huge foyers, living and dining rooms festooned with chandeliers, garages for four or five sports utility vehicles, a bathroom for every bedroom, a required swimming pool and jacuzzi, and manicured lawns with chemically treated grass exuding a preternaturally green color ("a greener green than real grass"). These residences are often maintained by teams of low-paid workers, usually immigrants from Central and South America, who do everything from house cleaning to swimming pool maintenance, to providing child care and the inevitable lawn service.[10] What has enabled this new Gilded Age to come into being, where a few benefit from riches that the overwhelming majority can only dream about?

The brief answer has to be that the new Gilded Age results from a combination of convictions now enshrined in American culture, in conjunction with the economic requirements of the neoliberal regime of accumulation. This "strategic coupling" of culture and economics has resulted in a new kind of politics, a "post-political politics," in which citizens are not really represented, but managed and cajoled in the interest of a ruthlessly pro-business political agenda. I take this "post-political politics" to be the core of the insight made available by Deleuze in his account of the society of control. Most of the narrative and analysis provided below focuses on the United States, but the "managed citizen" of the United States has his or her counterparts in nearly every one of the advanced industrial countries, and so it behooves us to provide a characterization of this quintessential citizen of the society of control.

Thanks mainly to the means made available by the most recent mass media technologies and the internet, North American, Antipodean, and most western European politics today are representational only in name. If we believe that the core principles of the American system of political representation are provided by the Constitution, then a brief but telling snapshot of what Americans believe regarding their constitutional freedoms is provided by the nonpartisan annual State of the First Amendment survey, conducted since 1997 by the University of Connecticut.[11] The 2005 survey revealed that 23 percent of Americans said "the First Amendment goes too far in the rights it guarantees," compared to 49 percent in 2002 (the first survey done after 9/11) and down from 30 percent in 2004. The 2003 survey showed that 46 percent of those polled believed that the press had too much freedom, and almost one-third of those surveyed in 2003 believed that anti-war protests should be forbidden when America was fighting a war. About 50 percent of those surveyed in 2003 said the American press had been too aggressive in asking government representatives for information about the war on terrorism. The 2002 survey showed that more than 40 percent wanted to curb the academic freedom of professors and prohibit criticism of US military policy. Around 50 percent of those polled in 2002 said the government should be permitted to monitor religious groups in the interest of national security, even at the cost of violating the Constitution's provisions regarding religious freedom. More than 40 percent in the 2002 survey said the government should be given greater power to monitor Muslims living in the United States more than other religious groups. So much for the "American love of freedom" touted by George W. Bush and his handlers! But what such survey numbers visibly indicate is the very high level of insecurity (with or without an associated threshold of low information) evinced by the respondents involved. The question of the causes that underlie this anxiety-driven condition of the American citizenry has to be posed.

Of course, data of the kind provided above are merely symptomatic, and a more complete account of the system that allows such responses as the ones conveyed in these surveys to be "normalized" has to be forthcoming before a clearer sense of the political subjectivities displayed in these survey responses can be gleaned. How can a country that has an apparently inviolable belief in its status as a free and democratic country, a "shining city on the hill" which also happens to be the wealthiest nation in the world, nonetheless have so much social and economic inequality, a patently racialized system of incarceration and the imposition of the death penalty, with over 20 percent of its population lacking health insurance (while it spends vast sums of money on its military), as well as having a much poorer record of environmental protection than all other industrialized countries, while also being burdened by a system of institutionalized and legalized political corruption that would scarcely be credible if an attempt were made to introduce it to another advanced industrial nation?[12] What is the nature of the typical modes of political subjectivity that allow such a "post-political" polity to function in the way that it does? Here, at least a sketch of the model responsible for the production of these political subjectivities is needed.

In its ideal and most general form the notion of a representational democracy requires "an informed and involved" citizenry to choose in "free and fair" elections representatives who will then convene with other similarly elected representatives to determine what the laws of that country should be. Hence, it is a truism that the degree to which citizens are not able to participate in this system in the prescribed way will indicate that this system is not truly capable of undertaking the functions required by this "ideal type" of representational democracy. How near is the Western model of government to this "ideal type" of representational democracy?

There is nowadays a widespread acknowledgment, irrespective of political affiliation, that the resources for political mobilization afforded by the latest mass media technologies and the internet have drastically transformed the nature and forms of political involvement—at least in comparison with the alternatives associated with previously regnant media forms and the strategic opportunities they provided for a putative electorate. The "informed and involved"citizen of the previous paradigm of representational democracy has effectively given way to a new kind of citizen, sometimes referred to as "the managed citizen," "the citizen of governmentality," and so on.[13]

Citizenship in the United States today is basically "thin, shadowy, and privatized," to use the description provided by Philip N. Howard in his absorbing study of the ways in which objects for political consumption are produced through the application of today's hypermedia technologies. Howard's study draws attention to a fact that has been overlooked in many discussions of citizenship—that historically the United States has had many kinds of citizens, each with different "informational needs," and that hypermedia technologies have if anything added to this differentiation.[14] These new technologies "remove the burden of being informed while expressing public opinion" by privileging voices expressive of outrage at the expense of those that are informed (p. 185). Such voices are invariably required to provide preset responses to political options that have been simplified in advance (e.g., a decade after the US invasion of Iraq, the US media still provides very little scope for those who want to say that Saddam Hussein's regime was without qualification morally unacceptable while also holding to the view that the American invasion of Iraq was a flagrant breach of international law, and that Tony Blair and George W. Bush and their senior aides should therefore be charged in an international tribunal for war crimes).

The quintessential manifestation of "thin citizenship" is the computer-generated signature campaign, which requires only a few strokes of the keyboard to make someone feel they are involved in a political movement. Government in such a setting then becomes primarily a matter of being seen to redress grievances, and thus of providing a few "sound bite" positions that can easily be assimilated by "low information" subjects who have relatively crude benchmarks for feeling that the grievances in question are being addressed by officials.

A prime-time television appearance by George W. Bush in a Potemkin village setting in New Orleans (with special floodlighting of the cathedral background while most of New Orleans was still without electricity, etc.) and a couple of other presidential "appearances" quickly reduced the numbers of those who said in opinion polls that the government was not doing enough to expedite relief after Hurricane Katrina, and helped foster the completely erroneous impression that the (legitimate) grievances of those needing help in New Orleans were being addressed by the Bush administration, when in fact they were not. The floodlights did not shine on the mountains of debris a short distance from where Bush made his reassuring noises in front of the television cameras. The aim of such media orchestrations is less to "convince" those with firmly settled convictions, who are apt to regard themselves as "activists," and much more to draw on those less committed factions whose opinion-poll responses can tilt the balance this or that way ("the marginal voter"). The target in these new-media political campaigns tends therefore to be those who are less informed and somewhat wavering in their attitudes—those who, as with their choice of beverage, may in all likelihood want any political option served up to them to be "lite" (and nothing but "lite"). "Political choice" in this kind of media-fuelled "representational democracy" has metamorphosed into the ability to register one's opinions and little else (the individuals with the real choices in such a system are the ones with money bags heavy enough to induce politicians to do their bidding). The difference between a "politics lite" or "thin democracy" (to use Perry Anderson's phrase), favoring "hot button" single issues and little else, and its real alternative, is stated thus by Philip Howard:

> [The hypermedia campaigns] allow citizens to manage their distance from political issues. Candidates must remain ideologically competitive, and they use hypermedia to present different and sometimes conflicting ideological packages to different communities or supporters. The thin polity may have an immense total supply of information that is only sparingly shared among citizens. Information is unevenly distributed among communities, except for citizens with good search skills or those who can hire consultants with good information management skills. Conversely, a thick public sphere would have consistent, rich sources of political information in which all citizens can be immersed. (Howard 2006, p. 186)

It would be foolish however to think that the way to restore a "thicker" practice of citizenship is by going back to a Golden Age (which in any event never did exist), in which more people read serious newspapers, took the trouble to be informed about politics, and were more concerned about a candidate's position on the issues of the day than they were about his or her smile, hair color, jawline, lack of height, the rock stars or sports personalities supporting the candidate, etc., etc. Howard makes the point that what did happen in previous times was not anything that accorded with this mythical Golden Age. Rather, what existed then in the United States was a system that enabled patronage networks to be lined up behind party positions that were more or less loosely demarcated by ideology, so that to vote "left" generally meant being mildly in favor of worker's rights, welfare transfers, increased spending on education, taxes on corporate profits, etc., and to vote "right" meant voting for lower taxes, reduction of the social safety net, the implementation of pro-business policies, etc. The merits of these patronage networks should not be exaggerated, since they were primarily machines for getting voters to the polls and had little or sometimes nothing to do with bringing about radical social change. But they did serve the minimal purpose of giving voters effective clues about party alignments on social and economic issues. These patronage networks have now dissolved, as both American parties have become unrelentingly pro-business, hostile to wealth redistribution of even the most restrained kind, in favor of wholesale marketization, reflexively pro-military, and so forth, and can only separate themselves from each other by the populist stances they take on such "value issues" as gun control, gay marriage, the "right to die," abortion, the death penalty, hanging the Ten Commandments in courthouses, prayer in schools, teenage chastity pledges, teaching evolution in schools, schooling for the children of undocumented immigrants, and so on. Both parties are now appendages of the military-industrial-entertainment-Wall Street complex and make no pretense whatsoever of being otherwise. The outcome in the United States is a diminished public sphere, with "thin citizenship," culminating in what Tom Mertes has rightly called a "Republican proletariat."[15]

This public sphere is further eviscerated by another practice that defines "thin citizenship"—in this case the use made by political organizations of our "data shadow" to shape and predict the preferences of voters. This "shadow" is the "data trail" left behind by citizens as they negotiate life in an electronic society—credit card purchases, magazine subscriptions, polling information, organization memberships, voter registration data, etc.—that can be used by political organizations to "deduce" the different kinds of "political personality" that can then be appealed to through the hypermedia in specifically tailored ways (such as election advertisements with an anti-gun control pitch in districts with a high proportion of licensed hunters, etc.). To quote Howard again:

What is meaningfully represented in contemporary political institutions is not you but your data shadow, the political personality deduced from data about you. Sometimes your opinion diverges from what statistically derived models say your opinion is, and some of us know how to manage our data shadows while others do not. Some of us know what our data shadow looks like, while others do not. However, the data that constitutes [sic] our political personalities, including explicit citizenship acts and the implicit political meanings of consumer behavior, are bought and sold in the market. In this sense, hypermedia campaigns have "privatized citizenship." (Howard 2006, p. 189)

The informational needs of citizens have thus become commoditized by private businesses which sell the resultant commodities to political organizations for their campaigns. This information is then packaged into a media format that can be "narrowcast" to personalized voter niches (using such labels as "security mom," "town and gown," "pool and patio," "Nascar dad," "New Age and granola," etc., to specify these niches), and the result is an informational political culture that more and more resembles the kind of "infotainment" peddled on cable television. As a consequence, says Howard,

> the incentive to participate is not the public service but relief from private wrongs, as framed by hypermedia campaigns. Political hypermedia are designed to move democratic conduct from the public sphere of rallies, town hall meetings, newspaper editorials, and coffee shop debates to the private sphere of screens, key strokes, and highly personalized news services. For campaign managers and policy makers, commercial data about voter preferences make it easier to evaluate and push both public and individual sentiments .... [P]olitical hypermedia are deliberately designed to privatize in multiple senses of the word: to move the logistics of citizenship from the public to the private sector, into the private world of home and work space, where individuals act more out of private discontent on select issues than out of public duty for collective welfare. (Howard 2006, p. 190)

As a result, citizens are increasingly likely to be mobilized by a "backlash" populism, evinced by the Tea Party for instance, that trades on the resentments of voters, whether real or (as is more likely to be the case) trumped up by a demagogic hypermedia campaign. Hypermedia campaigns can also be used to destroy the credibility of political opponents, as shown by the Willie Horton episode that helped get Bush Senior elected, or the "Swift Boat" Veterans media campaign in the 2004 presidential election which deflected attention from Bush Junior's patchy record in the National Guard during the Vietnam War. The use of hypermedia in US elections was taken to another level by Barack Obama in his presidential campaigns. In his *New York Times* article "Data You Can Believe In: The Obama Campaign's Digital Masterminds Cash In," Jim Rutenberg gives us the following insight into contemporary "retail politics." Rutenberg shows how Obama's campaign team are now trying to commercialize the techniques they used during the 2012 election campaign, and describes their company's (they formed a company named AMG. for this purpose) meeting with their first potential client, a Las Vegas casino chain:

> The potential client was Caesars. The casino chain was looking for ways to induce semiregular visitors to show up more routinely at its other casinos around the country and to keep regulars from defecting to new competitors. A.M.G. was making the pitch that keeping gamblers loyal to Caesars was not all that different from keeping onetime Obama voters from straying to Mitt Romney. It was all a matter of figuring out how to get their message in front of the right customers at the right time.[16]

"Thin citizenship" is amplified by the growing contribution cybertechnology makes to the society of the spectacle, which now so thoroughly permeates American politics that political campaigns are effectively reduced to a set formula, namely, "spin plus spectacle." Thus, George W. Bush was seen landing on an aircraft carrier in his flight suit; an uncomfortable-looking Michael Dukakis was televised riding in the turret of a massive tank in the 1988 presidential campaign; the toppling of the statue of Saddam Hussein (with the Stars and Stripes attached to its head), when the first phase of the American invasion was completed, turned out to be a well-staged media event and not a spontaneous act on the part of Iraqi citizens. Tony Blair had his "I'm the uniter of the nation" moment in front of the television cameras when Princess Diana died, and politicians flock to disaster sites like vultures, knowing the cameras will be there to show them in their "leadership roles." Even the refusal of the US Department of Defense to allow cameras to film the arrival of the caskets of US military personnel killed in Iraq testifies to the power of the society of the spectacle: in this case, of course, the fear of the government is that the true nature of the price being paid by poorer Americans who join the military to have what they think will be a better life will be shown all too clearly.[17]

In the era of managed citizenship, as described above, political advantage is perceived or projected to lie in "the center" (Clintonite "triangulation," Blair's "Third Way," and so on), and this perception has two consequences: parties gravitate toward the right while giving the illusion that it is their opponents who have in fact abandoned the center, and political élites become increasingly disconnected from their voters. Thus the United States has two right-wing parties, a no-holds-barred right-wing party, and an indistinctly right-wing party ("I support the centre, but I'm leaning, leaning to the centre right" would be the appropriate refrain for most Democratic politicians in the United States today); and the same is true in Britain of both Blair's "New" Labour and the Conservative Party.[18] If there is a serious third party in an election in the United States or UK (these countries being the prime exemplars of the Anglo-Saxon model of neoliberal capitalism, and thus of the control society), it has invariably to struggle to fit itself into this schema which allows the two main parties to move to the right while conveying the impression that the "third" or "alternative" party is by its very nature too "extremist" to belong to the fictitious center defined by the two established parties. The Rainbow Coalition's efforts in the 1988 US presidential election and Ralph Nader's campaign in the 2000 presidential election were both portrayed by "mainstream" Democrats and Republicans alike as too "extremist" to deserve votes.

Similarly, any attempt in British politics by the third-party Liberal Democrats to make a move away from this fictitious "center" in a more progressive direction is immediately stigmatized by both Labour and Conservative politicians as an unacceptable "lurch to the left."[19] Another consequence of this shift to a system of managed citizenship has been to move the emphasis away from parties and ideological platforms and place it instead on the "personalities" (already shaped by the "behavior technologies" of the hypermedia system) of candidates—who must then have the money to run a protracted media campaign if they are to get anywhere. But candidates per se are never as durable as traditional parties and the ideologies they embody and, with the deemphasizing of the latter, electorates have weak and tenuous links to the parties they notionally vote for: if a "more attractive" candidate shows up for the opposing party in the next election, then one simply changes one's allegiance and "splits the ticket" at the next election. Hence, a significant number of working-class Democrats voted for George W. Bush in 2004, enticed by his "moral stance" on gay marriage, just as they voted in overwhelming numbers for Ronald Reagan in 1980 and 1984 on the basis of his airy proclamations to the effect that it was "morning again in America" (Reagan's pronouncements were even then characterized by pundits and "opinion shapers" as part of the "feel good" factor in politics that can win elections for those who in truth are singularly uninformed and not very intelligent candidates, but who can prevail electorally if they make enough voters "feel good").

In an era where citizenship is now managed, the question of political transformation poses itself even more urgently. A managed citizenry, beholden to the seemingly endless succession of spectacles that are now the focal point of contemporary political campaigning in such control societies, will in all probability not be in a position to initiate a radical political shift in favor of those who are impoverished and socially marginalized. The government in such a control society has sufficient resources to neutralize opposition to its ruling élites by changing its strategies of citizen management and by putting on new spectacles. The high proportion of respondents in polls taken around the start of the American occupation of Iraq who believed that Saddam Hussein was responsible for the World Trade Center bombings is a telling reminder of the American state's power to dragoon its people into compliance through media manipulation and fear-instilling propaganda.

This indicates that the impetus for comprehensive and radical social change will have to come from those parts of the world where there is no such system of managed citizenship, nor the resources for launching a society of the spectacle. This points to the countries of the South, who have a considerably greater incentive to overthrow an economic system that confers systemic advantages on the wealthy industrialized countries to the disadvantage of the South, even if at the same time not all these advantages are reflected in the incomes of the poorest citizens of the countries of the North (and the United States in particular). But the managed citizenry which increasingly populates the wealthy countries of the North and West is of course not really interested in bringing about significant changes that will help the countries of the South and East, especially if these changes involve substantial wealth transfers from the North to the South. Moreover, the attempts by the richer nations to promote a "low-intensity democracy" in the poorer countries (which will not really change much in a poor country, but which will do enough to ensure the modicum of stability required to let multinational corporations get on with their business) have their exact complement in their governments' own efforts to manage their citizens in order to ensure compliancy.[20] In both zones, North/West and South/East, what is fundamentally being sought is the wholesale quiescence of citizens. Is this the pass that things have come to in the age of control societies: a citizenry managed through the cybernetic technologies in the North/West, while the countries of the South/East make do with a promised patina of democratic and human rights while having to toe the line set down by the IMF and World Bank, or else face ostracism from the international economic order?

14

The Undecidable and the Fugitive: *Mille Plateaux* and the State-Form

> When intuitionism opposed axiomatics, it was not only in the name of intuition, of construction and creation, but also in the name of a calculus of problems, a problematic conception of science that was not less abstract but implied an entirely different abstract machine, one working in the undecidable and the fugitive. It is the real characteristics of axiomatics that lead us to say that capitalism and present-day politics are an axiomatic in the literal sense. But it is precisely for this reason that nothing is played out in advance. (*TP*, p. 461)

The last decade has seen a remarkable resurgence of interest in the state.[1] We need only think of the influential contributions of Michael Mann and Anthony Giddens in comparative historical sociology; the "autopoieticist" theory of Nikolas Luhmann and his associates; the influential "discourse analysis" of Ernesto Laclau and Chantal Mouffe; and the efforts of Bob Jessop, building initially on some of the formulations of Nicos Poulantzas, and now providing one of the most interesting Marxist or neo-Marxist reflections on the state.

While the work of these thinkers has been much discussed, a very different treatment of the State has gone totally unnoticed by "State-theorists." I refer of course to the one provided in *Capitalisme et schizophrénie* by Deleuze and Guattari. There is a striking difference between *Capitalisme et schizophrénie* and the work of the above-mentioned State-theorists; this is the resolutely metaphysical character of Deleuze and Guattari's treatment of the State. Theirs is decidedly the metaphysics of a counter-tradition, as Deleuze and Guattari themselves acknowledge—one marked by its eschewal of anything resembling the traditional metaphysical attempt—associated above all with Hegel—to think the *absolute* and/or the *categorical*. However, State-theory today appears to have banished any trace of metaphysics from its purview. It is not difficult to appreciate why this is so: "metaphysics" (as the age-old project of thinking the *absolute*/the *categorical*) is commonly thought to be inextricably bound up with discredited "universal histories," with narratives of progress that have died with the death of the "grand narratives," with a traffic in all kinds of unacceptable "essentialisms," with mythic teleologies and necessities, and so forth. My intent is not to show how and why Deleuze and Guattari are not vulnerable to such strictures, but to proceed directly to their treatment of the State-form. I am chiefly concerned in this paper with those sections of *Mille Plateaux* which deal with the relation between the State and the War Machine (Plateau 12—"Treatise on Nomadology") and with the forms of the State in particular relation to the axiomatics of capitalism (Plateau 13–"Apparatus of Capture").[2]

Deleuze and Guattari are unabashed in their espousal of a "universal history." This universal history, which is "rhizomatic" and hence "non-systematic," is associated with three different forms of the State:

> Imperial archaic States, which are paradigms and constitute a machine of enslavement by overcoding already-coded flows (these States have little diversity, due to a certain formal immutability that applies to all of them); (2) extremely diverse States—evolved empires, autonomous cities, feudal systems, monarchies—which proceed instead by subjectification and subjection, and constitute qualified or topical conjunctions of decoded flows; (3) the modem nation-States, which take decoding even further and are models of realization for an axiomatic or a general conjugation of flows (these States combine social subjection and the new machinic enslavement, and their very diversity is a function of isomorphy, of the eventual heteromorphy or polymorphy of the models in relation to the axiomatic). (*TP*, p. 459)[3]

Of particular interest is the depiction by Deleuze and Guattari of the form of the modern nation-state and its relation to the axiomatics of capitalism which they propound. Their approach furnishes theoretical resources which enable us to move beyond a pervasive—and "theological"—conception of the State which extends from Rousseau and Kant via Hegel down to Habermas today.

Central to this "theological" account of the State is the category of reconciliation. Allied to this category are a whole series of reflections on the construction of a transfigured social and political order. These lines of thought may extend in ostensibly different directions, but they invariably converge upon the same point, for example, the State as the "appropriate" polity for establishing a general will (*volonté générale*) out of the particular wills (*volonté de tous*) of its citizens (Rousseau), or as the site of the resolution of the antagonisms which pervade civil society (Hegel's *sittlichkeit*). This approach to the State (more so in Hegel than in Rousseau, perhaps) effectively regards it as a *deus ex machina* which overcomes the otherwise unresolvable dichotomies of a "disorganized civil society." The outcome is a theodicy of the State.[4] It would be a mistake, however, to suggest that the treatment of the State in *Mille plateaux* is merely a repudiation of this age-old theology of the State. The breadth of *Capitalisme et schizophrénie* ranks it alongside Hegel's *Phenomenology of Spirit*. That work sought above all to express in a philosophically comprehensive way the "spirit" of Hegel's age. Deleuze and Guattari certainly harbor no such ambition: theirs is an attempt to furnish a repertoire of concepts that will enable us to construct "lines of escape" from precisely such notions as that of the "spirit" of this (or any) age. But what both projects have in common is an expansiveness and a reach, which prompt one to think that if the *Phenomenology* had to be conceptually undone, it would take a work of the extraordinary scope and philosophical ingenuity of *Capitalisme et schizophrénie* to do it.

> *Before Being, there is politics.* (TP, p. 203)

Mille plateaux continues and extends the critique, made in *L'Anti-Oedipe*, of the evolutionist framework almost universally invoked by State-theorists in their attempts to portray the rise and growth of the State. The gist of their critique of evolutionism is that it is implausible to hold that the State arises out of agricultural communities with their already existing forces of production. For Deleuze and Guattari, the state springs up directly in hunter-gatherer groups which have no existing agriculture or metallurgy. The upshot is that it is

> the State that creates agriculture, animal raising, and metallurgy; it does so first on its own soil, then imposes them upon the surrounding world. It is not the country that progressively creates the town but the town that creates the country. It is not the State that presupposes a mode of production; quite the opposite, it is the State that makes production a "mode." The ... reasons for presuming a progressive development are invalidated. (*TP*, p. 429)

The claim that the State-form prevailed even during the earliest hunter-gatherer groups seems insupportable in the light of what social evolutionists would regard as the "historical evidence."[5] It becomes more convincing, however, when Deleuze and Guattari's espousal of the principle of "reverse causality" is brought into the picture. This causal principle is borrowed by them from biology and physics. Such reverse causalities, they say,

> testify ... to an action of the future on the present, or of the present on the past ... which imply an inversion of time. More than breaks or zigzags, it is these reverse causalities that shatter evolution. (*TP*, p. 431)

So, it is possible, given reverse causality, to say that in hunter-gatherer societies the (Paleolithic) State was

> already acting before it appeared, as the actual limit these primitive societies warded off, or as the point toward which they converged but could not reach without self-destructing. These societies simultaneously have vectors moving in the direction of the State, mechanisms warding it off, and a point of convergence that is repelled, set outside, as fast as it is approached. To ward off is also to anticipate. Of course, it is not at all in the same way that the State appears in existence, and that it pre-exists in the capacity of a warded-off limit; hence its irreducible contingency. (*TP*, p. 431)

The relation between the State and the "primal" peoples (*les primitifs*) is thus to be understood in terms of two inverse "moments" or "waves"—one prior to the appearance of the State (in which the hunter-gatherers are brought to a point of convergence that destabilizes the prevailing socius), the other subsequent to its manifestation (in which the State, now an apparatus, generates agriculture, the division of labor, animal husbandry, etc.). The two unfold "simultaneously in an 'archaeological', micropolitical, micrological, molecular field" (*TP*, p. 431).

This contention is significant and radical.[6] For it is evidently not the case, where *Mille plateaux* is concerned, that a molecular or micropolitics merely comes to appear at a relatively late stage in response to an already constituted State (which qua State is molar, macrological, etc.). On the contrary, the State, when it "arrives," is an arrestation or "caging" of something that is irreducibly molecular or micropolitical. Both State and non-State exist in a field of perpetual interaction, so that the State cannot be viewed as being in sole and absolute possession of a field that has been exhaustively molarized in consequence. In the beginning is politics, which has an intrinsic propensity to be micrological and micropolitical.[7]

This positioning of the State in a molecularized field means that the appearance of the State is not the outcome of its own efficacy or of its having its own grounds. The State is an invention, an invention of thought. But it is an invention that has to show itself precisely as its "opposite"—that is, an *unthought* (at least where "origins" are concerned): "Only thought is capable of inventing the fiction of a State that is universal by right, of elevating the State to the level of *de jure* universality" (*TP*, p. 375). *Thought* confers on the State the character of a singular and universal form, the fullest and most decisive expression of the rational-reasonable (*le rationnel-raisonnable*).

The foremost proponent of this understanding of the State is Hegel, who views the State as an explicit embodiment of the universal, as the realization of reason, and thus as the spiritual community that integrates all individuals within itself. This Hegelian view of the State as the "necessary" realization of the rational-reasonable is overturned by Deleuze and Guattari. They maintain that, on the contrary, it is the rational-reasonable itself that is derived from the State. The State provides the formal conditions for the enactment of the rational-reasonable (*TP*, pp. 375–81), and thought (as the rational-reasonable) in turn necessarily confers on the State its "reason" (*lui donner nécessairement "raison"*) (*TP*, p. 556 n42). To wrest thought from the State and to return the State to thought, thereby "fictionalizing" the State (which is a fiction before it is anything else)—this is the demanding task set for those who would live out the nomadology of Deleuze and Guattari.

To return the State to thought—In *Mille plateaux* this requires the State-form to be further conceptualized in terms of the axiomatics of capitalism formulated by Deleuze and Guattari. In *L'Anti-Oedipe* they had spoken of the need to rediscover everywhere the force of desiring production; to renew, on the level of the Real, the tie between the analytic machine, desire, and production ... (*TP*, p. 53). Here are the primary features of the relation between the State and capitalism, as identified by Deleuze and Guattari:

1. The State "comes into the world fully formed and rises up at a single stroke, the unconditioned *Urstaat*" (*TP*, p. 437).
2. The State that thus arises is an imperial, despotic machine of overcoding. This imperial State brought about a deterritorialization of the primitive territorial codes, codes which it then reterritorialized, through its Overcoding, in a way that instituted an organized production which brought with it the creation of "a particular kind of property, money, public works ... " (*TP*, p. 448).
3. The archaic imperial State which arose in this way then mutated. The principle of this mutation is internal, regardless of the external factors that may contribute to it. The archaic State was an overcoding apparatus, but it was not able to prevent a substantial quantity of decoded "flows" to escape from it:

> The State does not create large-scale works without a flow of independent labor escaping its bureaucracy (notably in the mines and in metallurgy). It does not create the monetary form of the tax without flows of money escaping, and nourishing or bringing into being other powers (notably in commerce and

banking). And above all, it does not create a system of public property without a flow of private appropriation growing up beside it, then beginning to pass beyond its grasp; this private property does not itself issue from the archaic system but is constituted on the margins, all the more necessarily and inevitably, slipping through the net of overcoding. (*TP*, p. 449)

5. This transformation confronts the succeeding State apparatuses with a new task. Where the archaic imperial State had to overcode already coded flows, the new State apparatuses had to organize conjunction of the decoded flows that had escaped their predecessor. These were the apparatuses of the extremely diverse State. But even here, decoded flows continued to escape, until they reached a point where the diverse State was no longer able to contain them, and the decoded flows attained an "abstract," "generalized" conjunction which overturned the more recent State apparatuses and created capitalism "at a single stroke" (*TP*, pp. 452–3). *Capital* thus represents a new threshold of deterritorialization. This "force of deterritorialization infinitely [surpasses] the deterritorialization proper to the State" (*TP*, p. 453). But capital's superiority did not spell the end of the State. Rather, the State underwent a further mutation, and the modern nation-State was born.

6. The relation between the State and capital is thus a reciprocal one. Capitalism is an "independent, worldwide axiomatic that is like a single City, megalopolis, or 'megamachine' of which the States are parts, or neighborhoods" (*TP*, pp. 434–5). The State is not totally displaced by the "worldwide, ecumenical organization" of capital, but it has, in its modern mutation, become "a model of realization" for capital. As such, it is the function of each State today to "[group] together and [combine] several sectors, according to its resources, population, wealth, industrial capacity, etc." (*TP*, p. 454). Under capitalism, the State serves "to moderate the superior deterritorialization of capital and to provide the latter with compensatory reterritorializations" (*TP*, p. 455). It becomes a site for the effectuation of capital, and it does this by reterritorializing flows which capitalism connects and deterritorializes (*TP*, p. 221). Capitalism will even sustain and organize States that are not viable, for its own purposes (mainly the crushing of minorities through integration and extermination) (*TP*, p. 472).

7. International capitalism is able to ensure "isomorphy" (not to be confused with "homogeneity" in Deleuze and Guattari's scheme) of very diverse formations. As a molar multiplicity, an abstract machine, capital is situated at the crossing point of all kinds of formations, and thus has the

capacity to integrate and recompose non-capitalist sectors or modes of production. A case in point would be a country like Brazil, in which there is every conceivable kind of production, from the tribal production of the Amazonian Indians to advanced computer technology. It would seem that in such a country, every and any kind of production can be mediated and placed at the "disposal" of capital.[8] This is a form of capitalism generated by the progressive and inexorable internationalization of the circuits of capital since the 1960s. It is an abstract machine which ensures several factors: the interpenetration of capital within international corporations, the existence of an international debt economy, the introduction of flexible manufacturing systems and labor processes associated with an international standardization of production. (Of course, the "benefits" of this development are confined to those who belong to the managerial and technocratic strata; thus, there are "third worlds right in the centre of overdeveloped Nations".)[9]

The great merit of the "universal history" outlined in Plateaus 12 and 13 lies in its almost uncanny ability to chart developments that have become more manifest in the thirty years since its publication. State-theory today is grappling with the phenomenon of "post-Fordism" and its practical and theoretical repercussions, but no one (except Toni Negri, who is affiliated with Deleuze and Guattari) has addressed the new conjuncture "theorized" under the auspices of "post-Fordism" (or its cognates) with the conceptual subtlety and the unwavering political commitment of the authors of *Mille plateaux*. Guattari and Negri (1990) write:

> The revolution continues. The irreversible character of the hitherto completed processes affirms itself. The new subjectivities rearrange their political identity by "assimilating" (that is, semiotizing and smothering) the obstacles posed by the adversary-including those that the adversary has made them introject. The changing characteristics of the collective force of labor, the living forces of the non-guaranteed urban proletariat, the transfinite network of dissident discursive arrangements set themselves up as so many protagonists of the new cycle of struggle. (p. 84)

According to Deleuze and Guattari, capitalism today has the character of an "international ecumenical organization." As such, it is the ubiquitous, intermediate milieu which assures—"simultaneously"—the isomorphism of even the most heterogeneous orders (commercial or economic, religious, artistic, etc.) (*TP*, p. 435ff). In this milieu, productive labor is formed in every component of society: the ubiquity of capital is simultaneous with the omnipresence of everything that yields surplus value for capital. The absolute spatial division between exploiters and exploited posited by a more conventional marxism has been eliminated. In the current regimes of accumulation, the whole of society is imbricated in the reproduction of capital. In the present regimes of capitalist accumulation, the work of the State is the essentially negative one of reterritorialization.

The State deflects and dissipates, through such reterritorialization, the efforts of resistance on the part of social subjects. This point is well made in a passage of *Mille plateaux* that bears extended quotation:

> One of the fundamental tasks of the State is to striate the space over which it reigns, or to utilize smooth spaces as a means of communication in the service of striated space. It is the vital concern of every State not only to vanquish nomadism but to control migrations and, more generally, to establish a zone of rights over an entire "exterior," over all of the flows traversing the ecumenon. If it can help it, the State does not dissociate itself from a process of capture of flows of all kinds, populations, commodities or commerce, money or capital, etc. There is still a need for fixed paths in well-defined directions, which restrict speed, regulate circulation, relativize movement, and measure in detail the relative movements of subjects and objects. This is why Paul Virilio's thesis is important, when he shows that "the political power of the State is polis, police, that is, management of the public ways," and that "the gates of the city, its levies and duties, are barriers, filters against the fluidity of the masses, against the penetration power of migratory packs," people, animals, and goods. Gravity, gravitas, such is the essence of the State. (*TP*, pp. 386–7)[10]

The State subserves the processes of accumulation by representing social production and reproduction to its subjects as "natural" and inevitable. The State undertakes its integrative and neutralizing role in a way that accords with what Deleuze and Guattari (following Virilio) have identified as the fundamental law of the State-war and the fear of war. (The productive organization of this terror is the State's *modus operandi* when it seeks social integration.) The traditional wielders of power are more and more obliged to resort to war and the preparation for war to quell or slow down social revolution, while their subjects (positioned "nomadically" within social space) are the carriers of this revolution, and must further it through strategies of stabilization, and especially the struggle for peace. This is a struggle to construct "*revolutionary connections* in opposition to the *conjugations of the axiomatic*" (*TP*, p. 473. Emphasis in the original). Through the construction of such "revolutionary connections" a new kind of social power is organized which cannot be mobilized by war or the fear of war.

The goal here is the creation of a "postbourgeois" civil society. This is not necessarily more "proletarian" in the standard sense of "productive labor," nor is it the *societas civilis* of Locke or the *bürgerliche Gesellschaft* of Hegel. It becomes possible to create this new civil society because in global capitalism, there is no State into which this new and nomadic socius can be adequately sublimated. The State still has the function of providing capitalism with its models of realization, but there is one thing, according to Deleuze and Guattari, that it cannot do: it cannot alter an ineluctable element in the axiomatics of capitalism—"While capitalism would like for us to believe that it confronts the limits of the Universe, the extreme limit of resources and energy," it can however do no more than confront "its own limits (the periodic depreciation of existing capital); all it repels or displaces are its own limits (the formation of new capital, in new industries with a high profit rate)" (*TP*, p. 463). And adjacent to "the limits of the Universe" is schizophrenia—that which signals the limit of capitalism by being its "exterior." Schizophrenia is also the "exterior" of the State. This is the "exteriority" of the emergence of new collective subjectivities. It will, of course, take ceaseless human effort and human transformation to create a fully fledged socius populated by these new subjectivities. Subjectivities that are the loci of a multiplicity of affects and potentials, the lines of which escape the coding of the state apparatuses. Packs and singularities, rather than model societies and individuals.

There is as yet no theory of the State-form which has brought itself to the point where it can dispense with the idea of a "model society." Nearly every version of marxism has to affirm something like a "withering away" of the State, which involves a fairly drastic decoding if it is to be given any substance. But far more radical, and perhaps more politically productive, would be the expression of that which cannot be codified—the revolutionary forces, the intensities that elude the codes of the State apparatus and its surrogates. This of course hints at a productive convergence between Marx and Spinoza and perhaps Nietzsche. It is not enough to discredit the proposition that the State is not (and cannot be) the model society. Most versions of marxism do this much. We need to go further. The notion of a "model society" itself needs to be dismantled. In its place must be put what Guattari and Negri (1990) describe as

> the task of organizing new proletarian forms ... concerned with a plurality of relations within a multiplicity of singularities—a plurality focused on collective functions and objectives that escape bureaucratic control and overcoding, in the sense that the plurality develops towards optimizing the processes of involved singularities. What is at stake here then is a functional multicentrism capable,

on the one hand, of articulating the different dimensions of social intellection, and on the other hand of actively neutralizing the destructive power of capitalist arrangements. (p. 107)

The project is revolutionary because *Capitalisme et schizophrénie* is the most politically engaged and intellectually powerful conceptual cartography of these new collective subjectivities. For all the strictures against Marx and marxism that it contains, *Capitalisme et schizophrénie* is plausibly to be seen as a renegade and deviant member of this tradition of theory and practice. A tradition that it subverts and rewrites even as it stakes its (unspoken) claim to be positioned within it.

15

"Reinventing a Physiology of Collective Liberation": Going "Beyond Marx" in the Marxism(s) of Negri, Guattari, and Deleuze

We want to reinvent a living, real body, to live and to experience a philosophy of collective liberation.[1]

In several different works, and from somewhat (though not entirely) different intellectual and practical trajectories, Toni Negri, Felix Guattari, and Gilles Deleuze can be said to have sought to present an answer to a question that perhaps underlies any project of radical social transformation, namely, "what is it to live in a society completely constituted on the basis of freedom?"[2] *Their approaches to this question have in large part taken the form of an attempt to reorient the marxist "project," though this is perhaps more discernibly so in the case of Negri than in that of his counterparts.*[3] *The intellectual impetus behind this particular reconstructive undertaking derives as much from Spinoza as from Marx (Nietzsche and/or Bergson, in the case of Deleuze).*

Spinoza, on this view, sought to delineate a metaphysical response to the crisis of the Renaissance and post-Renaissance utopia. This is the bourgeois utopia which—"impossibly"—used the myth of the market, the capitalist myth *par excellence*, to underpin the aspiration toward a transformed and fulfilled human subjectivity (the creation of this subjectivity being very much the propelling aspiration of Renaissance humanism). The immediate source of this understanding of Spinoza's intellectual and historical context is of course Negri's great work on Spinoza, but this reading of that context is also consonant with the one provided by Deleuze in some of the essays published as *Spinoza:*

Philosophie pratique (*SPP*).⁴ Both Negri and Deleuze (and by extension Guattari) treat Spinoza as the philosopher who more than any other sought to provide a materialist ontology of the constitution of political practice.

I make this point about the centrality of Spinoza for Negri and Deleuze/Guattari because this dimension of their work is self-avowedly a response to another, subsequent, crisis of utopia, in this case the crisis of the utopia generated by the revolutions of 1917 and 1968. (Here 1968 is viewed as an expression of the crisis of the utopia of 1917, although the utopia of 1968 underwent a crisis of its own in the Reagan-Thatcher years: the Reagan-Thatcher *épistémè* or imaginary being the expression of the crisis of the utopia of 1968.)

If the crisis of the bourgeois utopia addressed by Spinoza was situated in the conjuncture marked by a transition from mercantile to industrial capitalism, the crisis that is the "occasion" of the reconstructive projects of Negri, Deleuze, and Guattari is the one brought into being by the passage from the social democratic form of capitalism sponsored by Keynesianism to the one that exists today, that is, the form that Negri and Guattari have called "integrated world capitalism."⁵ This particular transition from one phase of capitalism to another is manifested in several different registers: the reconstitution of the subject of labor, the creation of new regimes of accumulation, the inauguration of a new semiotics of value, the transformation of the capitalist state, the generation of new forms of antagonism and struggle, and so forth. These and other associated developments are taken by Negri, Deleuze, and Guattari to signal different readings of Marx. But the reconstitution of the marxist "project" which the crisis of the socialist (but not the communist⁶) utopia instigates is an undertaking that, in their eyes, requires us to attend to the question of an ontology of constitutive political practice (the question that, as we have seen, was Spinoza's question *par excellence*).

There are of course substantial differences of theme and emphasis between Negri and the authors of *Capitalism and Schizophrenia* which cannot be overlooked by the attentive reader. The perspective of Deleuze and Guattari is unabashedly that of a "universal history"—*Capitalism and Schizophrenia* is arguably an endeavor that involves something like an "unwriting" of Hegel's *Phenomenology of Spirit*. In elaborating this "universal history" *Capitalism and Schizophrenia* uses a schema of periodization that situates the rise and development of capitalism in a network of subjectifications, conjunctions, and appropriations which extend as far back as the Paleolithic and Neolithic Ages. As Deleuze and Guattari see it, capitalism emerged when a substantial quantity of flows (of labor, of money, of private property) escaped the overcoding apparatus that was the archaic state. The decoded flows continued to escape, until they reached a point where they attained an "abstract," "generalized" conjunction which overturned the existing archaic state-form and created capitalism "at a single stroke."[7] Deleuze and Guattari do not explicitly state the time when capitalism emerged, but it is clear from their discussion of the state-form in *A Thousand Plateaus* that they believe capitalism to have developed some time after the end of the Middle Ages, though certainly at a time prior to the rise of the modern nation-state. (In their view the presence of capitalism was the condition of possibility for the emergence of the modern nation-state.)[8]

Negri, somewhat by contrast, is not overtly interested in the question of the rise of capitalism and the relation that capitalism has to previous forms of production and accumulation. He is more concerned with a historical periodization that begins with the rise of capitalism. Negri considers Marx to have studied capitalism in its first two periods of development: the first, which existed before 1848, was regarded by Marx as the period of "manufacture"; the second, which began in about 1848 (and which according to Negri lasted until 1968), was seen by Marx as the period of "large-scale industry." The period of "large-scale industry" can be divided into two phases. The first phase, from 1848 to 1914, was the epoch of what Negri calls "the professional worker," that is, it was a period when the worker belonged to a qualified labor force with a knowledge of the labor cycles, and when workers' parties were formed. The second phase of "large-scale" industry extended from 1918 to 1968. It was the period of "the mass worker," when the labor force was technically reorganized according to Taylorist principles in ways that made it completely abstract with regard to its productive activity. This was also the phase in which Fordism was instituted, thereby enabling the wage to be conceived for the first time as a specific instrument for enabling and promoting consumption. This Keynesian version of capitalism put in place a state project that was interventionist, a state form that sought to regulate economic cycles in ways that maintained full employment and guaranteed social assistance.

After 1968 Keynesian capitalism started to move into crisis, and in response a new epoch of capitalist development was inaugurated. From 1968 onwards, laboring processes were radically restructured and altered by automation and computerization, so that productive labor, now socially organized along "post-Fordist" lines in the metropolitan nations, was no longer central to the process of production. (Negri is careful to acknowledge that there is a "peripheral" Fordism and Taylorism.) This is the age of "the socialized worker," of a new situation in which productive cooperation is diffused throughout society and productive networks are rendered entirely social in nature. The form of the state also changed in this new phase: the "planner state" of Keynesianism gave way to the "crisis state" in the sense that the state now had to have recourse to crisis (in the form of war and the preparation for war, "low intensity conflict," the orchestration of "moral panics," etc.) in order to re-establish its domination. Postmodernism became the ideology adequate to this new mode of production. This mutation of capitalism, which Negri calls the phase of "real subsumption," also involved the creation of a fully integrated world economy.[9]

There are very direct indications in *A Thousand Plateaus* that Deleuze and Guattari find Negri's periodization to be compatible with their own perspective on capitalist development. I do not wish to dwell for too long on these periodizations—I mention them primarily in order to provide a backdrop or context for subsequent discussion. But, as I shall try to show, there is a possible difference in their conceptions of the logic of capitalist command which may be due to differences that inhere in these periodizations.

If 1968 marks something like a crisis of utopia where Negri, Deleuze, and Guattari are concerned, a "theorization" of this crisis along marxist or marxisant lines is possible only if there is a recognition that the most recent mutation of capitalism has altered the historical conditions that subtended Marx's analysis of capitalism; that a recasting of the content of this analysis is necessitated by the realization that radically new relations of production and their concomitant productive antagonisms have come into existence since 1968. Negri has taken this changed state of affairs into account in at least two major ways.

First, he has seen the need to shift his own focus as a reader of Marx from *Capital* (with its negative emphasis on the irresolvably contradictory nature of capitalist production) to the *Grundrisse* (with its positive stress on the constitutive capacity of the proletariat to appropriate social wealth); and second, he has turned to Spinoza in his quest for an ontological foundation for the new revolutionary subjectivity that has emerged since 1968. Deleuze and Guattari, while apparently not following Negri in imputing anything like a new and decisive significance to the *Grundrisse*, have nonetheless also turned to Spinoza. The motivations for these respective "turns to Spinoza" appear to be somewhat different. In the case of Negri, the turn derives from what he takes to be a consequence of the "real subsumption" of society in the current phase of capitalist production and accumulation. With the direct absorption by capital of all the conditions of production and reproduction, capital, through its command over the logic of social cooperation, envelops society and hence becomes social: capital has to extend its logic of command to cover the whole of society, but in doing this it also necessarily enlarges the terrain of antagonism to cover society in its entirety.[10] The "real subsumption" of society thus guarantees antagonism a maximum of continuity and flexibility. If capitalist command becomes universal, then antagonism becomes correspondingly ubiquitous. The sites of struggle become fluid, generalized, and diffused. This situation has an important implication for Negri. Antagonism in the phase of "real subsumption" cannot be understood dialectically (i.e., in the Hegelian manner) because the proletariat is constitutively—that is, "autonomously"—opposed to capital and so the opposition between labor and capital cannot in principle be understood along the lines of the negation-retention (or "sublation") typical of the Hegelian dialectic. Capitalist exploitation consists in command, and capital has to resort to political operations to secure and maintain this command. Labor is opposed to capital because its constitutive power has to be ceaselessly harnessed by (capitalist) systems of social cooperation which pervade the whole of society, thereby ensuring an exponential intensification of the composition of the working class and a massive extension of its potentiality. The dialectic cannot encompass the very many kinds of antagonism that constitute this proletarian intensification and extension.[11]

Negri turns to Spinoza because the latter presents a "metaphysics of being" as "a physics of power (*potentia*) and an ethics of constitution" (1991, p. 219). In this metaphysics

> being and nonbeing affirm each other and negate each other simply, discretely, immediately. There is no dialectic. Being is being, nonbeing is nothing. Nothing: phantasm, superstition, shadows. It is opposition. It is an obstacle of the constructive project. (1991, p. 220)

Using the lineaments of this metaphysics, Negri is able to understand capitalism precisely as the "obstacle of the constructive project," as wasteful, dissipative "nonbeing" in the strict Spinozist sense.

Negri has another reason for undertaking the turn to Spinoza. A whole philosophical tradition, extending from Hobbes to Rousseau to Hegel, has posited a dialectic between the ineffective power of the individual and the compelling or coercive social power of the state or sovereign as a transcendental zone in which the ineffective and contradictory powers of individuals can be reconciled into a singular collective power (*potestas*). Against this bourgeois myth, says Negri, Spinoza posits the strength (*potentia*) of the multitude, the strength that counters the dominative, negative power of the state/sovereign (1991, pp. 195–202).[12] In the phase of "real subsumption" the whole of society is imbricated in the reproduction of capital and so, with respect to some more standard marxist accounts, the state is not, on the one hand, a political "agent" capable of shaping and maintaining classes nor, on the other, an essentially neutral instrument at the disposal of the various classes (although invariably this political instrument is deemed to be most readily available to the dominant class).[13] In "real subsumption" the state possesses no power on its own: it is, instead, the primary site or field for the exercise of capitalist command (whether bourgeois or socialist). In this phase, the work of the state is the essentially "negative" one of decomposition, that is, the modification and neutralization, primarily through the production and "management" of crisis, of the efforts of resistance on the part of social subjects.[14] In this society-state complex (the term is Negri's) there cannot be a "vertical" resolution of the manifold contradictory individual wills (as maintained by the Hobbes-Rousseau-Hegel tradition), because in an integrated world–capitalism which is essentially "paranational" in form, there is no state, no "new" state, into which the contradictions of civil society can be sublimated by negative power.[15] In a situation in which the state and civil society have dissolved into a single complex, there can be a zone of possibility in which the strength of the multitude is left intact. Spinoza formulated a physics of the power of this multitude, but in his time there was no possibility of this physics being brought to its point of historical operativeness. In the phase of "real subsumption," however, we finally have the politics that brings precisely this physics, and hence its attendant ethics, to its point of material instantiation, its moment of "truth." Spinoza's philosophy of the constitution of the structural movement of the multitude had thus to await its politics, the politics of a new kind of revolutionary subjectivity which arrived ("after 1968") in the phase of "real subsumption," the time when there is finally the possibility of the multitude being actualized as something real and irreducible. This, very briefly and somewhat schematically, is Negri's warrant for using Spinoza's philosophy to provide an ontological foundation for this new revolutionary subjectivity.[16]

(There are several affinities between Negri's reading of Spinoza and the one provided in Etienne Balibar.) Like Negri, Balibar views Spinoza as a revolutionary thinker who adopted, albeit only "in theory," the standpoint of the masses/multitude. Unlike Negri, however, Balibar believes that Spinoza's notion of constitutive power is compatible with the (Althusserian) dialectical mediation. It is impossible to deal with this important and vexed question in so brief a space. (Certainly, Spinoza's account of constitution cannot do without the category of opposition, but it is not clear that this category is necessarily to be wedded to the dialectic.)

Where Deleuze and Guattari are concerned, any imputation to them of a turn to Spinoza has to be justified on somewhat different grounds. Like Negri, they too want to eschew dialectics. But the motivation for Negri's repudiation of the dialectic is resolutely and explicitly political (as Michael Hardt has pointed out).[17] For Negri, as I have already said, there is no possibility of a synthesis emerging from the relation between labor and capital, but only pure antagonism: if there is a synthesis, then it is one that can only be maintained on the side of capital, because capital has ceaselessly to contain and incorporate (i.e., sublate, if one looks at it in Hegelian terms) the proletarian antagonism in order to perpetuate itself. The proletariat, by contrast, is not behoved by any political imperative to establish a synthesis of this kind in its struggles with capital. Quite the reverse.[18] For Deleuze (Guattari can be left out of this for the moment), perhaps by contrast, the bypassing or deliberate overlooking of the Hegelian dialectic is necessitated, at least initially, by a more recognizably philosophical exigency. As Deleuze sees it, Hegelian contradiction is ultimately subsumed by a logic of identity, a logic that disastrously collapses "difference" into the rational "same," and that therefore ensues inevitably in a disavowal of multiplicity.[19] I do not want to push this putative difference between Deleuze and Negri too far because if anything it is one of starting point and emphasis, of research strategy (so to speak); it is not in the end a difference of real philosophical principle. This has to be said because Deleuze's philosophical project clearly intersects at certain points with Negri's—they are both concerned (as indeed is Guattari) to formulate, albeit by different theoretical routes, a constitutive ontology of political practice. This affinity cannot be overlooked, because the Deleuze I am talking about here is very much the figure who wrote the earlier philosophical works, such as the one on Nietzsche; the more recent Deleuze can be said to have moved to a position much closer to Negri's, especially in his writings on "societies of control."

In his depiction of the society of control, Deleuze points to a contrast between such societies and their predecessors, the disciplinary societies and the societies of sovereignty. He follows Foucault in locating disciplinary societies in the eighteenth and nineteenth centuries, although they reached their culminating point at the outset of the twentieth. Societies of sovereignty existed prior to the Napoleonic era, and their goals and functions were very different (according to Deleuze, to tax rather than to regulate production, to command death rather than to organize life).[20]

In characterizing the relationship that societies of control have to capital, Deleuze says the following:

> Nineteenth-century capitalism is a capitalism of concentration, for production and for property. It therefore erects the factory as a space of enclosure, the capitalist being the owner of the means of production but also, progressively,

the owner of other spaces conceived through analogy (the worker's familial house, the school). As for markets, they are conquered sometimes by specialization, sometimes by colonization, sometimes by lowering the costs of production. But, in the present situation, capitalism is no longer involved in production, which it often relegates to the Third World, even for the complex forms of textiles, metallurgy, or oil production. It's a capitalism of higher-order production. It no longer buys raw materials and no longer sells the finished products; it buys the finished products or assembled parts. What it wants to sell is services and what it wants to buy is stocks. This is no longer a capitalism for production but for the product, which is to say, for being sold or marketed. Thus, it is essentially dispersive, and the factory has given way to the corporation. (1992, p. 6)

It is clear from this passage that Deleuze is talking about a manifestation of capitalism confined to the overdeveloped nations—at any rate, it would be very problematic if this account of capitalism were generalized in ways that covered the developed and underdeveloped nations. It is just as obvious that Deleuze is identifying a phase of capitalist "advance" that is precisely the one that Negri terms "real subsumption." In which case, the politically driven rejection of the dialectic that is to be found in Negri can properly be said to be applicable to Deleuze's analysis of the societies of control: it therefore becomes a political complement to the philosophical rejection of the Hegelian dialectic to be found in Deleuze's earlier writings.[21]

The phase of "real subsumption" and of the societies of control, as I have already indicated, creates a situation in which there has to be a recourse to philosophical reflection of the kind engaged in by Spinoza (and nineteenth-century German speculative Idealism and Romanticism). If marxist theory is a set of axioms or principles that governs the field that is capitalism, then the onset of the new phase that is "real subsumption" poses, urgently, the question of the compliance of this field with the axioms or principles that constitute marxism. Marxism is explicitly characterized by Deleuze and Guattari as an algorithm or axiomatic in the following passage:

If Marx demonstrated the functioning of capitalism as an axiomatic, it was above all in the famous chapter on the tendency of the rate of profit to fall. Capitalism is indeed an axiomatic, because it has no laws but immanent ones. It would like for us to believe that it confronts the limits of the Universe, the extreme limit of resources and energy. But all it confronts are its own limits (the periodic depreciation of existing capital); all it repels or displaces are its own limits (the formation of new capital, in new industries with a high rate of profit). This is the history of oil and nuclear power. And it does both at once: capitalism confronts its own limits and simultaneously displaces them, setting them down again farther along. (*TP*, pp. 463)

This passage provides an inkling of what it will take to resolve the question that underlies the (putative?) "crisis" of marxism, namely, how will we know that capitalism in its current manifestations is congruent with this axiomatic? This compliance or congruence can only be accounted for by a principle, a second-order principle, that is not "marxist"; and this is necessarily so because the applicability of marxism to this field can only be specified metatheoretically: it is this metatheoretical or "transcendental" specification that tells us in virtue of what conditions and principles is *this* field (i.e., capitalism) governed, universally and without exception, by *this* axiomatic (i.e., marxism).[22] The resort to a constitutive ontology of political practice on the part of Negri, and Deleuze, and Guattari can be seen as precisely the attempt to provide a metatheoretical elaboration of the kind just mentioned. But—and this is a question that needs to be posed in regard to Deleuze and Guattari at this point—what is the pertinence of this ontology for any conceivable reorientation of the marxist paradigm?

An undeniable accomplishment of the *Capitalism and Schizophrenia* project has been to put the topic of the modes of production back on the agenda for marxist scholarship. The intervention in marxist theory that goes under the name of the Frankfurt School has been in many ways an immensely productive one. But the Frankfurt School, in its much-publicized efforts to steer clear of the economic reductionism associated with a Second or Third International "vulgar marxism," tended to place a one-sided emphasis on the commodity-form and the commodity-fetish (and their effect on the consciousness of human beings dazed by the various culture industries). As a result, the Frankfurt School was disposed to give less weight in its analyses to the question of the nature and function(s) of the modes of production. The work of Deleuze and Guattari can therefore be viewed as a salutary rectification of this state of affairs (which is certainly not to suggest that this is how they themselves conceive of their task: the Frankfurt School is barely mentioned in any of their works).

Yet, while they deal with the modes of production in terms of a problematic that is central to their project, Deleuze and Guattari do not themselves ascribe any primacy, whether analytical or otherwise, to the modes of production as such. Instead they bestow this primacy on machinic processes, that is, the modes of organization that link all kinds of "attractions and repulsions, sympathies and antipathies, alterations, amalgamations, penetrations, and expressions that affect bodies of all kinds in their relations to one another" (*TP*, p. 90). The modes of production depend on these machinic processes (*TP*, p. 435). This is another way of saying that the modes of production are expressions of desire, that what is truly productive is desire, so that the modes of production are (merely) the outcome or derivation of this ceaselessly generative desire.[23] The mode of production is on the same level as any other expression of the modes of desire, in which case, as Brian Massumi points out, there is for Deleuze and Guattari neither base nor superstructure in society, but only stratifications, that is, accumulations or concatenations of ordered functions which are expressions of desire.[24] What enables each mode of production to be constituted is a specific aggregation of desires, forces, and powers: it is this accumulation that produces the mode (of production).

Deleuze and Guattari effectively reverse the traditional marxist conception of the mode of production: it is not the mode that enables production to take place (which is what the traditional account maintains); rather it is desiring production itself that constitutes this or that mode as the mode it is. It is therefore important for Deleuze and Guattari to resort to a practical ontology of desiring production, because it is this ontology that gives us the requisite account of the organization of productive desire. This sounds highly abstruse, but the insight expressed in this part of the *Capitalism and Schizophrenia* project is quite simple and indeed is perfectly congruent with what Marx himself said: namely, that it is necessary for society, in this case the state, to exist before capital can receive its condition of possibility; that a society/state with stockpiled labor has already to exist already if the extraction of surplus value is to take place.[25] As Deleuze and Guattari put it, it is the state that gives capital its "models of realization" (*TP*, p. 434). The politics that organizes the proletariat into a constitutively antagonistic productive force is what makes capitalist the "transcendental" (and other "nontranscendental") conditions of this politics of proletarian constitution. Before anything can be generated by capital there is politics, and this is why the resort to a materialist political ontology, involving in this case a turn to Spinoza (though Nietzsche and Bergson are just as central for Deleuze), is unavoidable.

Capitalism, on this conception, is an apparatus that transcodes or rearticulates a particular space of accumulation. Basic to the constitution of this space of accumulation is the organized labor power that is the enabling condition of accumulation. The aimed-for production of surplus value is made possible only by the ("prior") realization or regulated expenditure of labor power. It is the function of the state to organize its members into a particular kind of productive force, a force capable of generating surplus value. Deleuze and Guattari take the position of Pierre Clastres in making this point:

We follow Clastres when he demonstrates that the State is explained neither by a development of productive forces nor by a differentiation of political forces. It is the State, on the contrary, that makes possible the undertaking of large-scale projects, the constitution of surpluses, and the organization of the corresponding public functions. (*TP*, pp. 358-9)

The state uses its dominative power to bring together labor power and the conditions of labor, thereby enabling the production of surplus value. There is thus a constitutive antagonistic relation between labor and the state, and since the state supplies capital with its models of realization, this antagonism is necessarily one that holds also between labor and capital. Capitalism exists and maintains itself by organizing itself to control and subjugate this proletarian antagonism, and it is from this process of organization, hitherto undertaken by the apparatuses of the state, that surplus value is generated and accumulation is made possible. Capital and the state are under constant internal pressure to contain and defuse the antagonism that, "paradoxically," is the very thing that enables it to exist. The assemblages created and maintained by the state and capital create a collective subjectification which establishes the material aspects of the productive figures who generate surplus value and who thereby make production and accumulation possible.[26]

It should perhaps be noted here that the state form that uses its dominative power "directly" to regulate and suppress the proletarian antagonism is the one that prevailed prior to the onset of integrated world capitalism. In the age of integrated world capitalism the function of the state is still dominative, in that the state is required to regulate the flows of production and to reproduce the forms of accumulation. But this dominative power of the state is no longer mediatory (as had been the case prior to "real subsumption"), inasmuch as the state is not needed anymore to create and maintain classes and class fractions. Rather, the function of capitalist state in the current dispensation is to engage in the work of disaggregation, to segment (through administrative procedures and the use of media and informational systems) the countervailing powers that the proletariat has developed. Capital/state has a negative relationship to the forces and forms that oppose it. Where Negri is concerned this indicates that what marxism needs now is not "a theory of the capitalist mode of production and of the division of labour, but, quite simply, a theory of administrative functions and types of domination."[27] The state subserves the imperatives of capital by inserting—"reactively"—the countervailing initiatives of the proletariat into its system(s) of domination.

Here I think there is a divergence or at least a tension between Negri and Deleuze and Guattari. According to Negri, while it has always been the case that capital has specified the form of productive social cooperation presupposed by it, this form of social cooperation has not, until the current phase of "real subsumption," preexisted capitalism's economic and political movements. Negri is worth quoting at length on this point:

> In every moment of the development of the capitalist mode of production, capital has always proposed the form of cooperation. This form had to be functional with the form of exploitation, when it did not actually inhere within it. It was only on this basis that labor became productive. Likewise, in the period of primitive accumulation, when capital enveloped and constricted pre-existent labor forms to its own valorization, it was capital which posed the form of cooperation—as this consisted in the emptying of the pre-constituted connections of the traditional laboring subjects. Now, instead, the situation has changed completely. Capital has become a hypnotizing, bewitching force, a phantasm, an idol: around it revolve the radically autonomous processes of auto-valorization, and only political Power can succeed in forcing them, with the carrot or with the stick, to begin to be molded into capitalist form. The transfer of the economic into the political, which comes about here, and in global dimensions with respect to the productive social life, is accomplished not because the economic has become a less essential determinant, but only because the political can tear the economic away from the tendency which leads it to mix with the social and realize itself in auto-valorization. The political is forced to be the value-form of our society because the new laboring processes are founded on the refusal to work and the form of production is its crisis. The social worker's [i.e., the kind of worker created by "real subsumption"] productive cooperation is the consolidation of the refusal to work, it is the social trench where the producers defend themselves from exploitation. (1992, pp. 154–5)

Today, according to Negri, social cooperation is "autonomous" from the economic and the political—it is a condition of capital being able to constitute the economic and the political that it makes a prior appropriation of the social, that it "command" social cooperation. That is to say, for Negri command of the social is today a condition of the existence of capital (and this because capital has to manage the constitution of labor power, a constitution that extends throughout the socius), whereas in the past it was capital, expressed in the form of the economic and the political, that produced social cooperation. Negri sees the state as "the form in which the process of extracting surplus value takes place" (1989a, pp. 186–7). He also maintains (as we have seen) that in the phase of "real subsumption" the state has the function of symbolizing the world of social production (and thus segmenting that world and submitting it to the logic of capital) (1989a, p. 187).

The argument of Deleuze and Guattari seems to be somewhat different, at least when it comes to specifying the function of the state in capitalist production and accumulation. For them, the prior command of social cooperation has always been an "ontological" condition of any such production and accumulation (although of course the forms of this "ontological" condition are necessarily historically variable and specific). This is why for them the state emerged not with the development of agricultural societies but came into being even in hunter-gatherer groups during the Paleolithic Age— it was the state that commanded social cooperation and so made hunting and gathering into a productive "mode" (*TP*, pp. 429ff.). The state had to exist, qua capitalism's "model of realization," even before surplus labor and surplus value existed. The state, it would seem, has for Deleuze and Guattari never ever been "autonomous" in relation to the social, whereas it seems plausible to say that for Negri this imbrication of the state in the social is a development specific to the phase of "real subsumption." This is perhaps why Michael Hardt is right to suggest that, at least in regard to Negri's position, something like the dissolution of civil society is a defining feature of "real subsumption." At any rate, for Negri, the "withering away" of civil society is a condition for the state to cease being autonomous in relation to the social; whereas for the writers of *Capitalism and Schizophrenia* the demise of civil society is not something that necessarily enables the state to be imbricated in the social. For Deleuze and Guattari, the dissolution of civil society of course affects the character of the relation between the state and the social, but it does not serve as a condition of possibility for the imbrication of the former into the latter.[28]

A particular difficulty for someone who wants to insist on this particular difference or tension between Negri and Deleuze and Guattari is that Negri (as I have already indicated) does not try to situate capitalism in the frame of a universal history. I will refrain from speculating about what he would do with such a universal history, but it could be argued (as indeed I have just tried to) that what is truly significant in Negri's characterization of the phase of "real subsumption" is not so much the issue of the insertion per se of the state in the social (for, as Deleuze and Guattari suggest, there has always been an imbrication of this kind) but that in the phase of "real subsumption" the forms and functions of this confluence of the state and the social have been radically transformed, have acquired a character they never possessed before. In the foregoing discussion we have seen that this revolutionary transformation has, for Negri, involved the creation of the "society-state complex" (to use his term), and this is a situation that did not exist until the current phase of capitalist development.

Deleuze and Guattari likewise acknowledge a shift of this kind in the present capitalist conjuncture. They say that capitalism is an "independent, worldwide axiomatic that is like a single City, megalopolis, or 'megamachine' of which the States are parts, or neighborhoods." (*TP*, pp. 434–5). It is the function of each state today to "[group] together and [combine] several sectors, according to its resources, population, wealth, industrial capacity, etc." (*TP*, p. 434). Under capitalism, the state serves "to moderate the superior deterritorialization of capital and to provide the latter with compensatory reterritorializations" (*TP*, p. 455). The state becomes a site for the effectuation of capital, and it does this by reterritorializing flows that capitalism connects and deterritorializes (*TP*, p. 221). Capitalism will even sustain and organize states that are not viable, for its own purposes (mainly the crushing of minorities through integration and extermination) (*TP*, p. 472).

Capitalism today has the character of an "international ecumenical organization." It is the omnipresent, intermediate milieu that secures ("simultaneously") the isomorphism of even the most heterogeneous orders (commercial or economic, religious, artistic, etc.) (*TP*, pp. 435ff). In this milieu, productive labor is inserted in every component of society: the universality of capital is simultaneous with the ubiquity of everything that yields surplus value. Deleuze and Guattari hold that the absolute spatial division between exploiters and exploited posited by a more traditional marxism has been superseded. In the current phase, they, like Negri, believe that the whole of society is inserted seamlessly into capital's nexus of reproduction. The outcome is that

> today we can depict an enormous, so-called stateless, monetary mass that circulates through foreign exchange and across borders, eluding control by the States, forming a multinational ecumenical organization, constituting a de facto supranational power untouched by governmental decisions ... [Capitalism] has from the beginning mobilized a force of deterritorialization infinitely surpassing the deterritorialization proper to the State. For since Palaeolithic and Neolithic times, the State has been deterritorializing to the extent that it makes the earth an object of its higher unity, a forced aggregate of coexistence, instead of the free play of territories among themselves and with the lineages. But this is precisely the sense in which the State is termed "territorial." Capitalism, on the other hand, is not at all territorial, even in its beginnings; its

power of deterritorialization consists in taking as its object, not the earth, but "materialized labor," the commodity ... That is why capitalism marks a mutation in worldwide or ecumenical organizations, which now take on a consistency of their own ... From all these standpoints, it could be said that capitalism develops an economic order that could do without the State. (*TP*, pp. 453–4)

So, determining whether or not there is a tension or incompatibility between the accounts given by Negri and Deleuze and Guattari of the relation that capital has to the administrative forms that command the social is something that may or may not be an unproductive undertaking. But on the decisive question of the nature of this relation as it exists in late capitalism Negri, Guattari, and Deleuze share the conviction that capital today operates in a domain where the separation between state and society can no longer be maintained.

In the phase in which state and society constitute a single, unitary complex, the assemblages/apparatuses that make up this complex use a dominative power to secure the social cooperation that makes it possible for capital to operate. It is this cooperation that puts in place the conditions that enable production to have its "modes." In effect all capital has become social capital. The issue of the production of social cooperation—that is, social capital—thus becomes a crucial one for this line of marxist thought and practice.

Given this conception of the relation between the logic of social command and capital, the limits that circumscribe the production of social cooperation will also be the limits that circumscribe capitalism. We have seen that for Deleuze and Guattari capitalism's "ruse" is to get us to believe that its limits are coextensive with those of "the Universe" (*TP*, pp. 23–4).

In Negri's scheme of things, the limits of capital are coextensive with the limits of social capital and of subsumption, and these are constituted by the pervasive, "structural," antagonism that exists between capital and the socialized worker.[29] The question of the constitution of the socialized worker is therefore paramount: the limits to capitalism are set by the constitution of this worker. An inquiry into the limits of capitalism, in this scheme of things, will therefore take the form of an ontological specification of the constitution of the socialized worker. This "constitutive ontology" is an analytics (Negri in one place calls it a "phenomenology") that sets out to specify what powers, forces, and effects are received and disseminated by the socialized worker; it will specify the organization of the accumulations of these energies and impulses in the socialized worker.[30] And the writings of Spinoza are for Deleuze, Guattari, and Negri a rich (meta)theoretical resource the construction of this ontology.

It should perhaps be pointed out that Negri believes that this ontology of constitutive, countervailing power will enable him to overcome a limitation in the theories of power developed by Deleuze and Foucault (interestingly enough he does not mention Guattari in the course of making this criticism). According to Negri, the problem with the accounts of power provided by Deleuze and Foucault is that while they move in the right direction by understanding antagonism in terms of an ontology of productive force (as opposed to the dialectic), they nonetheless "err" in posing "the critique of power as a line of flight, as the splendor of the event and of the multitude, and they refuse to identify a constitutive Power which would be the organ of the subversive minority" (1992, p. 170).[31] The productive force identified by this ontology will be one that is subjected to nothing but itself and here we have the gist of Negri's important notion of *auto-valorization*.

So this, "finally," is the theoretical underpinning of the answer provided by Negri, Deleuze, and Guattari to the question posed at the start of this essay, namely, "What is it to live in a society completely constituted on the basis of freedom?" Their precise answer (and it is one that perforce can only be given metatheoretically), which is Spinoza's answer too, is: "It will be a society in which the productive force of its members is subject to nothing but itself."

In speaking of a metatheoretical reorientation of the marxist project along the lines I have discussed it must be stressed that this is only one possible route among several that can be taken if one is working within the kind of theoretical armature supplied by Negri, Deleuze, and Guattari. And here there is a great deal I have not talked about. For instance, it is clear from *Communists Like Us* that the accounts of constitutive power and collective subjectivity given by Guattari and Negri in that work can be approached via a theory of singularity. ("Singularity" being the category that more than any other goes beyond the "collective" versus "individual" polarity that is essential to the Hobbes-Rousseau-Hegel tradition of reflection on the state/sovereign.) This account of singularity, and here I have to be very brief and schematic, can in turn be connected up with the theory of simulation given in Deleuze's *Logique du sens* and *Différence et Répétition*; since for Deleuze simulation (or the simulacrum) is the basis of singularity.[32] In a universe of absolute singularities, production can only take the form of repetition: each singularity, in the course of production, can only repeat or proliferate itself. In production each simulacrum can only affirm its own difference, its distanciation from everything else. Production, on this account, is a ceaselessly proliferative distribution (of all the various absolute singularities).

Production is always repetition of difference, the difference of each thing from every other thing.

Capitalism, though, also embodies a principle of repetition. The axiomatic of capitalism is one predicated on identity, equivalence, and intersubstitutability (this being the underlying logic of the commodity form as analyzed by Marx). In which case, repetition in capitalism is always repetition of the nondifferent; or, rather, the different in capitalism is always only an apparent different, because it can be overcome and "returned," through the process of abstract exchange, to the same, the fungible. Capitalism, as the *Capitalism and Schizophrenia* project indicates, effects a deterritorialization only to make possible a more powerful reterritorialization: it breaches limits only in order to impose its own limits, which it "mistakenly" takes to be coextensive with those of the universe. The power of repetition in capitalism is therefore negative, wasteful, ultimately nonproductive. Capitalistic repetition is nonbeing in Spinoza's sense. An analysis of the commodity form along these lines will have to be provided as a complement to the account of production and constitution mentioned in this paper. But this, as they say, is another story.[33]

16

Mao's "On Contradiction," Mao-Hegel/Mao-Deleuze

Mao Tse-Tung's 1937 essay "On Contradiction" is a landmark contribution to Marxist philosophy, although it is more often praised than analyzed.[1] Mao, like Lenin and Marx before him, was interested in the logic(s) of change, and for all three "dialectical materialism" was the preeminent of these logics. For Marx, Lenin, and Mao, the defining feature of dialectical materialism as a logic of change was the pivotal role it gave to the notion of antagonism, cast by them in terms of contradiction. My aim in this paper is to give an account of Mao's position on contradiction, and then to suggest that his insights on this issue can be retained, more or less faithfully, if recast in terms of a post-Hegelian conception of antagonism, involving the replacement of contradiction by a suppler set of categories which encapsulate all the principles associated with antagonism, but without the conceptual and practical inflexibility built into the notion of contradiction. Mao greatly modified the Hegelian-Marxist notion of contradiction to take China's unique situation into account, but he was still beholden to an orthodoxy represented by these Hegelian-Marxist rubrics. That is to say, Mao was absolutely correct to say that historical, social, political, and economic processes are riven by antagonism, but, to depart from Mao, these antagonisms are not necessarily, or best, explained by the concept of contradiction.

For the Marxist philosopher, all the above-mentioned processes are in a state of constant transformation—transformations which reflect, even as they purport to resolve, the antagonisms integral to these processes. Mao sought ways to theorize the Chinese embodiment of these (for him, antagonistic and contradictory) transformations, at a level both abstract and yet attentive to the uniquely specific.

Mao begins "On Contradiction" by retaining Marx's insight that capitalism involves a social system beset by contradictions because the social classes within it have incompatible class-bound goals. Following Marx and Lenin, Mao said these incompatibilities would lead to class conflict, economic crisis, and eventually revolution. In this revolution, the existing order would be supplanted by the oppressed classes, who would now possess the means to obtain political power. To quote Mao:

> Changes in society are due chiefly to the development of the internal contradictions in society, that is, the contradiction between the productive forces and the relations of production, the contradiction between classes and the contradiction between the old and "the new," it is the development of these contradictions that pushes society forward and gives the impetus for the supersession of the old society by the new. (p. 70)

Mao believed, somewhat simplistically, that there were two opposing worldviews, which he called the "metaphysical" and the "dialectical-materialist" (pp. 68–71). The former, deeply idealist (in the pejorative sense), had long prevailed in both the east and west.

Again perhaps simplistically, Mao maintained that historical forces enabled the European proletariats to find their way toward dialectical materialism, while the European bourgeoisie remained resolutely immured in the realm of "metaphysical," and thus were unable to grasp how historical forces really operated. This blinded them to how exploitation takes place, not just in their own capitalist societies, but even in precapitalist societies (e.g., in slavery).

Mao next follows Lenin in suggesting that contradiction is universal:

> Contradiction exists in the process of development of all things, and ... in the process of development of each thing a movement of opposites exists from beginning to end .... There is nothing that does not contain contradiction; without contradiction nothing would exist .... Contradiction is universal and absolute, it is present in the process of development of all things and permeates every process from beginning to end. (pp. 72–4)

This, to say the least, is a highly metaphysical claim. Mao was of course addressing his argument to comrades in a revolutionary situation, in which volatile and ever-changing conditions were the norm. "Contradiction" was a theoretical tool available to him at that time and in that circumstance, one extremely useful for a sense-making of these conditions and his revolutionary political practice, especially the need to form a united front, between the Communists and their sworn enemies the Nationalists, to counter the invasion by Japan in 1937. Today, in very different circumstances and very different intellectual formations, we have the advantage of being able to use a different theoretical nomenclature to express (hopefully) Mao's insights into a revolutionary political practice, for our time as much as Mao's.

At the same time as he asserts the universality of contradiction, Mao acknowledges the sheer particularity inherent in the practical instances of contradiction:

> In considering each form of motion of matter, we must observe the points which it has in common with other forms of motion. But what is especially important and necessary, constituting as it does the foundation of our knowledge of a thing, is to observe what is particular to this form of motion of matter, namely, to observe the qualitative difference between this form of motion and other forms. Only when we have done so can we distinguish between things. Every form of motion contains within itself its own particular contradiction. This particular contradiction constitutes the particular essence which distinguishes one thing from another. (p. 76)

The flexibility in Mao's notion of contradiction comes to the fore in his discussion of the difference between the "the principal contradiction and principal aspect of contradiction." Under capitalism the principal contradiction is between the proletariat and the bourgeoisie, whereas in feudalism the principal contradiction was the one between the emerging bourgeoisie and the feudal overlords (p. 78). The former contradiction is resolved by the socialist revolution, the latter was overcome by the democratic revolution.

From the principal contradiction stem secondary contradictions ("its aspects"). For instance, according to Wang Hui the principal contradiction in China today is the one between entry into the capitalist world market ("globalization") and the project of a democratic socialism (Wang Hui 2016). From this primary contradiction other contradictions arise, such as the developmental disparity between regions (China's eastern coastal region and provinces in the far interior), a disparity between rural and urban incomes, and the growing disparity between the rich and poor. Another disparity is the one between China's two development models, the "Guangdong model" (focused on export-oriented development) and the "Chongqing model" (focused on internally driven development).

Mao said that "processes change, old processes and old contradictions disappear, new processes and new contradictions emerge, and the methods of resolving contradictions differ accordingly" (p. 78). With such change, what was a secondary contradiction can become a principal contradiction, and vice versa.

Mao emphasizes the need to pay the utmost attention to the often complex and not always self-evident relationships between the primary and secondary contradictions, since only in this way can the revolutionary find ways conducing to their "resolution." The revolutionary response to such an upheaval in the always specific configuration of contradictions involved has necessarily and unavoidably to be political:

> When we speak of understanding each aspect of a contradiction, we mean understanding what specific position each aspect occupies, what concrete forms it assumes in its interdependence and in its contradiction with its opposite, and what concrete methods are employed in the struggle with its opposite, when the two are both interdependent and in contradiction, and also after the interdependence breaks down. It is of great importance to study these problems. Lenin meant just this when he said that the most essential thing in Marxism, the living soul of Marxism, is the concrete analysis of concrete conditions. (p. 79)

Mao at this point is a firm Hegelian, retaining Hegel's stress on identity and unity, even while acknowledging difference. A contradiction depends on the existence of one or more of its opposites, complexity thus involves an increased number of these opposites, simplicity only one or a few of them:

> Without life, there would be no death; without death, there would be no life. Without "above," there would be no "below," without "below," there would be no "above." Without misfortune, there would be no good fortune; without good fortune, there would be no misfortune. Without facility, there would be no difficulty; without difficulty, there would be no facility. Without landlords, there would be no tenant-peasants; without tenant-peasants, there would be no landlords. Without the bourgeoisie, there would be no proletariat; without the proletariat, there would be no bourgeoisie. Without imperialist oppression of nations, there would be no colonies or semi-colonies; without colonies or semi-colonies, there would be no imperialist oppression of nations. It is so with all opposites. (p. 94)

Identity differentiates the contradictions, and establishes a space for the antagonism between the contradictions. Identity is thus the underlying basis for the maintenance of contradictions.

Identity has a second characteristic—in the appropriate situation, the contradictory aspects within a thing can be transformed into their opposite, and when this occurs an aspect changes "its position to that of its opposite" (p. 94). Mao at this point posits what is clearly a metaphysical logic:

> By means of revolution the proletariat, at one time the ruled, is transformed into the ruler, while the bourgeoisie, the erstwhile ruler, is transformed into the

ruled and changes its position to that originally occupied by its opposite. This has already taken place in the Soviet Union, as it will take place throughout the world. If there were no interconnection and identity of opposites, in given conditions, how could such a change take place? (pp. 94–5)

For all Mao's emphasis on the concreteness of revolutionary praxis, is there not something of an incipient teleology at work in his argument, precisely because of his staunch a priori adherence to the principle of "the identity of opposites"? If revolutionary agency is "contained" within an a priori metaphysical logic, is the latter not somehow bound within the terms of this logic?

My (undogmatic) intuition here is that Mao was invoking this Hegelian-Marxist-Leninist theoretical armature because it had been employed so fruitfully in the most successful revolution at that point in the twentieth century (the October Revolution of 1917), and that even as he did this, he sought to widen it in profound and original ways when adapting it to China's proto-revolutionary circumstances.

This is clear from the admittedly brief section of Mao's essay titled "The Place of Antagonism in Contradiction" (2007c), where for me he undoes, fundamentally, the metaphysical logic that had guided him up to this point. To quote him:

> We must make a concrete study of the circumstances of each specific struggle of opposites and should not arbitrarily apply the formula discussed above [the identity of opposites] to everything. Contradiction and struggle are universal and absolute, but the methods of resolving contradictions, that is, the forms of struggle, differ according to the differences in the nature of the contradictions. Some contradictions are characterized by open antagonism, others are not. In accordance with the concrete development of things, some contradictions which were originally non-antagonistic develop into antagonistic ones, while others which were originally antagonistic develop into non-antagonistic ones. (p. 100)

Mao makes it clear here that contradiction and antagonism do not imply each other, and that there are contradictions which do not "mature" into antagonisms. An antagonism develops when a contradiction, hitherto dormant in its manifestations, grows into an openly visible enmity.

In his 1957 essay "On the Correct Handling of Contradictions among the People" (2007c), Mao, with a successful revolutionary insurrection having by now taken place in China, still acknowledged, with uncanny Althusserian echoes, that communist China was even then not without its contradictions, and that indeed "such struggles will never end" (p. 155). Also in this essay, the phrase "the unity of antagonism" was developed alongside "the identity or unity of contradiction"—antagonism existed between communism/socialism and their enemies, whereas contradictions (which Mao said were non-antagonistic) still existed in the worker–peasant alliance that was revolutionary China's bedrock (as the Cultural Revolution showed a few years later, Mao was being somewhat optimistic in calling this situation "non-antagonistic"). Writing and speaking in 1957, Mao was very alert to the 1956 Hungarian uprising, and thus conscious of the importance of acknowledging that while contradictions exist in a communist society, these contradictions nonetheless do not reach the point of antagonism, the latter a not absolutely convincing claim, given that the Cultural Revolution that was to take place a few years later.

Mao's 1957 essay addressed, sometimes in a very forthright manner, the social and economic impasses existing in communist China. At the same time, with the Hungarian situation in mind, Mao was concerned to show the Chinese people he accepted the existence of contradictions in China's communist project (which the Hungarian communist leadership had failed to do in its abject kneeling before the USSR), while mitigating or even denying the possible mutation in China of these contradictions into outright antagonisms (which had of course reached the point of explosion in Hungary). As a result, the central tenets of "dialectical materialism" are applied more loosely and flexibly in the 1957 essay, in contrast to its 1937 counterpart, which had of course addressed many of the same themes as the 1957 essay.

Given all this, is there a more productive way to conceptualize antagonism in the revolutionary conjuncture, both Mao's and the ones confronted by such present-day revolutionaries as Subcomandante Marcos (a university teacher in philosophy who wrote his dissertation on Althusser and Foucault)?

Let a Hundred Flowers Blossom, Let a Hundred Schools of Thought Contend—Mao Tse-Tung

As Mao himself said, the notions of contradiction and antagonism do not imply each other. This suggests the possibility of developing a concept of antagonism freed of the theoretical shackles imposed by the dialectical method, and its key category of contradiction.

Some forms of antagonism involve contradiction, many others do not. Mao was only concerned with contradictions which do or do not ensue in antagonism, but it would be helpful if we considered the reverse possibility, namely, that many antagonisms do not necessarily involve contradiction.

Here it is important to safeguard against anachronism. There is no way the historical Mao can be cast, or recast, as a Deleuzean—this would be stupid, as stupid as depicting the historical Ho Chi Minh or Che Guevara as Deleuzeans.

Better, therefore, to refer to Mao from now on in this essay as an embodied form of consciousness, a conceptual persona, and to see if this form of consciousness or conceptual persona can be rendered compatible with an "Deleuzean inflection of Mao-consciousness as 'Mao-Deleuze' (as opposed to, say, the very different 'Mao-Hegel' of full-blown dialectical contradiction)." That is to say, can there be something approximating to a political materialism, as opposed to a dialectical materialism in which contradiction always forms a theoretical and practical arch over antagonism?

In according primacy to the notion of antagonism, we are remaining faithful to Mao's central insight that the most important feature of any materialism is "the concrete development of things" (Mao 2007a, p. 100).

It is axiomatic that antagonisms are bound up with configurations of power and force—if X and Y are antagonists in a relation of aversion or hostility toward each other, then X and Y transmit and receive forces accordant with aversion of hostility, even if these are merely ideational or verbal. Of course, every living thing, qua living entity, receives and transmits forces—bright sunlight impinging on an eye (which then transmits its own force by blinking), heavy rain falling on a leaf (which then transmits its own force by curling up to reduce the impact of the rain), and so on. Hostility or aversion are therefore specific modalities of the forces transmitted in an antagonistic relationship, just as conviviality and affection are specific modalities of the forces involved in a friendly relationship, and so forth.

Every reception and transmission of forces constitutes an event or assemblage, which is unique in its particularity. Take the event that is the 1917 October Revolution. This is really a mega-event, or event of events—involved here is the event we may term "Lenin" (which in turn is made up of other events), one termed "Trotsky" (likewise made up of other events), one termed "Tsar Nicholas II" (an event which transmits and receives radically different forces from "acting at the behest of the Bolsheviks," the events of this or that counter-revolutionary acting on behalf of the Tsar, the events of this or that spectator of a revolutionary episode (the seizing of a railway station, the arrest of a police chief loyal to the Tsar)), and so forth.

What Lenin and the Bolsheviks did, in conjunction with myriad others, was to harness and configure the forces available at that time to constitute the event subsequently known as "the October Revolution." Mao and his cohorts, in his army as well as the countless peasants who supported the army, likewise undertook an "eventive constitution" of the above-mentioned kind in China's communist revolution.

These revolutionary events were irruptions that broke into and broke up a prevailing order. These irruptions, although Lenin and Mao believed them to have a structure graspable in terms of the dialectic, really did not possess any such structure. Unless one assumes the virtual tautology that, under capitalism, forces transmitted by this or that capitalist structure or formation are always in a position to be countered by countervailing forces. Self-employed contractors stiffed by Donald Trump may only know of Marx by name, but they summon the merest countervailing forces the moment they sue Trump. Of course, it would be fanciful to pretend that this pushing back against Trump creates by itself potentials for revolution, but what Lenin and Mao, in their place and time, accomplished was an orchestration of antagonistic forces on a scale massive enough to precipitate a revolution. They did not need the dialectic to bring about this truly immense event.

What enabled the constitution of revolutionary forces in Russia and China was a combination of enabling conditions and a plenitude of forms of agency capable of mobilizing in these conditions. The dialectic is in essence a fiction intended to mobilize agency, by positing initial a priori contradictions, which may or may not ensue in antagonisms, that could then be mapped onto actually existing historical and political conditions. The dialectic is an idealized template for revolutionary practice, no less but no more. Both Lenin and Mao embarked on their revolutionary projects with the aim of capturing state power. This conception of revolution as state capture—involving the take over of the railways, tv and radio stations, post offices, and ultimately the parliament and presidential palace, etc.—has run its course.

Revolution today, for a Mao-Deleuze, will be more complex and multi-faceted than the ones brought about by Mao and Lenin—some aspects of it may be state-centered, but many of its components will come from mobilized concatenations of diverse "micro-experiences" (to use Raul Zibechi's term in his (2011)) not premised on the conquest of the state.

A theorization of revolution not predicated (entirely) on capturing state power will have as its focal point the irruptive event (which may fail or succeed as the basis for revolution), an event having the potentially countless attributes of antagonism (Mao-Deleuze), but without any overarching dialectical contradiction (Mao-Hegel). Mao-Hegel (and Marx!) had as his theoretico-practical terrain a capitalist system of accumulation bound up with a manifest imperialism and colonialism, whereas Mao-Deleuze operates in a terrain defined by neoliberalism and globalization (albeit possessing features belonging to a neocolonialism). Both terrains have deeply entrenched modes of capitalist expropriation and exploitation, but they operate with different politico-economic logics and ontological bases. In both cases, though, a Marxist analytical framework remains deeply salient.

The main shift required here is abandoning the dialectic as something of a transcendental entity underpinning Mao's (and Lenin's) ontology of revolutionary political practice. We note here that Mao endorses Lenin's statement that "dialectics in the proper sense is the study of contradiction in *the very essence of objects*" (Lenin (1958), p. 249). Instead of the dialectic (and its absolute reliance on the principle of contradiction or negation), we need a much more flexible and fluid mode of conceptual and practical organization which does justice to the dispositions of power and force operative in the present-day conjuncture, as opposed to the ones operating over a hundred years ago (Lenin) and eighty years ago (Mao). Historical context is of crucial importance here. While Mao was explicit in his disavowal of a mechanistic materialism, his writings on revolutionary practice focus overwhelmingly on the importance of objective processes, and the part played by "science" in validating knowledge of these processes. Processes identified as "subjective," even when these are generated collectively, do not receive much attention—in nearly every instance, subjectivity for Mao is individual or individualistic, and only the object and objectivity lend themselves to embodiments that are collective. Mao-Deleuze will seek to rectify this theoretico-practical imbalance (Deleuze and Guattari, *TP*, p. 90).

Mao-Hegel must give way to Mao-Deleuze; that is, the philosophy which prizes differentiation based on negation must give way to one that does justice to aleatory encounters, incommensurabilities, heterogeneities, and irruptions and disruptions that rupture prevailing socio-economic formations. It should, in the words of Deleuze and Guattari, link all kinds of "attractions and repulsions, sympathies, and antipathies, alterations, amalgamations, penetrations, and expressions that affect bodies of all kinds in their relations to one another" (*TP*, p. 90).

Before any surplus value can be realized by capital there is politics; that is, the strategic employment of various assortments of force, and hence an ontology of force (as opposed to one dealing primarily with contradiction), is central and unavoidable. Force is generated and shaped by desire, which is always social and collective. As Deleuze and Guattari argue, it is desire that makes the gun into a weapon of war, or sport, or hunting, depending on extant circumstances (*TP*, pp. 89–90). Desire is endlessly productive.

This recourse to a practical ontology of desiring production, derived from Deleuze and Guattari, is essential if we are to account for the organization of a productive desire that is revolutionary. All this sounds highly recondite, but the principle invoked here simply elaborates what Marx himself had said, namely, that a society of the appropriate kind has to exist before capitalist appropriation of a commensurate kind can take place, so that a society/state with already positioned labor of the appropriate kind has to exist if the realization of surplus value is to take place in that society. Put a Mongolian nomad-herder in a BMW car factory in today's Stuttgart and they will be in no position to realize surplus value, just as a cave-dweller would not know what a medieval wind mill was, let alone be able to use it to create surplus value.

Capitalism today is an immense array of apparatuses, operating on many levels at a planetary scale, that, thanks to globalization, today encompasses all reachable spaces of accumulation—as a result, its functioning is due to more than just the operation of forces at the institutional level of organizations and formations. Hence the need for the ontology of constitutive power which conceptualizes force, and not just in regard to its role in creating and consolidating a planetary-wide regime of accumulation.

Let us be reminded at this point of how Mao envisaged dialectical materialism's distinctive features:

> The Marxist philosophy of dialectical materialism has two outstanding characteristics. One is its *class nature*: it openly avows that dialectical materialism is in the service of the proletariat. The other is its *practicality*: it emphasizes the dependence of theory on practice, emphasizes that theory is based on practice and in turn serves practice. The truth of any knowledge or theory is determined not by subjective feelings, but by objective results in social practice. Only social practice can be the criterion of truth. The standpoint of practice is the primary and basic standpoint in the dialectical materialist theory of knowledge. (2007b, p. 54. Emphases are mine.)

This conceptualization of force we are about to identify with Mao-Deleuze, in retaining Mao's emphasis on practicality and those who create surplus value for capitalism (Mao's proletariat), also encompasses two complementary facets: on one hand, the ways in which this force enables at once the emergence and consolidation of the various forms of collective subjectivity (as was pointed out, Mao-Hegel dealt primarily with the dialectical object, and hardly at all with the formation of collective subjectivity); on the other hand, the ways in which these forms make possible the means for capitalism to fashion the kinds of collective subjectivity required for collective functioning.

Next, we have to follow Deleuze (and Guattari) in connecting the notion of force with the concept of a singularity, primarily because it takes a psychic investment, and thus the activation of a force or ensemble of forces, to constitute a singularity. (The *locus classicus* of this account of psychic or libidinal investment in the writings of Deleuze and Guattari is their *Anti-Oedipus*.)

If the universe is composed of absolute singularities, then production, any kind of production, can only take the form of repetition: each singularity, as production unfolds, can only repeat or propagate itself. In production, each singularity can only express its own difference, its distance or proximity, from everything else. Production, on this view which is adapted for Mao-Deleuze, is a ceaselessly proliferating distribution of all the myriad absolute singularities. Desiring production is thus necessarily repetition of difference, the difference of each singularity from everything else, while these singularities are capable at the same time of being brought together in assemblages that constitute social groupings such as classes, clans, extended families, and nations.

Capitalism, however, also requires the operation of repetition. A capitalist logic, premised as it is on the notion of the exchange of commodities, can only base itself on notions of identity, equivalence, and intersubstitutivity, as Marx himself pointed out in his analysis of the logic of the commodity form. This being so, capitalist repetition is always repetition of the sheerly nondifferent; the different in capitalism can never be more than the mere appearance of difference, because capitalist difference can always be overcome, and returned through the processes of abstract exchange, to what is always the same, the utterly fungible. (You buy a Toyota Corolla, I buy a Nissan Sentra, both of which are virtually identical in terms of appearance and performance, and yet the capitalist car companies who sell them must convince us that a world of difference, simulated of course, exists between the Toyota and Nissan. Mao-Hegel never was in the position of having to address this aspect of the capitalist simulacrum.)

Capitalism, and this is a decisive principle in Deleuze and Guattari's *Capitalism and Schizophrenia* project, only transforms in order to bring about a more powerful recuperation through exchange and exchange value. When capitalism breaches limits, it does so only in order to impose its own limits, which it projects as the limits of the universe (e.g., saying to us "only when the planet runs out of oil, coal, aluminum, etc.," but actually meaning "only when it is no longer viable for capitalists to extract oil, coal, aluminum, etc."). The power of repetition in capitalism is therefore entirely negative, wasteful, and lacking in any really productive force.

Any collective subjectivity constituted on the basis of this form of repetition will not be able to advance the cause of emancipation. The challenge, at once philosophical and political, posed by Mao-Deleuze has therefore to do with the supersession of this capitalist repetition by forms of a genuinely productive repetition that can break beyond the limits imposed on emancipation by those who rule us. Only force, that is, politics, which of course is not the same as violence (at least not necessarily), can accomplish this.

For Mao-Deleuze, therefore, the ontology of this anti-capitalist power of counter-constitution must take the form of an ontology of force, as opposed to contradiction. It will therefore eschew the dialectics of Mao-Hegel.

In whatever embodiment, Mao Tse-Tung is immensely significant—he was the first theorist of capitalism, with the possible exception of Nikolai Bukharin, to grasp the centrality of exploited peasants in the production of surplus value. On his theoretical shoulders stand such diverse contemporary Marxists as Samir Amin and Michael Taussig.

Notes

Chapter 1

1   Gilles Deleuze, "On Philosophy," in *N*, p. 136. The difficulty in writing on Deleuze's thought (as opposed to that of, say, Aristotle or Descartes or even Hegel) is that what he takes for granted is generally what we too will be disposed to take readily for granted, since his world is precisely our world, and vice versa.
2   The passage which contains Foucault's remark is perhaps worth quoting in full:

> I must discuss two books of exceptional merit and importance: *Différénce et répétition* and *Logique du sens*. Indeed these books are so outstanding that they are difficult to discuss; this may explain, as well, why so few have undertaken this task. I believe that these works will continue to revolve about us in enigmatic resonance with those of Klossowski, another major and excessive sign, and perhaps one day, this century will be known as Deleuzean.

See Foucault, "Theatrum Philosophicum," 1977a, p. 165. Foucault's essay originally appeared in *Critique*, #282 (1970), pp. 885–908. Interestingly enough, given his protracted engagement with Kant's thought, Foucault's own writings could be said to have an "enigmatic resonance" with the treatment of the three transcendentals afforded by the *Critiques*: the early histories of "mentalities" (*Les mots et les choses* and *L'archéologie du savoir*) have an affinity with *The Critique of Pure Reason* (dealing with judgment and truth), the works on disciplinary institutions and formations (the asylum, the prison, the clinic) align with *The Critique of Practical Reason* (dealing with duty or the good), and the late works on the aesthetics of existence (notably the three published volumes of *Histoire de la sexualité*) accord with *The Critique of Judgment* (dealing with beauty).
3   The obverse of this myth is that all philosophy culminated in Heidegger or Wittgenstein or whoever, a claim that is just as problematic as the complementary myth of origination.
4   Here I have in mind the following passage from Deleuze's *NP* (pp. 88–9): "Does the recuperation of religion stop us being religious? By turning theology into anthropology, by putting man in God's place, do we abolish the essential, that is to say, the place?" In other words, a truly critical philosophy would not seek simply to reverse the fundamental oppositions God-man, theology-anthropology, etc., but it would, more radically, abolish the very place from which these reversals emerge and from which they derive their force.

5 An excellent summary of these accomplishments and their import is to be found in the *Radical Philosophy* memorial symposium. See Patton, Braidotti, and Macey (1996), pp. 2–6.

   The reader familiar with Deleuze will know that several of the works associated with these achievements were coauthored with Félix Guattari. After the publication of *L'Anti-Oedipe* in 1972 it becomes virtually impossible to separate their accomplishments in terms of authorship, although of course both continued to publish individually. The neologism "deleuzoguattarian thought" has sometimes been used in the secondary literature to convey this conjugation of thought that defeats the imputation of individual authorship and all that that entails. I have avoided using this neologism here, but think it important to acknowledge the force and magnitude of Guattari's contribution to "Deleuzean thought," a thought that could never have been what it turned out to be had it been absolutely Deleuze's *own* (as he himself made clear when he acknowledged the crucial "intercessory" import of Guattari's thinking for him).

6 My point here is that the philosopher "expresses" worlds associated with this or that image of thought, and that some of these worlds can be expressed by a particular philosophy that happens to be congruent with that world or those worlds, but not by one that lacks this congruence. Hence, a Deleuze expresses our world, but not an Aristotle or Descartes—at any rate, this will be an implication of my argument. For Deleuze's notion of an image of thought as a kind of prephilosophical understanding that is the presupposition of philosophy, see the interview "On Philosophy," in *N*, pp. 135–55.

7 That the scope of *Capitalisme et schizophrénie* is putatively "world-historical" in a way that is "para-Hegelian" is perhaps evident from such remarks of Deleuze as: "*Délire* is world-historical … It fastens on the Chinese, the Germans, Joan of Arc and the Great Mogul, Aryans and Jews, money, power, and production …." See "*On Anti-Oedipus*," in *N*, p. 20.

8 See Deleuze, *FLB*. Deleuze links the rise of the Baroque with a specific crisis in capitalism (p. 110) and maintains that the "Baroque introduces a new kind of story … in which description replaces the object, the concept becomes narrative, and the subject becomes point of view or subject of expression" (p. 127). The "moment" of the Baroque is thus transposable: as an "operative conception" and not an "essence," the Baroque can come to have more than one place of realization, and so, according to Deleuze, it can come to reside in the latter part of the twentieth century. Calabrese (1992) has a suggestive discussion of these connections. Calabrese invokes the six features of the rhizome of Deleuze and Guattari—"multiple connectability at every point, heterogeneity of all components of the system, multiplicity without the generating unity, rupture without significance, cartographability, and transfer"—and takes them to evince a "*constructed* asystemicity" (his italics) seen by him to be emblematic of the new Baroque (p. 140).

9   For more on "the fold," see also Deleuze, F. The Deleuzean "fold" is perhaps best viewed as an allegory of "the always between," a ceaselessly mobile "between" which connects quite disparate entities and states. On page 13 of *FLB* Deleuze refers to Leibniz's conceptual vocabulary and gives as examples of such very different entities "inorganic bodies," "organisms," "animal souls," "reasonable souls," etc. Cyberspaces are of course computer driven, interactive feedback loops enfolding immense numbers and types of biological and technological components or dimensions. I have discussed these matters more fully in connection with the so-called globalization of culture in my (1995), from which this part of my essay is taken in modified form.

10 This much is evident from Serres (1995). Serres's characterization of philosophy is worth quoting in full:

> The philosopher is pulled between two poles—that of maximal accumulation of all knowledge and experience and, at the other extreme, the cancellation of all knowledge and experience, starting from zero ... Philosophy works on a two-layered cone, occupying its apex. I see the encyclopedia on the first layer, and, on the second, nothing—learned unknowing, the suspension of judgment, solitude, questioning, doubt, incertitude, reconstruction starting from zero. Philosophy is not a body of knowledge nor a discipline among the sciences, because it insists on this balance between everything and nothing. A philosophical work necessarily contains everything, and then everything starting from nothing, through a newness obtained by this leap aside. Thus, the difficulty is double and redoubtable: it concerns the accumulation of the totality and the foreignness of the leap aside. (p. 90)

11 These transformations have important implications for any attempt to extend the marxist paradigm in ways that take into account the latest phase of capitalist development. I have discussed some of these implications in my (1996). Also interesting are the essays in Ash Amin (1994) and Sklair (1994).

12 Samir Amin (1994), pp. 11ff. To quote Amin on the crisis of the system of accumulation that existed from 1945 to 1975:

> The crisis began in the capitalist West and called into question the myth of unlimited growth, with 1968 as the decisive turning point. The subsequent years offered hope for a possible revival of a Western left stupefied by a pro-imperialist recruitment from the end of the nineteenth century. Such hopes were rapidly extinguished in inconsistent projects. By 1980 the way was open for a neoliberal offensive that held sway but could not lead the Western societies out the dark tunnel of prolonged crisis or revive the illusions of unlimited growth.
>
> In turn a hardening of North-South relations accompanying the crisis of capitalist accumulation hastened the disillusionment with developmentalism in the third world. Radical regimes collapsed one after the other and surrendered to reactionary structural adjustment policies imposed by the West during the

1980s. The collapse was the result not of external aggression but a combination of the internal contradictions of the Bandung project and a new external crisis accompanying the overthrow of the existing world system.

The failure of the Bandung project also revealed the weakness of Soviet support. Sovietism ... had the most shattering collapse. The edifice seemed so solid that conservative ideologies described it as "irreversible totalitarianism." But it was gnawed away from within and collapsed in the space of a few months ... Here too ... collapse resulted from a dramatic acceleration in the Soviet Union's "conventional" capitalism, as well as from external factors, namely, Washington's victory in the arms race. (pp. 15–16)

13 The claim that marxism is an algorithm or set of axioms is made in *TP*:

If Marx demonstrated the functioning of capitalism as an axiomatic, it was above all in the famous chapter on the tendency of the rate of profit to fall. Capitalism is indeed an axiomatic, because it has no laws but immanent ones. It would like for us to believe it confronts the limits of the Universe, the extreme limit of resources and energy. But all it confronts are its own limits (the periodic depreciation of capital); all it repels or displaces are its own limits (the formation of new capital, in new industries with a high rate of profit). This is the history of oil and nuclear power. And it does both at once: capitalism confronts its own limits and simultaneously displaces them, setting them down further along. (p. 463)

14 Deleuze undertook a similar "transcendental" inquiry in regard to Freud in his *M*, pp. 112–13.
15 To quote from Deleuze's essay "On Philosophy," cited in note 1 above: "If our book [*Anti-Oedipus*] was significant, coming after '68, it's because ... we weren't trying to articulate or reconcile different dimensions but trying rather to find a single basis for a production that was at once social and desiring in logic of flows" (p. 144).
16 Deleuze and Guattari, *WP*, see especially p. 64.
17 The sense that the various projects of Deleuze (and Guattari) culminate in a kind of autopoesis is given in Foucault's famous Preface to *Anti-Oedipus*, and also most directly, indeed explicitly, in Guattari's last book (1995). This translation, it simply has to be said, is barely readable.

Deleuze has always made it clear in his interviews that he prefers to characterize his intellectual itineraries and work in this "eventive" way rather than in terms of a more conventional approach that deals with a thinker's influences, formation, shifts of interest, trajectory of publication, etc. See, in addition to *N*, Deleuze and Claire Parnet, *D*.

18 This preference for geography over history is most evident in *Mille plateaux*, although it comes through clearly in the following remark from "Many Politics" in *D*:

> The great geographical adventures of history are lines of flight, that is, long expeditions on foot, on horseback or by boat: that of the Hebrews in the desert, that of Genseric the Vandal crossing the Mediterranean, that of the nomads across the steppe, the long march of the Chinese—it is always a line of flight that we create; not, indeed, because we imagine that we are dreaming but, on the contrary, because we trace out the real on it, we compose there a plane of consistence. To flee, but in fleeing seeking a weapon. (pp. 135–6)

I am mindful here of the critique made by Antonio Negri of the accounts of power developed by Foucault and Deleuze. According to Negri, their accounts are problematic because they "pose the critique of power as a line of flight, as the splendor of the event and of the multitude, and they refuse to identify a constitutive Power which would be the organ of the subversive minority." See Negri (1992), p. 170. Although Negri notes in fairness that both Deleuze and Foucault were at the time of their respective deaths seeking to push their thought beyond this understanding of antagonism purely in terms of the line of flight.
19 See Paul Patton's obituary notice (1996), pp. 2–3.
20 I discuss this notion of concept-image-narrative more fully in Chapter 5.
21 It is not possible for me to develop this point here, but given the admittedly brief references in their writings to the work of Wilfred Bion and Donald Winnicott, there are significant resonances between the "object relations" theories of these British writers and Deleuze and Guattari. Bion and Winnicott (Bion especially) emphasize the role of intermediate links between desire or drive and instinct and concept or idea.
22 Antonio Negri (1996).
23 Deleuze, "Many Politics," in *D*, pp. 124–5.
24 Deleuze, *FLB*, pp. 130ff.
25 There is now a whole genre of anthropological writing that deals with this cross-cultural transposition of artifacts and forms. See, for instance, David Richards (1994) and Fritz Kramer (1993).
26 Here I have tried to convey in a rather leaden way the insight contained in the following passage from *LS*:

> Singularities are the true transcendental events, and Ferlinghetti calls them "the fourth person singular." Far from being individual or personal, singularities preside over the genesis of individuals and persons; they are distributed in a "potential" which admits neither Self nor I, but which produces them by actualizing or realizing itself, although the figures of this actualization do not at all resemble the realized potential. (pp. 102–3)

I have also benefitted from a reading of Agamben (1993) where a similar account of singularity is to be found.
27 *TP*, p. 203.

Chapter 2

1. It could be argued that a more serviceable substitute for "ontology" would be the French *problematique*, which conveys the sense that what we have in Deleuze is not something to be identified with this or that philosophical position (although this can be done), but rather by the attentiveness to a particular array of problems, whose conceptualizations are always undertaken when we are perforce "in the middle" (that favorite expression of Deleuze's), so that movement and a ceaselessly oscillating displacement/emplacement mark both the ensuing conceptualizations and their putative objects.
2. The impetus here to view the ontological dimensions of Deleuze's project in terms of a "problematic" is inspired in part by Daniel W. Smith's lapidary treatment of Deleuze's own category of "the problematic." On this see Smith, "The New," in his (2012), see especially the section titled "The Problematic, the Virtual, and the Intensive," pp. 250–5. Also helpful has been James Williams, "Distinguishing Problems from Questions," in his (2005), pp. 129–51.
3. We should recall that Deleuze is for Badiou not really the self-avowed proponent of multiplicity that he is typically and invariably taken to be by most commentators. See Badiou (1999). Badiou's reading of Deleuze receives a trenchant corrective in Clayton Crockett (2013).
4. See Sen (1977).
5. On the "crystalline regime," see *TI*, 127. See also Deleuze (1989c).
6. On the "organic regime," see *MI*, p. 11.
7. On the "power of the false," see *NP*, pp. 184–5. For helpful and interesting elaborations of this concept, see Flaxman (2011) and Massumi (1987).
8. Deleuze, "Immanence: A Life," in *PI*, p. 31.
9. On the virtual, see the entry "virtuel" in Zourabichvili (2003), pp. 89–91.
10. This incitement and solicitation is the function of the "attractor" that Deleuze and Guattari borrow from chaos theory. On the attractor, see Protevi (2006). Attractors not only establish new trajectories or lines of flight, but the interactions between attractors create new mutations in the attractors themselves, creating what Deleuze and Guattari call a "generalized chromatism."
11. On the three syntheses, see *AO*, pp. 1–21.
12. Patton (1996).
13. Deleuze and Guattari, *TP*, p. 203.

Chapter 3

1. It is tempting to think that Deleuze's seeming eschewal of materialism (but not empiricism) has something to do with a sense of wanting to stay as far away as possible from the aporiae of the hylomorphic formula that have bedeviled

Western philosophy since the time of Aristotle: that is, the view that the objects we experience and understand have as the condition of their constitution the imposition of form (*morphe*) on matter (*hyle*). The basis of this formula, even when repudiated, persists as a kind of tainted residue, since it is hard to dispel the notion, or philosophic curse even, that matter is inert and formless. But this is certainly not what a materialism is about, whether it be Fredric Jameson's depiction of it in terms of the *practices* of de-idealization, or an approximate Deleuzean view of it in terms of the *processes* or *events* of materialization. Both views are greatly distanced from the merely commonsensical superstition that matter in its essence is just "stuff." I'll try to develop this approximate Deleuzean materialism here, bearing in mind Deleuze's cautionary stipulation that "the event by itself is problematic and problematizing" (*LS*, p. 54). For Jameson, see his (1993), especially p. 175.

2   The sections below are indebted to *LS*, pp. 148–53; and *DR*, pp. 168–221.
3   A fuller discussion of Deleuze's understanding of the concept-narrative-image is provided in Chapter 5.
4   Sean Bowden, in his excellent (2011) quite rightly says that the Stoics were "the first philosophers to consider events as ontologically irreducible to 'things', whether material or ideal" (p. 17).
5   On Deleuze's anti-Platonism, expressed in the affirmation "The task of modern philosophy has been defined: to overturn (*renversement*) Platonism," see *DR*, p. 59. See also *LS*, pp. 53, 132, 253, 256, 262–3, 265. For helpful discussion of Deleuze's anti-Platonism, see Daniel W. Smith, "Platonism," in his (2012), pp. 3–26.
6   For Badiou's critique of Deleuze, see his (1999).
7   On the three syntheses of time, see *DR*, pp. 70–128. For helpful commentary, see James Williams (2003), pp. 86–110, see especially p. 162, to which I am indebted for my formulations.
8   See Wilfred Bion (2005), pp. 94–5.
9   For Davidson's rendition of the theory of "anomalous" monism, see his (1970), (1973), (1974), (1993). Davidson was one of the more intellectually flexible analytical philosophers (a possible legacy of his initial training as a classicist, culminating in a Harvard PhD on Plato's *Philebus*). However, his formulations of "anomalous monism" are confined to the "mind-body" problem that has vexed analytical philosophers for generations. Someone not bewitched by this particular Cartesian image of thought (the Deleuzean reference here is intended) is under no pressure to agonize over this particular "problem." It has also to be said that "anomalous monism" is less a doctrine and more a set of complexly related theses which can be approached from different angles. With this caveat in mind, what interests us, though, is the way Davidson's formulations can be expanded, productively, into the lineaments of a nonreductive materialism compatible with the thought of Deleuze. It would of course be pure conjecture to surmise whether Davidson's training as a classicist gave him a familiarity with Stoic thought in

ways that could have influenced his version of an "anomalous monism" seemingly accordant with the principles of Stoic doctrine.

10 For criticisms of anomalous monism, see Ted Honderich (1981); Fodor (1991); and de Pinedo (2006).

Chapter 4

1 Immediately before this quotation Deleuze says that "Goethe, and even Hegel in certain respects, have been considered Spinozists, but they are not really Spinozists, because they never cease to link the plan to the organization of a Form and to the formation of a Subject. The Spinozists are rather Hölderlin, Kleist, and Nietzsche" (*SPP*, pp. 128–9). Deleuze's book on Nietzsche is *Nietzsche and Philosophy* (*NP*).
2 An element of artificiality inevitably surrounds such attempts at periodizing an author's work. In 1989 Deleuze provided the following thematically arranged classification for his works: (1) from Hume to Bergson; (2) classical studies; (3) Nietzschean studies; (4) critique and clinical; (5) aesthetics; (6) cinematographic studies; (7) contemporary studies; (8) *The Logic of Sense*; (9) *Anti-Oedipus*; (10) *Difference and Repetition*; (11) *A Thousand Plateaus*. For this classification, see the editor's introduction to *Desert Islands and Other Texts* (*DI*, p. 292, n. 1). My typology, somewhat by contrast, aligns Spinoza with Nietzsche (at least on the matter of *conatus/macht*), and separates this alignment from the treatment of force provided after *Anti-Oedipus*.
3 To quote Spinoza, "To act absolutely in accordance with virtue is simply to act, live, and preserve one's being (these three mean the same) in accordance with the guidance of reason, and on the basis of looking for what is useful to oneself" (p. 243).
4 To quote Spinoza, "The mind is averse to imagining those things which diminish or hinder its own power, and the power of the body" (p. 175).
5 To quote Spinoza, "Our salvation, i.e. our blessedness, i.e. our freedom, consists … in a constant and eternal love for God, or, in the love of God for human beings. This love, i.e. blessedness, is called 'glory' in the Scriptures …. For whether this love is related to God or to the mind, it can rightly be called contentment of mind, which is not in fact distinguished from glory" (p. 310).
6 It would however be a mistake to assume that Deleuze believes Nietzsche to have superseded or surpassed in whatever way the insights of Spinoza. To do this would be to controvert a fundamental Deleuzean principle regarding the relation between philosophers of different ages. Deleuze insists repeatedly that great philosophers are first and foremost creators of concepts, and that an adequate philosophy of history consequently takes the form of a genealogy of concepts that positions concepts

in terms of the ways in which they transform and "contaminate" each other, and not simply in terms of a chronology or dialectical succession (the latter being the *modus operandi* of a traditional, and for Deleuze unsatisfactory, philosophy of history). Thus, it is possible for Nietzsche, or Deleuze for that matter, to employ a concept of Spinoza's in a rigorously Spinozist fashion, even though Spinoza himself would probably not have understood what Nietzsche and Deleuze were attempting to accomplish. For this principle, see the first paragraph of "Nomadic Thought" (*DI*, p. 252). Or as Deleuze said about his own collaboration with Guattari: "When I work with Guattari each of us falsifies the other, which is to say that each of us understands in his own way notions put forward by the other" (*N*, p. 126). On the collaboration between Deleuze and Guattari, see Dosse (2010).

7   See Deleuze, "On the Will to Power and the Eternal Return" (*DI*, p. 118). On the "dogmatic image of thought," see *NP*, pp. 103–5.

8   Deleuze maintains that the key Nietzschean principle here is asserted in *The Will to Power*, where Nietzsche says that there are nothing but relations of force in mutual "relations of tension" (Nietzsche (1968b), p. 635).

9   Here the following passage from *Nietzsche and Philosophy* comes to mind: "Does the recuperation of religion stop us being religious? By turning theology into anthropology, by putting man in God's place, do we abolish the essential, that is to say, the place?" (*NP*, pp. 88–9). In other words, a truly critical philosophy would not seek simply to reverse the fundamental oppositions God-man, theology-anthropology, etc., but it would, more radically, abolish the very place from which these reversals emerge and from which they derive their force. Deleuze consolidates this legacy of Nietzsche's.

10 See *AO* and *TP*. Deleuze has always made it clear in his interviews that he prefers to characterize his intellectual itineraries and work in this "eventive" way rather than in terms of a more conventional approach that deals with a thinker's influences, formation, shifts of interest, trajectory of publication, and so on. Besides Deleuze's *N*, see also Deleuze and Parnet's *D*.

11 This sketchy outline conforms to the narrative advanced in *WP*. Deleuze deals with structuralism in his "How Do We Recognize Structuralism?," *DI*, pp. 170–92. For a more general overview of structuralism's relation to philosophy, see Delacampagne (1999).

12 For Deleuze's critique of psychoanalysis, see, in addition to *AO*, the chapter "Dead Psychoanalysis: Analyse," in *D*, pp. 7–12, and "Five Propositions on Psychoanalysis," in *DI*, pp. 274–80. For works by other writers in this anti- or post-Freudian vein, see Lyotard (1983) and Julia Kristeva (1984). Also important for Deleuze and Guattari is the British "anti-psychiatric" school associated with R.D. Laing and David Cooper.

13 The Bandung Project got its name from the Indonesian City where the non-aligned movement, spearheaded by Indonesia, India, Egypt, and Yugoslavia, held its first

meeting. The aim of the movement was to form an international bloc that would not be subsumed by either the capitalist "West" or the Soviet-led "East."

14 An important retrospective analysis of this French social and political conjuncture is to be found in Kristin Ross (2002). See also Sunil Khilnani (1993) and Michael Kelly (1982).

15 Paul Patton, in his excellent (2000), pp. 103–8, correctly points out that is possible to extract "anti-political" propositions from nearly all of Deleuze's texts, and that these propositions show Deleuze (and Guattari) to be more concerned with a generalized form of social being rather than with capitalism per se. Patton, and I agree with him, insists however that it would be a mistake to take this for the whole story, since the *Capitalism and Schizophrenia* project also provides an "axiomatics" for constructing assemblages that are explicitly political.

16 This point is made in Brian Massumi's useful analysis of Deleuze and Guattari's mode of production in his (1992), p. 194, n. 51.

17 In the words of Deleuze and Guattari, it is the State that gives capital its "models of realization" (*TP*, p. 428).

18 *Anti-Oedipus* is perhaps the *locus classicus* of this account of libidinal investment in the writings of Deleuze and Guattari.

Chapter 5

1 The position developed below borrows a number of formulations from my (1995).

2 *WP*, pp. 5–6. The quotation from Nietzsche is in his (1968b), section 409. Emphases as in original.

3 I use the term "concept" here, though to conform to the position developed later in this essay "concept" should of course be replaced by "image-narrative-concept." But since it is advisable to wait for this argument to be spelled-out before introducing what seems to be a novel piece of terminology, "concept," and not "image-narrative-concept," will be used in the next few paragraphs.

4 I mention Foucault as the exemplary figure in the development of this new "theoretics" of knowledges, but Pierre Bourdieu also did significant work in this area. The most important figure for my account, however, has been Gilles Deleuze; see especially his interpretations of Foucault in his *Foucault*. For a more detailed treatment of the notions of concept, function, and field, see Deleuze and Guattari, *WP*. Deleuze has analyzed cinema as a "crystalline regime," in his two-volume work on cinema; see also his (1989c). I am deeply indebted to Deleuze's texts for my account of conceptual practice.

5 A useful account of this distinction between the "rational concept" and "sensible intuition" is to be found in Levi R. Bryant's excellent (2008), pp. 5ff. Like me,

Bryant wants to argue that Deleuze's major philosophical achievement resides in the overcoming of this age-old distinction. It is impossible to do justice to Bryant's book in an endnote, but I think it is possible to account for the essential features of Deleuze's transcendental empiricism without pushing his thought in the direction of a "hyper-rationalism" of the kind proposed by Bryant. But there are many "Deleuzes," and Bryant's "Deleuze" is certainly among the more noteworthy of them—I am much indebted to his rigorous and thought-provoking book.

6 According to Deleuze positioning something as a pure exteriority necessarily grants that pure exteriority an a priori ontological superiority because that exteriority then becomes the ground for any reflection on the character and function of the empirical particular. The function of such concepts as Being, Unity, Matter, etc., is thus to order and group phenomena that would be disparate and unconnected if not placed "under" these regulative concepts. "Brute" phenomena need these regulative concepts in order to make any sense to the subject of consciousness.

7 *WP*, p. 20.

8 *WP*, p. 23. Deleuze derives the notion that "concepts are centers of vibrations" from Gilbert Simondon. On Simondon, see Deleuze, "Gilbert Simondon," in *DI*, pp. 86–9. See also the essay "The Method of Dramatization," in *DI*, pp. 94–116.

9 Deleuze, *TI*, pp. 161–4. Emphases as in original. The next few quotations from Deleuze will be from this text. A lucid overview of Deleuze's philosophy of cinema is to be found in Felicity J. Colman (2005).

10 The "suspension of the world" invoked here by Deleuze may appear to have affinities with the phenomenological "epoche," in which the productions of consciousness are "bracketed" in a critical gesture that will ground these productions even more firmly in the consciousness once the "bracketing" is lifted. The key difference is that Deleuze is not making a critical gesture of the kind made by Husserl and Merleau-Ponty (say) when they employ the "epoche," but is instead referring to a process inherent in the movement of the concept-image itself. In this strictly involuntary movement, thought or consciousness is directed to that which is unthought (and hence can never be in consciousness). The phenomenological "epoche" is a voluntary (indeed, a quite deliberate) movement of thought intended above all to safeguard the philosophy of consciousness, whereas Deleuze's primary interest is in bypassing this very philosophy by espousing the notion of an involuntary propensity constitutively situated at the very heart of thought.

11 The key metaphysical principles adverted to by Deleuze include the notion of an absolute immanence (anathema to those who believe immanence cannot be the basis of an adequate account of "the way things are"); a repudiation of the dialectic (unacceptable to those who maintain that an adequate theory of process and movement has to invoke the dialectic, even if only to do justice to its complexity); a rejection of any philosophy based on the form of God (theology) or Man (anthropology) in the name of a "monstrous" form that has not yet been tried

(unacceptable to those wedded to religious and humanistic ideologies); an unrelenting empiricism (problematic for those who believe that reality cannot be accounted for if our conceptions of it are confined to the empirical domain). How Deleuze is able to obviate these possible charges has to be left to another time and place.

Chapter 6

1. *AO*, p. 4. After their collaboration in *Anti-Oedipus* it becomes virtually impossible to separate the positions of Deleuze and Guattari. But since the pivot of my discussion is Deleuze's "Anglo-American Literature" piece, I shall refer throughout to "Deleuze" rather than resort to the neologism "deleuzoguattarian," while bearing in mind at the same time Guattari's function as an indispensable "intercessor" for Deleuze's thinking.

2. In the interview published as "On *Anti-Oedipus*" (*N*, p. 23), Deleuze says that in comparison to the "great English and American novelists … [a]ll we've got in France is Artaud and half of Beckett." It is clear however from other texts and interviews that Deleuze's list of French writers who approximate to the Anglo-Americans is considerably less abbreviated than this passage indicates—elsewhere Deleuze has characterized Lautréamont (as interpreted by Bachelard), Genet, Villon, and Tournier as having significant affinities with the Anglo-American novelists. The omission of Proust from this list is perhaps surprising, but Proust is indicted in *A Thousand Plateaus* for seeking a salvation through art, "a still Catholic salvation," as opposed to finding a salvation "in real life," which is where the Anglo-American novel locates it (*TP*, pp. 186–7). The question of the criteria used by Deleuze (and Guattari) to determine the composition of the Anglo-American "canon" will be taken up in note 21 below.

    The absence of any engagement with "magical realism" in Deleuze's *oeuvre* is striking and may need to be accounted for. Would there be room in an expanded "Anglo-American canon" for such writers as Garcia Márquez and Wilson Harris? It is hard to see why these writers should not in principle have a place in this heteronomous "canon," and Deleuze's apparent failure to take them into account will be taken up later.

3. As Deleuze and Guattari say humorously: "The French are like landowners whose source of income is the cogito." See *WP*, p. 104.

4. As Paul Patton points out in his "Notes for a glossary," Deleuze and Guattari often proceed by enumerating a list of contents, perhaps the best known being the filigree of notions that begins the plateau titled *Rhizome* in *Mille plateaux*:

    All we talk about are multiplicities, lines, strata and segmentarities, lines of flight and intensities, machinic assemblages and their various types, bodies without organs and their construction and selection, the plane of consistency, and in each case the units of measure. *Stratometers, BwO units of density, BwO units of convergence.* (*TP*, p. 4)

My delineation of the differences between "French" and "Anglo-American Literature" follows this *modus operandi*, and simply enumerates their respective characteristics as identified by Deleuze (and Guattari).

5 Where literary criticism or the philosophy of criticism are concerned, the clear implication of Deleuze's position is that someone like Lukács must generally be reckoned "French" on account of the canonical primacy he accords such "classical realists" as Balzac, Scott, Tolstoy, Thomas Mann, and Gorky. The writers preferred by Deleuze tend invariably to belong to the experimental wing of a broadly defined modernism, and this would certainly set him apart from Lukács, who, for instance, contrasted the "mixture of decadence and reaction" displayed by Deleuze's favorite Kleist with Goethe, whom Lukács esteemed for "wrestling to create glorious islands of human culture against the pressing flood of bourgeois barbarism," and this despite being a "representative" of his class. See Lukács, *Essays on Realism*. I am grateful to Ian Buchanan for urging me to try to contrast Lukács and Deleuze, and for making several suggestions that helped improve this essay.

6 Elsewhere in this essay Deleuze says:

To fly is to trace a line, lines, a whole cartography. One only discovers worlds through a long, broken flight. Anglo-American literature constantly shows these ruptures. These characters who create their line of flight, who create through a line of flight ... In [Hardy, Melville, Stevenson, Woolf, Wolfe, Lawrence, Fitzgerald, Miller, Kerouac] everything is departure, becoming, passage, leap, daemon, relationship with the outside. (*D*, p. 37)

7 See also the interview-essay "Dead Psychoanalysis: Analyse," in *D*, p. 120, where it is asserted that "Brönte designates a state of winds more than a person."
8 For Melville and Lawrence, see *D*, pp. 68ff and p. 118, respectively.
9 *TP*, p. 5. Deleuze says that "an assemblage may have been in existence for a long time before it receives its proper name which gives it a special consistence as if it were thus separated from a more general regime to assume a kind of autonomy: as in 'sadism', 'masochism.'" See "Dead Psychoanalysis," in *D*, p. 120. Fredric Jameson's suggestion that the Hegel of *The Phenomenology of Spirit* be regarded as the prescient "inventor" of the category of *reification*, albeit before it got its name, while not concerned with this aspect of Deleuze's work, provides another interesting example that provides grist for a Deleuzean characterization of the assemblage. See Jameson (1996), pp. 393–4.
10 *D*, pp. 70–1. Deleuze says of the regime of utterances that in them "signs are organized in a new way, new formulations appear, a new style for new gestures

(the emblems which individualize the knight, the formulas of oaths, the system of 'declarations', even of love, etc.)" (*D*, pp. 70–1).

11 Derrida (1976), p. 158. It has to be said however that the claim that "there is no outside-text" is sometimes willfully misrepresented by Derrida's more intemperate critics, who seem more eager to make him sound ridiculous than to find ways of understanding what this assertion may be about. (It could after all be the quite benign insight that an irreducible element of "constructiveness" or "contingency" goes into the constitution of the text. The problem for Deleuze (and Guattari) would then not be with this claim in itself, since they would in all likelihood be disposed to regard this version of it as salutary and anodyne, but with the ontological edifice used by Derrida and others to buttress it.) Another target of this polemics could be Jean Starobinski, well-known for his proposal, which is something like an axiom for the Geneva School, that "data" lodged in the interior of the text can be suitably transcoded to reveal marks of the author's consciousness or imagination. See Starobinski (1991), pp. 158–9. As "founding" proponents of the doctrine of intertextuality, Julia Kristeva and Roland Barthes would also be susceptible to criticism on the grounds adduced by Deleuze (and Guattari).

12 François Dosse is right therefore to depict Derrida as a "superstructuralist," that is, someone intent—when he reads texts by philosophers, ethnologists, and representative structuralists—on working within the terms of the structure of the text in order to expose its impasses and undecidabilities. See Dosse (1997), pp. 17ff.

13 I am grateful to Janell Watson for drawing my attention to the relevance of this passage from *Logique du sens* for an understanding of the claims made by Deleuze (and Guattari) about the text's "outside" in *Mille plateaux* and in the "Anglo-American Literature" essay.

14 Of Deleuze's many commentators, Keith Ansell Pearson is perhaps the one who has most explicitly brought out the part played by his Bergsonism in his elaboration of the notion of *multiplicity*. Ansell Pearson has also stressed (perhaps over-stressed from some) the importance of Deleuze's Bergsonism for his critique of dialectics. See Ansell Pearson (1999), especially p. 156.

15 *TP*, p. 240. This therefore is an ethics of writing, but also a politics (more about which later).

16 Deleuze, "A Conversation: What Is It? What Is It For?," in *D*, pp. 34–5. Although Deleuze does say that some lines of flight can be motionless. See "Anglo-American Literature," in *D*, p. 37.

17 Brian Massumi uses the term "hyperdifferentiation" to describe the position of Deleuze and Guattari, and contrasts it with the "identity-undifferentiation" that is more typical of the viewpoints of Lacan, Barthes, Althusser, Derrida, Kristeva, and Baudrillard. I am inclined therefore to agree with Massumi when he says that these thinkers "can still be said to repose in the shadow of Saussure's tree, even if they claim to have closed the door on it." See Massumi (1992), pp. 77–8 n. 73. See also p. 78 n. 74.

18 An "intensity" communicates a difference, and the *haecceity* is either an "assemblage *haecceity*," that is, an individuated multiplicity that receives and projects intensities, or an "interassemblage *haecceity*," that is, the expression of the potential becoming-other that resides in an assemblage when it enters into combinations and conjunctions with another assemblage or group of assemblages. See *TP*, pp. 262–3. Deleuze and Guattari say that the two kinds of *haecceity* cannot really be separated from each other.

19 "A flight is a sort of delirium." See Deleuze, *D*, p. 40. In his "Literature and Life" (*D*, p. 1), Deleuze says:

> Writing is a question of becoming, always incomplete, always in the midst of being formed, and goes beyond the matter of any livable or lived experience … These becomings may be linked to each other by a particular line, as in Le Clezio's novels, or they may coexist at every level, following the doorways, thresholds, and zones that make up the entire universe, as in Lovecraft's powerful oeuvre. Becoming does not move in the other direction, and one does not become Man, insofar as man presents himself as a dominant form of expression that claims to impose itself on all matter, whereas woman, animal, molecule always has a component of flight that escapes its own formalization. The shame of being a man—is there any better reason to write?

20 *WP*, p. 66. Deleuze and Guattari remind us that "affects" and "percepts" are not to be confused with "affections" and "perceptions," respectively. An affect is not a state of being in the way that an affection is, rather it is the becoming that ensues when two sensations are coupled without resembling each other; and a percept is a bloc of sensations and relations that has an actuality that is independent of the perceiving subject (which is not the case with perceptions). For a succinct statement of this distinction see the interview "On Philosophy," in *N*, p. 137. The next few pages references in the main body of the text will be to *WP*.

21 In the interview "On Philosophy," Deleuze says that "the great English and American novelists often write in percepts, and Kleist and Kafka in affects" (*N*, p. 137). A similar demarcation seems to be at work in Deleuze and Guattari, *WP*, pp. 168–9. The conclusion that the English and Americans write essentially in "percepts" while the Continental Europeans who have affinities with them write in "affects" should however be resisted. Although Deleuze and Guattari do not say this in so many words, affects ("nonhuman becomings of man") and percepts ("nonhuman landscapes of nature") are not distributed in this neatly compartmentalized way. Indeed, it is clear from their accounts that Melville wrote in affects *and* percepts and D.H. Lawrence wrote almost exclusively in affects. Just as interesting, and this is a point that needs to be explored elsewhere, is Deleuze's suggestion that Spinoza's *Ethics* is written not just in concepts, but also percepts and affects. See "Letter to Reda Bensmaïa, on Spinoza," in *N*, pp. 164–6.

22 Deleuze goes on to say of principles that they "are not entities; they are functions. They are defined by their effects. These effects amount to this: the principles constitute, within the given, a subject that invents and believes … [T]he principles are principles of human nature. To believe is to anticipate. To communicate to an idea the vividness of an impression to which it is attached is to anticipate; it is to transcend memory and the senses" (p. 133).

23 In his essay "Spinoza and Us" Deleuze says: "[Spinoza's] approach is no less valid for us … because no one knows ahead of time the affects one is capable of; it is a long affair of experimentation, requiring a lasting prudence, a Spinozan wisdom that implies the construction of a plane of immanence or consistency. Spinoza's ethics has nothing to do with a morality; he conceives it as an ethology, that is, as a composition of fast and slow speeds, of capacities for affecting and being affected on this plane of immanence." See *SPP*, p. 125.

24 Deleuze and Guattari regard Hegel and Heidegger alike as "historicists" because they view history as the interior site in which the concept unfolds or reaches its point of completion. See *WP*, p. 95.

25 For Deleuze and Guattari on philosophy in the American university, see *WP*, p. 143.

26 We can still undertake a "reterritorialization" of ourselves among the Greeks, say Deleuze and Guattari, but, and this is something that Heidegger failed to understand, it will be "according to what they did not possess and had not yet become," that is, it will be more like a "reterritorialization" of the Greeks on us. See *WP*, p. 102.

27 Deleuze and Guattari provide a fascinating account of the temporality that subtends the Now of our becoming in this experimentation, which they distinguish from the present of history. This infinite Now runs counter to the past and the present, because (and here they follow Foucault) this Now is the actuality of our becoming which is incommensurate with the present of what we are. See *WP*, p. 112.

28 Of course Deleuze and Guattari's estimation of what it is that constitutes English philosophy is highly selective and, as I pointed out earlier, hardly approximates to the kind of thing that is purveyed in British philosophy departments. "English philosophy" for them encompasses all of Hume, Russell's doctrine of the externality of relations, and Whitehead's account of "the event" (which as Deleuze makes clear in *Le Pli* is heavily influenced by Leibniz in any case). The rest of English philosophy is done in hybrid fashion by its novelists.

29 For Deleuze's remark on writers, see "On Philosophy," in *N*, p. 143.

30 In arguing for this claim one must of course enter the caveat that problems unavoidably arise when we try to encompass so rich and diverse a body of work as that of Deleuze and Guattari within a single interpretive armature like that of an "axiomatics of desire."

31 Tom Conley (1997) has argued persuasively that this dynamism of the text and the image is characteristic of all of Deleuze's writings, with the possible exception of the more explicitly philosophical studies.
32 Deleuze therefore overturns Kant's separation of Vision from Ideas (Kant had assigned the former to the Sensibility and the latter to the Understanding), or rather he imputes this overturning to the cinematic conceptualizing of a Herzog.

Chapter 7

1 Deleuze, "Life as a Work of Art," in *N*, pp. 102–18.
2 When it comes to distinguishing "ethics" (l' éthique) from "morality" (la morale) Deleuze said the following:

> The difference is that morality presents us with a set of constraining rules ... ones that judge actions and intentions by judging them in relation to transcendent values (this is good, that's bad ...); ethics is a set of optional rules that assess what we do, what we say, in relation to the ways of existing involved. (Deleuze, *N*, p. 100)

3 For this see Deleuze, *N*, p. 100.
4 See Foucault, "Preface," in *AO*, p. xiii.
5 Smith, "Deleuze and the Question of Desire: Toward an Immanent Theory of Ethics" in his (2012).
6 Disputing the viability of this "immanent ethics" is of course a quite separate undertaking, which may or may not interest the interpreter of Deleuze. It does not interest Smith, nor does it this author. Smith's assessment of these two features of Deleuzean thought will be retained in this essay as a springboard for our ensuing discussion.
7 Deleuze, *KCP*, p. 47.
8 See Foucault (1994).
9 Two words of caution are needed here. First, in today's English "prudence" has strong overtones of wariness and circumspection. By contrast, Aristotelian φρονησις (*phronesis*), the basis for the medieval virtue of *prudentia*, had the connotations of adroitness, judiciousness, and forethought—connotations which may be lacking in the modern English definition. Deleuze's definition of ethics as "a set of optional rules that assess what we do, what we say, in relation to the ways of existing involved," is certainly compatible with the suggestion that these rules of assessment are guided by *prudentia*. Otherwise the person evaluating his or her life would in effect be saying that such important qualities as adroitness, judiciousness, and forethought—i.e., the defining features of *prudentia*—are somehow merely

accidental features of a life led ethically. Second, Dan Smith has pointed out to me several passages where Deleuze explicitly distances himself from the notion of transgression (with its parasitical relation to the figure of the Law). A breach of the law is a violation of the code, whereas Deleuzean (and Foucauldian) transgression is more like a *scrambling* of the code. Much more needs to be said about transgression, and I'm grateful to Smith for alerting me to the issues posed here.

10 There are of course many versions of the story of Tristan and Isolde, some so different from each other, that it could make just as much sense, given the appropriate rendition of the story, to view their bond as a doomed passion, less turbulent than Catherine and Heathcliff's certainly, but a passion nonetheless. Hence in Wagner's operatic rendition the love of Tristan and Isolde is fated from the outset to have a ruinous outcome. It would be futile for us to intervene in this debate—our purpose here is served by recognizing, if only for the sake of argument, the contrast between Tristan and Isolde and Catherine and Heathcliff that Deleuze wishes to make.

11 See Schultz (2006).

12 Foucault (1997b), p. 254.

13 On this *tekhnē tou biou* see Foucault (1997b), p. 258.

14 Foucault (1997b), p. 286.

15 The two *ēthoi* do part ways on the matter of sexual relations between men and women. For the Greeks, the noble *ēthos* was impossible to achieve in dealings between men and women. In the *ēthos* associated with the medieval *amour courtois*, by contrast, courtly chivalry was something that only a man could display toward his "fair lady."

16 Deleuze, "Immanence: A Life," in *PI*, p. 27.

Chapter 8

1 The inaugurator of the transcendental principle is of course Kant, who sought to obviate skepticism by making the conditions of possibility of cognition the starting point of any reflection on cognition, and providing a transcendental justification of knowledge-claims or judgments by grounding these claims or judgments in these a priori conditions. Kant soon drew criticism, by Fichte notably, who maintained that Kant's a priori principles were themselves metaphysical (Fichte's primary target here was Kant's distinction between noumena and phenomena), and thus begged the question of their own grounding. For Fichte see his (1970), p. 133. Nietzsche of course eventually dismissed the entire Kantian enterprise, saying that Kant had sought to ground claims to knowledge via an examination of the postulates of reason, but in so doing failed to provide a critique of knowledge and reason

themselves. See for instance the section "How the 'True World' Finally Became a Fable" in his (2005), p. 17.
2. For more on the socius, see Chapter 9 below.
3. For the English version of this essay, see "How Do We Recognize Structuralism?" in *DI*, pp. 170–92, the note which refers to Foucault's point about "structural mutation," is 308 (note 64).
4. For Althusser's "aleatory materialism" or "materialism of the encounter," see the essays collected in his (2006). The definitive overview of the work of Althusser's late period is Wal Suchting (2004). Also useful is Negri (1996).
5. The connections and differences between Williams and Deleuze and Guattari are examined in Chapter 11.
6. On Badiou and "evental fidelity" see his (2005), pp. 201–61.
7. For this comment of Bush's, see http://www.cbsnews.com/8301-503544_162-20014998-503544/a-look-back-to-2005-president-bush-and-katrina, accessed on June 13, 2013.

Chapter 9

1. For Althusser's account of interpellation, see his (1971).
2. See Althusser (1969), p. 113, where it is clearly stated that the "superstructure" exercises a "specific effectivity" on the base. It could certainly be argued on behalf of Deleuze and Guattari that the positing of such an "effectivity" on the part of the "superstructure" only compounds the original problem, since any significant "effectivity" on the part of the "superstructure" will only qualify or diminish the capacity of the "base" to serve as a determinant "in the last instance." This is too complex an issue to be resolved here, but it needs to be noted that Althusser is perhaps not quite the naïve proponent of the "base-superstructure" dichotomy that Deleuze and Guattari take him to be.
3. For further discussion of this philosophical tradition and its problems, see my (2009).
4. See Etienne Balibar (1991). In another work (1998), Balibar goes on to argue that it is Locke and not Descartes who invents the modern concept of the self as that which the "you" or the "I" possesses.
5. For Descartes's letter to Mersenne, see René Descartes (2000), p. 28. Also in (1987), p. 145. Balibar refers to this letter in his (1991), p. 36.
6. The importance of the Augustinian tradition for Descartes is stressed in Stephen Menn (1998), see especially p. 69. See also Nicholas Jolley (1992).
7. According to Balibar (2001), the notion of the transcendental subject arose from Kant's modification of the Cartesian *cogito*, with the Lockean self beginning a

second tradition that circumvents Kant before ending up with William James and Bergson.
8   Hobbes (1991), p. 230.
9   See (1991), pp. 122–3. See also David Runciman (2010), on the tension between this position on the state and sovereign and Hobbes's individualism, evidenced in his declaration that the State can't compel a subject to lose their life for it. See also Runciman (1997).
10 On this, see (1991), pp. 155–6.
11 See Immanuel Kant, "On the Relationship of Theory to Practice in Political Right (Against Hobbes)" in (1991), p. 84.
12 For this see Immanuel Kant, "On the Common Saying: 'This May Be True in Theory but It Does Not Apply in Practice,'" (1991), p. 71.
13 Balibar (1991), p. 55. Balibar says a great deal more about the Cartesian and medieval-theological *subjectus* than can be indicated here, rightly pointing out that a notion that had evolved over seventeen centuries from Roman times to the period of the European absolute monarchies is not easily encompassed in a single definition. He also rightly indicates that the supposed *novum* of the Citizen Subject has to be regarded with some skepticism, since under the aegis of bourgeois democracy this subject was always going to retain some traces of the old *subjectus*.
14 For Hegel's (early) view on the operation of "speculative" reason, see his (1997), p. 88. For excellent commentary on this aspect of Hegel's relation to Kant, see Terry Pinkard (2000), pp. 160ff.
15 The essential correlation between Reason and the Absolute entails that every operation of consciousness, practical as much as theoretical, is necessarily one which falls within the remit of the Absolute. The subject of thought then has to be the subject of morality and politics and vice versa—a connection previously established by Kant when he moved from the First to the Second *Critique*, that is, from the subject's understanding to the subject's willing and acting.
16 Like each of the plateaus in *Mille plateaux*, the "Treatise on Nomadology" has a date attached to it, in this case 1227, the year in which Genghis Khan died. Deleuze and Guattari give no explanations for their choice of such dates, and one can only surmise here that Genghis Khan's *Pax Mongolica* is for Deleuze and Guattari an emblematic instance of a counter-sovereignty to be posed against the sovereignty of the *polis* that he challenged from his movable base in the steppes. This much can be gleaned from *TP*, pp. 417–9.
17 *TP*, pp. 351–2. Emphasis as in original. The interior quotation is from Dumézil (1948), pp. 118–24, which deals with the difference between the bond and the contract.
18 For these properties, see *TP*, pp. 352 ff.
19 It would be interesting to contrast Balibar's Citizen Subject with Deleuze and Guattari's subject of the State apparatus. The central premise of Balibar's argument,

namely, that the *subjectus* of medieval polities had been supplanted by the post-Kantian *subjectum* or Citizen Subject, is not one that Deleuze and Guattari would readily accept. Balibar's cautionary note that under the remit of bourgeois democracy the Citizen Subject is always going to resemble in some important ways the *subjectus* of the dispensation that prevailed before the emergence of bourgeois democracy would be wholeheartedly assented to by Deleuze and Guattari.

20 *TP*, p. 90.
21 *TP*, p. 435.
22 *TP*, p. 434.
23 *TP*, p. 431. It should be pointed out though that the state is understood by Deleuze and Guattari in two senses. In one sense the state is to be identified with the formations and apparatuses that constitute it. In another, the state is, preeminently, a metaphysical conception, a machine of transcoding that (unlike the assemblages which embody it and which have to be constructed and positioned at this or that point in social space) "comes into the world fully formed and rises up at a single stroke, the unconditioned Urstaat." See p. 437.
24 It follows from this that there is a sense in which consciousness (taken here to include all the ramified outreachings of desire) constitutes something like a domain of the virtual, and so precedes the "actuality" of social apparatuses and formations. The "thinking" of the state is a function of consciousness par excellence, and is therefore the product of this virtuality. Clearly this has significant implications for any simplistic claims about the primacy of the "actually" material in a marxist thought and practice: the virtual, as Deleuze, following Bergson, has insisted, cuts across the division between the possible and the actual. "Before Being there is politics" (*TP*, p. 203), certainly, but inextricably bound up with politics is the thinking that is located in the realm of the virtual, and this thinking breaches the long-held distinctions between "thought" and "practice" and "materialism" and "idealism."
25 *TP*, pp. 375–6.
26 *TP*, p. 556n42.
27 Some of the ensuing formulations have been taken from Chapter 14.
28 *TP*, p. 448.
29 *TP*, pp. 452–3.
30 *TP*, p. 453.
31 *TP*, p. 453.
32 *TP*, p. 221.
33 *TP*, p. 472.
34 Deleuze, *FLB*, pp. 130–7.
35 To quote Deleuze and Guattari: "There is no universal capitalism, there is no capitalism in itself; capitalism is at the crossroads of all kinds of formations, it is neocapitalism by nature" (*TP*, p. 20). In *Anti-Oedipus* Deleuze and Guattari indicate how capitalism is able to perform this integrative function:

> Capitalism is in fact born of the encounter of two sorts of flows: the decoded flows of production in the form of money-capital, and the decoded flows of labor in the form of the "free worker." Hence, unlike previous social machines, the capitalist machine is incapable of providing a code that will apply to the whole of the social field. By substituting money for the very notion of a code, it has created an axiomatic of abstract quantities that keeps moving further and further in the direction of the deterritorialization of the socius. (*AO*, p. 33)

36 There have of course long been economic world-systems, as Andre Gunder Frank, Christopher Chase-Dunn, Janet Abu-Lughod, and others have pointed out. My claim that capitalism in its current dispensation takes the form of a meta-accord is not about the world-system as such, but rather about its present manifestation, that is, the way or ways in which the meta-accord that is capital gets to establish a world-system with a fundamentally isomorphic structure, something that did not occur with previous world-systems.

37 John Cage (1969, p. 22) thus describes his work as "music without measurements, sound passing through circumstances." Slavoj Žižek (1997) has, I believe, made a similar point about divergence and incompossibility when he says that many different sets can in principle be derived from the same collection. Several sentences in this section are reproduced from my "On Producing the Concept of a Global Culture."

38 *TP*, p. 253. Elsewhere Deleuze says that "the Anomalous is always at the frontier, on the borders of a band or multiplicity; it is part of the latter, but is already making it pass into another multiplicity, it makes it become, it traces a line-between." See *D*, p. 42.

39 In an interview on Foucault and his work, Deleuze refers to this movement between outside and inside as something which involves "subjectless individuations." See "A Portrait of Foucault," in *N*, p. 117. These "subjectless individuations" are of course a defining characteristic of the Anomalous. I am almost certainly going further than Deleuze and Guattari in my use of the Anomalous. They take this category to be a defining feature of the "line of flight," which is present wherever lines of flight are to be found. In the account given here, I take the Anomalous to be pervasively present in the epoch of the breakdown or dissolution of "transcendental" accords, that is, I view it as the operation of a currently regnant capitalist cultural logic. This however is entirely compatible with the positions set out in *Capitalisme et schizophrénie*. In *Dialogues*, Deleuze says:

> The State can no longer … rely on the old forms like the police, armies, bureaucracies, collective installations, schools, families … It is not surprising that all kinds of minority questions—linguistic, ethnic, regional, about sex, or youth—resurge not only as archaisms, but in up-to-date revolutionary forms which call once more into question in an entirely immanent manner both the global

economy of the machine and the assemblages of national States ... Everything is played in uncertain games, "front to front, back to back, back to front." (p. 147)

40 For his account of simulation, see Deleuze, *DR*, pp. 92ff, and *LS*, pp. 253–79. Deleuze's theory of simulation is complex, but its gist can be stated thus: If, contrary to Plato and the tradition of philosophy derived from him, there can be no primacy of a putative original over its copy, of a model over its representations, so that there can be no basis for differentiating between "good" original and "bad" copy, then everything is itself a "copy-original"—it is an "original" of itself, or rather, its "origin" is a copy or "shadow" of itself. In the absence of any possibility of separating copies from ostensible originals, each thing, in simulation, is thus an absolute singularity. Everything is different from everything else, and this in turn is the basis of multiplicity. It should be pointed out that a similar stress on the concept of a singularity is also to be found in Jacques Derrida's account of "political desire," to be found in his (1997), pp. 20ff.

41 To quote Deleuze and Guattari:

> If Marx demonstrated the functioning of capitalism as an axiomatic, it was above all in the famous chapter on the tendency of the rate of profit to fall. Capitalism is indeed an axiomatic, because it has no laws but immanent ones. It would like for us to believe that it confronts the limits of the Universe, the extreme limit of resources and energy. But all it confronts are its own limits (the periodic depreciation of existing capital); all it repels or displaces are its own limits (the formation of new capital, in new industries with a high rate of profit). This is the history of oil and nuclear power. And it does both at once: capitalism confronts its own limits and simultaneously displaces them, setting them down again farther along. (*TP*, p. 463)

42 Capitalism, by removing the conditions that enable "transcendental" accords to maintain themselves, in the process promotes a cultural logic that favors the description over the concept, and this cultural logic also contains within itself propensities that weaken or obviate the dichotomy between the individual and the collective, and thus creates the conditions for the emergence of a culture that, with the supersession of capitalist "nonbeing," will allow singularity potentially to become generalized as a cultural principle.

43 The sketchy account of singularity given here is taken from the much more substantial treatment in Giorgio Agamben (1993).

44 A point well-made in Daniel Lazare (1996 and 2001).

45 For discussion, see Bob Jessop (1997).

46 This formulation is owed to Jessop (1997), pp. 574–5.

47 Samir Amin has argued that only in this way can the system of a globalized economic polarization be neutralized and ultimately dismantled. See Amin (1999 and 2000).

48 Amin (2000), p. 84.
49 See Samir Amin (1990), p. 136.

Chapter 10

1. Deleuze, "Letter to Uno on Language," in *TRR*, p. 201.
2. See the plateau titled "On Several Regimes of Signs," in *TP*, pp. 111–48. Invaluable commentary on, and analysis of, the differences and affinities between Deleuze and Derrida are to be found in Patton and Protevi (2003).
3. See Deleuze, "Humans: A Dubious Existence," in *DI*, pp. 90–1. See also "Foucault's Main Concepts," in *TRM*, pp. 241–60. See also *F*.
4. On this appropriation of Hjelmslev's "double articulation," see *TP*, pp. 45, 108, and 402.
5. See Deleuze, "How Do We Recognize Structuralism?," in *DI*, pp. 170–92, for the quotation see note 64, p. 308.
6. For more on the account of part-objects given by Deleuze and Guattari, see my short piece "Partial Objects," in Parr (2010), pp. 202–4.
7. See Deleuze, "May '68 Did Not Take Place," in *TRM*, pp. 233–6, the quotation is on pp. 233–4.
8. Marchais, in an article titled "False revolutionaries who must be exposed," in *L'Humanité* on May 3, 1968, made a strident denunciation of the leaders of the movement, referring to one of the student leaders, Daniel Cohn-Bendit, as the "German anarchist."
9. See Carl Schmitt (2007), see especially the essay *"The Age of Neutralizations and Depoliticizations"* ((originally published in 1929), pp. 80–96); (1985); and (2003). Also important here is the work of Robert Michels (1915), who shared Schmitt's pessimism about liberal democracy, but who argued that because of the need in modern industrial societies for swift and complex decision-making, political parties are managed by cadres of professional "experts" who, with power in their hands, inexorably constitute themselves as an antidemocratic oligarchy. The parties are increasingly turned into machines for harvesting votes and become hollowed-out ideologically.
10. On "conceptual personae," see *WP*, chapter 3. A conceptual persona is a figure of thought that provides a concept with its unique and differentiating force. It is not to be identified with psychosocial types (*WP*, p. 67), and even when named after a philosopher, it cannot be identified with the philosopher in question (*WP*, p. 64). Deleuze and Guattari maintain that conceptual personae serve as an indispensable heuristic for grasping the significance of concepts and for creating concepts.
11. Alain Badiou has taken the figure of the *sans papiers* to be central to the configuration of our current political conjuncture. Badiou says:

Are those workers who do not have proper papers but who are working here, in France (or the United Kingdom, or the United States …) part of this country? Do they belong here? Yes, probably, since they live and work here. No, since they don't have the necessary papers to show that they are French (or British, or American …), or living here legally. The expression "illegal immigrant" designates the uncertainty of valence, or the non-valence of valence: it designates people who are living here, but don't really belong here, and hence people who can be thrown out of the country, people who can be exposed to the non-valence of the valence of their presence here as workers. (Badiou, 2004)

On the theme of *personnes sur les marges*, Paul Patton has several articles on human and land rights as they apply to the indigenous people of Australia, written from a broadly Deleuzean perspective. See Patton (2001a and b), (2004a and b).

Chapter 11

1 A more elaborate account of this notion of conceptual production is to be found in my (2009), from which several of my formulations are taken.
2 On this point, see Deleuze, "On the Superiority of Anglo-American Literature," in *D*, p. 60.
3 This is why Slavoj Žižek has been right to insist in his various writings that it is both futile theoretically and unsatisfactory politically to seek to distinguish between "ideology" and some brute facticity represented by "economy." To be confronted by the concepts or expressivities of capitalism is to confront the reality of capitalism (even if the "reality" overdetermines the expressivities in question), and vice versa.
4 It is possible to view this complexity in ways akin to Althusser's notion of an "overdetermined" relation between formations, and between formations and the points from which subject-positions are constituted.
5 There is no obvious affinity between the work of Raymond Williams and that of Deleuze and Guattari. I bring them together in this essay because their respective projects exist in a kind of creative tension. Williams always saw the project of solidarity in terms of a class-based politics (although toward the end of his life he did register the emergence of the new social movements), whereas the work of Deleuze and Guattari has as its context the situation after May 1968, when the new social movements mature and consolidate themselves. The category of "experience" is central to Williams, but he leaves it relatively untheorized, whereas the more philosophically adept Deleuze and Guattari theorize their key categories, but seem to have relatively little room for the notion of "experience."
6 Quoted in Dai Smith (2008), p. 220. I am deeply indebted to Smith for my subsequent formulations. Given access to Williams's papers, Smith furnishes the definitive account of the life and work of Williams.

7   Michael Orrom and Raymond Williams, quoted in Smith, p. 365. Emphases as in original. See also Williams (1977), pp. 128–37.
8   Williams (1985), pp. 268–9.
9   Axioms are constitutively foundational, in that their presuppositions are not derivable in principle from other statements. They function as protocols, in this way enabling other statements to be organized or orchestrated in specific ways. The resulting statements derive their meaning and saliency from the axioms which underpin them. Differentiating between different axiomatic formations can sometimes be difficult—the most common way of making this differentiation is to study the resulting statements. If these statements are in a relationship of contradiction or incompatibility with regard to each other, then all else being equal, it is likely that they are resting on different axiomatic formations. Axioms do not always possess a law-like character, since legal codes may themselves be premised on a particular axiomatic base.
10 See Deleuze, "A Portrait of Foucault," in *N*, p. 116.
11 There are evident affinities between the Deleuzean notion of the Anomalous used in this essay as the basis of an account of a countervailing constitutive power, and Antonio Negri's characterization of "the political monster." Negri's "political monster" emerges from a power that cannot be circumscribed by a putative essence, and as a result of this primal lack of circumscription is able to produce singularities that have the potential to be revolutionary. See Casarino and Negri (2008).

Chapter 12

1   See Thacker (2013). For a more detailed and programmatic elaboration of his position, see also Thacker (2005a and b).
2   The reference here is to Deleuze and Guattari's injunction: "A schizophrenic out for a walk is a better model than a neurotic laying on the analyst's couch. A breath of fresh air, a relationship with the outside world (*AO*, p. 2)". For background to the case of the Wolf-Man, see Karin Obholzer (1982) and Muriel Gardiner (1972).

Chapter 13

1   Deleuze, "Postscript on Control Societies," in *N*, pp. 177–82. I summarize Deleuze's "Postscript" in my "Control Society and State Theory," in Adrian Parr (2010), pp. 54–7, from which several formulations are taken for the paragraphs below.
2   See Bruno Théret (2007). The Regulationist approach allows for a "contestation" between societal groupings but does not view this "contestation" in terms of a

structural opposition that is class-based. The approach taken in this essay views this contestation to be primarily, though not exclusively, class-based. What is convincing about the Regulationist approach is its insistence that each of these spheres (the economic, the political, and the domestic) has its own internal operational logic, although each sphere also interacts with its counterparts. I argue more fully for this position in my (2009).

3 On this see Robert Brenner (2007).

4 Some would object that few Americans, if any, would approve of the business practices of Enron once they became aware of them. The obvious rejoinder to this objection is that we cannot be sure how many Americans would have objected to Enron's business practices if it had not gone out of business in a way that begged for its senior managers to end up in front of a judge. After all, relatively few Americans now seem to object to the business practices of the Wall Street bankers, involving as they do (officially documented after the 2008 financial crash) systemic overcharging, product misrepresentation, money laundering, fraud, various forms of governmental favoritism, and so forth.

5 For Gramm's election pitch, see David Plotz (2007). Gramm himself received $260,000 in campaign contributions from Enron, in return for which he expedited legislation which exempted firms like Enron from energy trading regulation. On this, see Robert Scheer (2006). Gramm's wife Wendy was also given a position on the Enron board of directors. Gramm by all accounts was thus an accomplished "rider, and not puller, of the wagon."

6 See "Jack Abramoff: The Lobbyist's Playbook," at http://www.cbsnews.com/8301-18560_162-57459874/jack-abramoff-the-lobbyists-playbook/?pageNum=3, accessed on June 22, 2013.

7 As Perry Anderson rightly points out, since the poorest Americans do not vote, what ensues in elections is functionally equivalent to a property franchise. See Anderson (2001), p. 8. See also Anderson (1992), p. 357, where he says:

> Democracy is indeed now more widespread than ever before. But it is also thinner—as if the more universally available it becomes, the less active meaning it retains. The United States itself is the paradigmatic example: a society in which less than half the citizens vote, ninety per cent of Congressmen are re-elected, and the price of office is cash by the million.

Anderson could have added that the *reward* of gaining office is also "cash by the million."

8 For the details needed to underpin this sketch of the American mode of societal regulation, I have consulted the following: Anatol Lieven (2004); Stefan Halper and Jonathan Clarke (2004); Jacob Hacker and Paul Pierson (2004); and Godfrey Hodgson (2004). I have deliberately chosen to cite works by those likely to be identified as "thoughtful" liberals (although both Halper and Clarke served

in the Reagan administration), as opposed to marxists—that is, liberals who give clear voice to the various "erosions" associated with the George W. Bush administration (and clearly continuing with the Obama administration). At the same time, there is a hand-wringing quality to these works, which manifests itself in their genuflections to "America's pluralistic traditions," "the centrality of the Constitution," "the vital centre ground," and so forth. Clearly the US Supreme Court putsch that brought George W. Bush to the White House has been a source of anguish for well-meaning liberals and/or mild conservatives, but an adequate understanding of the impulses and methods that brought people like Cheney, Rumsfeld, and Wolfowitz to positions of supreme power is not going to be achieved by pious references to the Constitution or to "pluralism" or to "the center." We are dealing with a political party that has abandoned all notions of the center, that will pay lip-service to the Constitution when this is convenient but not beyond that, and which, in the not-too-subtle words of Bush's "political strategist" Karl Rove, seems to think that those who decry the loss of American "pluralism" are really on the side of al-Qaeda. But the declarations or intimations of a sense of loss in these books should not be dismissed: what they convey in their sense of loss and foreboding, albeit at the same time quite inadvertently, is precisely what the American mode of societal regulation has truly managed to accomplish.

9   See Gérard Duménil and Dominique Lévy (2004).
10 As of January 20, 2006, the mayor of Atlanta, Shirley Franklin, placed a temporary ban on the construction of "McMansions" in her city.
11 For this and the subsequently detailed information regarding the First Amendment surveys provided in this chapter, see the Center for Survey Research & Analysis at the University of Connecticut Website at http://csra.stamford.uconn.edu/research.html, accessed on January 28, 2006.
12 A country so wealthy and powerful is in a position to influence the course of events just about anywhere in the world, and this in turn places a premium on the understanding its citizens have of the rest of the world—although here the indications are not reassuring. It is difficult to ascertain the extent to which the lack of a passport is indicative of a reduced interest in the world beyond one's country, but it is frequently noted that the citizens of other developed countries are much more likely to own passports than their American counterparts. It is estimated that only 21 percent of Americans currently own passports (in itself a record number for the United States, and of course a great many of these are naturalized citizens who need an American passport to travel to their country of origin). For a discussion of his ostensible American disinterest in the rest of the world, see Alkman Granitsas (2007).
13 For the "managed citizen," see Philip N. Howard (2006), and for the thesis that modern (i.e., Western) freedom does not counter government but is in fact one of

14 See Howard (2006), p. 184.
15 The book which more than any other charts this American capitulation to a right-wing populism is Thomas Frank's best-selling *What's the Matter with Kansas?: How Conservatives Won the Heart of America*. Franks, however, does look back to a Golden Age in which the Democratic Party stood for "real" social and economic change. Tom Mertes rightly takes him to task on this and suggests that the Democrats were never really a party with a deep interest in egalitarianism. See Mertes (2004).
16 See Jim Rutenberg (2013).
17 A powerful account of the way the society of the spectacle feeds the current US government's military-economic strategies in its endless "war on terror" is to be found in Retort (2005). But perhaps the most powerful and at the same time cynical manifestations of the spectacle have to do with the heavily media-focused responses of the richer nations to the plight of the African countries. G8 summits regularly make a point of "dealing" with the issue of African poverty, but beyond a few televised gestures of "compassion" very little is done to help African nations. On this, see Tom Nairn (2004).
18 On the British situation, see Ross McKibbin's informative (2006).
19 The current Conservative-Liberal Democrat ruling coalition in the UK is if anything reflective of a Lib Dem shift to the right.
20 On the part played by "low-intensity democracy" in US foreign policy, and its impact in Latin America and Asia, see William I. Robinson (1996). The United States practices its own kind of "low-intensity democracy," since it is a corollary of managed citizenship that the citizens thus managed show a high degree of political disengagement in the public sphere. This is exactly the conclusion drawn from the empirical studies discussed in Nina Eliasoph (1998).

Chapter 14

1 A bibliography of all the relevant works by these writers would be very substantial, and to save space I refer the interested reader to the one given in Bob Jessop (1990). I will follow Deleuze and Guattari's orthographic practice of using "State" in the upper-case.
2 Paul Patton, in his (1984), has provided an exemplary *explication de texte* of what he aptly calls "the conceptual politics" of Deleuze and Guattari. I am indebted to this essay for the light it casts on Plateau 12.
3 A similar triptych—tribal society/despotism/capitalist society—is to be found in the version of the "universal history" developed in *L'Anti-Oedipe*.

(the latter's least acknowledged inventions, see the Foucault-inspired argument in Nikolas Rose (2000).)

4   For a fuller discussion of this theodicy of the State, see my (2009).
5   Deleuze and Guattari are of course not the initiators of this critique of evolutionism. As they themselves acknowledge, the archeologist V. Gordon Childe, and in some ways even Marx himself (described by them as an "historian") are responsible for taking the first steps toward a critique of evolutionism. But the most important figure in this critique for Deleuze and Guattari is Pierre Clastres (1988). A rather different critique of general theories of social evolution is to be found in Michael Mann (1986).
6   Even Michael Mann, despite his brilliant critique of general theories of social development, does not contend that the State-form was present in the Paleolithic Age (as the authors of *Mille plateaux* do). See his (1986), pp. 49ff.
7   This is at variance with a certain conventional reading of a Foucault-like micropolitics which declares this politics to be a "new" development arising in response to modalities and formations of power that did not exist prior to the onset of modernity. Whether Foucault himself should be saddled with this position or whether his own view is really akin to the one elaborated in *Mille plateaux* is a vexatious problem.
8   I owe the example of Brazil to Toni Negri (1987), p. 83. Negri calls this kind of capitalism "Worldwide Integrated Capitalism."
9   See Saskia Sassen (1988) on the redeployment of "downgraded manufacturing" to South-East Asia, the Caribbean Basin, and Mexico. See also Herman M. Schwartz (1989), pp. 9–29, for discussion of the phenomenon of "compulsory underdevelopment."
10 The work in question by Paul Virilio is his (1986). The quotation within the passage just cited is taken from pp. 12–13.

Chapter 15

1   Guattari and Negri (1990), p. 91.
2   Negri views Spinoza's philosophy precisely as an attempt to delineate the ethics and politics of a society constituted on the basis of freedom. See Negri (1991, p. 221). A similar vision of a society constituted on the basis of absolute freedom is evinced in certain strands of German speculative Idealism and Romanticism. I refer here to the text titled "Das älteste Systemprogramms des deutschen Idealismus" [The Earliest System-Program of German Idealism], written it is commonly thought in 1796 and attributed to Friedrich Hölderlin (although the version of the text discovered by Franz Rosenzweig is in Hegel's handwriting). In this text we find a call for an "ethics" whose ruling idea is "the representation of myself as an absolutely free being." For this text, see Hölderlin (1989), pp. 154–6. Negri has noted this affinity between Hölderlin and Spinoza in his (1988b).

3   The description of Deleuze and Guattari as "marxists" may be challenged by some. To pronounce dogmatically on the question of who is legitimately a "marxist" (as opposed to a "postmarxist") in an age that is irreducibly one of "many marxisms" is not only problematic but also futile. Suffice it to say that Deleuze and Guattari view themselves as "marxists." On this, see Deleuze's affirmation in *N*, p. 171.
    It is necessary to be careful when placing these three thinkers in the same marxist bracket, because they diverge in some important respects. Negri is unquestionably a more devoted, even "intraparadigmatic," reader of Marx's *oeuvre*, whereas Deleuze and Guattari seek something like a "mutation" or strategic retention-displacement of this paradigm.
4   For Deleuze, see *EPS* in addition to *SPP*. See also Negri (1991).
5   See Negri (1987); (1988a); (1989a and b); and (1992). See also Guattari and Negri, *CLU*; and Deleuze and Guattari, *AO* and *TP*.
6   The distinction between "socialism" and "communism" adverted to here is made most forcefully in *CLU*. For Guattari and Negri "socialism" is the prisoner of an antiquated paradigm of production predicated on a bureaucratic-centralist model of organization, whereas "communism" is "the establishment of a communal life style in which individuality is recognized and truly liberated, not merely opposed to the collective" (p. 16). Negri and Guattari argue that the crisis of the socialist utopia is to be resolved through engagement in revolutionary communist forms of struggle.
7   See *TP*, pp. 452–3. To quote Deleuze and Guattari: "Capitalism forms when the flow of unqualified wealth encounters the flow of unqualified labor and conjugates with it" (p. 453).
8   See *TP*, pp. 454–5. I have discussed Deleuze and Guattari's treatment of the state-form more fully in Chapter 14.
9   By "real subsumption" Negri means the process whereby labor power and capitalist command are extended throughout the socius, a development that makes production inseparable from communication. On "real subsumption," see Negri (1989a), pp. 177–90. For a concise formulation of Negri's historical periodization, see his (1992).
10 It is not being claimed here that "real subsumption" precludes the existence of noncapitalist formations. Rather, in "real subsumption" a form of social cooperation exists that enables even noncapitalist formations to be inserted into a system of accumulation that renders them productive for capital.
11 Negri makes the claim that political struggles can no longer be defined in terms of contradiction in (1988a), pp. 222–5, and (1992), pp. 153–4.
12 This myth of the state is discussed in my (1990).
13 Nicos Poulantzas provides a sustained critique of both these positions on the state in his (1978). See also Bob Jessop's important study (1985), especially pp. 336ff.
14 The "managed" citizen who is the product of this negative function of the state is discussed in Chapter 13.

15 It may be interesting to compare Negri's position with the views of Samir Amin. In several works Amin has made proposals for the democratic management of production, some of which have been commented on in small ways by Deleuze and Guattari in the *Capitalism and Schizophrenia* project. But, in contrast to the thinkers we have been discussing in this paper, Amin insists that the state has a role to play in the democratic management of production and that there is a genuine dialectic between the state and civil society. He therefore opposes any notion of a "withering away of the state." See Amin (1990).

   In his paper "The Withering Away of Civil Society" presented at the "Marxism in the New World Order" conference at the University of Massachusetts (Amherst) on November 12, 1992, Michael Hardt places a somewhat different emphasis on this aspect of "real subsumption." According to Hardt, in "real subsumption" it is civil society, and not so much the state, that has "withered away." Hardt's argument, I believe, is not really incompatible with mine: the difference is one of emphasis, because in "real subsumption" both the state and civil society collapse into a society-state complex.

16 Negri has shown convincingly that Spinoza's *Political Treatise* is a philosophic concomitant of the political struggle that attended the curtailing of the humanistic revolution:

   > With the assassination of the de Witts, the Dutch anomaly begins to be recuperated in the master course and in the continental rhythm of capitalistic accumulation and the absolutist State. In this frame, the logical struggle, which has always developed in the Spinozian system, understood as the recuperation of the real conditions of constitution, becomes a political struggle, understood as the reconstruction of the historical conditions of revolution. (1991, pp. 204)

   Negri goes on to say why the *Political Treatise* remained a necessarily unfinished work (and this not only because Spinoza died before completing it):

   > The suspension of the work, due to Spinoza's death, coincides with its real, positive, and internal block. But the project lives: It is there, present, taut, ready to be grasped as a message. The temporal dimension, the concept of the future, is formed—an anticipation that the desire and the imagination contain, on the border of a determinate historical block. It continues to grow on itself, awaiting the revolution, the forceful reopening of philosophical possibility. Spinoza does not anticipate illusionism, he experiences and develops it fully. In order to be understood, however, Spinoza needs new, real conditions to be given: Only the revolution poses these conditions. The completion of the *Political Treatise*, the development of the chapter on democracy or, better, on the absolute, intellectual, and corporeal form of the government of the masses, becomes a real problem only within and after the revolution. Within this actuality of the revolution, the power of Spinoza's thought gains a universal significance. (p. 210)

For Negri of course this revolution occurs in the phase of "real subsumption." This issue is discussed more fully in my (2005).

17 See Hardt (1990).
18 I owe this formulation of Negri's rejection of the dialectic to Hardt (1990).
19 Deleuze's most extensively formulated repudiation of the dialectic is to be found in his *NP*. The temptation to think that Deleuze wishes to reject the Hegelian dialectic simply by pitting Nietzsche against Hegel has, however, to be resisted. Michael Hardt has convincingly shown that Bergson, Nietzsche, and Spinoza are read by Deleuze as part of an overall philosophical project. Thus, Deleuze derives from Bergson an ontology that is used in his approach to Nietzsche to constitute an ethics, and in his reading of Spinoza this ontology/ethics is used in turn to frame an ethico-ontological politics. Deleuze's jettisoning of the dialectic must therefore be seen as an element that is interlocked with the other components of this project. See Hardt (1993).
20 See Deleuze (1992).
21 The question of Deleuze's relation to the Hegelian dialectic is a vexed one. In this essay I have accorded a primacy to his work on Nietzsche while bearing in mind that some may argue that his other writings present a differential logic that has a least some affinity with Hegel's dialectic. Even so, I believe this view to be mistaken.
22 Deleuze has undertaken a similar "transcendental" inquiry in regard to Freud in his *M*.
23 There is an excellent description of Deleuze and Guattari's understanding of the mode of production in Massumi (1992), p. 194 n. 51. Desire is given a generative primacy in this scheme of things because it is desire, which is always social and collective, that makes the gun (say) into an instrument of war, or of hunting, or sport, and so forth (as the case may be). On this see *TP*, pp. 89–90.
24 Massumi (1992), p. 194, n. 51.
25 To quote from Deleuze and Guattari:

> Marx, the historian, and Childe, the archaeologist, are in agreement on the following point: the archaic imperial State, which steps in to overcode agricultural communities, presupposes at least a certain level of development of these communities' productive forces since there must be a potential surplus capable of constituting a State stock, of supporting a specialized handicraft class (metallurgy), and of progressively giving rise to public functions. This is why Marx links the archaic State to a certain [precapitalist] "mode of production." (*TP*, p. 428)

26 To quote from Deleuze and Guattari:

> The nation is the very operation of a collective subjectification, to which the modern State corresponds as a process of subjection. It is in the form of the nation-state, with all its possible variations, that the State becomes the model of

> realization for the capitalist axiomatic. This is not at all to say that nations are appearances or ideological phenomena; on the contrary, they are the passional and living forms in which the qualitative homogeneity and the quantitative competition of abstract capital are first realized. (*TP*, pp. 456)

27 See (1989a), p. 179. The pertinence of Foucault for such an analysis of the forms of administrative control and domination in the work of Negri, Guattari, and Deleuze should be obvious.
28 Some caution is needed here because, as has been noted, Deleuze moves to a position that is very like Negri's in his work on the societies of control, and Guattari in his collaboration with Negri does appear to endorse in nearly every detail the latter's "theorization" of the demise of civil society.
29 Negri (1989a), p. 113.
30 Negri gives an outline of the goals and methods of this ontology (1989a, pp. 127–39). To quote him:

> Antagonism, then, does not simplify, but increases the complexity which constitutes the subjects; and by establishing itself, this complexity creates antagonism. It is a very special form of ontology, one which we can here call a *constitutive* ontology, and which is able to arrive at the formation of collective identities through an accumulation of operations which are always analytic and always creatively efficient. (pp. 129; emphasis in original)

31 Negri quite fairly notes that Deleuze and Foucault were, however, seeking to push their thought beyond this point of conceiving antagonism purely in terms of the line of flight—an observation borne out by Deleuze's late work on the societies of control.
32 For an account of simulation, see Deleuze, *DR*, pp. 60–9 and *LS*, pp. 253–79. Deleuze's argument here is complex but reduced to essentials it goes something like this. If, contrary to Plato and the tradition of philosophy derived from him, there can be no primacy of an original over the copy, of a model over the representation, so that there can be no basis for differentiating between "good" original and "bad" copy, then everything is itself a "copy"-"original"; it is an "original" of itself, or rather, its "origin" is a copy or "shadow" of itself. In the absence of any possibility of demarcating copies from putative originals, each thing, in simulation, is thus an absolute singularity. Everything is different from everything else, and this is the basis of multiplicity.
33 I am grateful to Michael Hardt for conversations which helped improve the final draft of this paper. The printed version has benefitted from the criticisms of David Ruccio. The paper was originally presented at the "Marxism in the New World Order: Crises and Possibilities" conference at the University of Massachusetts at Amherst on November 12, 1992.

Chapter 16

1. All references to the English translation of Mao's 1937 essay "On Contradiction" will be to (2007a); as will be references to Mao's 1957 essay "On the Correct Handling of Contradictions among the People" (famous for containing the expression "Let a Hundred Flowers Blossom, Let a Hundred Schools of Thought Contend") will be to 2007b (the expression is on p. 153); and his 1937 essay "On Practice: On the Relation between Knowledge and Practice, between Knowing and Doing" will be to 2007c. Pagination to these essays will be given in the main body of my text. Useful background to Mao's 1937 text is to be found in Liu (1971).

Bibliography

Agamben, Giorgio. (1993) *The Coming Community*, trans. Michael Hardt (Minneapolis: University of Minnesota Press). Originally published as *La comunità che viene* (Turin: Bollati Boringhieri, 1990).

Althusser, Louis. (1969) "Contradiction and Overdetermination," in his *For Marx*, trans. Ben Brewster (Harmondsworth: Penguin), pp. 87–128. Originally published as "Contradiction et surdetermination (Notes pour un recherché)," *La Pensée* 106 (1962), pp. 3–22.

Althusser, Louis. (1971) "Ideology and Ideological State Apparatuses," in *Lenin and Philosophy and Other Essays*, trans. Ben Brewster (London: New Left Books), pp. 127–86. Originally published as "Idéologie et appareils idéologiques d'Etat," *La pensée* 151(May–June 1970), pp. 29–85.

Althusser, Louis. (2006) *Philosophy of the Encounter: Later Writings, 1978–1987*, eds. Oliver Corpet and François Matheron, trans. G.M. Goshgarian (London: Verso).

Amin, Ash (ed.). (1994) *Post-Fordism: A Reader* (Oxford: Blackwell).

Amin, Samir. (1990) *Delinking: Towards a Polycentric World*, trans. Michael Wolfers (London: Zed Books). Originally published as *La déconnexion: pour sortir du système mondial* (Paris: Éditions La Découverte, 1986).

Amin, Samir. (1994) *Re-Reading the Post-War Period: An Intellectual Itinerary*, trans. Michael Wolfers (New York: Monthly Review Press). Originally published as *Itinéraire intellectuel; regards sur le demi-siècle 1945–90* (Paris: L'Harmattan, 1990).

Amin, Samir. (1999) "For a Progressive and Democratic New World Order," in *Globalization and the Dilemmas of the State in the South*, eds. Francis Adams, Satya Dev Gupta, and Kidane Mengisteab (London: Macmillan), pp. 17–32.

Amin, Samir. (2000) "Conditions for Re-launching Development," in *Karl Polanyi: The Contemporary Significance of the Great Transformation*, eds. Kenneth McRobbie and Kari Polanyi (New York: Black Rose Books), pp. 73–84.

Anderson, Perry. (1992) *A Zone of Engagement* (London: Verso).

Anderson, Perry. (2001) "US Elections: Testing Formula Two," *New Left Review* 8 (new series), pp. 5–22.

Badiou, Alain. (1999) *Deleuze: The Clamor of Being*, trans. Louise Burchill (Minneapolis: University of Minnesota Press). Originally published as *Gilles Deleuze: La clameur de l'Être* (Paris: Hachette, 1997).

Badiou, Alain. (2004) "Eight Theses on the Universal," lacan.com (November), at http://www.lacan.com/badeight.htm, accessed on June 19, 2013.

Badiou, Alain. (2005) *Being and Event*, trans. Oliver Feltham (London: Continuum). Originally published *L'être et l'évènement* (Paris: Seuil, 1988).

Balibar, Etienne. (1989) "Spinoza, the Anti-Orwell: The Fear of the Masses," trans. Ted Stolze, *Rethinking Marxism* 2, pp. 104–39.

Balibar, Etienne. (1991) "Citizen Subject," in *Who Comes after the Subject?*, eds. Eduardo Cadava, Peter Connor, and Jean-Luc Nancy (London: Routledge), pp. 33–57.

Balibar, Etienne. (1998) *Identité et différence* (Paris: Seuil).

Balibar, Etienne. (2001) "Je/moi/soi," in *Vocabulaire européen des philosophies* (Paris: Seuil).

Bennington, Geoffrey. (1994) *Legislations: The Politics of Deconstruction* (London: Verso).

Bion, Wilfred. (2005) *The Italian Seminars*, ed. Francesca Bion, trans. Phillip Slotkin (London: Karnac Books).

Bourdieu, Pierre. (1985) "A Free Thinker: 'Do Not Ask Me Who I Am,'" trans. Richard Nice, *Paragraph* 5, pp. 80–89. Originally published as *Le plaisir de savoir*, in Le Monde (Paris), June 27, 1984.

Bowden, Sean. (2011) *The Priority of Events: Deleuze's Logic of Sense* (Edinburgh: Edinburgh University Press).

Brenner, Robert. (2007) "Structure vs. Conjuncture: The 2006 Elections and the Rightward Shift," *New Left Review* 43 (new series), pp. 33–59.

Bryant, Levi R. (2008) *Difference and Givenness: Deleuze's Transcendental Empiricism and the Ontology of Immanence* (Evanston, IL: Northwestern University Press).

Cage, John. (1969) "Diary: Emma Lake Music Workshop 1965," in *A Year from Monday: New Lectures and Writings* (Middletown, CT: Wesleyan University Press).

Calabrese, Omar. (1992) *Neo-Baroque: A Sign of the Times*, trans. Charles Lambert (Princeton: Princeton University Press). Originally published as *L'età neobarocca* (Bari: Laterza, 1987).

Casarino, Cesare, and Negri, Antonio. (2008) *In Praise of the Common: A Conversation on Philosophy and Politics* (Minneapolis: University of Minnesota Press).

Clastres, Pierre. (1988) *Society against the State*, trans. Robert Hurley (New York: Zone Books). Originally published *La Société contre l'État* (Paris: Minuit, 1974).

Colman, Felicity J. (2005) "Cinema: Movement-Image-Recognition-Time," in *Gilles Deleuze: Key Concepts*, ed. Charles J. Stivale (Montreal: McGill-Queen's University Press), pp. 141–56.

Conley, Tom. (1997) "From Multiplicities to Folds: On Style and Form in Deleuze", *The South Atlantic Quarterly* 96, pp. 29–46.

Crockett, Clayton. (2013) *Deleuze beyond Badiou: Ontology, Multiplicity, and Event* (New York: Columbia University Press).

Davidson, Donald. (1970) "Mental Events," in *Experience and Theory*, eds. Lawrence Foster and J.W. Swanson (Amherst: University of Massachusetts Press), pp. 79–101.

Davidson, Donald. (1973) "The Material Mind," in *Logic, Methodology, and the Philosophy of Science*, eds. P. Suppes, L. Henkin, G.C. Moisil, and A. Joja (Amsterdam: North-Holland), pp. 709–22.

Davidson, Donald. (1974) "Psychology as Philosophy," in *Philosophy of Psychology*, ed. S.C. Brown (London: Macmillan), pp. 41–52.

Davidson, Donald. (1993) "Thinking Causes," in *Mental Causation*, eds. John Heil and Albert Mele (Oxford: Clarendon Press), pp. 3–18.

De Pinedo, M. (2006) "Anomalous Monism: Oscillating between Dogmas," *Synthese* 148, pp. 79–97.

Delacampagne, Christian. (1999) *A History of Philosophy in the Twentieth Century*, trans. M.B. DeBevoise (Baltimore: Johns Hopkins University Press). Originally published as *Histoire de la philosophie au XXe siècle* (Paris: Seuil, 1995).

Deleuze, Gilles. (1983a) *Kant's Critical Philosophy: The Doctrine of the Faculties*, trans. Hugh Tomlinson and Barbara Habberjam (Minneapolis: University of Minnesota Press). Originally published as *La philosophie critique de Kant (La doctrine des facultés)* (Paris: Presses Universitaires de France, 1963).

Deleuze, Gilles. (1983b) *Nietzsche and Philosophy*, trans. Hugh Tomlinson (New York: Columbia University Press). Originally published as *Nietzsche et la philosophie* (Paris: Presses Universitaires de France, 1962).

Deleuze, Gilles. (1986) *Cinema 1: The Movement-Image*, trans. Hugh Tomlinson and Barbara Habberjam (Minneapolis: University of Minnesota Press). Originally published as *Cinéma 1: L'image movement* (Paris: Minuit, 1983).

Deleuze, Gilles. (1987) "On the Superiority of Anglo-American Literature," in Deleuze and Parnet (1987), pp. 36–76.

Deleuze, Gilles. (1988a) *Bergsonism*, trans. Hugh Tomlinson and Barbara Habberjam (New York: Zone Books). Originally published as *Le Bergsonisme* (Paris: Presses Universitaires de France, 1966).

Deleuze, Gilles. (1988b) *Foucault*, trans. Seán Hand (Minneapolis: University of Minnesota Press). Originally published as *Foucault* (Paris: Minuit, 1986).

Deleuze, Gilles. (1988c) *Spinoza: Practical Philosophy*, trans. Robert Hurley (San Francisco: City Lights). Originally published as *Spinoza: philosophie pratique* (Paris: Presses Universitaires de France, 1970).

Deleuze, Gilles. (1989a) *Masochism: Coldness and Cruelty*, trans. Jean McNeil and Aude Willm (New York: Zone Books). Originally published as Le *Froid et le Cruel* (Paris: Minuit, 1967).

Deleuze, Gilles. (1989b) *Cinema 2: The Time-Image*, trans. Hugh Tomlinson and Robert Goleta (Minneapolis: University of Minnesota Press). Originally published as *Cinéma 2: L'image-temps* (Paris: Minuit, 1985).

Deleuze, Gilles. (1989c) "On the 'Crystalline Regime,'" trans. D.N. Rodowick, *Art and Text* 34 (1989), pp. 18–22. Originally published as "Sur le regime cristallin," *Hors Cadre* 4 (1986), pp. 39–45.

Deleuze, Gilles. (1990a) *Expressionism in Philosophy: Spinoza*, trans. Martin Joughin (New York: Zone Books). Originally published as *Spinoza et le problème de l'expressionisme* (Paris: Minuit, 1968).

Deleuze, Gilles. (1990b) *The Logic of Sense*, trans. Mark Lester with Charles Stivale, ed. Constantin V. Boundas (New York: Columbia University Press). Originally published as *Logique du sens* (Paris: Minuit, 1969).

Deleuze, Gilles. (1991) *Empiricism and Subjectivity: An Essay on Hume's Theory of Human Nature*, trans. Constantin V. Boundas (New York: Columbia University Press). Originally published as *Empirisme et subjectivité: essai sur la Nature Humaine selon Hume* (Paris: Presses Universitaires de France, 1953).

Deleuze, Gilles. (1992) "Postscript on the Societies of Control," *October* 59, pp. 3–7.

Deleuze, Gilles. (1993) *The Fold: Leibniz and the Baroque*, trans. Tom Conley (Minneapolis: University of Minnesota Press). Originally published as *Le pli: Leibniz et le baroque* (Paris: Minuit, 1988).

Deleuze, Gilles. (1994) *Difference and Repetition*, trans. Paul Patton (New York: Columbia University Press). Originally published as Originally published as *Différence et Répétition* (Paris: Presses Universitaires de France, 1968).

Deleuze, Gilles. (1995) *Negotiations, 1972–1990*, trans. Martin Joughin (New York: Columbia University Press). Originally published as *Pourparlers* (Paris: Minuit, 1990).

Deleuze, Gilles. (1997) *Essays Critical and Clinical*, trans. Daniel W. Smith and Michael A. Greco (Minneapolis: University of Minnesota Press). Originally published as *Critique et clinique* (Paris: Minuit, 1993).

Deleuze, Gilles. (2000) *Proust and Signs: The Complete Text*, trans. Richard Howard (Minneapolis: University of Minnesota Press). Originally published as *Proust et signes* (Paris: Presses Universitaires de France, 1970).

Deleuze, Gilles. (2001) *Pure Immanence: Essays on a Life*, trans. Anne Boyman, intro. John Rajchman (New York: Zone Books).

Deleuze, Gilles. (2004) *Desert Islands and Other Texts*, ed. Sylvère Lotringer, trans. Michael Taomina (New York: Semiotext(e)).

Deleuze, Gilles. (2006) *Two Regimes of Madness: Texts and Interviews 1975–1995*, ed. David Lapoujade, trans. Ames Hodges and Mike Taormina (New York: Semiotext(e)).

Deleuze, Gilles, and Guattari, Félix. (1977) *Anti-Oedipus*, trans. Robert Hurley, Mark Seem, and Helen R. Lane (New York: Viking). Originally published as *L'Anti-Œdipe: capitalisme et schizophrénie* (Paris: Minuit, 1972).

Deleuze, Gilles, and Guattari, Félix. (1987) *A Thousand Plateaus: Capitalism and Schizophrenia*, trans. Brian Massumi (Minneapolis: University of Minnesota Press). Originally published as *Mille plateaux: capitalisme et schizophrénie* (Paris: Minuit, 1980).

Deleuze, Gilles, and Guattari, Félix. (1994) *What Is Philosophy?*, trans. Hugh Tomlinson and Graham Burchell (New York: Columbia University Press). Originally published as *Qu'est-ce que la philosophie?* (Paris: Minuit, 1991).

Deleuze, Gilles, and Parnet, Claire. (1987) *Dialogues*, trans. Hugh Tomlinson and Barbara Habberjam (New York: Columbia University Press). Originally published as *Dialogues* (Paris: Flammarion, 1996; original edition in 1977).

Derrida, Jacques. (1976) *Of Grammatology*, trans. Gayatri Chakravorty Spivak (Baltimore: Johns Hopkins University Press). Originally published as *De la Grammatologie* (Paris: Minuit, 1967).

Derrida, Jacques. (1978) "Structure, Sign, and Play in the Discourse of the Human Sciences," in his *Writing and Difference*, trans. Alan Bass (London: Routledge & Kegan Paul). Originally published as *L'écriture et la différence* (Paris: Seuil, 1967).

Derrida, Jacques. (1997) *Politics of Friendship*, trans. George Collins (London: Verso). Originally published *Politiques de l'amitié* (Paris: Éditions Galilée, 1994).

Descartes, René. (2000) *Philosophical Essays and Correspondence*, ed. Roger Ariew (Indianapolis: Hackett). Also in *Oeuvres de Descartes* (Paris: J. Vrin, 1987), vol. 1.

Dosse, François. (1997) *History of Structuralism (vol. 2): The Sign Sets, 1967–Present*, trans. Deborah Glassman (Minneapolis: University of Minnesota Press). Originally published as *Histoire du structuralisme, II. Le chant du cygne, de 1967 á nos jours* (Paris: Éditions La Découverte, 1992).

Dosse, François. (2010) *Gilles Deleuze and Félix Guattari: Intersecting Lives*, trans. Deborah Glassman (New York: Columbia University Press). Originally published *as Gilles Deleuze et Félix Guattari: Biographie croisée* (Paris: Éditions La Découverte, 2007).

Duménil, Gerard, and Lévy, Dominique. (2004) "Neoliberal Income Trends: Wealth, Class and Ownership in the USA," *New Left Review* 30 (new series), pp. 105–33.

Dumézil, Georges. (1948) *Mithra-Varuna* (Paris: Gallimard).

Eliasoph, Nina. (1998) *Avoiding Politics: How Americans Produce Apathy in Everyday Life* (Cambridge: Cambridge University Press).

Fichte, Johann Gottlieb. (1970) *Fichtes Sämmtliche Werke: Vol 1*, ed. I.H. Fichte (Berlin: W. de Gruyter).

Flaxman, Gregory. (2011) *Gilles Deleuze and the Fabulation of Philosophy: Powers of the False*, Vol. 1 (Minneapolis: University of Minnesota Press).

Fodor, Jerry. (1991) "You Can Fool Some of the People All of the Time, Everything Else Being Equal: Hedged Laws and Psychological Explanations," *Mind, New Series* 100, pp. 19–34.

Foucault, Michel. (1965) *Madness and Civilization: A History of Civilization in the Age of Reason*, trans. Richard Howard (New York: Pantheon). Originally published as *Folie et déraison: Histoire de la folie à l'âge classique* (Paris: Plon, 1961).

Foucault, Michel. (1970) *The Archaeology of Knowledge*, trans. A.M. Sheridan Smith (New York: Pantheon). Originally published as *L'archéologie du savoir* (Paris: Gallimard, 1969).

Foucault, Michel. (1970) *The Order of Things: An Archaeology of the Human Sciences*, trans. A.M. Sheridan Smith (New York: Pantheon). Originally published as *Les mots et les choses* (Paris: Gallimard, 1966).

Foucault, Michel. (1973) *The Birth of the Clinic: An Archaeology of Medical Perception*, trans. Alan Sheridan (London: Tavistock). Originally published as *Naissance de la clinique: une archéologie du regard medical* (Paris: Presses Universitaires de France, 1963).

Foucault, Michel. (1977a) *Discipline and Punish: The Birth of the Prison*, trans. Alan Sheridan (New York: Pantheon). Originally published as *Surveiller et punir: naissance de la prison* (Paris: Gallimard, 1975).

Foucault, Michel. (1977b) *Language, Counter-memory, Practice: Selected Essays and Interviews*, ed. Donald F. Bouchard, trans. Bouchard and Sherry Simon (Ithaca, NY: Cornell University Press).

Foucault, Michel. (1977c) "Preface," to Gilles Deleuze and Félix Guattari, *Anti-Oedipus*, in AO, pp. xi–xiv.

Foucault, Michel. (1979) *The History of Sexuality, vol. 1: An Introduction*, trans. Robert Hurley (New York: Pantheon). Originally published as *La Volonte de savoir* (Paris: Gallimard, 1978).

Foucault, Michel. (1980) "Georges Canguilhem: Philosopher of Error," *Ideology and Consciousness* 7, pp. 51–62.

Foucault, Michel. (1985) *The Use of Pleasure*, trans. Robert Hurley (New York: Pantheon). Originally published as *L'Usage des plaisirs* (Paris: Gallimard, 1984).

Foucault, Michel. (1986) *The Care of the Self*, trans. Robert Hurley (New York: Pantheon). Originally published as *Le Souci de soi* (Paris: Gallimard, 1984).

Foucault, Michel. (1989) *Foucault Live (Interviews, 1966–84)*, trans. John Johnston, ed. Sylvère Lotringer (New York: Semiotext(e)).

Foucault, Michel. (1991) *The Foucault Effect: Studies in Governmentality: With Two Lectures by and an Interview with Michel Foucault*, ed. Graham Burchell, Colin Gordon, and Peter Miller (Chicago: University of Chicago Press).

Foucault, Michel. (1991) *Remarks on Marx (Conversations with Duccio Trombadori)*, trans. R. James Goldstein and James Cascaito (New York: Semiotext(e)).

Foucault, Michel. (1994) "Conversation avec Werner Schroeter," in *Michel Foucault: Dits et écrits 1954–1984*, vol. IV, eds. Daniel Defert and François Ewald (Paris: Gallimard).

Foucault, Michel. (1997a) "The Ethics of the Concern for Self as a Practice of Freedom," in *The Essential Works of Michel Foucault 1954–1984, vol. I (Ethics)*, ed. Paul Rabinow, trans. R. Hurley and others (New York: The New Press), pp. 281–301.

Foucault, Michel. (1997b) "On the Genealogy of Ethics: An Overview of Work in Progress," in *The Essential Works of Michel Foucault 1954–1984, vol. I (Ethics)*, ed. Paul Rabinow, trans. R. Hurley and others (New York: The New Press), pp. 253–80.

Foucault, Michel. (2006) *History of Madness*, trans. Jonathan Murphy and Jean Khalfa, ed. Jean Khalfa (London: Routledge). Originally published as *Folie et déraison: Histoire de la folie à l'âge classique* (Paris: Plon, 1961).

Frank, Thomas. (2004) *What's the Matter with Kansas?: How Conservatives Won the Heart of America* (New York: Metropolitan Books).

Gardiner, Muriel. (1972) *The Wolf-Man and Sigmund Freud* (London: Karnac).

Gordon, Colin. (1981) "The Subtracting Machine," *I & C* 8, pp. 27–40.

Granitsas, Alkman. (2007) "Americans Are Tuning Out the World," Yale Center for the Study of Globalization Website, at http://yaleglobal.yale.edu/display.article?id=6553, accessed on January 28, 2007.

Guattari, Félix. (1995) *Chaosmosis: An Ethico-Aesthetic Paradigm*, trans. Paul Bains and Julian Pefanis (Bloomington: Indiana University Press). Originally published as *Chaosmose* (Paris: Éditions Galilée, 1992).

Guattari, Félix, and Negri, Antonio. (1990) *Communists Like Us: New Spaces of Liberty, New Lines of Alliance*, trans. Michael Ryan (New York: Semiotext(e)). A postscript by Negri has been added for the English edition. Originally published as *Les nouveaux espaces de la liberté* (Paris: Dominique Bedou, 1985).

Hacker, Jacob, and Pierson, Paul. (2004) *Off Center: The Republican Revolution and the Erosion of American Democracy* (New Haven: Yale University Press).

Halper, Stefan, and Clarke, Jonathan. (2004) *America Alone: The Neo-Conservatives and the Global Order* (Cambridge: Cambridge University Press).

Hardt, Michael. (1990) "Review of Toni Negri, Revolution Retrieved," *Rethinking Marxism* 3, pp. 171–81.

Hardt, Michael. (1993) *Gilles Deleuze: An Apprenticeship in Philosophy* (Minneapolis: University of Minnesota Press).

Hegel, Georg Wilhelm Friedrich. (1989) *Science of Logic*, trans. A.V. Miller (Atlantic Highlands, NJ: Humanities Press).

Hegel, Georg Wilhelm Friedrich. (1997) *The Difference between Fichte's and Schelling's System of Philosophy*, trans. Horton S. Harris and Walter Cerf (Albany, NY: State University of New York Press).

Hobbes, Thomas. (1991) *Leviathan*, ed. Richard Tuck (Cambridge: Cambridge University Press).

Hodgson, Godfrey. (2004) *More Equal than Others* (Princeton, NJ: Princeton University Press).

Hölderlin, Friedrich. (1989) *Essays and Letters on Theory*, ed. and trans. Thomas Pfau (New York: State University Press of New York).

Honderich, Ted. (1981) "Psychophysical Lawlike Connections and Their Problem," *Inquiry* 24, pp. 277–303.

Howard, Philip N. (2006) *New Media Campaigns and the Managed Citizen* (Cambridge: Cambridge University Press).

Jameson, Fredric. (1993) "Actually Existing Marxism," *Polygraph* 6/7, pp. 170–95.

Jameson, Fredric. (1995) "On Cultural Studies," in *The Identity in Question*, ed. John Rajchman (New York: Routledge), pp. 251–95.

Jameson, Fredric. (1996) "Marxism and Dualism in Deleuze," *South Atlantic Quarterly* 96, pp. 393–416.

Jessop, Bob. (1985) *Nicos Poulantzas: Marxist Theory and Political Strategy* (New York: St. Martin's Press).

Jessop, Bob. (1990) *State Theory: Putting the Capitalist States in Their Place* (Cambridge: Polity Press).

Jessop, Bob. (1997) "Capitalism and Its Future: Remarks on Regulation, Government and Governance," *Review of International Political Economy* 4, pp. 561–81.

Jolley, Nicholas. (1992) "The Reception of Descartes' Philosophy", in *The Cambridge Companion to Descartes*, ed. John Cottingham (Cambridge: Cambridge University Press), pp. 393–423.

Kant, Immanuel. (1991) *Kant: Political Writings*, ed. Hans Reiss, trans. H.B. Nisbet (Cambridge: Cambridge University Press).

Kelly, Michael. (1982) *Modern French Marxism* (Baltimore: Johns Hopkins University Press).

Khilnani, Sunil. (1993) *Arguing Revolution: The Intellectual Left in Postwar France* (New Haven: Yale University Press).

Kramer, Fritz. (1993) *The Red Fez: Art and Spirit Possession in Africa*, trans. Malcolm R. Green (London: Verso). Originally published as *Der rote Fes: Über Besessenheit und Kunst in Afrika* (Frankfurt am Main: Athenäum, 1987).

Kristeva, Julia. (1984) *The Revolution in Poetic Language*, trans. Margaret Waller (New York: Columbia University Press). Originally published as *La révolution du langage poétique: l'avant-garde à la fin du XIXe siècle. Lautréamont et Mallarmé* (Paris: Seuil, 1974).

Lazare, Daniel. (1996) *The Frozen Republic: How the Constitution Is Paralyzing Democracy* (New York: Harcourt Brace).

Lazare, Daniel. (2001) *The Velvet Coup: The Constitution, the Supreme Court, and the Decline of American Democracy* (London: Verso).

Lenin, V.I. (1958) "Conspectus of Hegel's *Lectures on the History of Philosophy*," in his *Collected Works* (Moscow: Progress Press), vol. 38.

Lieven, Anatol. (2004) *America Right or Wrong: An Anatomy of American Nationalism* (Oxford: Oxford University Press).

Liu, Joseph. (1971) "Mao's 'On Contradiction,'" *Studies in Soviet Thought* 11, pp. 71–89.

Lukács, Georg. (1981) *Essays on Realism*, ed. and intro. Rodney Livingstone, trans. David Fernbach (Cambridge, MA: MIT Press). Originally published in Georg Lukács, *Werke, vol. 4: Essays über Realismus* (West Germany: Luchterhand, 1971).

Lyotard, Jean-François. (1983) *Libidinal Economy*, trans. Ian Hamilton Grant (Bloomington, IN: Indiana University Press). Originally published as *Économie libidinale* (Paris: Minuit, 1974).

Mann, Michael. (1986) *The Sources of Social Power: Vol. 1: A History of Power from the Beginning to AD 1760* (Cambridge: Cambridge University Press).

Mao, Tse-Tung. (2007a) "On Contradiction," in *On Practice and Contradiction: Mao Tse-Tung*, ed. Slavoj Žižek (London: Verso), pp. 67–102.

Mao, Tse-Tung. (2007b) "On Practice: On the Relation between Knowledge and Practice, between Knowing and Doing," in *On Practice and Contradiction: Mao Tse-Tung*, ed. Slavoj Žižek (London: Verso), pp. 52–66.

Mao, Tse-Tung. (2007c) "On the Correct Handling of Contradictions among the People," in *On Practice and Contradiction: Mao Tse-Tung*, ed. Slavoj Žižek (London: Verso), pp. 130–66.

Massumi, Brian. (1987) "Realer than Real: The Simulacrum According to Deleuze and Guattari," *Copyright* #1, pp. 90–97.

Massumi, Brian. (1992) *A User's Guide to Capitalism and Schizophrenia: Deviations from Deleuze and Guattari* (Cambridge, MA: MIT Press).

McKibbin, Ross. (2006) "The Destruction of the Public Sphere," *London Review of Books* 28:1, pp. 3, 6.

Menn, Stephen. (1998) "The Intellectual Setting," in *The Cambridge History of Seventeenth-Century Philosophy*, eds. Daniel Garber and Michael Ayers (Cambridge: Cambridge University Press), pp. 33–86.

Merleau-Ponty, Maurice. (1968) *The Visible and the Invisible, Followed by Working Notes*, trans. Alphonso Lingis (Evanston, IL: Northwestern University Press). Originally published as *Le visible et l'invisible, suivi de note travail*, ed. Claude Lefort (Paris: Gallimard, 1964).

Mertes, Tom. (2004) "A Republican Proletariat," *New Left Review* 30 (new series), pp. 37–47.

Michels, Robert. (1915) *Political Parties: A Sociological Study of the Oligarchical Tendencies of Modern Democracy*, trans. Eden Paul and Cedar Paul (New York: Hearst's International Library). Originally published as *Ur Soziologie des Parteiwesens in der modernen Demokratie: Untersuchungen über die oligarchischen Tendenzen des Gruppenlebens* (Leipzig: W. Klinkhardt, 1911).

Morris, Meaghan. (1994) "Banality in Cultural Studies," in *Contemporary Literary Criticism: Literary and Cultural Studies*, eds. Robert Con Davis and Ronald Schleifer (New York: Longman, 3rd ed.), pp. 642–66.

Nairn, Tom. (2004) "At the G8," *London Review of Books* 27:15, pp. 19–20.

Negri, Antonio. (1987) "Interview with Alice Jardine and Brian Massumi," *Copyright* #I, pp. 74–89.

Negri, Antonio. (1988a) *Revolution Retrieved: Selected Writings on Marx, Keynes, Capitalist Crisis and New Social Subjects (1967–83)*, trans. Ed Emery and John Merrington (London: Red Notes).

Negri, Antonio. (1988b) "Between Infinity and Community: Notes on Materialism in Spinoza and Leopardi," trans. Michael Hardt, *Studia Spinozana*, pp. 151–75.

Negri, Antonio. (1989a) *The Politics of Subversion: A Manifesto for the Twenty-First Century*, trans. James Newell (Cambridge: Polity Press).

Negri, Antonio. (1989b) *Marx beyond Marx: Lessons on the Grundrisse*, trans. Harry Cleaver, Michael Ryan, and Maurizio Viano (New York: Autonomedia). Originally published as *Marx oltre Marx: Quaderno di lavoro sui Grundrisse* (Milan: Feltrinelli, 1979).

Negri, Antonio. (1991) *The Savage Anomaly: The Power of Spinoza's Metaphysics and Politics*, trans. Michael Hardt (Minneapolis: University of Minnesota Press). Originally published as *L'anomalia selvaggia* (Milan: Feltrinelli, 1981).

Negri, Antonio. (1992) "Twenty Theses on Marx: Interpretation of the Class Situation Today," trans. Michael Hardt, *Polygraph* #5, pp. 136–70.

Negri, Antonio. (1996) "Notes on the Evolution of the Thought of the Later Althusser," trans. Olga Vasile, in *Postmodern Materialism and the Future of Marxist Theory: Essays in the Althusserian Tradition*, eds. Antonio Callari and David F. Ruccio (Hanover, NH: Wesleyan University Press), pp. 51–68.

Nietzsche, Friedrich. (1968a) *Basic Writings of Nietzsche*, trans. Walter Kaufmann (New York: Modern Library).

Nietzsche, Friedrich. (1968b) *The Will to Power*, ed. Walter Kaufmann, trans. Kaufmann and R.J. Hollingdale (New York: Vintage Books).

Nietzsche, Friedrich. (2005) *The Anti-Christ, Ecce Homo, Twilight of the Idols and Other Writings*, ed. Aaron Ridley, trans. Judith Norman (Cambridge: Cambridge University Press).

Obholzer, Karin. (1982) *Wolf Man—Sixty Years Later: Conversations with Freud's Patient*, trans. Michael Shaw (London: Routledge & Kegan Paul). Originally published as *Gesprache mit dem Wolfsmann* (Hamburg: Rowohlt, 1980).

Orrom, Michael, and Williams, Raymond. (1954) *Preface to Film* (London: Film Drama)

Parr, Adrian (ed.). (2010) *The Deleuze Dictionary* (Edinburgh: Edinburgh University Press).

Patton, Paul. (1981) "Notes for a Glossary," *I & C* 8, pp. 41–8.

Patton, Paul. (1984) "Conceptual Politics and the War-Machine in Mille Plateaux," *SubStance* #44/45 (vol. XIII), pp. 61–80.

Patton, Paul. (1996) "One of the Saints," *Radical Philosophy* 76, pp. 2–3.

Patton, Paul. (2000) *Deleuze and the Political* (London: Routledge).

Patton, Paul. (2001a) "The Translation of Indigenous Land into Property: The Mere Analogy of English Jurisprudence," *Parallax* 6, pp. 25–38.

Patton, Paul. (2001b) "Reconciliation, Aboriginal Rights and Constitutional Paradox in Australia," *The Australian Feminist Law Journal* 15, pp. 25–40.

Patton, Paul. (2004a) "Political Liberalism and Indigenous Rights," in *Philosophy and Aboriginal Rights: Critical Dialogues*, eds. Sandra Tomsons and Lorraine Mayer (Ontario: Oxford University Press Canada), pp. 151–60.

Patton, Paul. (2004b) "Colonisation and Historical Injustice—The Australian Experience," in *Justice in Time: Responding to Historical Injustice*, ed. Lukas H. Meyer (Baden-Baden: Nomos Verlagsgesellschaft), pp. 159–72.

Patton, Paul, and Protevi, John (eds.). (2003) *Between Deleuze and Derrida* (London: Continuum).

Patton, Paul, Braidotti, Rosi, and Macey, David. (1996) "Gilles Deleuze, 1925–95," *Radical Philosophy* 76, pp. 2–6.

Pearson, Keith Ansell. (1999) *Germinal Life: The Difference and Repetition of Deleuze* (London: Routledge).

Pinkard Terry. (2000) *Hegel: A Biography* (Cambridge: Cambridge University Press).

Plotz, David. (2007) "Phil Gramm," Slate Website, at http://www.slate.com/id/114972/#ContinueArticle, accessed on January 22, 2007.

Poulantzas, Nicos. (1978) *State, Power, Socialism*, trans. Patrick Camiller (London: New Left Books). Originally published as *L'État, le pouvoir, le socialism* (Paris: Presses Universitaires de France, 1978).

Protevi, John. (2006) "Deleuze, Guattari, and Emergence," *Paragraph: A Journal of Modern Critical Theory* 29, pp. 19–39.

Retort (Boal, Iain, Clark, T.J., Matthews, Joseph, and Watts, Michael). (2005) *Afflicted Powers: Capital and Spectacle in an Age of War* (London: Verso).

Richards, David. (1994) *Masks of Difference: Cultural Representations in Literature, Anthropology and Art* (Cambridge: Cambridge University Press).

Robinson, William I. (1996) *Promoting Polyarchy: Globalization, US Intervention, and Hegemony* (Cambridge: Cambridge University Press).

Rose, Nikolas. (1998) *Powers of Freedom: Reframing Political Thought* (Cambridge: Cambridge University Press).

Rose, Nikolas. (2000) "Governing Cities, Governing Citizens," in *Democracy, Citizenship and the Global City*, ed. Engin F. Isin (London: Routledge), pp. 95–109.

Ross, Kristin. (2002) *May '68 and Its Afterlives* (Chicago: University of Chicago Press).

Runciman, David. (1997) *Pluralism and the Personality of the State* (Cambridge: Cambridge University Press).

Runciman, David. (2010) "Hobbes's Theory of Representation: Anti-democratic or Proto-democratic?," in *Political Representation*, eds. Ian Shapiro, Susan C. Stokes, Elisabeth Jean Wood, and Alexander S. Kirshner (Cambridge: Cambridge University Press), pp. 15–34.

Rutenberg, Jim. (2013) "Data You Can Believe In: The Obama Campaign's Digital Masterminds Cash In," *New York Times*, accessed on June 20, 2013, at http://www.nytimes.com/2013/06/23/magazine/the-obama-campaigns-digital-masterminds-cash-in.html?_r=0, accessed on June 25, 2013.

Sassen, Saskia. (1988) *The Mobility of Capital and Labor: A Study in International Investment and Labor Flow* (Cambridge: Cambridge University Press).

Scheer, Robert. (2006) "Put the Politicians in the Enron Docket," Truthdig.com, at http://www.truthout.org/docs_2006/020106O.shtml, accessed on January 2, 2007.

Schmitt, Carl. (1985) *The Crisis of Parliamentary Democracy*, trans. Ellen Kennedy (Cambridge, MA: MIT Press). Originally published as *Die geistesgeschichtliche Lage des heutigen Parliamentarismus* (Berlin: Duncker and Humblot, 1923).

Schmitt, Carl. (2003) *The Nomos of the Earth in the International Law of the Jus Publicum Europaeum*, trans. G.L. Ulmen (New York: Telos). Originally published as *Der Nomos der Erde im Völkerrecht des Jus Publicum Europaeum* (Cologne: Greven Verlag, 1950).

Schmitt, Carl. (2007) *The Concept of the Political*, Expanded Edition, trans. George Schwab (Chicago: University of Chicago Press). Originally published as *Der Begriff des Politischen* (Munich: Duncker and Humblot, 1932).

Schultz, James A. (2006) *Courtly Love, the Love of Courtliness, and the History of Sexuality* (Chicago: University of Chicago Press).

Schwartz, Herman M. (1989) *In the Dominions of Debt: Historical Perspectives on Dependent Development* (Ithaca, NY: Cornell University Press).

Sen, Amartya. (1977) "Rational Fools: A Critique of the Behavioral Foundations of Economic Theory," *Philosophy & Public Affairs* 6, pp. 317–44.

Serres, Michel, with Latour, Bruno. (1995) *Conversations on Science, Culture, and Time*, trans. Roxanne Lapidus (Ann Arbor: University of Michigan Press). Originally published as *Eclaircissements* (Paris: Éditions François Bourin, 1990).

Sklair, Leslie (ed.). (1994) *Capitalism and Development* (London and New York: Routledge).
Smith, Dai. (2008) *Raymond Williams: A Warrior's Tale* (Cardigan, Wales: Parthian Press).
Smith, Daniel W. (2012) *Essays on Deleuze* (Edinburgh: Edinburgh University Press).
Spinoza, Baruch. (2000) *Ethics, Demonstrated in Geometrical Order* (1677), ed. and trans. G.H.R. Parkinson (Oxford: Oxford University Press).
Starobinski, Jean. (1991) *L'Oeil Vivant*, vol. 2 (Paris: Gallimard).
Suchting, Wal. (2004) "Althusser's Late Thinking about Materialism," *Historical Materialism* 12, pp. 3–70.
Surin, Kenneth. (1990) "Marxism(s) and 'the Withering Away of the State,'" *Social Text* #27, pp. 35–54.
Surin, Kenneth. (1991) "The Undecidable and the Fugitive: *Mille Plateaux* and the State-Form," *SubStance* [USA] #66, pp. 102–13.
Surin, Kenneth. (1995) "On Producing the Concept of a Global Culture," *South Atlantic Quarterly* 94, pp. 1179–99.
Surin, Kenneth. (1996) "'The Continued Relevance of Marxism' as a Question: Some Propositions," in *Marxism Beyond Marxism*, eds. Saree Makdisi, Cesare Casarino, and Rebecca Karl (London and New York: Routledge), pp. 181–213.
Surin, Kenneth. (2005) "'Now Everything Must Be Reinvented': Negri and Revolution," in *The Philosophy of Antonio Negri*, eds. Timothy Murphy and Abdul-Karim Mustapha (London: Pluto Press), pp. 205–42.
Surin, Kenneth. (2009) *Freedom Not Yet: Liberation and the Next World Order* (Durham, NC: Duke University Press).
Surin, Kenneth. (2010) "Partial Objects," in *The Deleuze Dictionary*, ed. Adrian Parr (Edinburgh: Edinburgh University Press), pp. 202–04.
Surin, Kenneth. (2011) "A Genealogy of Comparative Literature in the USA," in *Blackwell Companion to Comparative Literature*, eds. Ali Behdad and Dominic Thomas (Oxford: Wiley-Blackwell), pp. 65–72.
Thacker, Eugene. (2004) *Biomedia* (Minneapolis: University of Minnesota Press).
Thacker, Eugene. (2005a) *The Global Genome: Biotechnology, Politics, and Culture* (Cambridge, MA: MIT Press).
Thacker, Eugene. (2005b) "Biophilosophy for the 21st Century" (2005), at http://www.ctheory.net/articles.aspx?id=472, accessed on June 15, 2013.
Thacker, Eugene. (2013) "Bats, Rats and Packs," at http://lmc.gatech.edu/~broglio/animality/bats.html, accessed on June 15, 2013.
Théret, Bruno. (2007) "Theoretical Problems in International Comparisons: Toward a Reciprocal Improvement of Societal Approach and Regulation Theory by Methodic Structuralism," in Association Recherché & Régulation, at http://web.upmfgrenoble.fr/regulation/Journees_d_etude/Journee_1998/theret.htm, accessed on January 22, 2007.
Virilio, Paul. (1986) *Speed and Politics: An Essay on Dromology*, trans. Mark Polizotti (New York: Semiotext(e)). Originally published *Vitesse et politique: essai de dromologie* (Paris: Éditions Galilée, 1977).

Wang, Hui. (2016) "Contradiction, Systemic Crisis and Direction for Change: An Interview with Wang Hui," in *Foreign Theoretical Trends* (in Chinese), English trans at Verso Blogs, at https://www.versobooks.com/blogs/2555-contradiction-systemic-crisis-and-the-direction-for-change-an-interview-with-wang-hui.

Williams, James. (2003) *Gilles Deleuze's Difference and Repetition: A Critical Introduction and Guide* (Edinburgh: Edinburgh University Press).

Williams, James. (2005) *The Transversal Thought of Gilles Deleuze: Encounters and Influences* (Manchester: Clinamen Press).

Williams, Raymond. (1977) *Marxism and Literature* (Oxford: Oxford University Press).

Williams, Raymond. (1985) *Towards 2000* (Harmondsworth: Penguin).

Zibechi, Raúl. (2011) "The Revolution by Ordinary People," in *Johannesburg Workshop in Theory and Criticism*, trans. Cristina Cielo, at http://jwtc.org.za/volume_4/raul_zibechi/revolutions_of_ordinary.htm.

Žižek, Slavoj. (1997) *The Plague of Fantasies* (London: Verso).

Zourabichvili, François. (2003) *Le vocabulaire de Deleuze* (Paris: Ellipses).

Index

abjection 140, 144, 145
Abramoff, Jack 150, 229 n.6
abstraction 2–5, 7, 9, 60, 88, 126, 139, 168, 169, 175, 189
   and capital 236 n.26
   and concepts 5, 48
   and essences 86
   and exchange 39, 111, 201
   and flows 105
   and individuals 55
   and quantity 224 n.35
Abu Ghraib prison 128
Abu-Lughod, Janet 224 n.36
acceleration 39, 153, 206 n.13
accords 11–12, 76–7. *See also* concerts
   and capital 106, 107
   meta-accords 11, 77, 224 n.36
   transcendental 108, 111–13, 224 n.39, 225 n.42
accumulation 6–7, 9, 11, 36–8, 106–7, 115, 147–8
   and desire 182
   and energies 187
Aceh 113
act 139, 159–60
   and being 83, 87, 125, 137
   Hobbes 95
   Kant 98
   and speed 24
   Spinoza 210 n.3
action 17, 25, 34, 38, 82, 102, 125, 140, 166, 197, 201, 219 n.2, 222 n.15
   and Herzog, Werner 70, 165
   and Kant 98
   political 96–7
   and thought 47
activity 19–20, 26, 32, 60, 80, 95, 172, 175
   and concept 35
   and force 34, 52, 83
   and Kant 7, 93, 96
   and political action 86, 89
   vs. passivity and reactivity 75

actuality 25, 43, 56, 86, 89, 103, 107, 128, 223 n.19, 233 n.13
   the actual 19, 46, 64, 86, 88, 121–2, 140, 166, 217 n.19, 223 n.24
actualization 18, 25, 88, 178, 207 n.26
   and possibility 11
Adorno, T.W. 4
aesthetics 15, 45, 54, 71, 74–7, 80–3, 85–6, 130, 203 n.2, 210 n.2
aisthesis 45
affect 4, 9–10, 20, 28, 31, 37, 54–5, 58, 60–9, 70–1, 102, 127–8, 141, 171, 181, 185, 199, 217 n.20
   and affection 32, 58, 62–3, 217 n.20, 218 n.23
affiliation 12, 20–1, 156
Africa 145, 231 n.17
Agamben, Giorgio 87, 99, 207 n.26, 225 n.43
Albright, Madeleine 151
algorithm 7, 107, 180, 206 n.13
al-Qaeda 230 n.8
Althusser, Louis 10, 86–7, 91–2, 101, 109, 127, 178, 195–6, 218 n.21, 221 n.1, 221 n.2
   aleatory materialism 87, 128, 221 n.4
   interpellation 86–7, 91–2, 101–2, 221 n.1
   overdetermination 44, 227 n.4
America
   Anglo-American literature 51–71, 214 n.1, 214 n.2, 215 n.4, 215 n.6, 216 n.13, 227 n.2
   Anglo-American philosophy 41, 64–5
   South 154, 231 n.20
   U.S.A. 18, 53, 64, 112–13, 115, 117, 127–8, 137, 139, 140–1, 144, 148–9, 151–6, 158, 160–1, 214 n.1, 214 n.2, 217 n.18, 218 n.25, 229 n.4, 229 n.8, 230 n.8, 230 n.12, 231 n.15
Amin, Ash 205 n.11
Amin, Samir 6, 8, 114, 202, 205 n.12, 225 n.47, 226 n.48, 226 n.49, 234 n.15

animal 21, 58, 68, 71, 139–43, 165–6, 217 n.19
  becoming-animal 139–42
  packs 58, 100, 140–3, 170–1
anomalous 53, 62, 66, 110, 134, 136, 143, 224 n.38, 224 n.39, 228 n.11
apparatus 7, 19, 38, 44, 53, 91–2, 96, 99, 101, 103–5, 113–14, 120–2, 125–6, 131, 164, 166–8, 171, 174, 182–3, 187, 200, 222 n.19, 223 n.23
arborescence 52–3, 65, 100. *See also* rhizome
Aristotle 15, 92
Arnauld, Antoine 94
Artaud, Antonin 18, 48, 52, 54, 61, 66, 100, 214 n.2
Asia 231 n.20, 232 n.9
assemblage 11, 23, 27–9, 43, 51–2, 54–63, 68–9, 76, 91–2, 114, 119–20, 128–9, 131, 135, 181, 183, 187, 197, 201, 212 n.15, 215 n.9, 217 n.18, 227
  super-assemblage 28, 64, 71
Augustine 94, 221 n.6
Austin, J.L. 64
Australia 144, 227 n.11

Bachelard, Gaston 214 n.2
Bacon, Francis 3, 70
Badiou, Alain 16, 26, 28, 87, 208 n.3, 209 n.7, 221 n.6, 226 n.11, 227 n.11
Balibar, Etienne 93–8, 145, 178, 221 n.4, 221 n.5, 221 n.7, 222 n.13, 222 n.19, 223 n.19
Ballard, J.G. 144
Balzac, Honoré 215 n.5
Bandung project 36, 205–6 n.12, 211 n.13
Bangladesh 129
Baroque 5, 12, 76, 105, 108–9, 204 n.8
Barthes, Roland 216 n.11
Basques 113
Baudrillard, Jean 12, 49, 216 n.17
beauty 1, 74, 77, 81–2, 85, 87, 97, 107, 203 n.2
Beckett, Samuel 52, 70, 214 n.2
becoming 5, 7–8, 16, 18, 20–1, 25, 34, 53–4, 58–60, 62–3, 66, 69, 98, 100, 108, 139–42, 146, 215 n.6
  becoming-active 34

becoming-animal 139, 141–3, 146
becoming-imperceptible 139
becoming-insect 58, 139, 141
becoming-mineral 146
becoming-minor 139
becoming-molecular 139, 146
becoming-other 58–9, 66, 68, 140, 142, 217 n.18
becoming-people 66
becoming-rat 58, 141
becoming-reactive 34
becoming-revolutionary 10, 20–1, 34, 53, 139, 141
becoming-wolf 58, 81–2, 141
becoming-woman 53, 101, 139, 141, 146
becoming-writer 58, 141
Beddoes, Thomas Lovell 69
being 13, 20, 24, 31–2, 45, 51, 62–3, 71, 92–3, 95, 100, 111, 139, 142, 147, 165, 210 n.3, 212 n.15, 215 n.6, 223 n.24, 232 n.2
  and act 83, 87, 125, 137
  human 62, 113, 119, 134, 140, 181, 210 n.5
  minor 123
  non-being 21, 34–5, 39, 111, 136, 177, 189, 225 n.42
  stylistics of 76
  supreme or divine 1, 35, 92–3, 95–6
belief 12, 27, 33, 49–50, 57, 62, 67, 85, 92, 132–3, 136, 141, 155, 160, 171, 175, 180, 186–7, 198, 203 n.1, 206 n.13, 213 n.11, 218 n.22, 224 n.37, 225 n.41
  faith 49, 197
Bennett, Jonathan 64
Bensmaïa, Reda 217 n.20, 217 n.21
Bergson, Henri 3, 9, 38, 42, 58, 63, 71, 117, 175, 182, 210 n.2, 216 n.14, 222 n.7, 223 n.24, 235 n.19
Berkeley, George 64
Berlusconi, Silvio 152
Bey, Hakim 4
Bion, Wilfred 27, 207 n.21
Bismarck, Otto von 129
Blacksburg 46
Blair, Tony 113, 122, 152, 156, 160–1
Blanchot, Maurice 48

bodies 16, 27–8, 31, 37, 42–3, 55–6, 59, 63, 93–4, 99, 102, 120, 141, 173, 181, 199, 205 n.9, 205 n.10, 210 n.4, 214 n.4, 217 n.20, 218 n.30, 237 n.1
  without-organs 55
Bolivar, Simon 108
Bolsheviks 197
Borges, Jorge Luis 9, 49, 108
Bourdieu, Pierre 212 n.4
bourgeois 139, 222 n.13
  class 53, 114, 192–4
  democracy 97, 222 n.13, 223 n.19
  post-bourgeois 143, 169
  utopia 173–4, 177
Bowden, Sean 209 n.4
Braidotti, Rosi 204 n.5
Brazil 145, 149, 169, 232 n.8
Brenner, Robert 128, 229 n.3
Britain 64, 109, 120, 133, 151–2, 161, 207 n.21, 211 n.12, 231 n.18
Broch, Hermann 64
Brontë, Charlotte 52, 55, 68, 215 n.7
Brontë, Emily 52, 57
  Wuthering Heights 80–3, 220 n.10
Brown, Gordon 152
Bryant, Levi R. 212–13 n.5
Buchanan, Ian 215 n.5
Bukharin, Nikolai 202
bureaucracy 105, 135, 167, 224 n.39
Burkina Faso 88
Burroughs, William 52
Bush, George W. 89, 113, 122, 155–7, 159–61, 221 n.7, 230 n.8

Caesar, Julius 63
Cage, John 108, 224 n.37
Camus, Albert 145
capitalism 6–8, 10–13, 21, 36–9, 53, 67, 91, 97, 103, 105–7, 110–15, 121, 128, 132–7, 147, 152, 156, 162, 168–89, 193, 198–202, 204 n.8, 205 n.11, 205 n.12, 206 n.13, 212 n.13, 212 n.15, 212 n.16, 223 n.35, 224 n.36, 224 n.39, 225 n.41, 225 n.42, 227 n.3, 231 n.3, 233 n.7, 233 n.9, 234 n.15, 236 n.26. *See also* globalization
  and accumulation 148–9, 152, 156, 170
  axiomatics of 5, 7, 11, 21, 38, 105, 108, 110, 135–6, 163–5, 167–8, 170–1, 180–1, 186, 206 n.13, 224 n.35, 225 n.41, 228 n.9, 236 n.26
  corporations 162, 186
  counter-capitalism 114
  debt 6
  development 6–7, 36, 104, 107, 147, 165, 169, 174–6, 183–6, 192–3, 195, 205 n.11, 205 n.12, 233 n.9, 235 n.25
  disorganized 6
  financial 115, 128, 135, 137, 146–7, 152–3, 171, 186, 224 n.35, 229 n.4
  Fordist and post-Fordist 6, 175
  hypercapitalism 6–8, 11
  and management 152, 159, 169, 184, 229 n.4, 234 n.15
  manufacturing 6, 55, 169, 177, 232 n.9
  markets 6, 8, 106, 111–12, 113, 128, 152, 158–9, 173, 180, 193
  neoliberal 98, 112, 152, 154, 156, 161, 168, 198, 205 n.12
  post-capitalism 111, 136
  precapitalism 6, 38, 103, 107, 192, 235
  social capital 147, 176, 187
  speculative bubbles 128
Cardinale, Claudia 145
Carpenter, Edmund 52
Carroll, Lewis 52
  Alice in Wonderland 89
Casarino, Cesare 228 n.11
Castoriadis, Cornelius 8
Catalonians 113
Cervantes, Miguel de 17, 118
chaos 6, 12, 21, 111
  chaosmos 15
  theory 208 n.10
Chechnyans 113
Cheney, Dick 137, 230 n.8
Childe, V. Gordon 38, 103, 232 n.5, 235 n.25
China 113, 144, 191–202
Christianity 12, 21, 49, 78, 112, 123, 129, 139, 149, 151
Churchill, Winston 109
cinema 17, 42–3, 47–9, 70, 210 n.2, 213 n.9, 219 n.32. *See also* film
  action-image 47

crystalline regime 17–18, 208 n.5, 212 n.4
  of the sublime 3
citizen 88, 133, 137, 149, 164, 229 n.7, 230 n.12, 231 n.20
  citizenry 3, 155
  citizenship 112–14, 156–62
  Citizen Subject 93–9, 102, 222 n.13, 223 n.19
  managed 147–62, 226 n.9, 230 n.13, 231 n.20, 233 n.14
city 46, 96, 105, 155, 168, 170, 211 n.13, 230 n.10
  megalopolis 105, 168, 186
clan 12, 21, 111–13, 201
Clarke, Jonathan 229 n.8
class 38, 103, 118, 132, 153, 155, 167, 177–8, 180–1, 183, 192, 201–2, 215, 227 n.5, 229 n.2, 235 n.25
Clastres, Pierre 182–3, 232 n.5
Clinton, Bill 152
codes, coding 8, 18–20, 33, 35, 53–4, 60, 86, 89, 100, 104–5, 121, 141, 149, 151, 168, 171, 220 n.9, 224 n.35, 228 n.9
  over-coding 38, 103, 105, 164, 167–8, 170, 174, 235 n.25
  recoding 18–19, 86, 104
Cohn-Bendit, Daniel 226 n.8
collective 7, 13, 21, 36–9, 56, 78, 97, 110, 113–14, 120, 135, 143, 159, 169, 171–3, 177, 183, 188, 199–200, 202, 224 n.39, 225 n.41, 233 n.6, 235 n.23
  collection 53, 62, 119, 224 n.37
Colman, Felicity J. 213 n.9
colonialism 180, 198
  colonies 194
commodity 5, 159, 170, 181, 187, 201
  commodity form, principle 21, 38, 110, 135, 189, 201
commonwealth 85–6, 89
communism 8, 107, 109, 188, 196, 233 n.6
  Chinese 192, 195–6
community 12, 21, 38, 68, 99, 103–4, 112, 131–3, 165, 235 n.25
complexity 44, 120, 194, 209 n.9, 213 n.11, 227 n.4, 236 n.28
concept 3, 8, 10, 13, 16–18, 20–1, 24–5, 28, 31–3, 36–9, 41–50, 54, 59–63, 65, 67–9, 71, 91, 93–5, 109, 112, 119, 125–31, 139–40, 142, 144–5, 165, 191, 196, 201, 204, 207 n.21, 208 n.7, 210 n.6, 211 n.6, 214 n.3, 214 n.4, 217 n.21, 218 n.24, 221 n.4, 224 n.37, 225 n.40, 225 n.41, 226 n.3, 226 n.10, 227 n.3, 234 n.16
  concept-image 20, 25, 213 n.10
  concept-image-narrative 20, 28, 207 n.20, 209 n.3
conception 10, 17, 33, 35, 37–8, 46, 57, 68, 70, 77, 85–6, 91, 101, 112–14, 120–3, 134, 149, 163–4, 176, 182, 187, 191, 198, 204 n.8
conceptual 1, 4–6, 8, 41, 43, 59–61, 65, 68, 70, 79, 82, 97, 117, 123, 126, 130, 144, 169, 172, 191, 197, 199, 205 n.9, 212 n.4, 219 n.32, 226 n.10, 227 n.1, 231 n.2
conceptualization 17, 37–8, 101, 118, 122–3, 127, 144, 167, 196, 200, 208 n.1
concerts 5, 9, 11, 82, 106–7. *See also* accords
Conley, Tom 219 n.31
consciousness 4, 28, 63, 67, 83, 88, 93, 108, 120, 131, 147, 181, 197, 213 n.10, 216 n.11, 222 n.15, 223 n.24
conservatives 149, 161, 205 n.11, 230 n.8, 231 n.15, 231 n.19
constellation 36, 54, 60, 97, 139
cooperation 129, 147, 175–7, 184–5, 187, 233 n.10
Corsicans 113
Cortázar, Julio 69
crisis 37, 96–7, 120, 173–6, 178, 181, 184, 192, 204 n.8, 205–6 n.12, 233 n.6, 236 n.30
critique 1, 17, 33, 39, 41, 45, 66, 74–7, 97–8, 165, 188, 203 n.1, 207 n.19, 209 n.5, 211 n.9, 211 n.12, 216 n.14, 220 n.1, 222 n.15, 232 n.5, 232 n.6, 233 n.13
Crockett, Clayton 208 n.3
culture 215 n.5
cyberpunk 108, 205 n.9

Davidson, Donald 25, 28–9, 209 n.9
death 16, 18, 20, 49, 57, 63, 66, 78–9, 87, 98, 123, 127, 155, 158, 164, 179, 194, 207 n.18, 234 n.16

decoding 18–19, 86, 100, 104–5, 164, 167–8, 171, 174, 223 n.35
de Gaulle, Charles 36, 121
democracy 65, 114–15, 123, 133, 155–7, 159, 161–2, 172, 229 n.7, 231 n.20, 234 n.15, 234 n.16
  bourgeois 97, 222 n.13, 223 n.19
  French 36
  liberal 102, 122–3, 226 n.9, 231 n.19
  social 8, 10, 12, 21, 133, 174, 193
Derrida, Jacques 58–9, 216 n.11, 225 n.40
Descartes, René 1, 64, 93–5, 203 n.1, 204 n.6, 221 nn.4–6
  Cartesian 3, 35, 94–5, 221 n.7, 222 n.13
  cogito 52, 65, 214 n.3, 221 n.7
  res cogitans 1, 93
desire 8, 10, 16, 20–2, 26, 32, 35, 37, 51–71, 73, 77, 88, 97, 102, 113–14, 119, 121, 139, 140, 142, 144, 146, 167, 182, 199–200, 207 n.21, 216 n.13, 218 n.27, 219 n.5, 223 n.24, 225 n.40, 234 n.16, 235 n.23
  production 16, 22, 37, 86–7, 102, 119, 122, 126, 167, 182, 200–1, 206 n.15
desiring machines 21
deterritorialization 7, 21, 39, 53, 60, 65–6, 100, 105, 111, 135, 167–8, 186–7, 189, 224 n.35. *See also* reterritorialization
de Villepin, Dominique 145
dialectic 2, 25, 47, 51, 59, 121, 141, 146, 154, 177–9, 191–2, 196–9, 200, 202, 211 n.6, 216 n.14
dichotomy 23–4, 41–2, 44–5, 110, 135, 165, 221 n.2, 225 n.42
difference 13, 15, 27, 34, 38–9, 58–9, 110–11, 135, 140, 144–5, 179, 188–9, 194, 199, 201, 203 n.2, 210 n.2, 217 n.18, 225 n.40, 235 n.21, 236 n.32
Dostoevsky, Fyodor 17, 123
dramatology 8, 32, 49, 213 n.8
drives 35–6, 119, 121–2, 207 n.21
dualism 29, 99
Duménil, Gérard 152
Dumézil, Georges 99–100, 222 n.17
dynamism 11, 17, 20, 22, 25–6, 32, 77, 93, 101, 107, 122, 133, 136, 219 n.31

earth 22, 65–9, 94, 123, 140, 186–7
economy 6–7, 91–3, 109, 113–15, 128, 130, 133, 135, 148, 148–9, 151, 152, 154–5, 158, 162, 165, 169, 176, 179, 181, 184, 186–7, 191–2, 196, 224 n.36, 225 n.39, 225 n.47, 227 n.3, 229 n.2, 231 n.15, 231 n.17
effect 25, 31, 33, 54, 57–8, 71, 85, 87, 103, 105, 111–12, 119, 127–8, 130, 135, 141, 145–6, 161, 168, 181, 186–7, 189, 218 n.22, 219 n.9, 221 n.2
elections 122, 148, 150, 155–6, 158–9, 161, 229 n.5, 229 n.7
elite 81, 112, 115, 122
emancipation 36, 39, 120–1, 125, 202
emergence 3–6, 8–9, 15–16, 34–6, 38, 58–9, 63, 65, 67, 74, 80, 86–7, 95, 109, 111, 113, 136, 140, 171, 175, 200, 223 n.19, 225 n.42, 228 n.11, 229 n.5
empiricism 23–4, 28, 42–4, 51, 52, 54, 61–2, 64, 68, 87, 88, 118, 126, 210 n.1, 213 n.6, 213 n.5, 214 n.11, 231 n.20
energy 77, 120, 133, 136, 171, 180, 187, 206 n.13, 225 n.41
England 109, 129, 144
English 15, 31, 52–3, 61–3, 65, 67, 68, 108–9, 111, 144–5, 214 n.2, 217 n.20, 218 n.27, 219 n.9, 221 n.3, 237 n.1
Enron 149–50, 229 n.4
ensemble 8, 11, 31, 38, 42, 54, 63, 129, 201
epistemology 28–9, 45, 67, 75, 85, 93, 95, 97–8, 142
epoch 3–5, 10, 15, 95, 107, 132, 147, 175, 224 n.39
Erasmus 17
Eribon, Didier 74, 78
Eritrea 113
Esposito, Roberto 87
ethics 31, 54, 63, 69, 73–83, 81, 97, 102, 123, 130, 177–8, 216 n.15, 217 n.21, 218 n.23, 219 n.2, 219 n.9, 220 n.9, 232 n.2, 235 n.19
European 107, 121, 149, 153, 192, 217 n.21, 222 n.13

event 9–10, 17–20, 23–8, 42, 54, 57, 59, 63, 64, 78–83, 87, 89, 100–1, 117, 120–3, 127, 157, 160, 188, 197, 198, 206 n.15, 207 n.18, 209 n.1, 211 n.10, 218 n.28, 221 n.6
evolution 59, 159, 164–5, 222 n.13, 232 n.5
exchange 39, 66, 71, 111, 135, 140, 141, 145, 147, 187, 189, 201
existence 8–9, 18–19, 25–6, 31, 34, 37, 42, 48, 51, 55, 62, 73, 75, 77–8, 81–2, 89, 91, 93, 99, 103–4, 107, 114, 117, 120, 125–31, 139, 157, 166, 168–9, 177, 182–6, 192, 194, 196, 200, 203, 204 n.6, 209 n.5, 215 n.9, 226, 232 n.7. *See also* being
experience 8, 33, 41, 44–6, 49, 58, 67–8, 71, 87, 94, 121, 127, 131–2, 141, 173, 205, 209, 217, 227, 234 n.16
expression 3, 5, 8, 11, 18, 21–2, 25, 26–8, 31, 37–8, 43, 46–7, 48, 56, 62, 68, 75–6, 80–1, 91–2, 97, 99, 102, 104, 106–7, 125, 127–8, 130–1, 147–8, 151–2, 156, 165–6, 171, 174, 181–2, 193, 199, 201, 204 n.8, 208 n.1, 217 n.18, 217 n.19, 227 n.3, 227 n.11, 237 n.1
externality 26, 44, 56, 62, 100–1, 114, 130, 167, 206 n.12, 218 n.28

fabulation 1, 5, 49, 220 n.1
faciality 45–6, 54–5, 98
family 133, 141–3, 149, 151, 201, 224 n.39
Farah, "Mo" 109
Faulkner, William 52, 54
feeling 12, 27, 47, 58, 63, 76, 79, 110, 112, 125, 132, 134, 141, 156–7, 161, 200
Fichte, Johann Gottlieb 220 n.1
figuration 2, 5, 8, 38, 48, 54, 56, 60–1, 64–5, 95–7, 100, 102, 123, 153, 179, 207 n.26, 213, 220 n.9, 226 n.10
film 16, 47, 49, 70–1, 80, 127, 160. *See also* cinema
Fitzgerald, Scott 52, 215 n.6
Flaubert, Gustave 18–19, 53
force 31–5, 37–9, 57–8, 61, 70, 78, 95, 97, 105, 107, 108, 119, 120, 122, 133, 167–9, 175, 182, 184, 186, 188, 197, 200–2, 203 n.4, 204 n.5, 210 n.2, 211 n.8, 211 n.9, 226 n.10

formations 2, 11, 13, 38, 44, 103, 106, 114, 126, 128, 130, 136, 147, 168, 171, 180, 193, 198–200, 203 n.2, 206 n.13, 210 n.1, 211 n.10, 223 n.23, 225 n.41, 228 n.9, 232 n.7, 233 n.9, 236 n.30
Foucault, Michel 44, 74–82, 87, 96–7, 102, 118, 139, 147, 179, 188, 196, 203 n.2, 206 n.17, 207 n.18, 212 n.4, 218 n.27, 219 n.4, 219 n.8, 220 nn.9–10, 220 nn.12–14, 221 n.3, 226 n.3, 228 n.10, 231 n.13, 232 n.7, 236 n.27, 236 n.31
  biopower 99, 104
  on Deleuze 2–3, 9
  and micropolitics 103–4
  practices of subjectivation 86, 125, 134, 224 n.39
France 35–6, 54, 75, 120–1, 145–6, 152, 214, 227 n.11
Frankfurt School 181
Frank, Thomas 128
freedom 32, 46, 50, 68, 76–7, 82, 85, 86, 94–6, 113, 120, 152, 155, 173, 186, 188, 196, 210 n.5, 224 n.36, 230 n.13, 232 n.2
Frege, Gottlob 41, 64
Freud, Sigmund 33, 35–7, 97–8, 206 n.14, 211 n.12, 235 n.22
  wolf-man 139, 141–3, 228 n.2
Fukuyama, Francis 12

Garcia Márquez, Gabriel 69, 214 n.2
Genet, Jean 52, 54
geoliterature 51–71. *See also* novels
Ghérasim, Luca 52
Gibson, William 5
Giddens, Anthony 163
globalization 6, 11, 36, 38, 67, 105–6, 135, 169, 171, 174, 193, 198, 200, 205 n.9, 225 n.47. *See also* capitalism
Glyn, Andrew 128
Goethe, G.W. 100, 210 n.1, 215 n.5
Gombrowicz, Witold 52
goodness 1, 31–2, 74–7, 82, 85, 97, 107, 119, 149, 203 n.1, 219 n.2
Gordian Knot 2, 18, 42, 45, 50, 89, 117, 126
Gorky, Maxim 215 n.5

government 112–14, 121, 155–7, 162, 186, 229 n.4, 230 n.13, 231 n.17, 234 n.16
   meta-governance 113–14
Greenham Common women's peace camp 123
Guevara, Che 196
Guerin, Michel 61

Habermas, Jürgen 164
Hacker, Jacob 229 n.8
haecceity 20, 60–1, 110, 134, 217 n.18
Halper, Stefan 229 n.8
Hardt, Michael 99, 179, 185, 234 n.15, 235 nn.17–19, 236 n.33
Hardy, Thomas 52–4, 215 n.6
Harris, Wilson 214 n.2
Hegel, G.W.F. 1–4, 54, 62–5, 71, 144–5, 164–5, 167, 174, 177, 193, 203 n.1, 212 n.1, 215 n.9, 218 n.24, 222 n.14, 232 n.2
   bürgerliche Gesellschaft 171
   Hegelian 3, 64, 93, 104, 167, 177, 179–80, 191, 194–5, 204 n.7, 235 n.19, 235 n.21
hegemony 112–15
Heidegger, Martin 1–2, 35, 43, 45, 57, 63, 65, 85, 94, 97, 203, 218 n.24, 218 n.26
Herzog, Werner 70, 219 n.32
   Fitzcarraldo 7, 71
history 5–7, 9–10, 12, 20, 33, 38, 53, 63, 65, 71, 101, 103, 105, 108, 120–3, 129–30, 136, 156, 163, 165, 173, 175–6, 178, 181, 185, 191–2, 196, 198–9, 206 n.13, 210 n.6, 218 n.24, 218 n.27, 225 n.41, 232 n.4, 233 n.9, 234 n.16
   of philosophy 1–3, 43, 64, 70, 92, 94, 97, 210 n.6, 211 n.6
   universal 123, 164, 169, 174, 185, 231 n.3
   world-historical 137, 204 n.7
Hjelmslev, Louis 56, 118, 226 n.4
Ho, Chi Minh 196
Hobbes, Thomas 92, 95, 110, 130, 135, 177–8, 222
Hodgson, Godfrey 229 n.8
Hölderlin, Friedrich 52

Howard, John 152
human 53, 80, 133, 141, 148, 171, 175
   autopoesis 9
   being 77, 93, 95, 113, 119, 140–1, 181, 210 n.5
   humanity 58, 141
   intuition 44
   life 147
   nature 218 n.22
   rights 115, 162
   sciences 57
   subjectivity 173
humanism 58, 86, 173, 234 n.16
Hume, David 3, 38, 52, 62–5, 68, 71, 88, 92, 210 n.2, 218 n.28
hunter gatherers 103–5, 165–6, 183, 185
Hurricane Katrina 89, 157
Hussein, Saddam 156, 160, 162

ideal, idealism 3, 24, 27, 43, 81, 86, 94, 149, 155–6, 192, 209 n.4
identity 7, 21, 23, 38, 47, 59, 100, 109–10, 118–19, 135, 140, 141, 144–5, 148–9, 169, 179, 189, 194–5, 201, 216 n.17, 236 n.28
ideology 56, 86, 91–2, 112, 126, 149–50, 152, 157–8, 161, 176, 206 n.12, 214 n.11, 227 n.3, 228 n.9, 236 n.26
illusion 45, 47, 120, 160, 205 n.12, 234 n.16
image 4, 8, 16–20, 24–5, 31–3, 35, 41–3, 47–9, 54, 60–1, 70, 102, 108, 117, 130, 148, 204 n.6, 209 n.3, 211 n.7, 219 n.31
   image-concept 41–50
   image-object 43
imagination 7, 51, 62, 76, 210 n.4, 216 n.11, 234 n.16
immanence 7, 16–18, 21, 23, 25, 49, 60–1, 65–9, 75, 77, 83, 117, 135–6, 180, 206 n.13, 208 n.8, 213 n.11, 218 n.23, 219 n.5, 219 n.6, 220 n.16, 224 n.37, 225 n.41
immigrant 109, 123, 154, 158, 227 n.11
imperialism 38, 103, 164, 167–8, 194, 198, 235 n.25
incorporeality 8, 21, 25, 29. *See also* matter
India 66, 71, 144–5, 211 n.13

individual 5, 7, 9, 15, 33, 83, 91, 93, 100, 104, 110, 118, 126, 129, 134–5, 142, 144, 149, 154, 157, 159, 167, 171, 177–8, 188, 199, 204 n.5, 207 n.26, 216 n.10, 222 n.9, 225 n.42, 233 n.6
individuation 9, 11, 13, 15, 78–80, 82–3, 110–11, 134, 142, 217 n.18, 224 n.39
industrialization 36, 105, 112, 154–5, 162, 168, 174, 186, 226 n.9. *See also* capitalism
  industries 136, 147, 171, 175, 180–1, 206 n.13, 225 n.41
inequality 55, 151, 152–3. *See also* poverty
intensity 7, 20, 26, 28, 33, 35–6, 46–7, 55, 60–1, 78–80, 82, 86, 110, 134, 171, 176, 208 n.2, 214 n.4, 217 n.18, 217 n.19
interiority 53, 100, 143, 216 n.11, 218 n.24
international monetary fund 152, 162
internet 4, 147, 149, 154, 156
intuition 44–6, 49–50, 163, 195, 212 n.5
Iraq 128, 149, 157, 160, 162
Irian Jaya 113
Ishiguro, Kazuo 109
isomorphism 5, 7, 106, 108, 164, 168–9, 186, 224 n.36
Italy 122, 152

James, C.L.R. 8, 137
James, Henry 52, 69
James, William 9, 222 n.7
Jameson, Fredric 12, 209 n.1, 215 n.9
Japan 111, 144, 152, 192
Jessop, Bob 108, 149, 163, 225 n.45, 231 n.1, 233 n.13
judgment 4, 17, 35, 41, 45, 76, 85, 92, 94, 203 n.2, 205 n.10, 219 n.2, 220 n.1
justice 96, 99, 132

Kafka, Franz 3, 9, 55, 61, 64, 70–1, 217 n.21
  insect-man 139–41
Kant, Immanuel 3, 41, 44–5, 64, 66, 74–7, 92–8, 164, 203 n.2, 219 n.32, 220 n.1, 221 n.7, 222 nn.11–12, 222 n.15
  Kantian 75–6, 82, 92–5, 96, 98, 220 n.1, 222 n.19
Kashmir 113

Kelly, Michael 212 n.14
Kerouac, Jack 52, 63, 107, 127, 215 n.6
Kesey, Ken 55
Keynesianism 6, 152, 154, 174–5
Khan, Genghis 222 n.16
Khilnani, Sunil 212 n.14
Khrushchev, Nikita 36
Kierkegaard, Søren 61, 64, 123
kingship 53, 94–6, 98, 100, 120, 164, 222 n.13
Kipling, Rudyard 144
Klein, Melanie 119
Kleist, Heinrich von 55, 61, 64, 68, 100, 210 n.1, 215 n.5, 217 n.21
Klossowski, Pierre 203 n.2
knowledges 1, 4–5, 12, 21, 32, 49, 75–9, 85, 87, 99, 115, 118–19, 136, 175, 193, 199, 200, 205 n.10, 212, 220 n.1, 237 n.1
  knowing 1, 7, 23, 32, 47, 53–4, 56, 64, 78, 81, 85, 87, 89, 97, 112, 125, 132, 148, 159–60, 181, 198, 200, 204 n.5, 237 n.1
Koizumi, Junichiro 152
Kristeva, Julia 211 n.12, 216 n.11
Kurds 113

labor 1, 6, 36–7, 105, 132, 147, 152, 166–7, 169, 172–5, 177, 181, 182–7, 200, 224 n.36, 233 n.7, 233 n.9
Lacan, Jacques 129, 216 n.17
Laclau, Ernesto 163
Laing, R.D. 211 n.12
language 5, 12, 15, 25, 35, 45, 47, 59, 69, 117–18, 130, 226 n.1
  meaning 35, 55–7, 65, 88, 118, 120, 125, 139, 158–9, 194, 201, 228 n.9, 229 n.7, 233 n.9
Las Vegas 160
Lautréamont, Comte de 52, 108
Lawrence, D.H. 52, 61–2, 215 n.6, 215 n.7, 217 n.19
Lawrence, T.E. 52, 55
Le Clézio, Jean-Marie Gustav 217 n.19
Leibniz, G.W. 3–5, 11, 15–16, 63–5, 92, 94, 106–9, 205 n.9
Lenin, V.I. 191–2, 194, 197–9
Le Pen, Jean-Marie 107, 109, 145
Lévy, Dominique 152

liberalism 12, 21, 98, 102, 122–3, 136, 149, 161, 226 n.9, 229 n.8, 230 n.8
liberation 34, 36, 65, 126, 140, 173
  as project 99, 114, 125
libidinal 35–6, 38, 201, 212 n.18
Lieven, Anatol 229 n.8
  and Jonathan Clarke (2004); Jacob Hacker and Paul Pierson (2004); and Godfrey Hodgson (2004)
Locke, John 64, 71, 92–4, 221 n.4, 221 n.7
  societas civilis 171
logos 1, 33
love 21, 49, 55, 63, 80–1, 155, 210 n.5, 216 n.10, 220 n.10
  amour courtois 81–2, 220 n.15
Lovecraft, H.P. 52, 68, 217 n.18
Lowry, Malcolm 52
Luhmann, Nikolas 163
Lukács, György 215 n.5
Luxemburg, Rosa 137
Lyotard, Jean-François 211 n.12

Macey, David 204 n.5
Machiavelli, Nikolai 87
machine 17, 20–2, 26, 28, 33–4, 37, 54–5, 57, 100–2, 135, 142, 158, 163–4, 165, 168–9, 181–2, 214 n.4, 223 n.20, 224 n.35, 225 n.39
  analytic 167
  bureaucratic 55
  capitalist 224 n.35
  delirious 55
  despotic 167
  fog 55
  literary 51–71
  mad war 55
  for manufacturing giants 55
  wave 55
  wind 55
Madoff, Bernie 135, 137
majoritarian 123, 139, 145–6. *See also* minoritarian
Malaysia 11, 106–7
Malebranche, Nicolas 94
Mallarmé, Stéphane 61
man 9, 35, 41, 47, 58, 66, 82, 101, 123, 132, 139, 217 n.20, 220 n.15. *See also* human

and God 35, 203 n.4, 211 n.9, 213 n.11
Mann, Michael 163, 232 n.5, 232 n.6
Mann, Thomas 215 n.5
Mao, Tse-tung 191–202
Marchais, Georges 121
Marcos, Subcomandante 196
Marx, Karl 1, 21, 37–9, 91, 97–8, 103, 136, 171–6, 182, 191–2, 197–8, 200, 225 n.41, 232 n.4, 233 n.3, 235 n.25
  analysis of commodity form 21, 107, 110, 135, 189, 201
Marxism 7, 9, 37, 97, 99, 102–3, 125, 163, 170–4, 176–7, 180–2, 183, 186–8, 191, 194, 199–200, 202, 205 n.9, 223 n.24, 230 n.8, 233 n.3, 234 n.15, 236 n.33
  as axiomatics of capitalism 6–7, 180, 189, 206 n.13, 225 n.41
  base-superstructure 91–2, 221 n.2
  postmarxism 97, 233 n.3
  vanguardism 120–1
Massumi, Brian 182, 208 n.7, 212 n.16, 216 n.17, 235 n.23
materialism 3–13, 15–29, 32–5, 43, 174, 182, 191–2, 196–7, 199–200, 208 n.1, 209 n.9, 223 n.24
  aleatory 87, 126, 221 n.4
  anomalous 23
matter, material 9, 23–29, 42–3, 45, 122, 127, 131–2, 148, 178, 180, 183, 187, 193, 209 n.1, 209 n.4, 213 n.6, 217 n.19, 223 n.24
  immaterial 26, 28
McKibbin, Ross 231 n.18
Mead, Margaret 130
media 149, 151, 154, 157, 160–2, 183, 213 n.10, 231 n.17
  hypermedia 155–7, 159–62
Melville, Herman 52, 215 n.6
Mendes, Sam 107
Menn, Stephen 221 n.6
mentality 113, 141, 203 n.2
Merleau-Ponty, Maurice 2, 35, 117
Mersenne, Marin 94, 221 n.5
Mertes, Tom 158, 231 n.15
metallurgy 38, 103, 105, 165, 167, 180, 235 n.25

metaphysics 15, 45, 49–50, 70–1, 78, 91–2, 96–7, 99, 163, 173, 177, 192, 194–5, 213 n.11, 220 n.1, 223 n.23
Middles Ages 175, 222 n.13
　medieval 74, 82, 93–5, 107, 129, 200, 219 n.9, 220 n.15, 222 n.19
Miller, Arthur 52, 107
Miller, Henry 52
mind 16
minoritarian 8, 21, 123, 135, 139–40, 144–6, 168, 186, 188, 206–7 n.18, 224 n.39. *See also* majoritarian
mode of production 37, 102, 106–7, 169, 181–2, 187
modernity 4, 49, 104, 118, 232 n.7
　modernism 65, 68–70, 215 n.5
molarity 103, 139, 143, 166, 168. *See also* majoritarian; molecularity
　vs. micrological 103, 166
molecularity 103, 143, 166. *See also* molarity
Mona Lisa 85
money 104–5, 118, 155, 157, 161, 166–7, 170, 174, 186, 204 n.7, 223 n.35, 229 n.4
monism 23–4, 26, 28–9, 47
　anomalous 23, 29, 209 n.9, 210 n.10
morality 63, 74, 78, 80, 85, 92, 149, 156, 218 n.23, 219 n.2, 222 n.15
Morgan, J.P. 135
Moritz, Karl Philipp 58
Mouffe, Chantal 163
multiplicity 4, 7, 9, 12, 15, 22, 26, 48, 52, 54–6, 58–60, 62, 65, 70–1, 98, 108, 110, 129, 134, 140, 143–4, 159, 168, 171, 179, 204 n.8, 208 n.3, 214 n.4, 216 n.14, 217 n.18, 224 n.38, 225 n.40, 236 n.32
myth 12, 98–9, 122–3, 164, 173, 177, 203 n.3, 205 n.12, 233 n.12

Nairn, Tom 231 n.17
nation 13, 21, 96, 105, 111–14, 145, 151, 155, 160, 164–5, 168, 175, 235 n.26
　national 52, 65, 67–8, 114, 122, 135, 155, 159, 224 n.39
nature 29, 32, 47, 58, 62, 70, 94, 118, 141, 217 n.21
　natural 47, 62, 110, 118, 134, 170

Negri, Antonio 10, 99, 111, 136, 170–1, 173–81, 183–8, 207 n.18, 207 n.22, 221 n.4, 228 n.11, 232 n.1, 232 n.2, 232 n.8, 233 nn.3–9, 234 n.15, 234 n.16, 235 n.16, 235 n.18, 236 nn.28–31
networks 107, 114, 141, 147–9, 158, 169, 174–5
neurosis 53, 123
Nietzsche, Friedrich 1–3, 8–10, 31–4, 38–9, 42, 49, 52, 57–8, 61, 63–5, 73, 75, 77–9, 85, 97–8, 123, 171, 174, 179, 182, 210 nn.1–2, 210 n.4, 210 n.6, 211 nn.7–9, 212 n.2, 220 n.1, 235 n.19, 235 n.25
Nissan 201
nomadology 99, 131, 164, 167, 222 n.15
　nomads 67, 170, 200, 206–7 n.18
novels 17, 52–3, 59–61, 64, 71, 214 n.2, 217 n.19. *See also* geoliterature
　novelist 52, 60–2, 68, 71, 109, 127, 214 n.2, 217 n.21, 218 n.28

Obama, Barack 113, 159–60, 229 n.8
objects 12, 18, 20, 23–9, 41–2, 44, 48–9, 55–6, 60, 76, 83, 88–9, 96–8, 107, 118–19, 121–2, 126–8, 130–1, 156, 170, 186–7, 199–200, 204 n.8, 207 n.21, 208 n.1, 226 n.6. *See also* subjects
　part/partial 20, 55, 119, 121–3, 226 n.6
ontology 8, 15–16, 18–19, 21–2, 25–6, 32, 35, 36–9, 45, 56–7, 125, 134, 142, 174, 179, 181, 183, 187–9, 200, 202, 208 n.1, 235 n.19, 236 n.30
　ontological 8, 16–17, 23, 35, 45, 91, 98, 100, 117, 120, 176, 178, 185, 187, 199, 208 n.2, 213 n.6, 216 n.11, 219 n.4

Pakistan 144
parliament 120, 127, 198
Parnet, Claire 61, 134, 206 n.17, 211 n.10
passion 19, 32, 62, 75–6, 80–2, 89, 102, 220 n.10, 235 n.25
Patton, Paul 212 n.15, 214 n.4
people(s) 11, 21, 29, 65, 88, 95, 106, 111–14, 127, 133, 136, 140, 144, 157, 162, 166, 170, 195–6, 226 n.11, 237 n.1

masses 120, 170, 178, 234 n.16
multitude 177-8, 188, 207 n.18
new 22, 65-6, 68-9, 140
perception 7, 118, 217 n.20
  percepts 4, 60, 62, 64-5, 67-9, 217 n.20
periodization 174-6, 210 n.1, 233 n.9
Pessoa, Ferdinand 61
phantasm 2, 53, 110, 134, 177
phenomena 28, 43, 76, 106-7, 117-18, 120-1, 169, 213, 220, 232 n.8, 235 n.26
phenomenology 4, 35, 45, 64, 151, 165, 174, 187, 213 n.10, 215 n.9
philosophy
  analytical 209 n.9
  geophilosophy 65, 67-70, 123
  history of 1-3, 43, 64, 70, 92, 94, 97, 210 n.6, 211 n.6
  scholastic 93-4
Pierce, C.S. 67, 70
Pierson, Paul 229 n.8
Pinochet, Augusto 152
Plato 2-3, 9, 26, 41, 59, 63, 92, 95, 209 n.5, 209 n.9, 225 n.40, 236 n.32
politics 6-8, 10-13, 20-1, 33, 35-9, 43-4, 54, 63, 66, 68-9, 86-8, 91-9, 101, 104, 108, 111-15, 117, 119-23, 123, 130, 133-4, 136-7, 139, 142-4, 146, 148-9, 150-1, 154-62, 164-6, 169-70, 172, 177-84, 191-4, 197-9, 202, 206-7 n.18, 207 n.23, 211-12 n.13, 212 n.15, 216 n.15, 222 n.11, 222 n.15, 222 n.19, 223 n.24, 225 n.40, 226 n.9, 227 n.5, 228 n.2, 228 n.11, 229 n.8, 231 n.20, 232 n.2, 233 n.11, 234 n.16, 235 n.19
  biopolitics 87
  depoliticized 226 n.9
  macropolitics 103
  micropolitics 20-1, 103-4, 166, 232 n.7
  polity 94, 102, 155, 157, 164
  and representation 110-11, 122, 154-7
  voters 122, 150-1, 157-61, 226 n.9, 229 n.7
  western European 154
potentiality 16, 19, 32, 36-7, 43, 177
Poulantzas, Nicos 152, 163, 233 n.13
poverty 149, 162
Powell, Enoch 109

power 2, 7, 11, 13, 17, 21, 31-9, 47-8, 53, 57-8, 63, 71, 75, 78-9, 83, 91-2, 94, 97, 99-101, 104, 106, 111-14, 120-1, 127-9, 131, 133-4, 136, 141, 148, 150, 155, 160, 162, 170, 172, 177-8, 181-4, 186-9, 192, 197-202, 204, 206-8, 210-11, 225-6, 228, 230, 232, 232-4
  powerlessness 48, 76
pragmatics 56-7, 100
praxis 47, 89, 195
proletariat 121, 158, 169, 171, 176-7, 179, 182-3, 193-4, 200
prudence 17, 80-1, 218 n.23, 219 n.9
psychoanalysis 2, 27, 35, 110, 119, 134, 141, 143, 211 n.12, 215 n.7, 215 n.9, 228 n.2. See also neurosis
  Oedipus complex 41-3, 53, 119
Putnam, Robert 127

Quine, W.V.O. 41, 64

race 66, 112-13, 145-6
Reagan, Ronald 112, 161, 229 n.8
reality 15, 18-19, 23, 33, 45-8, 53, 64, 89, 91, 94, 108, 119-20, 122, 125, 133, 142-3, 153-4, 159, 163, 167, 173, 178, 206-7 n.18, 213 n.11, 214 n.2, 227 n.3, 231 n.15, 234 n.15
  realism 69, 71, 108, 214 n.2, 215 n.5
reason
  Bolshevik 197
  human 1
  rationality 17, 63-4, 83, 92, 94-6, 104, 111, 121, 123, 136, 166-7, 179, 212 n.5
Reich, Wilhelm 36
religion 42-3, 101, 147, 151, 203, 211 n.9
Renaissance 120, 173
repetition 15, 21, 27, 38-9, 49, 59, 100, 110-11, 135-6, 188-9, 201-2, 203 n.1, 210 n.2
representation 33, 46, 48, 56, 60, 86, 93, 113, 118-19, 130, 225 n.40, 232 n.2. See also language
resistance 65-6, 78-9, 100, 170, 178
reterritorialization 7, 21, 38, 65-7, 105, 167-8, 170, 186, 191, 218 n.26. See also deterritorialization

revolution 10, 18, 53, 63, 88–9, 112, 121, 132–3, 136, 169–70, 174, 193–8, 234 n.16
   counter-revolution 89, 197
   revolutionaries 196, 226 n.8
   revolutionary 10, 13, 37, 53, 55, 77, 88–9, 98, 112, 114–15, 120, 135, 137, 144, 170–2, 176, 178, 186, 192–200, 224 n.39, 228 n.11, 233 n.6
   revolutionary-becoming 112, 136
rhizome 5, 7–8, 52, 54, 56, 100, 164, 204 n.8, 214 n.4. *See also* arborescence
Richards, David 207 n.25
Riesman, David 107
Rimbaud, Arthur 61
Rodman, Dennis 4
Romanticism 96, 180, 232 n.2
Romney, Mitt 160
Rose, Nikolas 230 n.13
Rosenzweig, Frank 232 n.2
Ross, Kristin 212 n.14
Rousseau, Jean-Jacques 96, 110, 164, 177
Rove, Karl 122, 230 n.8
Rumsfeld, Donald 229 n.8
Runciman, David 222 n.9
Rushdie, Salman 69, 71
Russell, Bertrand 4, 41, 64, 218 n.28
Russia 127, 198
Rutenberg, Jim 160
Rwanda 88

Sabah 11, 106
Saint-Beuve, Charles Augustin 52
Sarawak 11, 106
Sarkozy, Nicolas 152
Sartre, Jean-Paul 2, 35
Sassen, Saskia 232 n.9
Saussure, Ferdinand de 35, 70, 216 n.17
Savile, Jimmy 20
Schelling, F.W.J. 64
Schizophrenia 19, 32, 35–9, 49, 67–70, 85, 143, 171, 174, 181–2, 185, 189, 201, 212 n.15, 228 n.2, 234 n.15
Schmitt, Carl 122, 226 n.9
Schopenhauer, Arthur 64
Schroeter, Werner 80
Schwartz, Herman M. 232 n.9
Schwarzenegger, Arnold 4
science 5, 7, 35, 43, 57, 67, 87, 142, 144, 147, 163, 199, 205 n.10

Scott, Walter 54, 215 n.5
Scotus, Duns 52
semiology 2, 15, 100, 117
semiosis 5, 19–20, 56, 70
   semiotic 6, 10, 16, 18, 22, 57, 59, 70, 169, 174
Sen, Amartya 17
sensation 3, 5, 9, 53, 217 n.18
sense 3, 27, 33–4, 71, 77, 80, 93, 119, 144–5, 192, 210 n.2
sensibility 5, 34, 45, 219 n.32
Serres, Michel 5, 205 n.9
sexuality 120, 203 n.2
Shah of Iran 127
Shakespeare, William 132
shaman 99, 101, 122
signification 15, 55, 118, 131
   signified 33, 55, 57, 117–19
   signifier 33, 55, 57, 117–19
signs 19, 43, 87, 91, 117–19, 130, 215 n.10, 226 n.2
Sikhs 113
Simondon, Gilbert 213 n.8
simulacrum 57, 59, 110, 135, 188, 201. *See also* simulation
   copies 57–9, 225 n.40, 236 n.32
simulation 57–9, 110, 135, 188, 225 n.40, 236 n.32. *See also* simulacrum
singularity 4, 7, 9, 13, 15, 18, 20, 26, 38, 60, 86, 89, 100, 104, 110–13, 133, 135–6, 166, 171, 177, 188, 201, 207 n.26, 225 n.40, 225 n.41, 225 n.42, 228 n.11, 236 n.32
Sklair, Leslie 205 n.11
socialism 8, 10, 12, 21, 98, 113, 133, 174, 177–8, 193, 196, 233 n.6
   social democracy 36
society 37, 99, 103, 114, 120–1, 123, 125, 129, 132, 147–8, 150–2, 154, 158, 160–2, 164–6, 169–71, 173, 175–80, 182, 184–8, 192, 196, 200, 206 n.15, 226 n.9, 228 n.1, 229 n.7, 231 n.17, 232 n.2, 234 n.15, 236 n.28
   of control 147–62
   of the spectacle 160, 162, 231 n.17
socius 21, 85–7, 89, 119, 166, 171, 184, 221 n.2, 223 n.24, 233 n.9
Socrates 8
solidarity 13, 21, 101, 111–12, 125–7, 129–31, 135–6, 227 n.5

Somalia 109, 114
sorcerer 58, 122, 140–1
sovereignty 95–6, 100, 102, 112–13, 129, 222 n.16
 divine 93–4, 96
 political 92–4, 96, 99, 101
Soviet Union 6, 8, 12, 21, 36, 113, 195, 205–6 n.12, 211–12 n.13, 233 n.6
 sovietism 6, 8, 10, 205–6 n.12
space 7–8, 16, 25, 38, 100, 103, 108, 142–3, 159, 170, 179–80, 182, 186, 194, 200, 205–6 n.12
space-time 26, 34
Spain 122
speech 5, 9–10, 24, 46–7
Spinoza, Baruch 3, 9, 16, 18, 23–4, 29, 31–3, 38–9, 51–2, 54, 59, 61–5, 71, 75, 83, 92, 111, 127, 136, 171, 173–8, 180, 182, 187–9, 210 nn.1–6, 217 n.21, 218 n.23, 232 n.2, 234 n.16, 235 n.19
 conatus 31–3, 210 n.1
Spivak, Gayatri Chakravorty 99
Sri Lanka 113
Stalin, Josef 36
Starobinski, Jean 216
state 6, 95–6, 100, 103–6, 110, 112–15, 121–2, 135, 139, 147, 165, 171–2, 176–7, 198, 200, 222 n.9, 223 n.23, 223 n.24, 224 n.39, 228 n.1, 231 n.1, 232 n.4, 233 n.12, 233 n.14
 archaic 38, 103, 167, 235 n.25
 and capitalism 37, 65, 103, 105–6, 108, 110, 167–9, 171, 174, 178, 182–7, 212 n.17, 233 n.9, 234 n.15, 234 n.16
 despotic 94, 101–2, 167, 231 n.3
 modern 65, 163, 175
 Palaeolithic 103, 165–6, 174, 185–6, 232 n.2
 socialism 6, 8, 12, 233 n.6
 state-form 9, 103, 105, 114, 163–5, 167, 171, 175, 232 n.6, 233 n.8
 theodicy of 65, 232 n.4
 vs. non-state formations 103, 166
 vs. war machine 100–1, 163
 withering-away of 175, 185, 234 n.15
Stephenson, Neal 5
steppes 122, 142, 206–7 n.18, 222 n.16
Stevenson, Robert Louis 52, 215 n.6
Stone, Oliver 107
Stoppard, Tom 144

Strawson, P.F. 64
structuralism 35, 57–8, 87, 126, 211 n.11, 216 n.12, 221 n.3, 226 n.5
Stuttgart 200
subjects 2, 9, 18, 23–9, 36, 53, 56–7, 62–71, 78–80, 82–3, 86–9, 91–9, 102, 110, 121, 126, 131, 134, 144, 156, 170, 174, 178, 184, 199–200, 204 n.8, 210 n.1, 213 n.6, 217 n.20, 217 n.21, 221 n.7, 222 n.9, 222 n.13, 222 n.15, 222–3 n.19, 227 n.4, 236 n.30. *See also* objects
 subjectification 9, 29, 55, 78–9, 91, 110, 134, 164, 174, 183, 235 n.26
 subjectivities 4, 7, 13, 35, 102, 148–9, 155, 169, 171–2
 subjectum 93, 95, 222 n.19
 subjectus 93–5, 98, 222 n.15, 222 n.19
substance 3, 25–7, 29, 60, 97, 171

Takemitsu, Toru 108
Tamils 113
Taussig, Michael 202
Taylorism 175
technology
 cybernetic 5, 160, 162
teleology 164, 195
television 41, 149, 158–60
Texas 150
textuality 56–8, 70, 216 n.13
Thacker, Eugene 142, 228 n.1
Thatcher, Margaret 20, 152
theology 1, 77, 94–5, 165, 203 n.4, 211 n.9, 213 n.11
Théret, Bruno 228 n.2
Thesiger, Wilfred 52
Thought 60
Tilly, Charles 129
time
 Aeon 101
 eternity 32, 34, 86, 210 n.5, 211 n.7
 future 12, 27, 53, 65–7, 65, 234 n.16
Tokyo 147
Tolstoy, Leon 215 n.5
Tournier, Michel 52
Toyota 201
tradition 12, 28, 41, 43–5, 52, 54, 63–5, 69, 71, 93, 110, 125, 135, 172, 177–8, 198, 221 n.3, 221 n.6, 221 n.7, 225 n.40, 236 n.32

transcendence 23, 75, 86
    transcendent 45, 219 n.9
    transcendentals 1, 75, 77, 107, 203 n.2
transcoding 8, 38, 129–30, 182, 216 n.11, 223 n.23
tribes 11–12, 20–1, 111, 169, 231 n.3
Trollope, Anthony 52
Trotsky, Leon 197
Trump, Donald 198
truth 1, 17, 33, 45, 57, 66, 74, 76–7, 86, 93, 97, 107, 123, 149–50, 161, 179, 200, 203 n.2
Turks 107
Tzara, Tristan 51

Unger, Roberto Mangabeira 129
unity 45, 215 n.6
universal 4, 9, 15, 41, 49, 57, 96, 104, 123, 152, 164–5, 166, 169, 174, 177, 181, 185, 194–5, 223 n.35, 229 n.7, 231 n.3, 234 n.15
    universality 106, 168, 188, 195
unthought 104, 166, 213 n.10
    unthinkability 43, 48, 129
Utopia 37, 96, 135, 143, 173–4, 176, 233 n.6

Vargas Llosa, Mario 69
Verdi, Giuseppe 71
vibrations 47, 49, 63, 213 n.8
Villon, François 52
violence 39, 47, 58, 62, 78, 101, 142, 202
Virgil 64
Virilio, Paul 170, 232 n.10
virtuality 18–19, 87, 89, 125, 208 n.9, 223 n.24
    the virtual 18–19, 22, 27, 88–9, 121, 199, 208, 223 n.24

wages 132, 152–3, 175
Wagner, Richard
    Tristan and Isolde 80–1, 220 n.10
Wang Hui 193
war 26–8, 37, 49, 53, 55, 100–1, 113, 131–3, 151, 155–6, 159, 164, 170, 176, 199, 231 n.17, 235 n.23
    man of war 53
    World War One 27
Watson, Janell 216 n.13
wealth 105, 128–9, 141, 150–1, 155, 158, 162, 168, 176, 186, 230 n.12, 233 n.7

Weber, Max 130
welfare 150, 158–9
Western
    freedom 230 n.13
    left 205–6 n.12
    philosophy 1, 41, 209 n.1
    rationality 123
    world 36
Whitehead, A.N. 2, 15
Whitman, Walt 52
will
    general 96, 164
    inner 33
    to live 81
    to power 71, 97, 211 n.7, 211 n.8
    to truth 1
Williams, James 208 n.2, 209
Williams, Raymond 87, 125, 133, 218 n.28
Winnicott, D.W. 207 n.21
Wittgenstein, Ludwig 64, 203 n.3
Wittig, Monique 4
Wolfe, Thomas 52, 215 n.6
Wolf, Naomi 128
Wolfowitz, Paul 230 n.9
Woolf, Virginia 51, 52, 54, 215 n.6
worker 130, 151, 153–4, 158, 175, 180, 184, 187, 196, 224 n.35, 226 n.6
working class 131–3, 161, 177
World 2, 8, 11–12, 18, 25, 47, 49–50, 55–6, 62–3, 67, 89, 93, 96, 106–7, 109, 111, 113–14, 117–18, 131–3, 136, 149, 151–2, 153, 159, 162, 165, 167, 184–5, 195, 201, 203 n.1, 204 n.5, 204 n.6, 205 n.12, 213 n.10, 215 n.5, 221 n.1, 223 n.23, 228 n.2, 230 n.12
    New and Old 53
    possible 9, 45–6
    Stone Age 11, 106
    -system 6, 10, 224 n.36
    Third 6, 36, 169, 180
    -view 192
    -wide 105, 115, 168, 186–7, 232 n.8
World Bank 152, 162
Write 5, 9–10, 16, 19, 41, 45, 52, 56, 60–3, 65–6, 69, 75, 87, 92, 94, 97, 108, 127, 136, 148, 169, 179–80, 187, 199, 217 n.20, 217 n.21, 226 n.11, 232 n.2

Writing 5, 9–10, 41, 51–71, 87, 92, 94, 96, 99, 108, 127, 136, 141, 179–80, 187, 196, 199, 201, 203 n.1, 203 n.2, 207 n.21, 207 n.25, 212 n.18, 216 n.15, 217 n.19, 219 n.31, 227 n.3, 235 n.21

Zibechi, Raúl 198
Zidane, Zinadine 107, 145
Zola, Émile 54
Zourabichvili, François 208 n.9

www.ingramcontent.com/pod-product-compliance
Lightning Source LLC
Chambersburg PA
CBHW070023010526
44117CB00011B/1689